THE
STOLEN
CROWN

THE STOLEN CROWN

TREACHERY, DECEIT,
and the DEATH *of the*
TUDOR DYNASTY

TRACY BORMAN

Atlantic Monthly Press
New York

First published in 2025 in Great Britain by Hodder & Stoughton Limited
An Hachette UK company

First Grove Atlantic hardcover editon: November 2025

Typeset in Plantin Light by Hewer Text UK Ltd, Edinburgh

Printed in the United States of America

Library of Congress Cataloging-in-Publication data is available for this title.

ISBN 978-0-8021-6590-9
eISBN 978-0-8021-6591-6

Atlantic Monthly Press
an imprint of Grove Atlantic
154 West 14th Street
New York, NY 10011

Distributed by Publishers Group West

groveatlantic.com

25 26 27 28 10 9 8 7 6 5 4 3 2 1

In loving memory of Maureen (Mo) Wilkins

HENRY VII *m.* ELIZABETH OF YORK
1457–1509 *1466–1503*

ARTHUR
Prince of Wales
1486–1502

MARGARET *m.1* JAMES IV
1489–1541 King of Scots
1473–1513

m.2 ARCHIBALD DOUGLAS
6th Earl of Angus
c.1489–1557

JAMES V *m.* MARY OF GUISE
King of Scots *1515–1560*
1512–1542

MARGARET *m.* MATTHEW
1515–1578 STUART
1516–1571

MARY I
1516–1558

MARY *m.1* FRANCIS II
Queen of Scots King of France
1542–1587 *1544–1560*

JANE GREY *m.* GUILDFORD
Queen of England DUDLEY
1537–1554 *c.1535–1554*

m.2 HENRY STUART
Lord Darnley
c.1545–1567

CHARLES *m.* ELIZABETH
STUART CAVENDISH
6th Earl of Lennox *1555–1582*
c.1557–1576

m.3 JAMES HEPBURN
Earl of Bothwell
c.1536–1578

JAMES VI *m.* ANNE
King of Scots of Denmark
1566–1625 *1574–1619*

ARBELLA STUART *m.* WILLIAM
1575–1615 SEYMOUR
Duke of Somerset
1588–1660

THE TUDORS AND THE STUARTS

HENRY VIII
King of England
1491–1547

m.1 **CATHERINE OF ARAGON**
1485–1536

m.2 **ANNE BOLEYN**
c.1501–1536

m.3 **JANE SEYMOUR**
c.1508–1537

m.4 **ANNE OF CLEVES**
1515–1557

m.5 **CATHERINE HOWARD**
c.1518/24–1542

m.6 **KATHERINE PARR**
1512–1548

MARY *m.1* **LOUIS XII**
1496–1533 King of France
1462–1515

m.2 **CHARLES BRANDON**
Duke of Suffolk
c.1484–1545

ELIZABETH I
1533–1603

EDWARD VI
1537–1553

FRANCES BRANDON *m.* **HENRY GREY**
1517–1559 Duke of Suffolk
1517–1554

ELEANOR *m.* **HENRY CLIFFORD**
1519–1547 Earl of Cumberland
1517–1570

KATHERINE GREY *m.* **EDWARD SEYMOUR**
c.1540–1568 1st Earl of Hertford
c.1539–1621

MARY GREY *m.* **THOMAS KEYES**
c.1545–1578 *c.1524–1571*

MARGARET STANLEY *m.* **HENRY STANLEY**
1540–1596 Earl of Derby
1531–1593

EDWARD *m.* **HONORA ROGERS**
Lord Beauchamp *d. after 1608*
1561–1612

THOMAS *m.* **ISABELLA ONLEY**
1563–1600

FERDINANDO
Earl of Derby
1559–1594

WILLIAM
Earl of Derby
1561–1642

EDWARD
c.1586–1618

FRANCIS
c.1590–1664

The Claimants to Elizabeth's Throne

✝ James VI

Mary Queen of Scots

Lady Jane Grey

Lady Mary Grey

Bess of Hardwick

Arbella Stuart

Elizabeth Cavendish *m.* Charles Stuart

Margaret Douglas

Elizabeth Stanley

Ferdinando Stanley

William Stanley

Lord Strange *m.* Margaret Stanley

Edward
Seymour

Thomas
Seymour

Lady   *m.* Edward
Katherine   Seymour
Grey

Elizabeth I

⊞ ✝

Henry
Hastings

Philip II
King of Spain

Isabella Clara
Eugenia

✝
▱

Alexander
Farnese

CONTENTS

'When I am dead, they shall succeed that have the most right.'

(Elizabeth I, September 1561)

'A DROP OF DOUBTFUL ROYAL BLOOD'

In March 1603, Queen Elizabeth I, the last Tudor monarch, lay dying at Richmond Palace, her favourite retreat west of London. She had reigned for forty-four years, longer and more successfully than any of the other Tudor monarchs. The forgotten younger daughter of Henry VIII, Elizabeth had had her right to the throne withdrawn in 1536 following the execution of her mother, the 'Great Whore', Anne Boleyn, and had been declared a bastard. The stain of illegitimacy could not easily be scrubbed away, as her grandfather, Henry VII, had found to his cost. Even when he was well established on his throne, the founder of the Tudor dynasty had been scorned by one foreign ambassador for having 'a drop of doubtful Royal blood'.[1] Furthermore, Elizabeth had had two siblings ahead of her in the line of succession: her younger half-brother Edward and her elder half-sister Mary, with the 'nine days' queen' Lady Jane Grey sandwiched in between. Yet within just eight years of her father's death in 1547, all three had followed him to the grave, leaving Elizabeth as the sole heir to the Tudor dynasty. A brilliant propagandist, she had turned the widespread horror at her unmarried state into a dazzling virtue, becoming the Virgin Queen of legend.

Elizabeth may have been celebrated for her virginity, but the price she and her subjects had paid was uncertainty over who would succeed her. Her determination not to settle the succession had given rise to fierce rivalry between the blood claimants to the English throne, among them Mary, Queen of Scots and her son James VI; Arbella Stuart; Lady Katherine Grey and her descendants; and Henry Hastings, Earl of Huntingdon. The discord had spilled out into the court and across the kingdom as a whole.

By 1603, James VI had apparently emerged as the favourite. His legitimacy, lineage, gender and religion gave him the edge over his rivals, even if there were still doubts over the legality of his claim. 'I hear none almost call it in question,' the Earl of Northumberland assured him at the time. The fact that the King of Scots had two sons also worked in his favour: if he should succeed, the future of the monarchy seemed secure. Even the Queen's adoring godson, Sir John Harington, looked forward to the day when England would no longer be governed by an elderly and increasingly reclusive woman 'but by a man of spirit and learning, of able body, of understanding mind, that in the precepts he doth give to his son shows what we must look for, what we must trust to'. In ever greater numbers, Elizabeth's subjects flocked north to ingratiate themselves with the Queen's likely successor. According to her earliest biographer, William Camden: 'They adored him as the sun rising, and neglected her as now ready to set.'[2]

It was also Camden who described how, when the dying Queen's anxious ministers clustered around her bed, Charles Howard, Earl of Nottingham and Lord High Admiral, urged her to settle the succession once and for all. At length, she replied that her closest blood relative, James VI, should inherit her crown, declaring: 'I'll have none but him.'[3] She died shortly afterwards and the throne of England passed peacefully to the King of Scots.

This scene has been replayed (and embellished) numerous times in the four hundred or so years since Elizabeth's death.

It first appeared in 1615, when Camden published the first instalment of his monumental work *Annales: The True and Royall History of the Famous Empresse Elizabeth*. His account soon became the official version of the Stuart succession as a rightful and smooth transition from one monarch – one dynasty – to the next. Given that Camden was close to some senior members of Elizabeth's court, historians have relied on his manuscript as one of the most important and accurate sources for the period. It has therefore shaped our view of the last years of Elizabeth and the early reign of her successor.

But detailed analysis of Camden's original manuscript published by the British Library in 2023 revealed that key passages were pasted over and rewritten after Elizabeth's death to make them more favourable to her successor. Thanks to advances in enhanced imaging, concealed lines can be read for the first time, offering a deeper insight into the political machinations of Elizabeth's court. They suggest that Camden was so concerned not to offend the new king that he rewrote key sections of his manuscript, pasting new pages over his original text. Among the findings are that Elizabeth's last-gasp naming of James as her heir was a work of fiction, designed to make his accession appear more predetermined than it had been. The real story of the Elizabethan succession was altogether darker and more turbulent than Camden's fiction.

If the truth had been more widely known at the time, it would have had profound repercussions for the Stuart succession. Rather than welcoming James as the king to whom 'Good Queen Bess' had given her blessing, the people of England might have refused to accept him. After all, England and Scotland had been bitter enemies for centuries, the fleeting periods of peace cut abruptly, bloodily short by the clash of arms or threat of invasion. William Camden had lived through the reigns of all three of Henry's children and was also the author of *Britannia,* a detailed history of Great Britain, so was well versed in Anglo-Scottish hostility. He therefore would have appreciated the crucial importance of smoothing the path for the new Stuart regime which, by the time that his biography of Elizabeth was published, was already looking dangerously unstable.

Using this new research as a springboard, *The Stolen Crown* will tell the dramatic story of the end of the Tudor dynasty and the rise of the Stuarts. Far from being a peaceful transition, it was a time of turbulence and uncertainty, conspiracy and persecution, witchcraft and gunpowder. With the accession of England's first Stuart monarch, everything was transformed: from court culture to royal ceremony, religious tolerance to parliamentary authority, morality to witch hunting. Two countries that had been fierce rivals for centuries were now forged into an uncomfortably United Kingdom.

And it had all begun with a lie.

CHAPTER 1

THE THISTLE AND THE ROSE

On 24 January 1502, the optimistically named Treaty of Perpetual Peace was signed by Henry VII, the first Tudor monarch of England, and representatives of the Scottish king, James IV, at Richmond Palace, the magnificent Thames-side residence that Henry had completed the previous year. It was the first alliance between England and Scotland in well over a hundred years. The two countries had been bitter enemies for almost half a millennium. Fierce rivalry, bloody battles and uneasy truces had marked their relationship ever since the Anglo-Scottish border was formed in the early 1000s. This border itself quickly became a lawless territory, blighted by frequent raids as each kingdom tried to make incursions into the other.

In size and wealth, England was superior to its northerly neighbour. The monarchy's annual income was around nine-teen times that of its Scottish counterpart. Scotland was a poor country and regarded as something of an outpost by the rest of Europe. In the late fifteenth century, its population was around 700,000, compared with three million in England, and the majority of people lived in rural areas. Edinburgh was the only major city, and the Highlands and Borders were domi-nated by clans and powerful lords.

The English had pushed home their advantage in 1296 when Edward I (thereafter known as the 'Hammer of the

Scots') invaded Scotland and crushed the Scottish force at
the Battle of Dunbar. Within a few months he had all but
conquered the entire country. In a highly symbolic gesture, he
ordered that the Stone of Destiny, on which all Scottish
monarchs had been crowned for centuries, be removed to
Westminster Abbey. Revolts led by William Wallace and other
Scottish nobles sparked the Wars of Scottish Independence,
one of the bloodiest and most protracted conflicts of the medieval period. They culminated in the accession of Robert II,
the first monarch of the House of Stuart (originally spelled
Stewart), in 1371.

In 1488, a little under three years after Henry VII became
King of England, the fifteen-year-old James IV inherited the
throne of Scotland. Traditionally regarded as the most successful of the Stuart monarchs, James enjoyed an advantage over
his English rival, who was already struggling to hold on to
power. Henry VII was the last of the Lancastrian claimants
and his right to the throne was weak enough to spark dangerous challenges from the outset. The first came from a young
man named Lambert Simnel, who claimed to be Edward
Plantagenet, Earl of Warwick, nephew of the popular Yorkist
king, Edward IV. He soon garnered support from some of the
most powerful members of the House of York and was
crowned King Edward VI in Ireland. But the promised
support in England did not materialise and Henry VII defeated
Simnel's forces at the Battle of East Stoke in 1487.

Having fought off one pretender to his throne, the English
king faced a more potent threat with another: Perkin Warbeck,
who claimed to be the younger of the Princes in the Tower, the
sons of Edward IV who were presumed murdered by their
uncle, Richard III. He garnered considerable support in both
England and Europe and was welcomed with open arms in
Scotland, where the wily James spied an opportunity to stir up

trouble for his English rival. He treated the pretender as an honoured guest at the Christmas celebrations of 1495 and subsequently arranged a marriage between Warbeck and Lady Catherine Gordon, the daughter of one of his nobles.

Choosing diplomacy over warfare, on 5 May 1496 Henry VII opened negotiations for a marriage between his eldest daughter Margaret and the King of Scots. At first, James seemed to lend a willing ear to Henry's proposal. But all the while he was preparing to invade England with Warbeck. A red, gold and silver banner was made for the pretender as Duke of York, and James was fitted for gilded and painted armour. In September, his royal artillery was made ready while men and munitions arrived from France, Germany and other parts of Europe.

On 14 September, James and Warbeck offered prayers at Holyrood Abbey in Edinburgh. A week later, they crossed the River Tweed at Coldstream. But the hoped-for support for Warbeck in Northumberland failed to materialise and upon hearing that a superior English force was marching north from Newcastle, James and his men retreated to Scotland. They did not have far to travel: the invasion force had advanced just four miles into England during its four-day expedition.

Having failed to use Warbeck to further his ambitions towards his southerly neighbour, James quickly lost interest in the pretender and provided a ship for him to escape to Ireland. Henry VII's army proceeded to rout Warbeck's supporters during another failed invasion attempt and the pretender himself was taken prisoner. Anglo-Scottish peace talks resumed shortly afterwards and the Treaty of Ayton was signed on 30 September 1497. Now that the English king had regained the initiative, James was more inclined to consider marriage with Henry's daughter, so negotiations were revived.

It took more than four years for the union to be formally agreed in the Treaty of Perpetual Peace. On 10 December 1502, almost a year after the treaty had been confirmed, James IV pledged to keep its terms at a ceremony held in Glasgow Cathedral. Despite the painstaking preparations that had gone into this moment, however, it was found that 'France' had been inserted into the text of the King's oath instead of 'England', so the whole thing had to be repeated.[1]

The English version of the treaty was decorated with roses; the Scottish with thistles. The language was no less decorative, with each king pledging to uphold 'the bond and amity, truce, friendship and alliance which presently exists between our most illustrious princes . . . that there be a true, sincere, whole and unbroken peace, friendship, league and alliance . . . from this day forth in all times to come, between them and their heirs and lawful successors'. Anxious to guard against any future pretenders, it was likely Henry VII who insisted on including the clause that neither king would offer refuge to any 'rebels, traitors or refugees' who threatened the other.[2] To make the alliance even more binding, both sides agreed that it should be ratified by the Pope. On 28 May 1503, Alexander VI issued a papal bull that threatened excommunication from the church if either king or their heirs and successors should break the peace.

The new treaty confirmed that the marriage between the King of Scots and the English king's daughter, first proposed six years earlier, should take place before the next Candlemas (2 February 1503). But while the Pope had granted a dispensation to allow the couple to marry, even though they were related within the prohibited degrees of consanguinity, there was opposition closer to home.

Deep-seated ethnic prejudices against the Scots were commonplace among Henry VII's subjects. The Scottish

Highlanders – or 'Redshanks' – were portrayed as a wild, barbaric people whose uncivilised culture, language and dress had much more in common with the Irish than the English. There were political objections, too. Polydore Vergil, an Italian scholar, historian and member of Henry VII's court, recorded that the council expressed concern that the marriage might lead to a future King of Scots becoming King of England. Henry's response was both historically inaccurate and predictably Anglocentric: 'What then? Should anything of the kind happen (and God avert the omen), I foresee that our realm would suffer no harm, since England would not be absorbed by Scotland, but rather Scotland by England, being the noblest head of the entire island, since there is always glory and honour in the less being joined to that which is far the greater, just as Normandy once came under the rule and power of our ancestors the English.' (In fact, it had been the Normans who had ruled the native English.) The same presumption about England's natural superiority over Scotland had been shown by centuries of Henry VII's predecessors. If his councillors had known that their fears would be realised almost exactly one hundred years later, they might not have praised the King's 'wisdom' or so readily and 'unanimously' approved the measure.[3]

Despite championing the match so robustly, Henry VII had harboured some misgivings himself. In July 1498, the English king had confided to Don Pedro de Ayala, the Spanish Ambassador, that both his mother, Lady Margaret Beaufort, and his wife, Elizabeth of York, were 'very much against the marriage'. They feared that Margaret would be sent to Scotland straightaway and that, given James IV was a known womaniser who had fathered several illegitimate children, he 'would not wait, but would injure her and endanger her health'. Margaret was thirteen years old by the time of her proxy marriage to James in January 1503, which was certainly considered old enough to marry. But Henry was heavily influenced by his mother, who had given birth to him at the same age. She claimed the experience had 'spoiled' her young body, rendering her incapable of bearing any more children. Henry had earlier declared that his daughter was 'so delicate and weak that she must be married much later than other young ladies' and said that James would have to wait another nine years.[4]

But a marriage that had been so long in the making could not be delayed any further. On 8 July 1503, Margaret left Richmond for Edinburgh, accompanied by a large retinue that included her father for the first stage of the journey. It was with great regret that she bade him farewell. Her mother had died a few months earlier and a letter that Margaret wrote after her arrival in Scotland betrayed her longing for home.[5] She had received a lavish reception in Edinburgh and the crowds who had gathered to welcome the English princess cheered as she progressed through the city's streets. A sumptuous ceremony was held in the chapel of Holyroodhouse Palace on 8 August to solemnify her marriage to the 30-year-old James. The young bride's notoriously parsimonious father had laid out a staggering 30,000 golden nobles (£10,000) on her dowry, equivalent to more than £6.6 million today. The union of two dynasties that the match represented was symbolised throughout the pageantry. The Scottish court poet William Dunbar wrote *The Thissil and the Rois* in celebration, in which he praised the beauty of 'this comely queen'.[6]

Perhaps out of consideration for Margaret's tender age, for the first two or three years of their marriage James visited his mistress's bed rather than his new wife's. It was not until the summer of 1506 that Margaret, then aged sixteen, fell pregnant. She gave birth to a son early the following year, but he died around the time of his first birthday. A daughter followed on 15 July 1508, but she died the same day.

Henry VII died in April 1509, not knowing that the alliance he had striven so hard for would eventually produce a healthy child. Prince James was born at Linlithgow Palace on 10 April 1512. Not everyone rejoiced. Margaret's brother, Henry VIII, was now on the English throne and was not so peaceably inclined towards Scotland as his predecessor had been. The feeling was mutual. In 1513, Henry VIII led a huge invasion force to France, eager to revive the glories of his medieval ancestor Henry V, who had conquered so much of the country that he had earned the title 'King of France' – one that English kings and queens had continued to use long after they had lost virtually all territory across the Channel. Spying an opportunity, James ignored his wife Margaret's pleas and revived the 'auld alliance', first established between Scotland and France in the thirteenth century, by leaping to Louis XII's defence and declaring war on England. His brother-in-law was enraged. 'It becometh ill a Scot to summon a King of England,' he ranted. 'One thing I ensure [assure] him [James IV] by the faith that I have to the Crown of England and by the word of a King, there shall never King nor Prince make peace with me that ever his part shall be in it.'[7]

With Henry on campaign in France, it was left to his consort Catherine of Aragon to superintend the English war effort as James IV prepared to invade. It was a task that this daughter of the formidable Spanish monarchs Ferdinand and Isabella rose to with gusto. Despite being heavily pregnant, she rode north in full armour to address her husband's troops. The two armies clashed at Flodden Field, on the English side of the border, on 9 September 1513. In the ensuing battle – the largest that had been fought between these two rival kingdoms – the English were victorious. The King of Scots was slain, securing him the dubious accolade of being the last monarch in Great Britain to die in battle. A triumphant Queen Catherine sent her husband Henry a piece of James's bloodied coat to use as a banner at the siege of Tournai.

The Anglo-Scottish alliance lay almost in tatters. The two kingdoms might have reverted to their accustomed hostility, but for as long as the new King of Scots drew breath, the Treaty of Perpetual Peace could not be entirely forgotten. James V was just one year and five months old when his father was killed at Flodden.[8] According to the terms of James IV's will, Margaret was regent during her son's minority, but only on the proviso that she did not remarry. Henry VIII was delighted with this arrangement, since it presented an ideal opportunity for him to influence Scottish affairs through his sister. But Margaret was not minded to remain single and within a year of her husband's death she married Archibald Douglas, sixth Earl of Angus, the most powerful magnate in Scotland, thus forfeiting her powers of regency. She gave birth to a daughter, Margaret, in 1515, but thereafter became alienated from her husband and spent long periods in England, which was once more at loggerheads with its northerly neighbour.

James V assumed personal rule in 1528 and soon after, ignoring his mother's persuasions to forge closer links with his uncle, Henry VIII, he renewed the alliance with France. Having rejected Henry VIII's daughter Mary as a potential bride, he went on to marry two French princesses: Madeleine, daughter of Francis I, who died less than two months after arriving in Scotland, and Mary, a noblewoman from the powerful House of Guise. In an attempt to prevent the second marriage, Henry VIII had offered himself as a husband to Mary of Guise. He told the French ambassador that he was a big man and had need of a big wife, to which

Mary responded: 'I may be a big woman, but I have a very little neck' – a reference to a macabre jest made by Henry's second wife, Anne Boleyn, prior to her execution, that her beheading would be swift because 'I have a little neck'.[9] Mary was crowned Queen of Scotland at Holyrood Abbey on 22 February 1540. James had offered her the title Queen of England too, but she chose not to take it, perhaps to avoid provoking her former suitor.

James's mother Margaret died in October 1541, thus removing any lingering incentive for peace between her native and adoptive kingdoms. Open hostilities resumed almost immediately. The Scots drew first blood at Haddon Rig in August 1542, then refused to hold talks with the English until James V's heavily pregnant wife had been delivered of her child. Their first two children (both sons) had died in infancy. Although he had fathered numerous healthy bastards by his many mistresses, James's lack of a legitimate heir set him at a disadvantage with his English rival, who finally had a son, Edward, after three wives and almost thirty years of trying. But Henry was not minded to wait and began preparing his army for another battle.

The two sides clashed at Solway Moss on 24 November 1542 and the Scots were routed. Their king, who had complained of feeling ill before the battle (possibly with cholera or dysentery), travelled to Falkland Palace after spending a few days with his wife. His condition rapidly worsened but he continued to plan his next move against the English from his sick bed. Then news arrived that his wife had given birth to a daughter, Mary, on 8 December. According to the Scottish theologian John Knox, upon hearing of this, James lamented: 'It cam wi' a lass, and it will gang wi' a lass' ('It began with a girl and it will end with a girl').[10] This has been taken as a reference to the Stuarts' accession to the throne through Marjorie Bruce, daughter of Robert the Bruce, and a prophecy that the dynasty would die out with James's newborn daughter Mary. James died on 14 December 1542, aged just thirty.[11]

With the King of Scots dead and his successor a six-day-old girl, Henry VIII was quick to push home his advantage. For once, he favoured diplomacy over warfare. The early sixteenth century had seen the introduction of resident ambassadors in courts across Europe. This dramatically changed the nature of diplomacy because it facilitated more regular correspondence between sovereigns and their advisers. Sir Ralph Sadler, who had come to prominence under the patronage of Henry VIII's former chief minister Thomas Cromwell, was one of the earliest regular (if not, quite, resident) English ambassadors to Scotland. Henry VIII sent him there after the Battle of Solway Moss to negotiate a marriage alliance between his son Edward and the infant Queen of Scots. 'King Henry VIII . . . desiring still this whole isle of Britain to be united in one monarchy, made a contract of marriage between the said two,' recorded Sir James Melville, later Scottish ambassador to England.[12] There was strong opposition to this among the Scottish government. Sadler, who was leading the negotiations there on the English king's behalf, reported a comment made by his Scottish counterpart, Adam Otterburn, which got to the heart of their objection:

Our people do not like of it . . . I pray you give me leave to ask you a question: if your lad was a lass, and our lass were a lad, would you then be so earnest in this matter? . . . And likewise I assure you that our nation will never agree to have an Englishman king of Scotland. And though the whole nobility of the realm would consent, yet our common people, and the stones in the street would rise and rebel against it.[13]

This echoed the English government's aversion to the proposed match between Margaret Tudor and James IV forty or so years earlier. The nub of the issue was gender. Whichever kingdom offered the bride was at a disadvantage because the groom would naturally take precedence – and, ultimately, might inherit the crown of his wife's native land. This was even more likely with Mary, Queen of Scots than it had been with Margaret Tudor because she was her father's sole legitimate heir, whereas Margaret had had a father and brother still living. The Treaty of Greenwich, which was signed on 1 July 1543, also made provision for a second marriage between the two kingdoms, involving Henry VIII's younger daughter Elizabeth and James Hamilton, son of the Scottish regent, the second Earl of Arran.

No sooner had the treaty been agreed than a group of influential Scottish lords signed a 'Secret Bond' against it. By the end of the year, the Parliament of Scotland had entirely renounced the fledgling Anglo-Scottish alliance. This led to eight years of war between the two nations, which the celebrated Scottish historian, novelist and poet Sir Walter Scott termed the 'Rough Wooing'. Henry VIII made the first aggressive move when he sent an army to invade Edinburgh in May 1544. During the conflict, the English commander Edward Seymour, Duke of Somerset, gave the order for the city to be burned. Almost all the houses within it were razed to the ground and considerable damage was inflicted on Holyrood Abbey, where James V lay buried. His tomb was destroyed by another English raid three years later.

In the meantime, Henry VIII took measures to prevent the Stuart line from ever inheriting the throne of England. In a hereditary monarchy, it was presumed that the closest blood descendant would succeed to the throne. But while England had had a more or less hereditary system for centuries (barring the occasional usurpation), there was no fixed law or rule governing the right to the throne. Furthermore, English common law stipulated that those born outside the realm could not inherit land or property – and so, by extension, the crown. This was not straightforward though, thanks to historic claims of overlordship dating back to Edward I's conquest of Scotland, which had temporarily forced it into allegiance to the English crown. Henry VIII certainly saw himself as the overlord of Scotland, with the king there paying him homage.

The succession was further complicated by Henry VIII's controversial and extensive marital history, which had resulted in three children by three different wives. His solution had been to create a series of Succession Acts in Parliament. The first was passed by Parliament in 1534 and disinherited his elder daughter Mary in favour of his younger daughter Elizabeth. The Second Succession Act of 1536 disinherited both Elizabeth and Mary in favour of any children from Henry's new marriage to Jane Seymour, who the following year obligingly produced the long-awaited son, Prince Edward. The Third Succession Act of 1543 confirmed Edward as Henry's immediate heir and reinstated Mary and Elizabeth after their new brother.

Significantly, both the 1536 and 1543 acts also stipulated that if the line of succession was not continued by the King's children, it would be regulated by the contents of his last will and testament. This ran contrary to common law, which did not allow for the nomination of heirs. But by now Henry was used to acting the absolutist monarch. After all, he had separated England from Rome to secure an annulment from his first wife, executed his second, created a new church and set in train a sweeping religious revolution. Naturally he viewed the succession as his to command. Future monarchs would be left to deal with the fallout from this seismic shift – his young-est daughter in particular.

It is perhaps not surprising that Henry should have been so concerned to secure the future of his throne. By the time the Third Succession Act was passed, Henry's health was deterio-rating rapidly. Incapacitated by a serious jousting accident in 1536, he was plagued by pain from his leg wounds, which turned ulcerous. Unable to undertake any form of physical exercise, he had rapidly gained weight. Complications from his injury had almost proved fatal in 1538 and frantic prepa-rations had been made for the succession.

By late 1546, it was obvious to everyone who saw him that the 55-year-old king did not have long left to live. He attended the Christmas celebrations at Greenwich only briefly before retreating to Whitehall Palace with a handful of private attend-ants. There, the final revisions were made to his will on 30 December – with Henry's knowledge or sanction is uncertain. Debate surrounding the authenticity of the will continues, but what is clear is how dominant the succession is within it, accounting for 60 per cent of the total text. The key clause, which would have profound ramifications for the succession during Elizabeth's reign, stated:

> For default of the issue of the several bodies of us and of our said son prince Edward and of our said daughters Mary and Elizabeth lawfully begotten shall wholly remain and come to the heirs of the body of the Lady Frances our niece, eldest daughter to our late sister the French Queen lawfully begotten.[14]

In other words, after Edward, Mary and Elizabeth would come the descendants of Henry's younger sister, Mary: Jane, Katherine and Mary Grey (the daughters of Frances Grey,

Duchess of Suffolk, Princess Mary's eldest child), and Margaret (the only surviving child of Eleanor Clifford, Countess of Cumberland, Princess Mary's second child). The descendants of Henry's elder sister Margaret – her grand-daughter Mary, Queen of Scots and her daughter Margaret Douglas – were conspicuously excluded. The clause therefore ran counter to inheritance based on primogeniture, which by now was firmly established in England – by tradition if not by law – as well as throughout Europe.

Introducing an element of personal choice into the succession rather than relying on the centuries-old system of hereditary monarchy meant the will was profoundly destabilising. Although Henry intended it as a potent tool to impose the royal will, once the genie was out of the bottle, there was always the prospect that it could be directed by others.

The Reformation that Henry VIII had set in train further exacerbated the already vexed issue of the succession. He had died a Catholic – albeit not a Roman Catholic – but had sign-posted his wishes for the future by ensuring that his son and heir was raised a Protestant, as was Elizabeth. This set them at loggerheads with their elder half-sister Mary, a staunch Roman Catholic. The choices that all three of Henry's children made regarding the succession would be heavily influenced by their religion.

Henry VIII's will was read to him on 27 January 1547, just hours before his death. He was incapable of signing it by hand, so the dry stamp was used. This held an impression of the monarch's signature and was used on official documents, then filled in by authorised clerks. It had been employed frequently during the last eighteen months of Henry's life. The potential for abuse was reduced by the introduction of a register to record that the monarch had checked the stamped document before it was dispatched.

The Third Succession Act had stipulated that although the final word on the succession would be given by Henry's last will, this was conditional on the will being signed by the King's 'most gracious hand'.[15] As a result, the seemingly insignificant detail of the dry stamp on Henry's will opened the door, just a crack, that the dying king thought he had slammed shut on any future Scottish claimants to his throne.

CHAPTER 2

'I AM RESOLVED NEVER TO MARRY'

Henry VIII had died content in the knowledge that his throne would pass to his 'precious jewel', Edward VI. He hoped that his son would enjoy a long and successful reign and sire male heirs of his own to continue the Tudor line long into the future. But in April 1552, after just five years on the throne, Edward contracted measles, and a few months later tuberculosis. In March the following year the Venetian envoy reported that the fifteen-year-old king was dying.

It was probably around this time that Edward drafted his 'Devise' for the succession.[1] By the terms of his father's will, and by nature, his successors were his two half-sisters. But the Succession Act of 1536 had given him the legal right to make his own choice. Influenced by John Dudley, Duke of Northumberland, the leader of Edward's government, he disinherited Mary and Elizabeth on the flimsy basis that they might marry a foreigner who would undermine both 'the laws of this realm' and 'his proceedings in religion'.[2] In the absence of any viable male heirs, he nominated his cousin, Lady Jane Grey, followed by her sisters Katherine and Mary. It is no coincidence that Dudley was scheming to marry his son Guildford to Jane. They were wed shortly after the Devise was finalised.

Edward VI died on 6 July 1553. Four days later the sixteen-year-old Lady Jane Grey was proclaimed queen. The bishop of London preached a sermon at Paul's Cross declaring her right to the throne. It was met with a muted reception by the capital's citizens, who were dubious about the new Queen's right to the Tudor throne. Jane herself shared their disquiet. Upon hearing that she was Queen, she was 'stupefied and troubled' and fell to the ground weeping and declaring her 'insufficiency'.[3]

Edward's elder half-sister Mary was quick to rally support from her base in Norfolk. Even those who favoured the religious reform that Queen Jane espoused preferred the Catholic Mary because her claim was stronger. Alarmed by rumours of the forces gathering in ever greater numbers to support Mary Tudor, on 19 July the council capitulated and abandoned Jane. Mary was proclaimed queen amid great rejoicing. Edward VI and his father might have ridden roughshod over the laws and customs governing the succession, but for the people of England, blood was most definitely thicker than water.

Mary's popularity quickly waned, however. Determined to return England to papal obedience, she ordered hundreds of Protestant heretics to be burned, ignoring the horrified reaction even among England's Catholics. Her choice of husband might have been natural to her – Philip of Spain was her cousin, and as the daughter of Catherine of Aragon she was half-Spanish. But it was anathema to her subjects, who feared that England would become a mere satellite of Philip's powerful kingdom. When Mary pressed ahead with the wedding in 1554, it sparked rebellion. Worse still, the union did not even serve the primary purpose of a royal marriage: the production of heirs. Aged thirty-eight when she married Philip (who was eleven years her junior), Mary was already approaching the end of her childbearing years.

'They had small hope of issue by the Queen, being now 40 years old, dry, and sickly.' This was William Camden's

withering verdict on Mary in the closing months of her reign.[4]
She had been queen for just five years. Despite experiencing
the physical symptoms of pregnancy during two prolonged
periods, by 1558 it was obvious that Mary would die without
issue. Her courtiers whispered that the swelling of her stomach was more likely caused by a 'tympany' or tumour than a
growing foetus.

In the summer of that year, the Queen invited her younger
sister to Richmond Palace. No expense was spared in preparing for Elizabeth's visit. Mary ordered a sumptuous pavilion
which was bedecked with gold and crimson cloth and resembled a mythical castle, and staged a sumptuous feast, followed
by dancing accompanied by a troupe of minstrels. The courtiers who gathered for this spectacular event were quick to draw
conclusions from all the magnificence. Surely Mary would
not have gone to such trouble or expense for anyone other
than her intended successor?

After the visit, Elizabeth returned to her residence at
Hatfield House, twenty miles north of London. A host of
ambitious ministers, courtiers and place-seekers beat a path
to her door, eager to ingratiate themselves with the dying
queen's successor. 'Many persons of the kingdom flocked to
the house of Miladi Elizabeth, the crowd constantly increasing with great frequency,' reported Michiel Surian, the
Venetian ambassador. Even while she still lived, Mary was
becoming obsolete, and she knew it. 'What disquiets her most
is to see the eyes and hearts of the nation already fixed on this
lady [Elizabeth] as successor to the Crown,' reported the
Count of Feria, envoy to the Queen's husband, Philip II.[5] It
was a lesson that her younger sister would never forget.

Philip urged his dying wife to name her sister as heir, not
least because he cherished hopes of marrying Elizabeth and
thereby remaining king consort in England. But the

beleaguered Queen was 'utterly averse to give Lady Elizabeth any hope of the succession'. Instead she railed against her sister, full of 'inveterate hatred' for all the wrongs that she had committed. Adoration of her husband soon overcame her aversion, however, and she sent Philip a message, expressing herself 'muy contenta [much pleased]' with his suggestion. 'Madam Elizabeth already sees herself as the next Queen,' Feria reported to Philip soon afterwards, 'and having come to the conclusion, that she would have succeeded, even if your Majesty and the Queen had opposed it, she does not feel indebted to your Majesty in this matter.'[6]

On 28 October 1558, Mary added a codicil to her will, finally acknowledging that there would be no 'fruit of her body' and confirming that the crown would go to the next heir by law. According to the Third Succession Act and her father's will, this was her half-sister. Even now, though, Mary could not bring herself to nominate her because Elizabeth was an avowed Protestant. Three weeks later, the Queen slipped from a life that had been marked by tragedy and heartache. A messenger was immediately dispatched to Hatfield with the news. Upon hearing that she was now Queen of England, Elizabeth proclaimed: 'My Lords, the law of nature moves me to sorrow for my sister; the burden that is fallen upon me makes me amazed.'[7]

When Elizabeth was proclaimed Queen in the City of London, there was great rejoicing. Across the capital, church bells were rung and at night bonfires were lit, around which thousands of people gathered to drink and make merry. The new Queen made a show of honouring her late sister. She arranged a lavish funeral at a cost of £7,763 (equivalent to more than £1.8 million today). But when it came to Mary's tomb, the mask of respect began to slip. The epitaph was more complimentary to the new Queen than to the old:

Marie now dead, Elizabeth lives, our just and lawful Queen
In whom her sister's virtues rare, abundantly are seen.

Elizabeth did not bother to commission a tomb above the
unmarked vault in which Mary was interred and during the
course of her reign pieces of stone from the alteration work
within Westminster Abbey were piled on top of it.[8]

During the weeks and months that followed her accession,
the new queen seized every opportunity to distance herself
from her predecessor. This was born less of arrogance than of
politics. Mary had courted widespread resentment during her
brief, bloody reign. Her marriage to Philip of Spain had
sparked rebellion, her attempts to return England to the
Roman Catholic fold had been opposed by Catholics and
Protestants alike, and her burning of hundreds of Protestant
heretics had earned her the sobriquet 'Bloody Mary'. Elizabeth
had learned from all of this: she would not marry at all, let
alone a foreigner, and she would seek compromise in religion.
But the greatest lesson that she drew from her sister's reign
was not to name her successor.

The widespread rejoicing at the accession of Henry VIII's
younger, more personable daughter quickly receded. She may
have been more popular than Mary but, like her, she was of
the wrong gender to rule effectively. In the same year that
Elizabeth came to the throne, John Knox published a tract
declaring that it was 'repugnant' and 'more than a monster in
nature that a Woman shall reign and have empire above Man'.[9]
Few of his contemporaries disagreed. Sixteenth-century society was a patriarchy in which women were considered the
weaker sex in every single respect: physically, emotionally,
spiritually and morally. They were entirely subject to the rule
of husbands, fathers, brothers and kings. At the apex of society, the system of primogeniture was well established: Henry

VIII would not have gone to so much trouble (or through so many wives) if he had been content for one of his daughters to succeed him.

Yet from the outset, Elizabeth made it clear that she had no intention of conforming to social conventions and declared that she was resolved to remain a virgin. The idea that any woman, let alone a queen, would not marry was preposterous to those present. As a self-confessed 'weak and feeble woman', Elizabeth could not possibly govern a kingdom without a husband dictating her every move. Besides, marriage was essential to produce an heir and secure the succession. Ruling alone as a 'sole queen' plunged both Elizabeth and England into jeopardy.

Elizabeth's accession brought the rivalry between England and Scotland back to the fore. Even though England's new Queen had been named as the rightful successor by her dying sister, and by the terms of their father's will (which Elizabeth had access to and believed to be valid), many of England's Catholics viewed Mary Stuart as the stronger claimant. Mary had inherited the crown of Scotland from her father James V in 1542, when she was only six days old, so she had been Queen for just shy of sixteen years when Elizabeth came to the English throne. The latter was also technically illegitimate, her father having annulled his marriage to Anne Boleyn before she was executed. Elizabeth was tainted by her mother's alleged adultery. Anne Boleyn was widely condemned as the 'Great Whore' and her daughter was often referred to as the 'Little Whore'. To make matters worse, as a teenager Elizabeth had been embroiled in a sexual scandal of her own, involving Thomas Seymour, husband of her former stepmother Katherine Parr. He was later executed. By contrast, Mary Stuart's legitimacy was beyond question: her parents' marriage was uncontested, she had lived a virtuous life, free from scandal, and her Catholic faith made her a more appealing prospect to at least half of Elizabeth's subjects than Anne Boleyn's heretical daughter.

Mary's hand was strengthened by the fact that as well as being Queen of Scots, she would one day be Queen of France. In 1548 the Scottish regent, James Hamilton, second Earl of Arran, had concluded a treaty with France. As well as sending a sizeable force to take up camp in Leith, from where they could either defend against or attack England, the French had agreed to a betrothal between the Dauphin Francis, eldest son and heir of King Henry II, and the five-year-old Queen of Scots. Mary had subsequently sailed to France and lived there for several years while a succession of regents ruled for her in Scotland. Peace with England had been declared in the spring of 1550, but the French had remained encamped at Leith.

In April 1558 Mary and the Dauphin were married. The very day after Elizabeth I's accession, Mary and her new husband began to style themselves King and Queen of England and included the English royal arms in Mary's shield. Her father-in-law, Henry II, always keen to wrong-foot his English rival, proceeded to denounce Elizabeth as an illegitimate usurper. At the wedding of his daughter, Princess Claude, in January 1559, he ordered Mary's servants to wear the arms of England on their livery, quartered with her own.

All this dealt Mary's relationship with Elizabeth a fatal blow. Highly sensitive to the merest hint of her illegitimacy, the new Queen of England had received enough provocation from the Queen of Scots to fuel a lifetime's enmity. With a healthy dose of hindsight, Camden opined: 'Hereupon Queen Elizabeth bore ... secret grudge against her [Mary], which the subtle malice of men on both sides cherished, growing betwixt them, emulation, and new occasions daily arising, in such sort, that it could not be extinguished but by death.'[10]

The threat posed by Mary was heightened in July 1559 when Henry II, in the prime of his life, was injured during a joust and died from his infected wound the following month, leaving the throne to his fifteen-year-old son Francis. Even though her Guise uncles assumed the power of regency, Mary's status and power had never been greater. She was now Queen in two countries, and sandwiched between them both was England. Sir Nicholas Throckmorton, the English ambassador to France, urged Elizabeth: 'The best means that has been thought on for the quietness of the two Queens is ... that Queen Elizabeth should for herself and her heirs peaceably enjoy the crown of England; and failing herself and her heirs, that the Queen of Scotland should be accepted next heir of England.'[11]

But centuries of history between England and Scotland had proved that neither enjoyed the ascendancy for long. Upon hearing of Mary's elevation to the throne of France, Elizabeth made friendly overtures, offering to send a portrait of herself. Mary expressed delight at the idea and assured her cousin 'her affection is fully reciprocated'.[12] Such diplomatic niceties disguised darker schemes. Mary's mother, Mary of Guise, who had acted as regent for her daughter in Scotland since 1554, had followed a pro-French, pro-Catholic policy, which had sparked growing opposition from the self-styled Lords of the Congregation, a group of powerful Protestant Scottish nobles.

In the autumn of 1559, Elizabeth dispatched seasoned diplomat Thomas Randolph to escort James Hamilton, son of the second Earl of Arran and a kinsman and former attendant to Mary, Queen of Scots, safely to Scotland. Hamilton, who had been mooted as a husband for Elizabeth in her youth, was a Protestant known for his opposition to the French-dominated regency in Scotland, had fled to Geneva in July that year with the help of Throckmorton. In arranging for Hamilton's safe passage to Scotland, the English queen hoped he would stir up trouble for Mary of Guise. It was all done with the utmost secrecy and those involved used code names to communicate.

After crossing the English Channel, Randolph and Hamilton made their way to Hampton Court, where the Scotsman had a private interview with the English queen. No record of their conversation has survived, but Gilles de Noailles, the French ambassador in England, reported that Elizabeth was plotting to make Hamilton King of Scotland by the consent of the Lords of the Congregation, with England as its superior kingdom. Scotland would pay England an annual fee and Elizabeth would add the arms of Scotland to her heraldry. Although there is no contemporary evidence to support this, an English document of 1583 claimed that the Scottish nobility were 'fully resolved to have deprived her [Mary] of her government, and established the same in . . . the Earl of Arran [Hamilton]'.[13]

If Elizabeth had devised such a scheme, it came to nothing. Upon his return to Scotland, Hamilton became embroiled in Scottish intrigues but was able to rally little support. Always an unstable character, his mental health soon deteriorated. '[He] is so drowned in dreams, and so feed[s] himself with fantasies, that either men fear that he will fall into some dangerous and incurable sickness, or play one day some mad part that will bring himself to mischief,' Randolph reported in 1562.[14]

In February 1560, the Lords of the Congregation signed a treaty with Elizabeth aimed at ousting the French from Scotland with the help of English troops. The following month, the English queen sent Randolph as her ambassador to Scotland. Randolph was able to exert considerable influence in encouraging the Protestants against Mary of Guise and effecting an understanding between them and Elizabeth. The success of his mission secured numerous other embassies to Scotland during the following twenty-six years. He also acted on behalf of William Cecil who, like him, was driven by ardent Protestantism.

On 11 June 1560, Mary of Guise died. There has been conjecture that she was poisoned on the orders of Elizabeth or those acting in her interests, but the evidence points to natural causes. Mary had been complaining of dropsy and her legs were so swollen that she was virtually lame. The following month, Elizabeth concluded an alliance with the Lords of the Congregation. The Treaty of Edinburgh was also signed by representatives of Mary Stuart's husband, Francis II, who agreed to withdraw French troops from Scotland and, with his wife, to stop quartering the English royal arms in their heraldry.

Mary's time as Queen of France would be brief. Her husband died of an ear infection in December 1560 and his mother, Catherine de' Medici, became regent for her younger son, Charles IX. The following summer, Mary decided to return to her native Scotland. The easiest passage was to cross the Channel and ride northwards through England. She duly made peaceable overtures to her English cousin, assuring her that she desired only 'amity', given 'they were both in one isle, of one language, the nearest kinswomen that each other had, and both queens'.[15] But when Elizabeth invited her to prove this by ratifying the Treaty of Edinburgh, Mary was evasive and the passage was refused.

Highly affronted, Mary returned to Scotland via a more circuitous route in August 1561. She was immediately confronted with a volatile political situation, in which Catholic and Protestant factions battled for supremacy. Having been in France since the age of five, she lacked the understanding and experience to bring matters under control. Rather than attempting to deal with the issues that threatened to tear her kingdom apart, she focused her attention on the English throne, which she persisted in viewing as hers by right.

The Scottish queen began by declaring her intention to form a 'strict and sisterly friendship' with her cousin Elizabeth. As Melville observed: 'There appeared outwardly no more difference, but that the Queen of England was the elder sister, and the Queen of Scotland the younger, whom the Queen of England promised to declare second person [her heir], according to her good behaviour.'[16] This behaviour soon proved otherwise. For all her effusive expressions of friendship and affection towards her cousin, Mary refused to ratify the Treaty of Edinburgh because it recognised Elizabeth as Queen of England. She would doggedly resist intense pressure to do so throughout her rule in Scotland.

The scene was set for a bitter rivalry that would dominate Elizabeth's reign for the next twenty-five years – and would, ultimately, decide the succession to her throne.

'In the end this shall be for me sufficient: that a marble stone shall declare that a queen, having reigned such a time, lived and died a virgin,' Elizabeth I had told the first Parliament of her reign, on 10 February 1559. Mistress of theatre as well as words, she stretched out her hand so that those present could see the coronation ring and exhorted them: 'Reproach me so no more, that I have no children: for every one of you, and as many as are English, are my children and kinsfolks.'[17]

It was a brilliant speech, demonstrating the new queen's mastery of theatre and words and evoking a positive, maternal image of female sovereignty. But few would have trusted the sincerity of her words. The Imperial emissary summed up the majority view when he opined: 'That she should wish to remain a maid and never marry is inconceivable.'[18] Elizabeth's subjects and advisers saw it as imperative that she find a husband as soon as possible so that he could take over the reins of government and enable her to fulfil a queen's foremost purpose of providing the kingdom with heirs.

Shortly after Elizabeth's accession, her former brother-in-law, Philip II, had told her that she should marry him in order to 'relieve her of those labours which are only fit for men'. His ambassador in England, Bishop Álvaro de la Quadra, smugly predicted: 'This woman's troubles are growing apace, and her house will be in a blaze before she knows it.' The inference was clear: for as long as Elizabeth remained single, England's downfall was inevitable. This was reinforced by Thomas Gargrave, speaker of the House of Commons, who in the 1559 Parliament reminded the new queen: 'The Kings of England have never been more careful of anything, than that the Royal Family might not fail of issue.' In reply, Elizabeth called on a higher authority: 'If I continue in this kind of life I have begun, I doubt not but God will so direct mine own and your counsels, that you shall not need to doubt of a successor which may be more beneficial to the Commonwealth than he which may be born of me, considering that the issue of the best princes many times degenerates.'[19]

Did Elizabeth mean it, or was this just statecraft: a ploy to increase her value on the international marriage market? Marriage can hardly have been an appealing prospect for a young woman whose mother and stepmother Catherine Howard had been executed on the orders of her father, and who had witnessed the rebellion, humiliation and, ultimately, fruitlessness that resulted from her half-sister Mary's union with Philip of Spain. According to Elizabeth's chief favourite and confidant, Robert Dudley, at the tender age of eight she had vowed: 'I will never marry.' Shortly after her accession to the throne, she had declared: 'It seemed unto me an inconsiderate folly to draw upon myself the cares which might proceed of marriage.' When pressed on the matter, her reaction occasionally veered towards the hysterical. She told a French ambassador that she would leave herself entirely vulnerable if she took a husband, as he could 'carry out some evil wish, if he had one'. On another occasion, she rounded on a German envoy, declaring that she would rather go into a nunnery or 'suffer death' than marry. As the pressure intensified, she hinted at the trauma that lay behind her resistance, confiding that she 'hated the idea of marriage every day more, for reasons which she could not divulge to a twin soul, if she had one, much less to a living creature'.[20]

Alongside the psychological reasons against marriage, there were the political. As the younger, bastardised daughter of Henry VIII, Elizabeth had grown up with little prospect of ever inheriting the throne. Yet she had battled through disgrace, imprisonment and the ever-present threat of execution to become queen regnant and was not about to give up her power to a husband. The Scottish ambassador Sir James Melville, who visited Elizabeth's court in 1564, quickly got the measure of her. 'Your Majesty thinks, if you were married, you would be but Queen of England; and now you are both King and Queen. I know your spirit cannot endure a commander.' As Elizabeth herself declared: 'I will have but one mistress here, and no master!' But if she alone knew that she was in earnest, she also knew the value of holding out the hope – or, in Mary Stuart's case, the threat – that she might change her mind. In the same conversation, she told Melville: 'I am resolved never to marry, if I be not thereto necessitated by the Queen my sister's harsh behaviour towards me.' Before long, her exasperated councillors were expressing their belief that 'no man can know the intention of her heart . . . but God and herself'.[21]

In the early months of Elizabeth's reign, the question of her marriage was quickly, if temporarily, superseded by that of religion. The product of Henry VIII's break with Rome and his marriage to Anne Boleyn, she had been raised a Protestant. But some of her closest companions were Catholic and she was not averse to hearing mass in private when the mood took her. Moreover, having lived through the turbulent reign of her half-sister, whose blind insistence on returning England to Roman Catholicism had sparked widespread opposition and rebellion, Elizabeth was more inclined to compromise. 'I would not open windows into men's souls,' she is often quoted as saying. Those words may have been Francis Bacon's rather than the Queen's, but they neatly summed up her approach.

However, in establishing an official state religion, compromise was not easily achieved. Not only did Elizabeth need to take account of the opposing views of her subjects, but those of her potential allies abroad. If she chose to uphold her predecessor's religion, alliance with the two superpowers, France and Spain, would be within her grasp. Returning to Protestantism would align England with some of the Dutch provinces, who had the commercial advantage as England's main trading partner.

At the opening of Parliament in January 1559, Sir Nicholas Bacon (father of Francis), as Lord Keeper of the Privy Seal, delivered a speech urging its members 'to unite the people of this realm into a uniform order of religion'. The following month, the House of Commons passed an act that joined together a bill of supremacy, confirming Elizabeth as head of the church, with a bill of uniformity, establishing the official religion. It was decisively rejected by the Catholic-dominated

House of Lords, forcing the Queen and her advisers to change
tack. When Parliament reconvened in April, a revised Act of
Supremacy was presented, which still abolished papal supremacy but defined Elizabeth as Supreme Governor, rather than
Supreme Head, of the church.[22] This slight but significant
amendment achieved its aim: the act was passed with a sizeable majority. The new Act of Uniformity was more conten-
tious. It restored the Protestant form of worship established
by Edward VI in 1552 but retained some Catholic practices.
Crucially, it also allowed for both a Catholic and Protestant
form of communion. It was an unsatisfactory compromise
and was passed by the narrowest of margins, with all twenty
bishops in the House of Lords, each of whom was Catholic,
voting against it.

The ambiguity of the new religious settlement was reflected
by the succession of Elizabeth's suitors, who were drawn from
both Catholic and Protestant camps. Although she was resolved
to preserve her 'single state', Elizabeth was shrewd enough to
give hope to these suitors in order to strengthen England's international position. Her former brother-in-law was the first in a
long line of European potentates to seek her hand in marriage.
Philip II had made little secret of his distaste for his first Tudor
bride, Mary I, telling an attendant that she was 'no good from
the point of view of fleshly sensuality'. But he had enjoyed being
King of England and was eager to regain that position through
marriage to his dead wife's sister. When Elizabeth refused to fall
in with his scheme, he promoted the suit of his cousin and fellow
Catholic Charles II, Archduke of Austria. Philip's agent in
England, Quadra, confidently predicted, 'If the Archduke comes
[to England] she will marry him', but in the next breath admitted that she was 'as fickle as ever'.[23]

A more peaceable but still futile proposal was made by the
Protestant Eric XIV of Sweden. He had inherited his father's

throne a little under two years after Elizabeth's accession and had already made clear his interest in her. But then, he had also made unsuccessful marriage proposals to several other royal women, among them Elizabeth's rival, Mary, Queen of Scots. What was more, he proved singularly unsuited to the task of governing a country and was overthrown in January 1569. By then, the idea of marriage with the Queen of England had been abandoned. After pretending to consider his suit for a time, Elizabeth had politely but firmly rejected it, telling him: 'We do not conceive in our heart to take a husband.'[24]

The Queen's reluctance had not been the only obstacle. Eric XIV was not alone among her various suitors in being concerned by the nature of her relationship with her chief favourite, Robert Dudley. 'All those who wished to see the Queen married, the whole nation in short, blamed him [Dudley] alone for the delay that had taken place,' the Spanish ambassador reported in February 1566. Kat Astley, one of Elizabeth's closest attendants, had been at pains to assure the Swedish king: 'The Queen was free of any man living, and that she would not have the Lord Robert.'[25] Elizabeth and Dudley's friendship was forged in childhood and strengthened by adversity: both were imprisoned in the Tower on suspicion of complicity in the Wyatt rebellion of 1554. As well as being one of the Queen's public advisers, Dudley was her constant companion in private. A year after her accession, she appointed him rooms next to her privy chamber so that they might meet away from the prying eyes of the court. The intimacy between them was obvious to all. When admitting her favourite to the Order of St George, Elizabeth tickled his neck. On another occasion, she mopped the sweat from his brow after a tennis match.

In the early years of their relationship, there was no question of the Queen marrying her favourite, even if she had

wished to, because he already had a wife. But in 1560, Amy
Dudley was found dead at the couple's Oxfordshire home.
The circumstances were suspicious. On the day of her death,
she had insisted that all her servants attend a local fair so that
she was left alone. They returned to find her at the bottom of
a short flight of stairs, her neck broken and two small wounds
to her head. The news spread like wildfire across the courts of
Europe. When Mary, Queen of Scots heard of it, she quipped
that her English rival was about to marry her 'horsekeeper',
who had killed his wife to make way for her.[26] In fact, the
suspicion of foul play ensured that far from leaving the way
clear for Dudley to pursue his matrimonial ambitions, Amy's
death destroyed them altogether. It was unthinkable that the
Queen would marry a man suspected of his wife's murder.

But then, Elizabeth had probably never intended to take
Dudley as a husband, so the situation suited her perfectly.
Queen and favourite soon resumed their former intimacy,
albeit with a little more discretion than before. In November
1561, she disguised herself as the maid of one of her ladies so
that she could enjoy the secret pleasure of watching Dudley
shoot at Windsor. In the letters that the pair exchanged, they
used the symbol 'ôô' as code for the nickname 'Eyes' that
Elizabeth had given her favourite. For as long as Elizabeth
remained unmarried, it was inevitable that the gossip
surrounding her relationship with Dudley would intensify.
Soon, there were rumours that he 'hath got the Queen with
child'. Years later, a young man going by the name of Arthur
Dudley arrived at Philip II's court in Spain claiming to be the
bastard offspring of their clandestine affair.[27]

The question of whether Elizabeth was really the Virgin
Queen is as hotly debated today as it was in the sixteenth
century. Unless fresh evidence comes to light, the truth will
probably never be known. But the practicalities of the Tudor

court made the chances of conducting an affair in secret slim at best. As Elizabeth herself pointed out: 'I do not live in a corner. A thousand eyes see all I do.'[28] Her former stepmother Catherine Howard had risked an illicit affair and paid for it with her life. By contrast, Elizabeth was a shrewd political operator with steely self-control. She had fought too hard for her throne to throw it away on the discovery of an affair or, worse, an unwanted pregnancy. In the international marriage market, reputation was everything and, as the daughter of the 'Great Whore', Elizabeth had more to prove than most.

CHAPTER 3

'NO QUEEN IN ENGLAND BUT I'

According to the terms of her father's will, if Elizabeth remained unmarried and childless then her throne would pass first to the surviving daughters of Henry VIII's niece, Frances Grey. The eldest of these was Katherine, who was about eighteen years old at the time of Elizabeth's accession and considered an attractive prospect by dint of her looks and royal blood. Katherine's sister Mary, who was five years younger, was a good deal less attractive. But the Grey sisters' claim to the throne was tarnished by a hint of bastardy. Their grandfather, Charles Brandon, Duke of Suffolk, had a wife living (albeit an estranged one) at the time that he married their grandmother, Henry VIII's sister Mary. Charles had proved that earlier marriage invalid and secured a papal bull that confirmed the legitimacy of his marriage to the King's sister. But, as Henry himself had known all too well, in the eyes of their contemporaries, papal bulls and annulments were mere smoke and mirrors compared with the solemnity of marriage vows.

Tainted or not, the Grey sisters had royal blood and Elizabeth's predecessor had shown them considerable favour. Mary had appointed them ladies of the bedchamber and had given their mother Frances shared precedence with Margaret Tudor's daughter and namesake, Margaret Douglas, at state occasions, ahead of Elizabeth – something that the latter neither forgot nor forgave. Queen Mary had seemed so fond of

Katherine that it had been rumoured she would name her as her successor. She had even overlooked the fact that the girls' father had supported the rebel Thomas Wyatt in 1554 – which Elizabeth was not prepared to do. From the very beginning of her reign, Elizabeth made it clear that she distrusted the Grey sisters, Katherine in particular. The Spanish ambassador noticed: 'The Queen could not abide the sight of her' and that she bore her 'no goodwill'. As well as demoting Katherine and Mary to maids of honour, she made it clear that she 'does not wish her [Katherine] to succeed, in case of her death without heirs'.[1]

The elder of the Grey sisters made no secret of the fact that she was 'dissatisfied and offended' by this treatment. Her resentment towards Elizabeth made her a natural ally of the Spanish envoys at court, who soon began to promote her as the rightful successor to the heretic queen. Philip II was rumoured to be plotting a marriage between Katherine and his degenerate son, Don Carlos, as a means of reclaiming the throne that he had briefly occupied as Mary's consort. One of his envoys reported 'that if the Queen were to die your Majesty [Philip II] would get the kingdom into your family by means of Lady Katherine'. By November 1559, the Spanish ambassador confidently predicted 'the ruin which, as I think daily threatens the Queen' and that she would be 'succeeded by Lady Katherine, who would be very much more desirable than this one'.[2]

Aware of the rumours, and conscious of the threat posed by another blood claimant, Mary Stuart, Elizabeth changed tack. She promoted the Grey sisters to her bedchamber and made a show of favouring the elder. She was fooling no one. 'The Queen calls Lady Katherine her daughter,' Camden recorded, 'although the feeling between them can hardly be that of mother and child, but the Queen has thought best to put her in her chamber and makes much of her in order to keep her quiet. She even talks about formally adopting her.'[3]

This uneasy truce was not to last. In the closing weeks of 1560, Katherine took the reckless step of marrying without the Queen's knowledge or consent, which was tantamount to treason for a person of royal blood. Worse still, her new husband was another blood claimant: Edward Seymour, Earl of Hertford, nephew of Henry VIII's third queen, Jane Seymour. His father of the same name had seized power as Lord Protector for Edward VI upon Henry VIII's death, which made Elizabeth and her advisers suspect Hertford would make a similar grab for the throne. Katherine and Seymour's combined claim to the English crown was impressive, but it spelled the end of Spanish support. Quadra scorned her new husband as being 'very heretical'.[4] This in turn heightened Katherine's appeal to England's Protestants. The couple managed to keep their marriage a secret for several months; by the time Elizabeth discovered it, Katherine was heavily pregnant. Incandescent with rage, the Queen ordered them both to the Tower while her officials set to work investigating the legality of their marriage.

A little over a month later, on 24 September 1561, Lady Katherine Grey gave birth to a son in the Tower. It had been a dangerous enough threat to have two rival claimants united in marriage. Now they had a male heir whose claim descended from two royal lines. Little wonder that the Queen was reported to be 'particularly embittered' by the news and 'already ... bent on having the child declared a bastard by Parliament'.[5] Lady Katherine countered this by arranging for her new son to be baptised in secret. He was named Edward, after his father, and was later given the courtesy title of Viscount Beauchamp. But until Katherine could prove that her marriage had been lawful – a challenge, since the priest

had disappeared without trace and the only witness was dead –
the boy's legitimacy would be in doubt.

The disgrace of Lady Katherine Grey bolstered the prospects of Henry Hastings, who had recently become third Earl
of Huntingdon, as a potential successor to Elizabeth.
Huntingdon was of the old Yorkist line, his great-grandmother
being Lady Margaret Pole, niece to King Edward IV. Born
around 1536, the eldest of six sons, Huntingdon was from a
new generation which had barely known a Catholic England,
except during the brief, bloody reign of Mary, when he had
suffered a spell in the Tower.[6] His grandfather, Henry Pole,
Lord Montague, had been a close personal friend of Henry
VIII before the King became suspicious of the whole family,
chiefly because of their royal blood, and had Pole executed.

While his grandfather was still in favour, Hastings had been
educated with Henry VIII's son and heir, the future Edward
VI. Given that Elizabeth had also shared her half-brother's
studies, she had probably been acquainted with Hastings from
an early age. All three children were profoundly influenced by
the evangelical Protestantism of Edward's tutors, a faith that
was strengthened for Hastings during his time at university.
His chief supporter on Elizabeth's council was his brother-in-
law Robert Dudley (he was married to Dudley's sister,
Katherine). The earl's staunch defence of the Protestant faith
attracted several other powerful councillors to his cause,
including William Cecil, Elizabeth's most trusted adviser.
Impressive though Huntingdon's lineage was, the fact that he
was not descended from Henry VII stood against him. The
earl himself insisted that he was 'inferior to many others both
in degree and any princely quality fit for a prince'.[7]

In January 1560, Quadra reported that the opponents of
Katherine Grey had declared that no woman should succeed
and had spoken in favour of Huntingdon. Two months later,

the ambassador predicted that the Queen might go so far as to formally name him her heir. The earl himself shrank from the idea, knowing Elizabeth's sensitivity about the subject and living in dread of being sent back to the Tower. Unusually for a courtier, he seemed free of political guile or ambition and never showed any desire for the throne. His brother described him as 'a loyal servant to his sovereign, and for her service would spare neither purse nor pains; a careful man for his country being in public causes most provident, and in private most upright, loathing and detesting to seek gain by either . . . as perfect a man as flesh and blood can afford'.[8] But his brother-in-law pushed his claim for him. The higher Robert Dudley rose in the Queen's favour, the more supporters flocked to Huntingdon's cause. The ever-watchful Quadra claimed that William Cecil had remarked that Huntingdon was the real heir of England and that all the Protestants wanted him as their next king.

While the controversy of Katherine Grey's clandestine marriage was at its height, another – of equal significance to the succession – was unfolding. Lady Margaret Douglas, Countess of Lennox, was the daughter of Henry VIII's elder sister Margaret by her second marriage and therefore Elizabeth's cousin. Her royal blood had already proved both a blessing and a curse. In 1535, Margaret, then aged nineteen, had contracted a secret engagement with a member of the powerful Howard family. When her uncle the King had discovered it, he had been so enraged at what he saw as a plot to 'interrupt, impede and let the said Succession of the Crown' that he had had an Act passed the following year forbidding any member of the royal family to marry without the sovereign's permission.

Henry had soon forgiven his niece. Margaret went on to enjoy great status as a princess of royal blood for the rest of his reign and that of his elder daughter Mary. This sharpened her ambition for the throne: she boasted that she was 'the second personage to the crown of England'.⁹ The fact that she had been born on English soil strengthened her claim, although her opponents argued that this was negated by the fact that her parents had not been under allegiance to Henry VIII at the time of her birth. More damaging still was that Henry had barred his Scottish relatives from the English succession and had also deemed his niece illegitimate, since her parents' marriage had been declared unlawful after one of the most bitter and public divorce battles in history. Upon Margaret's marriage to Matthew Stewart, Earl of Lennox, in 1544, she had been obliged to sign a contract that stipulated 'None of her issue were to claim any inheritance in England' given that, as one of Elizabeth's advisers put it, she was 'a mere bastard'.¹⁰

Even without such impediments, the chances of Elizabeth naming her cousin heir were slim. There was no love lost between them and Margaret had denounced Elizabeth as a bastard before she became queen. The Countess of Lennox therefore focused her energies on promoting the claim of her eldest son, Henry, Lord Darnley. Francis II was barely cold in his grave when she sent her son to offer his condolences to the widowed Mary, Queen of Scots, confident that Darnley's good looks and charm would work their effect. This was the second time he had travelled to France to meet Mary, as his mother had dispatched him to congratulate Francis and Mary upon succeeding to the French throne, rightly judging that the new King of France was too delicate to live long. A union between Mary and Darnley, both scions of the Stuart and Tudor dynasties, would surely produce an incontestable heir to the English throne. With Darnley as Mary's consort, he and his formidable Lennox family could build up resistance to the English queen from among Scotland's Catholic nobles and their European allies. One of Elizabeth's officials reported: 'The Countess, to allure the Queen of Scots to her purpose, set forth her own title here [in England], declaring what a goodly thing it were to have both the realms in one, meaning that her son should be King both of England and Scotland.'[11]

When Mary returned to Scotland in August 1561, Margaret went about boasting that her son would soon marry the Queen of Scots and that they would rule Scotland together and depose Elizabeth. When the English queen heard of this, she immediately summoned Margaret and her husband to London. The latter was sent to the Tower and Margaret and two of her younger children were kept under house arrest at Sheen.

Just two weeks after arriving in Scotland, Mary had dispatched her secretary of state William Maitland to the English court with the intention of securing 'a more strait knot' between the two countries – or, in other words, Elizabeth's agreement that Mary should be her heir.[12] Maitland received a lukewarm welcome when he arrived in London in September 1561. The English queen complained that Mary had not yet ratified the Treaty of Edinburgh and grumbled: 'I have long enough been fed with fair words.' Nevertheless, she assured Maitland that although his mistress 'had given me just cause to be most angry with her, yet could I never find [it] in my heart to hate her'. Neither did she deny the strength of Mary's claim: 'She is of the blood of England, my cousin and next kinswoman, so that nature must bind me to love her dearly.'[13]

On the matter of the succession, though, Elizabeth proved just as evasive as her cousin. 'Think you that I could love my winding-sheet?' she demanded of Maitland, likening a named heir to a shroud. 'As for the title of my crown, for my time I think she will not attain it, nor make impediment to my issue if any shall come of my body. For so long as I live there shall be no queen in England but I.' She concluded: 'The succession of the crown of England is a matter I will not mell [meddle] in ... I know the inconstancy of the people of England, how they ever mislike the present government and have their eyes fixed upon that person that is next in line to succeed ... If they knew a certain successor of our crown [they] would have recourse thither.' In other words, keeping the succession uncertain would help keep her subjects loyal; their focus on her, rather than her heir. She pointed out that she had had personal experience of this during her sister's reign and urged: 'If it were certainly known in the world who should succeed her, she would never think herself in sufficient surety.' Before Maitland could counter this, the Queen dropped in a sly mention of Mary's rival, Lady Katherine Grey, who, unlike the Scottish queen, had the advantage of a son and heir.[14]

The most Elizabeth would concede was: 'When I am dead, they shall succeed that have most right. If the Queen your sovereign be that person, I shall never hurt her; if another have better right, it were not reasonable to require me to do a manifest injury.' She then shrewdly pointed out that if she named Mary her successor, it was more likely to sour than strengthen relations between them. 'Ye think that this device of yours should make friendship betwixt us ... How then shall I, think you, like my cousin, being once declared my heir apparent ... And what danger it were, she being a puissant princess and so near our neighbour, you may judge; so that in assuring her of the succession we might put our present estate in doubt.'[15] In other words, giving Mary hope of the English throne would serve as a restraint; naming her heir might well unleash her. Far from creating stability in her realm, the latter scenario could lead to dissension and revolt, as had happened during the reign of Elizabeth's sister, when disaffected subjects had tried to oust Mary Tudor from the throne and replace her with the heir presumptive, Elizabeth. The latter's motives were therefore entirely at odds with those of her subjects. For her, settling the succession would cause the greatest anxiety; for them, not doing so would have the same result. Her conversation with Maitland made it clear that her own concerns weighed more heavily.

Although he had failed to secure a firm promise for his royal mistress, the Scottish envoy was convinced that Elizabeth 'likes better of the Queen of Scotland's title next herself than of all others, and failing of her own issue could best be content that she should succeed and that none of all others who had any interest were meet for the crown or yet worthy of it'.[16] But when he relayed the conversation to Mary, she reacted with irritation and impatience. 'We know how near we are descended of the blood of England,' she reminded her cousin, adding: 'We will deal frankly with you, and wish that you deal friendly with us.'[17] With the situation in danger of reaching an impasse, it was agreed that the two queens should meet. Mary was delighted with the idea of seeing her 'dear and natural sister' in the flesh for the first time and Elizabeth expressed similar eagerness.[18] Maitland left for Scotland shortly afterwards, satisfied that plans for the meeting were under way.

With the dawn of a new year, attention shifted to Elizabeth's other potential successor. On 31 January 1562, an ecclesiastical high commission headed by Matthew Parker, Archbishop of Canterbury, was appointed to judge the legitimacy of Katherine Grey's marriage to Edward Seymour. Its members were in no doubt as to the verdict that the Queen desired. Accordingly, on 12 May it found that in the absence of witnesses and documentary evidence to support its validity, the 'pretended marriage' was unlawful.[19] As a consequence, young Edward Seymour was deemed illegitimate.

However, because the commission had not been able to categorically disprove the marriage, many people believed that the Queen would seek to further undermine Lady Katherine's claim to the throne. A contemporary journal recorded: 'It was thought by the people . . . that they would attempt to prove the Lady Frances her [Katherine's] mother a bastard and so to disinherit her of the title to the crown, because it was said Duke Charles [Brandon] had a wife living when he married the French queen [Henry VIII's sister, Mary Tudor, Katherine's grandmother].'[20] In the event, Elizabeth took no further action, perhaps being content for the rumours to do their work in discrediting Lady Katherine's birthright.

Now that there seemed little prospect of Lady Katherine being named heir, there was speculation that the Queen would finally declare her intentions for the succession. The same contemporary journal noted: 'The common brute is that the Queen mindeth to establish the succession of the crown.' But its author added the shrewd observation: 'Some say that she will not do it because she is persuaded that if there were any heir apparent known the people would be more affectionate to him than to her, because the nature of Englishmen is variable, not contented with the state present but desirous of alterations. And that the people in hearing never so little fault in the prince would if the successor were known, exaggerate it.'[21]

While all this was happening, it had been agreed that the meeting between the English and Scottish queens should take place in August or September 1562 at York, which was roughly halfway between their two courts. However, the plans were disrupted by events in France in July that year, when civil war broke out. Elizabeth sent troops to support the Huguenots, while Mary remained neutral. With England and Scotland once more on opposing sides, the meeting between their queens was postponed.

When she heard of this, Mary took to her bed and wept bitterly for days. Elizabeth appeared more sanguine. The meeting was bound to spark more pressure on her to settle the succession in the Scottish queen's favour, something that she was even less inclined to do now than when she inherited the throne. Although the meeting had been postponed rather than cancelled outright, it would never take place.

In September 1562, Elizabeth and her court moved west of London to Hampton Court for negotiations with the Huguenot representatives. But on 10 October, the Queen complained of feeling ill. According to the Spanish ambassador, she took a bath to alleviate her symptoms, but instead this brought on a cold and fever. Still, there seemed no immediate cause for alarm. The Queen continued to conduct state business and several letters were sent out in her hand after she had been reported sick. The last of these, written on 15 October, was to the Queen of Scots. Elizabeth signed off the letter with an apology that a 'hot fever' prevented her from writing more at that time.[22]

The following day, the diagnosis that Elizabeth and her court had dreaded from the outset was confirmed: she was suffering from smallpox, one of the most feared diseases of the age. The death toll was high and those who survived were often left hideously disfigured. This latest epidemic quickly spread across the court, claiming the life of Margaret St John, the young Countess of Bedford. 'She is in great danger,' Quadra reported on 16 October. 'If the Queen die it will be very soon, within a few days at latest.' Nobody expected her to survive. The Queen's three predecessors had reigned for six years, nine days and five years respectively, and now it seemed the ill health that dogged the Tudor dynasty would claim another victim. 'Last night the palace people were all mourning for her as if she were already dead,' Quadra wrote in another hurried dispatch the following day, adding that Elizabeth was 'almost gone'.[23] Elizabeth herself later reflected: 'Death possessed almost every joint of me, so as I wished then that the feeble thread of life, which lasted, me thought, all too long, might by Clotho's hand have quietly been cut off.'[24]

Fearing that she was about to die, the Queen felt compelled to defend her reputation for posterity. Before witnesses, she vowed: 'Although she loved and had always loved Lord Robert [Dudley] dearly, as God was her witness, nothing improper had ever passed between them.'[25] The cynical might say that words are easy. But in this God-fearing age, when Catholics and Protestants alike strove to attain their place in heaven, few people would have risked their eternal salvation by uttering a lie as they prepared to meet their maker.

Elsewhere in the palace, an urgent meeting of the council was called, prompting frenzied speculation: 'Out of the 15 or 16 of them that are there were nearly as many different opinions about the succession to the Crown. It would be impossible to please them all.'[26] The new religious settlement seemed forgotten as the council divided itself between Catholic and Protestant claimants. On the Protestant side were Lady Katherine Grey and Henry Hastings, third Earl of Huntingdon, who were supported by two of the most powerful men on Elizabeth's council: William Cecil and Robert Dudley.

'Now all the talk is who is to be her successor', the Spanish ambassador reported.[27] He predicted that the Catholics would hold sway but admitted that they were divided among themselves, with some favouring Mary, Queen of Scots and others Lady Margaret Douglas, another of the English queen's cousins. But Henry VIII's will, drawn up just sixteen years earlier, was still fresh in people's minds and stated very clearly that his Stuart relatives should never inherit the crown of England. Furthermore, a law passed in 1351, during the reign of Edward III, decreed that 'aliens' (those not born on English soil) could not inherit any land there.[28] Pro-Stuart commentators argued that the English claim of suzerainty over Scotland meant that the latter was not, technically, a foreign country. But their opponents pointed out that at the time of Mary Stuart's birth her father James V was at war with Henry VIII and that she herself had never paid homage to Elizabeth I. On two very powerful counts, therefore, the Scottish queen and her descendants were effectively barred from inheriting the English throne.

Another Catholic claimant was Lady Margaret Stanley (née Clifford), wife of Henry, Lord Strange, and daughter of Eleanor Brandon, the younger daughter of Henry VIII's sister Mary and her husband Charles Brandon, Duke of Suffolk. As well as having a right to inherit thanks to Henry's will, Margaret had been named in Edward VI's 'Devise', after Lady Jane Grey and her sisters. Conscious of this, she reportedly alleged that her Grey cousins were debarred from the succession because of their sister Jane's treason, which made Margaret next in line by Henry VIII's will and 'as the nearest in blood . . . legitimately of English birth'.[29] Also in Margaret's favour was the fact that she had two living sons, Ferdinando and William. But for all her claims, she was of the junior Suffolk branch and a Catholic, which meant that her supporters were fewer in number than those of the Grey sisters and were mostly limited to her native Lancashire.

The ripples of unease spread beyond the court as news of the Queen's imminent demise was carried to cities and towns across England. At the same time, ambassadorial dispatches ensured that it became the talk of Europe. Elizabeth's greatest continental rival and former brother-in-law Philip II was quick to spy an opportunity to take back the kingdom that he had jointly ruled with Mary. Quadra urged that if the uncertainty continued, Philip could 'take steps in the matter'. Meanwhile, in France it was falsely reported that the beleaguered queen had already nominated Huntingdon as her successor.[30]

As the crisis reached fever pitch, on 23 October news arrived from the Queen's privy chamber. Against all the odds, Elizabeth had survived. The pus-filled sores had 'erupted', signalling that the contagion was almost over. There were conflicting reports as to whether she bore any scars. One member of the court reported that she had emerged virtually unscathed: 'The Queen is whole of the small-pox, not having had many signs on her face.' By contrast, Quadra claimed that she would 'not be visible for some time owing to the disfigurement of her face'.[31]

Either way, the experience had served as a salutary reminder of Elizabeth's mortality. The Spanish ambassador reported that the first thing she did upon regaining consciousness was to beg her council to make Robert Dudley protector of the kingdom with a title and an income of £20,000 per year (equivalent to more than £4.5 million today). 'Everything she asked was promised, but will not be fulfilled,' he added, knowing how much the Queen's favourite was resented by his fellow councillors. By 25 October, the Queen was sufficiently recovered to have a letter sent out in her name to the French ambassador.[32]

When Elizabeth heard that her councillors had met to discuss her successor, any sense of relief at her narrow escape quickly dissolved and she 'wept with rage'. Two months later, Quadra reported that her fury had still not abated. 'She was extremely angry with them, and told them that the marks they saw on her face were not wrinkles, but pits of small-pox, and that although she might be old God could send her children as He did to Saint Elizabeth.'[33] Although at twenty-nine years old the Queen was younger than her biblical namesake whom God had blessed with a child late in life, in an age when many women married and bore children in their mid-teens, she was considered to be running out of time.

The Queen's close attendant, Sybil Penn, who had nursed her through smallpox, contracted the disease herself. She died at Hampton Court on 6 November, which prompted Elizabeth to leave the palace shortly afterwards.[34] She seldom visited it again during the course of her long life, harbouring a superstitious dread of the place where her reign – and the Tudor dynasty – had almost been snuffed out. At around the same time as her departure, she received a petition from Lady Margaret Douglas for her husband's release from the Tower on the grounds of ill health. Perhaps minded to pay greater regard to her potential heirs, the Queen agreed that Lennox should join his wife at Sheen. They were released the following February.

Huntingdon was not so fortunate. Even though he had consistently refused to press his claim, he found himself out in the cold and his wife Katherine was given 'a privy nip' when she next appeared at court to serve the Queen. 'I perceive she hath some jealous conceit of me,' the earl complained to Robert Dudley. 'How far I have always been from conceiting any greatness of myself, nay, how ready I have always been to shun applauses both by my continual low sail and my carriage I do assure myself is best known to your lordship.' He therefore begged his brother-in-law 'to frame a new heart in her Majesty's princely breast . . . for never shall there be a truer heart in any subject than I will carry to her Majesty so long as I breathe'.[35] But even the Queen's closest favourite could not persuade her of Huntingdon's loyalty and he remained in the political wilderness for several years.

Elizabeth's brush with death had brought the succession to the fore and, once there, it would not recede into the shadows. Quadra shrewdly observed: 'The Queen will be glad to avoid having a parliament, as she knows they would like to discuss the question of the succession, and she has not the least wish that it should be opened. Public feeling, however, is so disturbed that I do not see how she can avoid it, and I am told by persons of position that they believe the matter will be dealt with whether the Queen wishes it or not.'[36]

He was right. Parliament met just three months after the Queen's recovery and was dominated by the question of who would inherit the throne after her. Both Houses petitioned their sovereign to follow her father's example and create an act of succession. Expectations about this had been raised in the first Parliament of Elizabeth's reign, which had passed an Act of Recognition of the Queen's Highness's Title to the Imperial Crown of this Realm. In asserting Elizabeth's position as England's rightful queen, the act not only referred to her hereditary claim but to Henry VIII's Third Succession Act, which confirmed her place in the succession. Parliament therefore anticipated that Elizabeth would pass a similar act to nominate her own heirs. At the same time, it urged her to marry so that the future of her realm was not left in doubt a moment longer.

However, Elizabeth's aversion to marriage remained so strong that even the recent, salutary reminder of her mortality had not shaken it. Rather than being cowed by the intense pressure from the all-male Lords and Commons, she reacted with fury. The draft of the speech she made in Parliament, written in her own hand, betrayed her impatience. Her usually neat script was hurried and untidy, and there were numerous crossings-out and underlined words as she tried to channel her anger into a more measured speech. She scorned the 'laboured orations out of such jangling subjects' mouths', but then tempered the insult by striking through the word 'jangling'.[37]

The final speech was a masterpiece of statecraft, one that played her ministers at their own game. If she, a mere woman, was too weak to govern a kingdom on her own, how could she possibly decide on such a momentous issue as marriage? Addressing the Speaker, Thomas Williams, she pleaded: 'The weight and greatness of this matter might cause in me being a woman wanting both wit and memory some fear to speak and bashfulness besides, a thing appropriate to my sex.'

Having assured Parliament that she appreciated their concerns, Elizabeth resorted to what would become a familiar delaying tactic, telling them: 'I am determined in this so great and weighty a matter to defer my answer until some other time, because I will not in so deep a matter wade with so shallow a wit.' She ended her speech by reminding those present that while she might not wish to fulfil her natural womanly duties by taking a husband, she would always fulfil her maternal role: 'I assure you all that though after my death you may have many stepdames, yet shall you never have any a more mother, than I mean to be unto you all.'[38]

According to Quadra, shortly after Elizabeth gave this speech, the Members of Parliament were presented with 'a proposition . . . made on behalf of the Queen to the lords . . . to regulate the succession . . . by a public Act, reducing the right to succeed to four families, amongst which the Queen might nominate the person who appeared nearest and fittest to succeed her'. He went on: 'They have been discussing this matter all the week, trying to discover some solution which will satisfy the needs of the nation, and at the same time fulfil the Queen's plans and keep the Queen of Scotland in suspense.'[39] If this was true, then nothing came of it.

Casting herself as a mother to her people, as she had in the 1563 Parliament, was a clever metaphor and one that Elizabeth would employ time and again as her reign progressed. But its power faded next to the reality of one blood claimant's motherhood. As the Queen had lain close to death at Hampton Court, one of her closest kin was about four months into another pregnancy. Even though Elizabeth had ordered that Katherine Grey and her husband be kept strictly separate in the Tower, their gaolers had evidently allowed the couple to meet in secret. A London tailor named Henry Machyn noted in his diary: 'On 10th day of February was brought a-bed within the Tower with a son my Lady Katherine Hertford, wife to the earl of Hertford.' He added that two of the yeoman warders stood as godparents at the christening.[40]

When news of this reached the Queen, she turned 'the colour of a corpse'. Now Katherine Grey, the woman whom many believed was the rightful heir to her throne, had two male heirs while Elizabeth herself remained unmarried and childless. The Queen's reprisal was swift and severe. Edward Seymour was hauled before the Court of Star Chamber and accused of compounding his original offence of 'deflowering a virgin of the blood royal in the Queen's house' by having 'ravished her a second time'. After being found guilty, he was fined the staggering sum of £15,000 – around £3.5 million in today's money.[41] The lieutenant of the Tower, Sir Edward Warner, was dismissed from his post but Elizabeth did not risk his successor showing a similar leniency. In August 1563, she had Katherine and her husband removed from the fortress on the pretence of protecting them from the plague and placed them under house arrest many miles apart. Heartbroken at being separated from her husband, Katherine wrote at once to Cecil, begging him to intercede with the Queen, whose forgiveness 'with upstretched hands and down bent knees from the bottom of my heart most humbly I crave'.[42] She received no answer.

But Katherine was not without her supporters. In the same year that she was moved from the Tower, John Hales, a Member of Parliament, wrote his *Declaration* in support of her right to the throne. As well as defending the legitimacy of Katherine's claim, it denounced those of her chief rivals, Mary Stuart and Lady Margaret Douglas.[43] Hales's work inspired another tract in support of the Suffolk claim that was published two years later. *Allegations Against the Surmised Title of the Quine of Scotts* made much of the traditional enmity between England and Scotland and pointed to Mary Stuart's alien status as the principal reason to discount her claim. The author concluded: 'The best remedy of all that may be thought of: were if it pleased god to grant a good husband and children to Queen Elizabeth.'[44]

Amid all the uncertainty of rival claimants and the Queen's dogged refusal to resolve the issue, Cecil began to draw up plans for something altogether more radical: a political future without a monarch. Quadra reported that 'in order to satisfy all these divergent interests', the lords of the council 'have agreed to pass an Act providing that in case the Queen dies no office, either judicial or in the household, shall become vacant, and twenty-four councillors are appointed to administer the Government'.[45] No formal record of this survives, but it is corroborated by Cecil's draft for a bill that if Elizabeth died without the succession being resolved, a council should be appointed to 'direct the public affairs of the realm'. He probably envisaged a temporary interregnum rather than a permanent republic, with the privy council taking the place of the sovereign until the succession was settled. The council, which had been dramatically reduced in size from Henry VIII's time and averaged about thirteen members, was the most important institution in government after the sovereign. It met three or four times a week but individual members were in almost constant attendance on their queen. The council's role was wide-ranging and included advising the monarch on all aspects of state and policy, undertaking routine administration, drafting diplomatic instructions, ordering the clergy, sheriffs and local officials, and coordinating myriad other areas of government. It was therefore a highly capable, powerful body that could step in to safeguard the kingdom against civil war, foreign intrigues and a Catholic monarch until a new incumbent was safely on the throne.

Cecil's scheme was pragmatic, but it was also unprecedented in England. Ever since the Anglo-Saxon king Æthelstan had been proclaimed 'King of the English' in 927, power had been centred upon the monarch. The evolution of Parliament in the 1200s had provided a check to royal authority, but there had never been any question that ultimate authority rested with the sovereign. This was certainly true of Elizabeth, who had always been careful to avoid the dangers of so much power being vested in a group of privy councillors. She favoured a policy of 'divide and rule', pitting one councillor against another – notably William Cecil and his fierce rival Robert Dudley. On occasion, she also acted without consulting the council at all.

The model that Elizabeth's chief adviser was proposing could therefore have overturned a system of monarchical rule that had existed for well over 600 years. And what began as a temporary measure could easily have signalled the end of the monarchy forever. Once a group of councillors had enjoyed untrammelled power, they would be unlikely to relinquish it and return to meek obedience. Even if the crown had endured, its authority might well have been permanently limited by government, as happened six decades after Elizabeth's death when Charles II restored the monarchy but wielded little more than symbolic power.

That William Cecil, an official whose loyalty to the crown was unshakeable, should even contemplate such a drastic step betrays the deep-seated anxiety within Elizabeth's government. It was a desperate measure but, Cecil judged, these were desperate times. For now, he let the scheme drop and nothing further was heard of it after Parliament had been dissolved and the white heat of the succession debate had begun to cool. But he had far from forgotten it.

CHAPTER 4

'TWO WOMEN WILL NOT AGREE VERY LONG TOGETHER'

In 1564, Sir James Melville, ambassador to Mary, Queen of Scots arrived at Elizabeth's court. His memoir of the visit betrays the deeply personal nature of the cousins' rivalry. Elizabeth seemed less concerned with the political situation in Scotland than with the famed beauty of its queen. 'She desired to know of me, what colour of hair was reputed best; and which of the two was fairest,' he recalled. 'I answered, They were both the fairest ladies in their countries; that her Majesty was whiter, but my Queen was very lovely.' Still Elizabeth persisted, asking next who was the tallest. When Sir James admitted that here Mary had the advantage, the English queen snapped: 'Then . . . she is too high; for I myself am neither too high nor too low.'[1]

But diplomacy was the order of the day. Elizabeth assured Melville that she had a great desire to meet his royal mistress, but that in the meantime she would console herself with looking at Mary's picture. Summoning him to her bedchamber, she opened a little cabinet and took out a miniature of Mary, then made a show of kissing it with great reverence. However, when Melville suggested that she should send her cousin the 'fair ruby, as great as a tennis ball' that he had spotted among her jewels, Elizabeth quickly refused and chose a much smaller diamond instead. Determined to leave the ambassador with a favourable impression, she repeated her earnest wish to meet her cousin. Taking her at her word, Melville offered to convey her to Scotland in secret, disguised as a page. 'She appeared to like that kind of language,' he recalled, but 'only answered it with a sigh, saying, "Alas! if I might do it thus."'[2]

The Scottish ambassador was not fooled by this display of regret, nor by the many protestations of 'great love' that Elizabeth made towards Mary. Upon his return to Scotland, he at once sought an audience with his royal mistress and relayed everything that had been said. With greater shrewdness than she showed on other occasions, Mary asked him: 'Whether I thought that Queen meant truly toward her inwardly in her heart, as she appeared to do outwardly in her speech.' Melville admitted: 'There was neither plain dealing, nor upright meaning; but great dissimulation, emulation and fear, lest her [Mary's] princely qualities should over soon chase her from the Kingdom.'[3]

The Queen of Scots was no less duplicitous. She pretended to use their sex as a means of uniting them in some kind of sisterly bond: two female sovereigns trying to make their way in a world dominated by men. 'It is fitter for none to live in peace than for women,' she once told her cousin. In fact, their sex proved a source of discord, adding a dangerously personal element to their already intense political rivalry. 'It is certain that two women will not agree very long together,' observed a Spanish envoy.[4]

Tension soon mounted over the issue of Mary's marriage. In contrast to her English cousin, the Queen of Scots viewed the position of an unmarried female ruler as something undesirable and therefore temporary. She told Elizabeth's ambassador that she was surprised her cousin had not yet taken a husband, given her advancing years, the 'wise counsel about her' and that she might have already been 'matched with the greatest'. In a deliberate sideswipe at her older rival, she added that her own years 'are not so many but she may abide'.[5] For Elizabeth, the stakes for Mary's marriage were almost as high as for her own. If her greatest rival married a prince of Spain or France, then England would face the threat of invasion by a Catholic potentate across her northern border, as well as from across the Channel to the south. Anxious to influence Mary's choice, Elizabeth used the succession to justify her role as adviser. After all, the child of this new marriage might well sit on the English throne one day.

Not surprisingly, when informed by her emissaries of the candidates for Mary's hand that had been proposed by Catholic Spain and its satellites, the English queen objected to each. She took particular exception to Archduke Charles of Austria, who was still in theory one of her own suitors. Neither did she wish Mary to become Queen of France once more by marrying the young Charles IX. Thomas Randolph, Elizabeth's ambassador to Scotland, predicted that if Mary persisted in favouring such candidates, it would 'dissolve the concord that is presently between the two nations' and disrupt 'such right or title as [Mary] might have to succeed in the crown of England'. Instead, Elizabeth tried to steer her cousin towards an English husband, 'with whom her Majesty would more readily and more easily declare, that she inclines that failing of children of her own body, you might succeed to her crown', as Melville reported.[6] In reality, of course, she had no authority to dictate Mary's choice, beyond the unspoken prospect that she might name the Queen of Scots her heir if she proved compliant.

But nobody was expecting the suitor whom Elizabeth put forward in 1563: her own great favourite, Robert Dudley. She even suggested that the three of them live together at the English court, presumably because she could not bear to be apart from him. Elizabeth told Mary that Dudley was the man 'whom she would have herself married, had she ever minded to take a husband. But being determined to end her life in virginity, she wished that the Queen her sister might marry him.'[7] Mary's first response was one of disbelief. The English queen assured her that she was in earnest and repeatedly hinted that she would at last name Mary as her successor if she agreed to the proposal. To further the match, Dudley was created Earl of Leicester the following year, by which time he had attracted a good deal of support among Mary's Protestant advisers. Finally, in January 1565, Mary herself agreed to the plan. But to everyone's amazement, her prospective husband refused. Randolph, who had spent many long months bringing the marriage to fruition, was dumbfounded. 'A man of that nature I never found any . . . he whom I go about to make as happy as ever was any, to put him in possession of a kingdom, to lay in his naked arms a most fair . . . lady.'[8]

By March 1565, Elizabeth had resumed her former position of decorous and evasive answers whenever the question of naming Mary her heir was raised. As for Dudley, all the time that he had been mooted as a husband for the Scottish queen, he had been busy furthering the suit of another candidate. Henry, Lord Darnley, and his mother Lady Margaret Douglas had become regular fixtures at the English court after the latter's release in February 1563. Elizabeth had decided not to make good her threat to have Margaret's claim to the throne annulled, perhaps fearing that the same threat could be directed at herself. She may also have been minded not to reduce the number of potential heirs at a time when relations with Mary, Queen of Scots were tense and Lady Katherine Grey was languishing in captivity.

The English queen was conspicuous in her favour towards Lord Darnley. His youth and good looks made him a natural companion for a queen who delighted in being surrounded by adoring male courtiers. But, as ever, there was statecraft at play. Showing preferment towards the son of a devout Catholic appeased those of the same faith both in England and abroad who were hostile towards the Protestant Queen of England. In Elizabeth's eyes, the claim of Darnley and his family also presented an obstacle between the Queen of Scots and the English throne. What she did not foresee was that he would prove to be the exact opposite.

In September 1564, the Scottish Parliament restored Darnley's father to his estates and titles as Earl of Lennox, which had been forfeited in 1545 when he had tried to advance Henry VIII's cause north of the border. With Lennox back in favour at the Scottish court, the way was now clear for Mary to take his son as her second husband. Even though the Queen of Scots had been persuaded to accept Robert Dudley as a suitor, for some time her preference had been for Lord Darnley. During his visit to Elizabeth's court, Melville had acted as a go-between for Mary and the Countess of Lennox, whose brush with the Tower had not dissuaded her from scheming behind the English queen's back.

Eager to seize the advantage, Margaret petitioned Elizabeth to allow her son to visit his father in Scotland. The Queen agreed on condition that Darnley must return if commanded, or else forfeit his English estates and titles. On 3 February 1565, he left London and was in Edinburgh nine days later. Thereafter, he was almost constantly in the presence of Mary, who declared him 'the lustiest and best proportioned long man that she had seen'. In preparation for the marriage that now appeared certain, on 15 May Darnley was made a knight, Lord of Ardmanoch and Earl of Ross. Philip of Spain declared his support for the match: 'The bridegroom and his parents being good Catholics and our affectionate servitors; and considering the Queen's [Mary's] good claims to the crown of England.'[9]

All this caused great consternation at the English court. Elizabeth sent Sir Nicholas Throckmorton to demand Darnley's return with the warning that if he went ahead with the marriage, it would be 'perilous to the sincere amity between Queens and their realms'.[10] She also had his mother placed under house arrest at Whitehall. At the same time, her council proposed that she show greater leniency towards Mary's rival for the throne, Lady Katherine Grey.

It was to no avail. On 28 July, a proclamation was made in Edinburgh that the government of Scotland would be in the joint names of the king and queen. In effect this meant that Darnley would take the same precedence over his wife as every other man in sixteenth-century society did over theirs. The following day, the pair were married in a Roman Catholic ceremony at Holyrood. When news of the marriage reached England, all the 'inward griefs and grudges' between the two queens 'bursted forth'. The pretence of sisterly affection was swiftly – and permanently – abandoned, replaced by 'so great a coldness . . . for in their hearts from that time forth there was nothing but jealousies and suspicions'. Just a few days after the wedding, Mary and Darnley pressed Elizabeth to formally recognise them 'as the persons by the law of God and nature next inheritable to the crown of England'.[11]

Having failed to prevent Mary's marriage to Darnley, Elizabeth's envoy Throckmorton resolved to make the most of his brief time in Scotland by addressing the vexed question of the succession. He was in the virtually unique position of being close to both queens. A cousin and servant of Henry VIII's last wife, Katherine Parr, he had become acquainted with Elizabeth during her sojourn in the household of Katherine and her new husband Thomas Seymour, who had soon become fatally attracted to his young stepdaughter. Soon after her accession, Elizabeth appointed Throckmorton ambassador to France and during his five-year stay he became close to Mary, despite the differences in their religion. He therefore now felt able to send her a long and frank letter about the succession.

'Your Majesty hath in England many friends of all degrees who favour your title,' Throckmorton assured her, 'but for divers respects.' His view was shared by Francis Russell, second Earl of Bedford, governor of Berwick and warden of the east marches of Scotland. In a letter to Robert Dudley of November 1565, Russell referred to 'The Queen of Scots, who I fear has too many friends at Court'. While some were genuinely persuaded by the justice of Mary's claim, by her 'virtues and liberality' and by her Catholic faith, others were motivated by their aversion to Lady Katherine Grey. Throckmorton went on to share, in cipher, the names of certain powerful nobles who stood ready to send men and arms if ever she needed to press her claim by force. He warned, though, that she also had 'divers enemies' who would miss no opportunity to ruin her chances of succeeding to the English throne. He concluded: 'In one point all concur, both friends and enemies, yea the whole people, that they are most desirous to have the succession of the crown declared and assured, that they may be at a certainty; only the Queen herself is of a contrary opinion, and would be glad the matter should always be in suspense.'[12] This was treason on the part of Elizabeth's ambassador and reveals the lengths to which her officials were willing to go in order to resolve what was rapidly becoming a succession crisis.

With Elizabeth still smarting about her cousin's marriage, it was the worst possible time for another claimant to marry without her permission. Lady Mary was the youngest of the Grey sisters and the least favoured. The Spanish ambassador described her as 'little, crookbacked, and very ugly'.[13] She may have suffered from scoliosis and was only about four feet tall. By contrast, her prospective husband was a giant of a man. Thomas Keyes was the sergeant porter at court, a trustworthy but low-ranking position. He did not have a drop of royal blood in his veins so hardly posed a threat to Elizabeth's crown, but the fact that he married Mary in secret immediately excited her suspicion, not to mention outrage. 'Here is an unhappy chance and monstrous,' reported William Cecil in the middle of August 1565. 'The Sergeant Porter, being the biggest gentleman in the Court, hath married secretly the Lady Mary Grey, the least of all the Court.'

While most of their fellow courtiers viewed the mésalliance as amusing, the Queen insisted that it was part of a wider plot and ranted that she would have no bastard of Keyes' on her throne. 'The offence is very great,' William Cecil noted.[14] Having learned from the example of Mary's sister Katherine, Elizabeth ordered that the newlyweds be imprisoned separately so that there would be no prospect of heirs from this marriage. They never saw each other again. Keyes' prolonged spell in Fleet prison broke his health and he died in 1571. His widow remained under arrest in a succession of different houses far distant from court.[15]

Elizabeth now had three claimants to her throne under lock and key. Lady Mary's sister Katherine was moved to a series of houses east of London and guarded by some of the Queen's most trusted courtiers. The Countess of Lennox was moved to the Tower in 1566. Elizabeth was deaf to Mary, Queen of Scots' pleas that her mother-in-law be released, considering her poor health and the fact that she was 'so tender of blood' to the English queen.[16] Mary continued to petition Elizabeth, even though her marriage to the Countess's son was already beginning to unravel.

Almost as soon as the crown of Scotland was on his head, Darnley's true character showed through the charming façade that had captivated his new wife. Even Mary's apologist, Sir James Melville, decried: 'No woman of spirit would make choice of such a man, who more resembled a woman than a man.'[17] Arrogant, feckless and vain, Darnley soon inflamed the already tense political situation in Scotland. When Throckmorton had been sent to Scotland the previous year to prevent Mary's marriage to Darnley, he had urged her to reconcile the warring factions in her kingdom in order to prove to the people of England what an able ruler she was and thereby strengthen her claim to Elizabeth's throne. Instead, the Scottish queen had ignored the ill-feeling against Darnley and doggedly insisted on taking him as her husband. The powerful Protestant lords, Mary's half-brother James Stewart, Earl of Moray, and James Hamilton, second Earl of Arran, had been opposed to the marriage from the start and now moved to open rebellion.

'I know now for certain that this Queen repents her marriage, that she hates Darnley and all his kin,' Elizabeth's ambassador reported.[18] Mary had married in haste but had little leisure to repent because the situation was rapidly spiralling out of control. She had become pregnant a few months after the wedding and in March 1566 Darnley subjected her to 'so odious a crime, as to hazard her life, together with his child which was in her belly'. Jealous of his wife's friendship with her Italian secretary, David Riccio, he joined a plot hatched by James Douglas, Earl of Morton, and other enemies of Mary to murder him.

The Queen of Scots was at supper at Holyrood Palace on the evening of 7 March when Lord Ruthven, George Douglas and their henchmen burst into her closet and stabbed Riccio to death as he clung to her waist, screaming for mercy. Fearing

for her own life, four nights later the heavily pregnant Queen
of Scots fled from Holyrood at midnight to Dunbar Castle.
Darnley, who had distanced himself from the murderers, all
of whom had escaped to England, went with her, but it was
obvious that her infatuation had turned to loathing. 'I could
perceive nothing from that day forth, but great grudges that
she entertained in her heart,' Melville observed.[19]

At first, Elizabeth seemed to sympathise with the plotters,
which prompted Mary to write a furious letter, demanding to
know if her cousin was minded 'to support them against her
as she boasts, for she is not so disprovided but that other
Princes will help her to defend her realm'.[20] The English queen
quickly changed her stance and took to wearing her cousin's
miniature on a chain about her waist, clearly visible to everyone at court. 'Had I been in Queen Mary's place, I would have
taken my husband's dagger and stabbed him with it,' she
declared.[21] But this display of female solidarity proved fleeting
and soon relations between the two queens were as testy as
before.

As the crisis in Scotland deepened, another developed
south of the border. 'The Queen of England was taken with a
great fever, that none believed she could live,' Melville
reported. 'All that kingdom was thereby in great perplexity.'
In alarm, two previously opposed factions at the English court
united in sending for Mary to 'set the crown of England upon
her head'.[22] Coming just four years after Elizabeth's brush
with death, when she contracted smallpox, this was yet another
salutary reminder that the fate of the kingdom rested entirely
on her shoulders.

But the Queen of Scots was too distracted by matters closer
to home to push her advantage. Desperate to avenge Riccio's
murder, she grew ever closer to James Hepburn, fourth Earl
of Bothwell, Lord High Admiral of Scotland, an ambitious

and volatile member of her court. Just as she had ignored the opposition to Darnley before their marriage, so she paid no heed to the 'great dissatisfaction of many' at her obvious favour towards Bothwell.[23] With the latter's help, she assembled an army and wrested back control from Moray and his faction.

The Scottish government was still riven with factions, though, and matters continued to teeter on a knife edge as Mary prepared for the birth of her child. She instructed Melville to write to Elizabeth, who had now recovered, requesting that she send some of her ladies to attend the Queen of Scots in her confinement. He was also to draft a letter announcing the birth, leaving a blank 'to be filled up either with a son or a daughter'.[24]

On 19 June 1566, Melville was informed that his royal mistress had given birth to a healthy son that morning, named James. Within minutes, he had mounted his horse and was riding south with the news. The Queen of England was at Greenwich and 'in great mirth, dancing after supper' when he arrived. He claimed that upon being told that her rival now had a son and heir, her good humour instantly evaporated and she lamented: 'The Queen of Scots was mother of a fair son, while she was but of barren stock.' Melville's account is not corroborated by any other source. Indeed, Philip II's envoy reported that 'the Queen seemed very glad of the birth of the infant'.[25] Whatever her personal feelings on the matter, the arrival of a male heir had added a dangerous new dimension to England's relations with Scotland.

The following day, Elizabeth greeted Melville with 'a glad and cheerful countenance', insisting 'that the joyful news of the Queen her sister's delivery of a fair son . . . had recovered her out of a heavy sickness which she had lain under for fifteen days'.[26] She accepted Mary's invitation to stand as godmother but excused herself from attending the christening because of pressing affairs of state. The Scottish envoy grasped the opportunity to press the matter of the succession. Anxious in case James's birth might encourage Elizabeth to have children of her own, he stressed that Mary's heir had been 'dear bought with the peril of her life, she being so sore handled that she wished she had never been married'. He admitted that he had embellished this peril 'to give her [Elizabeth] a little scare from marriage'. Seeing how the news had drawn other powerful English nobles to Mary's cause, notably Thomas Howard, Duke of Norfolk, and Henry Herbert, Earl of Pembroke, he entreated the Queen 'to embrace that fair offered opportunity of satisfying the minds of many, as well in England as in Scotland, who desired to see that matter out of doubt'. Elizabeth claimed 'that she wished from her heart that it should be that way decided'.[27] Melville was a seasoned enough ambassador to see through this and also recognised that Mary's chief opponent on Elizabeth's council was William Cecil, whom he rightly predicted would find ways to prevent the two queens from meeting.

News of the Scottish prince's birth spread rapidly across the continent. In Paris, a Scotsman named Patrick Adamson, who was in league with Hamilton, published a Latin poem describing James as prince of Scotland, England, France and Ireland. When the English Parliament met, a lawyer named James Dalton launched a furious tirade against the poem, declaring that he hoped never to see the day 'that ever any Scot or stranger shall have interest in the Crown of this realm, for it is against the law that any person other than such as be born the Prince's subjects hold merit in this land'.[28] Those assembled were in full agreement and demanded that Adamson be punished. The storm was eventually calmed by Mary's ambassador and by Elizabeth herself, but it had been a revealing episode. Today, the union between England and Scotland has been in place for well over four centuries, so it is easy to underestimate just how much the Scots in general – and James in particular – were viewed as foreigners by Elizabeth's subjects. An anti-Stuart tract of 1565 had warned that Mary's accession would make the English 'bound and subject unto a foreign nation' and condemned the Scots as 'a people by custom and almost nature our enemies, thirsty of our blood, poor and miserable by their country and envious of our welfare'.[29]

The same xenophobic attitude had condemned the marriage of Elizabeth's half-Spanish sister Mary to Philip of Spain, sparking widespread resentment and even revolt. When Elizabeth came to the throne, there had been a collective sigh of relief that here, at last, was a true Englishwoman born. The Spanish envoy noted: 'She is very much wedded to the people and thinks as they do, and therefore treats foreigners slightingly.'[30] Even the Catholic north, which would always prove most troublesome to her, had rejoiced at the accession of 'a princess . . . of no mingled blood of Spaniard, or stranger, but born mere English here among us, and therefore most natural unto us'.[31] When it came to the succession, blood was not necessarily thicker than water.

But there was no denying that the presence of a son and heir had considerably strengthened Mary's claim to the English throne. This intensified the pressure on Elizabeth to name her heir. By now, both her council and Parliament were fiercely divided between the supporters of Mary and those of Katherine Grey. 'Although the Scotch Queen has a large party in the House of Lords, it is thought that Katherine would have nearly all the members of the lower Chamber on her side,' reported the Spanish ambassador, Diego Guzmán de Silva. 'It seems, therefore, that everything tends to disturbance.'[32]

While Elizabeth played a more ambiguous game with the issue of her marriage to keep foreign suitors in play, she was much clearer when it came to naming her successor. In October 1566, the French ambassador reported her furious response to a parliamentary delegation sent to press the matter: 'As for handling the succession, not one of them [Elizabeth's subjects] should do it; for she would reserve that for herself. She had no desire to be buried alive, like her sister. Well she knew how people at that time had flocked to her [Elizabeth] at Hatfield: she wanted no such journeyings in her reign. Nor had she the slightest wish for their counsel on this subject.' The Queen upbraided the delegation for not considering the danger she would face if she named a successor and reflected bitterly: 'Nothing said for my safety, but only for themselves.' She went on to remind them again of the direct experience she had had as an heir in waiting during Mary's reign: 'I am sure there was not one of them that ever was a second person, as I have been, and have tasted of the practices against my sister . . . I stood in danger of my life, my sister was so incensed against me. I did differ from her in religion and I was sought for divers ways, and so shall never be my successor.' Whipped up into an indignant fury, she then roundly told those present that the succession was too important a matter to be considered by 'a knot of hare-brains'.[33]

But Elizabeth's subjects would not be silenced so easily. Just before the autumn Parliament in 1566, a pamphlet entitled 'The Common Cry of Englishmen' petitioned the Queen to name her successor in the opening session. Now that Elizabeth was in her thirties, the idea that by marrying she would resolve the issue had started to recede. 'It is not your marriage, most noble Queen, which can help this mischief, for a certain ruin cannot be stayed by an uncertain means. It is uncertain whether you shall marry; it is uncertain whether you shall have issue in your marriage; it is uncertain whether your issue shall live to succeed you . . . But this is most certain, that unless the succession after you be . . . appointed and ordered, England runneth to most certain ruin and destruction.' The tract urged Members of Parliament to take matters into their own hands if Elizabeth 'of timorousness to attempt a matter of so great weight' failed, which hardly recommended its author to her.[34]

De Silva was confident that the succession would be debated and claimed that the Protestants were divided between Lady Katherine Grey and the Earl of Huntingdon, 'who is the man to suit them best'. While Parliament was sitting, a group of law students at Lincoln's Inn held a disputation on the matter and found that the Scottish queen as an alien could not legally 'succeed to the crown, even if she were the nearest in birth and the ablest'.[35] But Parliament was dissolved before the succession could be discussed.

Shortly afterwards, Edmund Plowden, one of England's most eminent common lawyers, wrote a treatise in support of Mary Stuart's claim. Central to his argument was that Scotland was 'within the obedience of England', rather than being a foreign country, and that 'the realm of Scotland first came from and was first given by the crown of England'. This countered the argument that as an alien, Mary was unable to inherit property or land in England. Plowden also stressed the 'proximity of blood' between Mary and Henry VIII. But his fear of reprisal was evident: 'In dealing in titles of kingdoms there is much danger, and especially to the subjects, and in these cases I think the surest way is to be silent, for in silence there is safety but in speech there is peril, and in writing more.' Plowden's willingness to risk the consequences of speaking out indicates just how much anxiety surrounded the succession. He justified his defiance of the Queen's command on the basis that he hoped his expertise might help 'to conceive the right way in this dark mist'.[36]

Mary may have had the upper hand over Elizabeth after the birth of her son, but she was plagued by the worsening situation in Scotland and still heartbroken over Riccio's violent death. Melville advised her to focus less on her enemies there and more on 'the greater multitude of friends that she had got in England'. He urged that her priority should be 'joining the two kingdoms in a happy monarchy'.[37] Written after the events that he describes, Melville's account owes much to the wisdom of hindsight and cannot be relied upon as a wholly accurate source. If he did offer Mary this advice, she would have done well to heed it. Instead, she focused her energies on taking revenge against her estranged husband.

On 17 December 1566, Prince James was baptised at Stirling Castle. It was a Catholic service, which heightened the tensions among the Scottish nobles, most of whom absented themselves. The English ambassador also stayed away, as did James's father, Darnley. Alongside this public Catholic gesture, Mary made a concession to her Protestant adversaries by pardoning Morton and those who had joined him in murdering Riccio. She also seemed reconciled with her husband, who was ill and staying at his father's house in Glasgow, and persuaded him to accompany her to Edinburgh in January 1567. It would prove a fatal move.

In the early hours of 10 February 1567, the citizens of Edinburgh were woken by a huge explosion at Kirk o'Field, the house where Darnley was lodged. Although there were remarkably few casualties, two bodies were subsequently found in the grounds: Mary's husband and his servant. Neither bore any marks of the explosion but had been strangled or suffocated. 'Everybody suspected the Earl of

Bothwell,' Melville recorded, adding that he 'ruled all the court'.[38] When the Queen proved slow to act, suspicions about her own involvement were aroused. Elizabeth wrote at once to warn Mary that people were saying 'you will look through your fingers at the revenging of this deed, and that you do not take measures that touch those who have done as you wished'. Without naming Bothwell directly, she urged her cousin: 'I beseech you to take this thing so much to heart that you will not fear to touch even him whom you have nearest to you if the thing touches him . . . recognise this traitor and protect yourself from him as from the ministers of Satan.'[39]

Again, the English queen seemed genuinely to wish that Mary should safeguard her throne, rather than act on her own, often misguided instincts. Given all the false flattery and promises that had passed between the two rival queens while each tried to outdo the other, this might seem puzzling. In fact, it may be the closest that Elizabeth had ever come to revealing her true intentions for the succession. Instead of seizing the golden opportunity that Darnley's murder presented to see her greatest rival utterly disgraced, she was trying to rescue Mary's shattered reputation and shape her into a ruler fit to inherit the throne of England.

The idea that Elizabeth had the succession at the forefront of her mind is corroborated by a secret letter that she wrote to Throckmorton in July 1567. In it, the English queen proposed that Mary should send her infant son to England and offered the assurance: 'We shall not fail but yield to her as good safety therein for her child as can be devised for any that might be our child born of our own body.' Knowing it would take a great deal to persuade Mary, she instructed Throckmorton to make a thinly veiled promise regarding the succession: 'She may be by you reminded how much good may ensue to her son to be nourished and acquainted with our country.' In other words, if Mary allowed James to be raised in England, not only would Elizabeth confer the crown upon him one day, she would also be able to mould him into a future king of England. Elizabeth feared that Mary might send her son to France instead, so privately urged Throckmorton to 'stay her . . . from inclining to the French, and also to avoid any just offence that she may hereafter conceive if she should hear that we should deal with the Lords [of Scotland] for the Prince'.[40]

At around the same time, a document was prepared – likely on Elizabeth's orders – that both proved her own right to the English throne and helped pave the way for the Stuarts to succeed. An exquisitely illuminated, staggeringly detailed family tree that ran into numerous pages, it traced Elizabeth's descent all the way back to Count Rollo, the tenth-century founder of the Norman dynasty that would claim the throne of England in 1066. It also claimed: 'Your Majesty [Elizabeth] is chief sovereign of the realm of Scotland as hereafter appears by the several homages done by the kings of Scots to the kings of England, your Majesty's most noble progenitors.' It went on to narrate each of these occasions in detail, together with a full transcript of the oath of allegiance given by the Scottish kings.[41] On the face of it, this was a confident assertion of England's superiority over its northern neighbour. But by setting out such a fulsome justification for Scotland being subject to English sovereignty, it also challenged the most potent argument against the Stuart succession: that the Scottish monarchs were aliens and therefore had no right to inherit land or property in England. At a stroke, Elizabeth had safeguarded both her own right to the English throne and that of Mary and her descendants.

The English queen may have gone further still by acceding to a request from a Scottish diplomat that her father's will be examined to determine whether, as the 1543 Succession Act required, it was 'signed with [the king's] most gracious hand' or authenticated with the dry stamp. If so, then she probably already knew the answer: the dry stamp had indeed been used, which meant that the provisions the will had made for the succession were technically invalid. At a stroke, this deprived the Suffolk line of their trump card and reestablished the right of the Stuarts to inherit the English throne. Elizabeth did not make a song and dance about any of this – indeed, there is some doubt that she agreed to have the matter looked into at all. Instead, she kept the knowledge to herself, content that when it came to the succession, her choice would supersede that of her late father. There is no further mention of it in the Anglo-Scottish diplomatic papers.

All Elizabeth's attempts to advise her Scottish cousin were in vain. Following her husband's murder, the Queen of Scots seemed to suffer a nervous collapse and she went into complete seclusion. Bothwell was quick to seize the initiative. In April, he secured the support of a group of leading Scottish lords and bishops for an audacious plan to marry the newly widowed queen. When he put the proposal to Mary, she refused him without hesitation. What happened next has been the subject of intense debate ever since. On her return from visiting her infant son at Stirling a few days later, Mary was abducted and possibly raped by Bothwell and was thus forced to marry him. Her enemies claimed that she had indulged in a passionate affair and had incited her lover to murder her husband so that they could be together. Melville was of the former view and attested that Bothwell had 'ravished her and lain with her against her will'. Mary's own testimony strongly suggests this was the case. Unable or unwilling to speak out against him, she admitted: 'We found his doings rude' and was resigned to 'take the best of it'.[42]

Before he could marry Mary, Bothwell had to extricate himself from his wife, Jean Gordon, whom he had married the previous year. They were divorced on 7 May and he married the Queen of Scots at Holyrood eight days later. Her predicament plunged Mary into an even deeper depression and more than once she threatened suicide. Seeing Bothwell intent on grasping all the power to himself, his erstwhile allies – Morton and Argyll principal among them – turned against him. The so-called 'confederate lords' staged a successful coup to seize control of government and Mary and Bothwell were driven out of Edinburgh. Having amassed military support, the two sides clashed at Carberry Hill on 15 June 1567 and the Queen of Scots surrendered. While her new husband fled to exile, she was taken prisoner and led into Edinburgh, cries of 'Burn the whore' ringing in her ears.

Having been informed of the shocking events that had unfolded north of the border, Elizabeth wrote a letter to Mary that was at once sympathetic and condemnatory. 'Madam, to be plain with you, our grief hath not been small that in this your marriage so slender consideration hath been had . . . for how could a worse choice be made for your honour than in such haste to marry such a subject, who besides other and notorious lacks, public fame hath charged with the murder of your late husband.' But she promised to act as 'a good neighbour, a dear sister, and a faithful friend' by sending some 'trusty servants' to Scotland on her behalf.[43]

Sir Nicholas Throckmorton was duly dispatched with instructions to demand Mary's restoration. The seasoned ambassador knew as well as his royal mistress that he had little chance of success. Mary might have been forced to it against her will, but the fact that she had married the chief suspect in the murder of her husband was a scandal from which she could never recover. For a monarch – a queen in particular –

reputation was everything. By the time she sent Throckmorton to Scotland, Elizabeth had probably already decided that Mary was no longer a viable successor for her throne. But her ambassador did at least help preserve Mary's life at a time when her captors were considering having her tried and executed for murder.

After her arrest, the beleaguered Queen of Scots had been quickly moved to a more secure imprisonment on the island fortress of Lochleven. It was from there that on 24 July Mary was presented with the deeds of abdication. Prostrate with illness, having recently miscarried Bothwell's twins, and receiving encouragement from Throckmorton and others, she signed. Five days later, her thirteen-month-old son was crowned King of Scots at Stirling. Elizabeth forbade her ambassador from attending the coronation, fearing that his presence would be taken as her approval of Mary's deposition. A regency council was appointed to rule during James's minority, under the authority of the Earl of Moray, Mary's illegitimate half-brother. James's accession and the appointment of a regency council thwarted Elizabeth's plans to bring the young Scottish prince to England so that she could raise him herself.

The following month, Elizabeth received news of another claimant to the English throne. Lady Mary Grey had languished for two years at Chequers House, sending frequent pleas that the Queen might forgive her illicit marriage to Thomas Keyes. She lamented: 'The Queen's majesty's displeasure . . . makes me wish death rather than to be in this great misery.' In August 1567, Mary was sent to live in the custody of her step-grandmother, Katherine Willoughby, Dowager Duchess of Suffolk, a severe woman who deeply resented the disgrace that Mary had brought upon the Grey family. But Mary's sorrow soon excited her pity and she was concerned by her granddaughter's meagre appetite, confiding to William Cecil: 'I fear me she will die of her grief.'[44]

Lady Mary Grey's response to her ongoing imprisonment was strikingly similar to that of her elder sister. In January 1568, Elizabeth heard that Katherine Grey was seriously ill. Katherine had been moved to several different houses after leaving the Tower in 1563 and was now at Cockfield Hall in Yoxford, a remote estate in the Suffolk countryside with few amenities or comforts. Pining for her husband and despairing of ever being allowed her freedom, Katherine's health had begun to decline. From the very beginning of her separation from Edward Seymour, she had lapsed into a deep melancholy and, like her sister Mary, refused to eat. Her uncle and first custodian, Lord John Grey, had been shocked by her wan appearance and entreated her to take some food, but she had refused, saying: 'Alas, Uncle, what a life is this to me, thus to live in the Queen's displeasure. But for my Lord and children I would I were buried.'[45]

Elizabeth was persuaded to send her physician to Cockfield Hall. By the time he arrived, Katherine was dying. According to one of those present, the woman who for a time had looked set to be Queen of England seemed to welcome death, glad to be free at last from the sorrow of her earthly existence. When one of her attendants tried to reassure her that she would live for many years, she replied: 'No, no. No life in this world; but in the world to come I hope to live for ever. For here is nothing but care and misery.' Anxious to protect her sons' interests, she sent a message to the Queen via an intermediary, begging that she might 'be good unto my children and not impute my fault unto them ... For in my life they had few friends, and fewer they shall have when I am dead except her Majesty.' After pleading the same on behalf of her husband, she asked that her wedding ring be sent to him as a token of her affection. A few moments later, 'with a cheerful countenance', she murmured, 'Welcome, Death' and, offering her soul up to heaven, she died.[46] She was just twenty-seven years old.

'The Queen expressed sorrow to me at her death,' the Spanish ambassador reported, but shrewdly added: 'It is not believed that she feels it, as she was afraid of her.'[47] To her last breath, Katherine had maintained the validity of her marriage and in her will she left the 'necessary declarations' to prove it. Even though the situation with her potential Scottish successors remained precarious, Elizabeth had no intention of overturning the verdict that Katherine and Seymour's marriage had been unlawful, thereby restoring Katherine's sons to the order of succession. The only concession she made was to release their father Lord Hertford from his long imprisonment after Katherine's death. Nevertheless, the young Edward and Thomas Seymour remained a focus of attention for those who had favoured their mother's claim, and their names would continue to plague the Queen during the years to come.

With the Grey sisters out of the picture, Mary Stuart deposed, her son excluded from the English succession by the terms of Henry VIII's will, and Elizabeth showing no more inclination to marry than when she had ascended the throne, the stability of her regime rested entirely upon the safety and wellbeing of the Queen herself. Considering neither of her siblings had been long-lived, this seemed a precarious position indeed. A speaker in the House of Commons expressed the misgivings felt by many: 'If God should take her Majesty, the succession being not established, I know not what shall become of myself, my wife, my children, lands, goods, friends or country.'[48]

Then, in May 1568, events in Scotland took another dramatic turn. Having recovered from her illness, the ousted

Queen of Scots staged a daring escape from Lochleven and petitioned Moray to restore her to the throne. When he refused, she gathered her forces and a battle ensued at Langside, near Glasgow, on 13 May. Moray's forces were triumphant and Mary made the fateful decision to flee to sanctuary in England.

CHAPTER 5

'FAIR WORDS AND FOUL DEEDS'

Mary Stuart's arrival in England threw her relationship with Elizabeth into sharp relief. As queens of neighbouring kingdoms, their rivalry had dominated the first ten years of Elizabeth's reign. Now Mary was on English soil, she was within tantalising reach of those who wished her to succeed to the throne before her cousin had left it.

According to Melville, the former Queen of Scots' decision to seek refuge in England was born of hopeless naivety: 'Thinking herself sure of refuge there, in respect of the fair promises formerly made to her by the Queen of England.' The seasoned diplomats who had spent years travelling between the two kingdoms held a bleaker and arguably more realistic view. 'First they never will meet together, and next there will never be anything else but dissembling and secret hatred for a while, and at length captivity and utter wreck to our Queen [Mary] from England.'[1]

As soon as she had reached the safe haven of Workington Hall, where she spent her first night on English soil, Mary wrote a lengthy letter to her cousin. It is clear she expected nothing but support from the English queen: she expressed confidence that Elizabeth would invite her to court and organise aid against her enemies. Mary signed it (in French), 'Your faithful and affectionate sister and cousin and escaped prisoner', apparently oblivious that she had merely exchanged one prison for another.[2]

The following day, Mary was taken to Carlisle Castle. Elizabeth wrote to her there, congratulating her upon her escape and instructing the bearer to convey certain messages relating to Mary's 'estate and honour'. Enjoying the upper hand, she could not resist chiding her cousin that if she had had 'as much regard to her honour as she had respect for an unhappy villain, everyone would have condoled with her misfortunes, as to speak plainly not many have'.[3]

Mary's arrival had placed Elizabeth in a thorny predicament – not to mention very real danger. If she helped restore her to the Scottish throne, she would pose as great a threat as she had before she had been deposed. Likewise, if she gave Mary safe conduct to France, she might raise an army with which to invade not just Scotland but England too. Keeping the ousted Queen of Scots in England would mean that she was within reach of the many English Catholics who wished to see her on the throne in Elizabeth's place. It was with good reason that Cecil warned: 'The Queen of Scots is, and always shall be, a dangerous person to your estate.' While Elizabeth debated with her council over what to do with this 'daughter of debate', as she termed her, she ordered that Mary should be kept under close guard at Carlisle.[4] She was treated neither as an honoured guest nor a prisoner – yet.

If Mary's position remained uncertain, that of her one-year-old son appeared more settled. Young though he was, James had been confirmed as King of Scots upon his mother's abdication, which meant that he also stood to inherit her claim to the throne of England.

As the weeks dragged on, James's mother grew increasingly frustrated with her English cousin. She wrote a series of indignant letters to Elizabeth, complaining at her failure to invite her to court. The English queen's reply was equally tetchy. 'They have their signs and countersigns, and whilst they publicly unite and do one thing, they secretly order another,' reported de Silva in July 1568. He noted that the Scottish ambassador had complained: 'The Queen of England uses towards his mistress fair words and foul deeds'.[5]

Eventually, it was agreed that a conference would be held to inquire into Mary's grievances and those of her chief adversary, the Earl of Moray, in order to resolve their differences. Mary had hoped that this would be an opportunity to finally meet her English cousin and converse as equals, but she was forbidden to attend in person. It soon became clear that it was less a mediation than an investigation into Mary's conduct. The conference was terminated after several weeks, with nothing having been sufficiently proved on either side. Moray returned to Scotland but Mary was moved to Tutbury Castle in Staffordshire, under the charge of George Talbot, Earl of Shrewsbury, the fourth husband of Elizabeth Hardwick, better known as Bess of Hardwick. Any pretence of an honourable confinement was abandoned. It was clear that Mary was now Elizabeth's prisoner.

In a letter to Pope Pius V, Mary woefully referred to 'the Queen of England, in whose power I am'. But she was far from being the hapless victim that she liked to pretend. Her determination to reclaim not just her Scottish throne but also a promise of the English succession made her ruthless. 'The thing that most she thirsts after is victory,' remarked Sir Francis Knollys after visiting the captive queen, and added that she did not care how she attained it. Even though in theory Elizabeth held all the cards, Mary's unquestioned legitimacy, her Catholic faith and her powerful allies made her a troublesome presence in England. For as long as Elizabeth remained unmarried and without a nominated heir, the entire Tudor dynasty hung on the fragile thread of her life. She had now ruled for longer than both of her siblings combined, and with the ill health that dogged the Tudors, there was a sense that she was living on borrowed time. 'I am not free, but a captive,' Elizabeth lamented in despair. 'I am just as anxious to see Mary Stuart out of England as she can be to go!'[6]

Time and again, Mary pressed for a meeting with her cousin. But while she pretended to share the same desire, Elizabeth had no intention of making it happen. 'It is not believed that Queen Elizabeth, for her own reasons, will allow the Queen of Scotland to come to the Court, suspecting probably some ulterior motive, inasmuch as the Queen of Scotland is nearest in blood to the Crown of England, and beloved by some of the chief personages, although they dare not say so openly; and this is thought to be the cause why no interview will take place,' the Venetian envoy shrewdly observed.[7] As Mary besieged her English cousin with increasingly insistent demands for a meeting, Elizabeth lost her temper. 'In your letter I note a heap of confused, troubled thoughts, earnestly and curiously uttered to express your great fear and to require of me comfort,' she began. 'If I had not consideration that the same did proceed from a troubled mind, I might rather take occasion to be offended with you than to relent to your desires.'[8] She went on to remind Mary that she owed her life to Elizabeth. What provoked Elizabeth even more was the sympathy and support that her Scottish cousin was garnering in England. 'This Queen sees that all the people in the country are turning their eyes to the Queen of Scotland, and there is now no concealment about it. She is looked upon generally as the successor,' observed Philip II's envoy in July 1569.[9]

Plots soon began to swarm around the captive queen. Even though she was not allowed visitors, Elizabeth had agreed that Mary could send letters via the French embassy. However, Mary soon devised other, more covert ways to communicate with the outside world. She had been taught how to write in cipher at the age of nine and had used this system of coded letters throughout her life. She favoured a homophonic cipher, where each letter was replaced with a number, character, symbol or sign of the zodiac. She also shuffled the letters of the alphabet in a certain sequence so that once the key had been worked out, the message could be read quickly and easily. With the help of her attendants, she was able to smuggle these coded letters out of her prison, where they were secretly conveyed to such powerful friends as Michel de Castelnau de Mauvissière, a French emissary and later ambassador to England, who had spent time with Mary in Scotland and had tried to effect a reconciliation between her and Elizabeth.

Mary's methods were sophisticated, but so were those of Elizabeth's spymaster, Francis Walsingham. He rose from relative obscurity to become one of the most influential officials on the Queen's council. For the first few years of his service he was subordinate to William Cecil and Robert Dudley, but in 1573 he was appointed a privy councillor and principal secretary. Thereafter, his authority extended to foreign, domestic and religious policy, although it was his intelligence work for which he won greatest renown. An indication of the esteem in which Elizabeth held him was that she assigned him a nickname, 'the Moor', which was perhaps inspired by his dark hair and dress, as well as his sober demeanour.

Walsingham's world view was shaped by his staunchly Protestant beliefs. He had fled to exile in Basel during the reign of Elizabeth's Catholic half-sister Mary and had subsequently moved to Padua, where he enrolled as a student at the university and studied civil law. During his years on the continent, he built up a network of like-minded contacts and, as spymaster, would expand this into one of the most extensive and sophisticated networks in early modern espionage.[10]

'There is less danger in fearing too much than too little,' Walsingham wrote to Cecil on 20 December 1568.[11] This neatly encapsulated his ethos as Elizabeth's spymaster. His experience in Europe, both before and after entering her service in the late 1560s, imbued him with an implacable suspicion of Catholics. During an embassy to France in 1572, he witnessed the horror of the St Bartholomew's Day Massacre, when a Catholic mob slew thousands of Huguenots. This personal trauma, combined with his committed Protestantism, drove him to hunt down the seemingly endless succession of Catholic conspirators who plotted to assassinate his queen and put Mary Stuart on her throne.

A few months after Mary's move to Tutbury, Thomas Howard, fourth Duke of Norfolk, himself of royal blood, schemed to marry her and restore her to the Scottish throne. His expectation was that in time, they or their heirs would succeed to the English throne. He boasted 'that he would serve and honour the Queen his mistress so long as she lived, but after her decease he would set the crown of England upon the Queen of Scotland's head, as lawful heir . . . and the only means for eschewing of civil wars, and great bloodshed that might otherwise fall out'.[12] However, Norfolk's schemes were quickly discovered, likely by Walsingham and his associates, and he was consigned to the Tower.

Hot on the heels of the duke's treachery came news of a rebellion in the north of England led by a group of Catholic lords who planned to depose Elizabeth and replace her with Mary. It was easily crushed and, as a precaution, Elizabeth appointed the Earl of Huntingdon to take joint custody of the Scottish queen with the Earl of Shrewsbury. Huntingdon's staunch Protestantism made him deeply distasteful to Mary, who would also have been aware that he was a rival claimant to the English throne. Shrewsbury, meanwhile, resented the implication that he could no longer be trusted to keep sole watch over the captive queen, towards whom he had developed a warm sympathy.

After years in the political wilderness, Huntingdon was determined to prove himself worthy of the appointment and was a much stricter custodian than Shrewsbury. Throughout his guardianship of the Queen of Scots, he kept in almost daily contact with William Cecil, who was so impressed by his efforts that he became an advocate for him at court – a valuable connection, given the latter's pre-eminence. Elizabeth was similarly pleased with his service and kept him in post until she judged the danger had passed. In April 1570, she rewarded Huntingdon by having him elected a Knight of the Garter. His loyal service was perhaps not the only reason why Elizabeth had thawed towards him. By now, he had been married to Katherine Dudley for more than a decade and they were still childless. The couple were both in their thirties, so time was running out. The birth of Mary Stuart's son, who was being raised a Protestant, had also considerably lessened Huntingdon's appeal as a potential heir. And Elizabeth always found it easier to like those who were not expected to contest her throne.

In early 1570, events in Scotland appeared to be turning in Mary's favour. On 21 January, the Earl of Moray, who was acting as regent, was assassinated. He was succeeded by Matthew Stewart, fourth Earl of Lennox, the paternal grandfather of Mary's son James. The following month, Pope Pius V issued a bull of excommunication, declaring Elizabeth a usurper and absolving her subjects from allegiance. It also encouraged them to rise up against her and put her to death. At a stroke, this intensified the danger posed by the Scottish queen. The following year, the Venetian envoy reported that she was 'favoured by all the Catholic party in England'.[13] This was no exaggeration.

England's Catholics were quick to act on the Pope's sanction. Within a few short months of his bull, a deadly plot was gathering ground. Against the advice of her council, Elizabeth had pardoned the Duke of Norfolk and he was released in August 1570. Almost immediately, he began conspiring once more to marry the captive Queen of Scots, but this time to have her crowned Queen of England after deposing Elizabeth. To show her support for the scheme, Mary embroidered a cushion as a gift for the duke. The design showed a hand clipping off a barren vine so that the fruitful vine might flourish. The point was driven home by the Latin motto '*Virescit Vulnere Virtus*' (Virtue flourishes by wounding).[14] Early the following year, Mary wrote to the papal agent, Roberto Ridolfi (after whom the plot was named), urging him to solicit help from the Pope, Philip II of Spain and the Duke of Alva. She pleaded 'the jeopardy in which I stand of my life, menaced as I am with poisoning and other violent deaths' and claimed that Elizabeth had been 'many a time . . . on the point of compassing my death'.[15]

The letter, which was intercepted by Elizabeth's agents, was treasonous. When she heard of it, the Queen was 'mightily incensed'. The French ambassador bore the brunt of her fury. Evidently ignorant of the plot, he petitioned Elizabeth to improve the conditions under which her cousin was kept. 'The Queen burst into a most ferocious rage at this and dwelt very strongly upon the evils which she said were being brought upon this country by the Queen of Scotland,' he reported to the French king. 'She afterwards went on to speak of the plots which she [Mary] and the Duke of Norfolk were weaving jointly with your Majesty to turn her off the throne . . . She screamed all this out with so much vehemence that almost everybody in the palace could hear her.'[16]

The Ridolfi Plot had been uncovered thanks largely to the efforts of Elizabeth's naval commander and privateer, John Hawkins, rather than Walsingham, who was on an embassy to France at the time. Hawkins learned the details of the conspiracy after gaining the confidence of Guerau de Espés, the Spanish ambassador to England, and immediately notified the government. Elizabeth had also been sent a private warning by Cosimo I de'Medici, Grand Duke of Tuscany, who had learned of the plot. In April 1571, Ridolfi's messenger, Charles Baillie, was arrested at Dover for carrying coded letters. Under torture, he revealed the cipher that enabled Elizabeth's officials to read the letters' contents.

In January 1572, Norfolk was convicted of treason and was executed five months later. Elizabeth's councillors now urged her to do the same to Mary, variously referred to as 'the most dangerous enemy in the world to our Queen' and 'the monstrous and huge dragon'. But Elizabeth prevaricated. Mary was an anointed queen and, among the various claimants to her throne, her closest blood relative. In the end, the only action she took was to place the captive queen under much stricter supervision. Mary complained bitterly at this, but her cousin scolded her for 'filling a long letter with multitude of sharp and injurious words' and added: 'It is not the manner to obtain good things with evil speeches.'[17] The Ridolfi Plot had another, more serious, outcome for Mary. It had put paid to any lingering plans Elizabeth may have had to restore her cousin to the Scottish throne. She therefore formally recognised James VI as King of Scots.

The plot also motivated Parliament to pass a new Treasons Act. This restored the provisions of the Act passed by Henry VIII's Parliament in 1534. It was now high treason to intend bodily harm to the Queen, to levy war against her or challenge her right to the crown with either words or deeds. Furthermore, it was treason to assert that anybody other than the reigning monarch had a claim to the throne or that the laws enacted by Parliament did not govern the succession. The Act even went so far as to ban public debate about the succession, which betrayed both Elizabeth's personal aversion to such debates and the general climate of anxiety among her government. If any of Elizabeth's ordinary subjects dared to raise the subject thereafter, they were swiftly and severely dealt with, as Roger Edwardes discovered when he presented the Earl of Leicester with a New Year's gift in 1576 in the form of a manuscript entitled 'Cista Pacis Anglie' ('Chest of Peace in England'). This called for the succession to be settled immediately so that the people of England might avoid the sort of civil unrest that was afflicting France and the Low Countries. However, unlike almost every other author on the subject, Edwardes was of the firm belief that authority for such a decision rested not with Parliament but with the Queen. This was not enough to save him from her fury when she discovered that copies of the tract had been sent abroad. Edwardes was ordered to the Tower and fined £500 (equivalent to more than £100,000 today).[18]

At around the same time as the new Treasons Act was passed, the Queen singled out one of the claimants to her throne for promotion. Henry Hastings, Earl of Huntingdon, had proved consistently loyal and interested only in furthering the Protestant cause, rather than his claim to the throne. Although he had been disappointed of office, with the exception of his brief guardianship of Mary, he had attended all the major court events and had accompanied Elizabeth on her annual progresses. He also had two powerful allies in the form of William Cecil (now Lord Burghley) and Robert Dudley, Earl of Leicester. Finally assured that he could be trusted, Elizabeth appointed him President of the Council in the North in 1572, replacing the Earl of Sussex, whose brief tenure had been ineffective.

At a stroke, the promotion transformed Huntingdon into the most powerful royal official in the whole of northern England. A contemporary ballad recounted:

> His wisdom so pleased the Queen of this land,
> The sword of true justice she put in his hand:
> Of York he was president, made by her grace,
> Her laws to maintain, and rule in her place.[19]

As well as keeping order across a huge swathe of territory that had traditionally proved troublesome to the crown, the earl was responsible for helping to ward off invasion from Scotland and from Spain and other hostile Catholic powers. Initially, Huntingdon's fellow councillors considered him to be very inexperienced, but within a short time Edmund Grindal, Archbishop of York, was praising the way in which his new office had 'made manifest to many those excellent virtues and good gifts which afore were in a manner hid in him'.[20] Following Elizabeth's commands to the point of obsession (and near bankruptcy), Huntingdon also made it his mission to bring the northern counties to religious conformity. He became known for his relentless hounding of Catholics and his generous patronage of radical Protestants. His younger brother Francis asserted that his brother 'never set a straying foot in any place where he did not labour at the least to settle the preaching of the word to the people'.[21] The greatest testament to Huntingdon's abilities was that, in contrast to his predecessor, he held the

presidency for twenty-three years and was deprived of it
only by death.

Elizabeth continued to enlist Huntingdon's help in dealing
with those of his fellow blood claimants who stepped out of
line. Little had been heard of Margaret Douglas since 1571,
when her husband, the Earl of Lennox, had been assassinated
in Scotland. She seemed to have settled into a quieter life at
her house in Hackney, north-east of London, with regular
visits to court. But in 1574, she resumed her scheming for the
English throne. Her cousin the Queen had turned forty the
previous year and with no marriage in prospect was increasingly unlikely to produce any heirs. Margaret's grandson
James had one of the strongest claims to the English throne,
but the fate of his parents had proved how quickly things
could change. Margaret therefore focused her attentions on
her younger son, Charles, who had reached marriageable age.
If she could find him a bride of noble blood, it would make
him even more of a contender.

On the pretence of wishing to take Charles to visit his infant
nephew James, Margaret sought the Queen's permission to go
to Scotland. Elizabeth was immediately suspicious but eventually agreed to the request on the strict condition that the
countess must not visit her daughter-in-law Mary en route.
Margaret assured her: 'I was made of flesh and blood and
could never forget the murder of my child . . . for if I would, I
were a devil.'[22] After leaving London, Margaret had an apparently spontaneous change of plan when she accepted an invitation from the Countess of Shrewsbury to break her journey
at Rufford, one of Bess's estates in Derbyshire. The two
women were well acquainted from their days at court and
were united by their dynastic ambition. Bess had an unmarried daughter, Elizabeth, who, at eighteen, was just a year or
two older than Charles. They had almost certainly planned

the match from the outset. Margaret was all too well aware that her son would require the sovereign's permission before taking a wife, thanks to the Treasons Act of 1536, which had been prompted by her own mésalliance with Thomas Howard.[23] But she also knew that the Queen was unlikely to grant it, so she pressed ahead with her plan. Only a few days after arriving at Rufford, Charles and Elizabeth were married.

They could not hope to keep the secret for long. When the Queen found out, she was predictably enraged. She ordered Margaret and her son to London immediately and confined them initially to Lennox House in Hackney. Bess and her daughter were kept under guard at Rufford while the Earl of Huntingdon led an enquiry. The fact that the Queen enlisted his services again was at least as much to showcase her favour towards a rival claimant as to indicate her trust in him. When she learned that the newly married Elizabeth Lennox was pregnant, her anger deepened. Any child from their union would in theory have a claim to the throne, however distant, thanks to Charles's royal blood. The last thing the Queen needed was another potential claimant to her throne. She promptly threw Margaret into the Tower.

'Thrice have I been sent into prison not for matters of treason, but for love matters,' the countess lamented. But while she pleaded her case with Elizabeth, she also sent conciliatory letters to her estranged daughter-in-law, Mary, together with tokens of her affection. She signed her letters: 'Your Majesty's most humble and loving mother and aunt.' Eager to capitalise upon this potentially useful ally, Mary altered her will to include Charles and restored to her mother-in-law 'all the rights she can pretend to the earldom of Angus'. Elizabeth took a dim view of the correspondence but seemed to have no taste for detaining her cousin in the Tower this time, and by the end of 1574 Margaret was permitted to rejoin her son and daughter-in-law at Hackney. It was likely there that her grand-daughter Arbella was born the following year. On 10 November 1575, the countess wrote to the baby's aunt, Mary, Queen of Scots, thanking her 'for your good remembrance and bounty to our little daughter'.[24]

With the claimants circling around her throne, Elizabeth might have been tempted to strengthen her precarious position by marrying and producing an heir. But she was now in her early forties so the prospect of this was fading rapidly. Personal preference was in any case a stronger factor than biology, as it had been since the beginning of her reign. When Parliament once more petitioned her to marry in 1576, the Queen retorted: 'I must confess my own mislike so much to strive against the matter ... I would not forsake the single state to march with the greatest monarch in the world.'[25]

A month after Parliament closed, Arbella Stuart's father Charles died, aged just nineteen. His mother fell into a 'languishing decay', but the ambition that had driven her throughout her life was undiminished and now became focused firmly on her grandchildren. She wrote to her 'sweet jewel', the young James VI, assuring him that he was her chief hope for the future. She also worked tirelessly to secure the earldom of Lennox for Arbella, but this was in the gift of James, who refused to grant it. He was only ten years old at the time and was heavily influenced by his advisers, who would have made him aware that Arbella was his main rival for the throne.

Pursuing her dynastic schemes to the last, Lady Margaret died on 9 March 1578, aged sixty-two. Two days earlier, she had been taken violently ill after hosting a supper for Robert Dudley, Earl of Leicester. There were rumours of poisoning, but such talk often accompanied a sudden death in court circles at the time. In fact, Margaret had long been suffering from a digestive disorder. Determined that her status be recognised even in death, her will contained detailed instructions for an elaborate tomb to be erected in Henry VII's Chapel, Westminster Abbey. However, having died without the means to pay for it, Queen Elizabeth was obliged to meet the expense. It proved so great that the work was left half-finished for the remainder of Elizabeth's reign.

Despite Margaret's efforts, her English properties passed to the Queen rather than to her granddaughter. The crown might have taken Arbella's income, but it could not take her royal blood. She was the first cousin of James VI and the scarcity of other close relations made her a very real contender for the thrones of both England and Scotland. Indeed, her supporters argued that the fact that she had been born on English soil gave her the edge over her Scottish cousin. In the eyes of the Catholics, her ambiguous religious sympathies also made her more appealing than James, an avowed Protestant. The Pope himself backed her claim to Elizabeth's throne and encouraged England's Catholics to support her. Arbella also had support in Spain, thanks to James's predilection for an alliance with France. Philip II's new ambassador in England, Bernardino de Mendoza, who also acted as a spy, informed his master: 'The most learned lawyers consider that, failing the Queen of Scots and her son, this young lady [Arbella] is the nearest heir to the throne.'[26]

Arbella's ambitious grandmother, Bess, Countess of Shrewsbury, was instrumental in this. From the moment of Arbella's birth, she had resolved to make an advantageous match for her granddaughter, who was a regular visitor to Bess's Derbyshire home, Hardwick Hall, and moved there after her mother's death in 1582. Mindful that the now motherless young girl had no means to support herself, Bess's husband, the Earl of Shrewsbury, appealed to the Queen's better nature: '[I] humbly and lowly beseech her majesty, to have pity upon her poor orphan Arbella Stuart.' For her part, the countess petitioned Lord Burghley to persuade his royal mistress to contribute £600 per year towards the upbringing of 'my dearest jewel, Arbella', £400 of which was the allowance that Arbella's mother, Elizabeth, had been given during her lifetime. 'So trust I you will consider the poor infant's case, who, under her majesty, is to appeal only to your lordship for succour in all her distresses,' she pleaded. To strengthen her argument, Bess reminded Burghley of her granddaughter's credentials as an heir to the throne. 'I have special care not only such as a natural mother has of her best beloved child, but much more greater a respect how she is in blood to her majesty, albeit one of the poorest as depending wholly on her majesty's gracious bounty and goodness.'²⁷ Eventually, Elizabeth gave in to Bess's insistent requests and agreed to grant Arbella an annual income, although at £200 this was considerably less than her grandmother had hoped for.

Ignoring the fact that her granddaughter's title had been withheld, Bess referred to her as 'Countess of Lennox' and instructed all her servants to do the same. She also ordered her other grandchildren to curtsey whenever they met Arbella, to emphasise her superiority. In the portrait of Arbella at just shy of two years old that hangs at Hardwick Hall she wears a gold chain from which hangs a shield with a countess's coronet and the Lennox motto, *Pour parvenir, j'endure* (To achieve, I endure).

Arbella was a bright, precocious child who studied French, Italian, Spanish, Latin, Greek and Hebrew – a rare accomplishment for her sex, the other notable example being the Queen herself. She also shared Elizabeth's skill in music and, among other instruments, excelled at the lute and viol. Her grandmother proudly noted that she was 'very apt to learn, and able to conceive what shall be taught her'. The Queen's godson, Sir John Harington, commended 'her virtuous disposition . . . her choice education, her rare skill in languages, her good judgement and sight in music, and a mind to all these, free from pride, vanity and affectation'. He added that she had 'a gravity beyond her years', but that she also enjoyed the more light-hearted pastimes of dancing and sewing. In 1583, seven-year-old Arbella wrote to the Chancellor, Sir Walter Mildmay, who was so impressed with her 'learning' that he told Sir Francis Walsingham she was 'a very proper child, and to my thinking will be like her grandmother, my old Lady Lennox'. He added that 'the little lady' had included a request in her letter that Mildmay should present 'her humble duty to her majesty with her daily prayer for her majesty'.[28] When writing to her aunt and uncle, Mary and Gilbert Talbot, with whom she spent much of her youth, the young woman showed greater warmth and humour than is evident in her more courtier-like correspondence.

Arbella's birthright mattered a great deal more than her intellectual accomplishments. She was just two years old when, in 1577, the Countess of Shrewsbury lined up the first potential suitor for her granddaughter. Bess invited Robert Dudley, Earl of Leicester, to visit on his way to take the waters at Buxton in Derbyshire. She presented her infant granddaughter and proposed a match with Leicester's 'base son' Robert, the result of his affair with the courtier Douglas Sheffield. It was a curious choice, given the boy's illegitimacy, and came to nothing. Bess and Dudley remained in touch, however, and a few years later they plotted another marriage – this time with the earl's infant son Robert, Lord Denbigh by his new wife Lettice Knollys, a blood relative of the Queen on her mother's side. At around the same time, Dudley conspired to marry Lettice's daughter Dorothy to James VI. When word

of these schemes reached the Queen, she railed that she would
not allow the King of Scots to marry 'the daughter of such a
she-wolf'.[29] All Dudley's hopes now rested on the Arbella
match. But that was brought to a tragic end when his 'noble
imp' Denbigh died in July 1584, shortly after his third
birthday.

The Countess of Shrewsbury's ambitions for her granddaughter alienated another queen. She and her husband had
been the custodians of the captive Mary Stuart since the early
weeks of her arrival in England in 1568. Although the two
women became close companions for a while, Bess's schemes
to make an advantageous marriage for Arbella, and thus bolster
her claim to the throne above that of Mary's son, proved a
source of discord. When she introduced her granddaughter to
the Scottish queen, Bess was reported to have boasted that
Mary's claim to the throne was inferior to Arbella's. Mary
wrote a furious letter to the French ambassador, urging him: 'I
would wish you to mention privately to the Queen that nothing
has alienated the Countess of Shrewsbury from me more but
the vain hope which she has conceived of setting the crown of
England on the head of her little girl, Arbella.'[30]

Raised by her ambitious grandmothers, it was perhaps inevitable that Arbella should grow up convinced that she was
destined to be queen. At a time when even to mention a claim
to the throne was treason, such ambitions could be deadly.

CHAPTER 6

'THE BLOODY HAND OF A MURDERER'

On 19 October 1579, thirteen-year-old James VI of Scotland was proclaimed an adult ruler in an elaborate ceremony of entry to Edinburgh. Described as 'the bright star of the North', the young king was renowned for his intellect, having received an exceptional (if harsh) education at the hands of Scotland's leading scholars. He later claimed that they had taught him to speak Latin ''ere I could speak Scottish'.[1] James was a product of the strict Scottish Reformation, too, and grew up with a strong aversion to Catholicism. By the age of seventeen, he already had an extensive library which included classics, history, theology, political theory, geography and mathematics, as well as books on hunting and other sports.

Beneath the veneer of princely accomplishments lurked a fearful, suspicious and obsessive nature that became increasingly manifest in adulthood. In part, this derived from the strict and dangerously volatile childhood that James endured, with a rapid succession of regents who all met untimely or bloody ends.[2] But it was also thanks to the precariousness of the Scottish throne. Every Scottish monarch since 1406 had come to the throne as a minor and James was the third successive monarch to have acceded in infancy.[3] A succession of powerful magnates had controlled the affairs of the kingdom during the many minorities – a role they were not always willing to relinquish once the monarch reached the age at which they could rule alone. To make matters worse for James, whereas previous monarchs had inherited the throne on the death of a king, his predecessor (his mother Mary) was still alive. Her existence alone was a threat, but was made worse by her perpetual intrigues.

James could have had at most very little memory of the mother who had fled to England when he was less than two years old and he had been raised by men hostile to the ousted queen. He was therefore unlikely to have experienced any filial guilt in courting the friendship of her captor, the Queen of England. Like his mother, James never met Elizabeth, so their letters to each other were the only means of communicating directly, rather than through intermediaries.

Ideas about the form and use of letters had evolved during the sixteenth century with the spread of humanist learning. The influential Dutch scholar and humanist Desiderius Erasmus had encouraged individual expression and style over more formulaic templates. This sparked an unprecedented rise in letter writing by monarchs and other heads of state, and ushered in a more personal style of royal diplomacy than had been evident before. Erasmus's encouragement had been lost on one of his correspondents: Henry VIII confessed to finding writing 'tedious and painful'. But it was fully embraced by his daughter and the young King of Scots.[4] Elizabeth was a prolific letter-writer and produced an estimated 3,000 letters during her lifetime. James, who cherished a lifelong love of literature, composed a considerable number himself.

The earliest surviving letter between the two sovereigns is dated 1572, when James was just six years old. Their correspondence began in earnest from the late 1570s and endured until Elizabeth's death in 1603, making it the longest-running correspondence between two sovereigns in the early modern age – and one of the longest of all time. Two hundred and sixty of their letters have survived. Both monarchs had a powerful incentive to maintain the momentum. The exchange of royal letters was a highly ritualised process, and once a regular correspondence had been established it could not be broken without incurring dishonour or suspicion.

During the 1570s, Elizabeth relied on secretaries to write to James and simply signed the letters. But this changed completely in the 1580s when letters in her hand outnumbered those by her secretaries. From the early 1590s to the end of her reign, she hand-wrote the vast majority of her letters to James. By contrast, in each decade of their correspondence, the letters James wrote to Elizabeth in his own hand were consistently outnumbered by those produced by his scribes. Nevertheless, he wrote more letters to the English queen than to any other ruler during his reign in Scotland.

Even those letters which were not written by the monarchs themselves were carefully scrutinised (and often heavily amended) by them before signing. This made it highly unlikely that they would have allowed any letter to be dispatched unless they approved of its contents. Elizabeth was particularly exacting and frequently overrode the editorial advice of her secretaries. James was rather less so. On at least one occasion, he asked Sir James Melville, who was appointed his principal secretary, to draft a reply to a personally handwritten letter from Elizabeth, 'that he might write over it again with his own hand'.[5]

Even though both Elizabeth and James complied with the niceties of diplomatic exchanges, their letters were deeply personal. As such, they provide a unique and fascinating glimpse into a relationship that evolved over thirty years. The letters are awash with the flowery sentiments so typical of courtly correspondence. Elizabeth called James her 'dearest brother and cousin', while she was his 'dearest sister' and sometimes (notably when he hoped to persuade her to name him her heir) 'mother'. On occasion, James even penned clumsy poetry for Elizabeth – something that she quietly ignored. Despite being one of the most highly educated, articulate women of her generation, whose prose rivalled the likes of Edmund Spenser and even William Shakespeare, Elizabeth often ended her letters with an apology for her 'tedious' or 'long' 'scribbling'. Such self-deprecation was more likely aimed at softening the blow of the acerbic wit or reprimanding tone that characterised many of her letters. James also begged pardon for 'scribbling in haste', but given the often hurried style of his handwriting and less thoughtful construction of his prose, he was probably in earnest.[6]

Throughout their correspondence, there is a strong sense of superiority on the part of the English queen. She was thirty-three years older than James and had ruled successfully for almost a quarter of a century; he had been king since his earliest infancy but had been ruled by others until he reached maturity. 'You may believe me, for experience, though not to trust me for my wit,' she once told him in a tone that was typically condescending and falsely self-deprecating. On another occasion, Elizabeth expressed satisfaction that James had told her envoy that he intended to 'depend much upon our good advice and counsel for the settling of your affairs and the ordering of such causes of importance as do nearest concern you'. Although she often reminded James of the parental respect he owed her, she stopped short of referring to him as her 'son', despite him regularly calling her 'mother'. To do so would have been too strongly to imply that he was her heir. Instead, she employed more subtle language that maintained the uncertainty over the succession, such as when she told James: 'I find an old English proverb truly verified, that a feast long looked [for] is good when it cometh.'[7]

Although Elizabeth's letters to James could be read as an attempt to exert control over the governing of Scotland, her frequent, often insistent advice might have been more aimed at preparing him to inherit her throne in England. She once hinted: 'Remember that others may have many ends in their advice, but I think only of yourself.' She missed no opportunity to share her views of the qualities needed to succeed as a monarch of England, notably upholding one's honour, dealing honestly with all, maintaining the law and suppressing overmighty subjects. A brilliant propagandist who took exceptional care in cultivating her public image, she urged James: 'For your own sake play the king, and let your subjects see you respect yourself.'[8] It was a masterclass in monarchy, but not one that the Scottish king always – or even often – took to heart.

On the surface, though, James was careful to defer to Elizabeth in all things. His letters were full of deference and flattery, and for the most part he succeeded in suppressing his burning ambition for her crown. 'I will speak nothing of the state of England, as a matter wherein I never had experience,' he once declared. 'It could no ways become me, far inferior to her [Elizabeth] in knowledge and experience, to be a busybody in other princes' matters, and to fish in other folk's waters.' But he could not resist dropping the occasional hint. Insisting that he would not speak of the people of England, 'never having been among them', he added: 'I hope in that God, whoever favours the right, before I die, to be as well acquainted with their fashions.' He later told his eldest son and heir: 'I hope ye shall be King of more countries than this.'[9]

For the most part, James flagrantly ignored most of Elizabeth's advice. What did she, a mere woman, know about ruling a kingdom? In common with the vast majority of his subjects, including the outspoken theologian John Knox, his stout conviction was that women were inferior to men in every respect – intellectually, physically, spiritually and morally – and was appalled at the idea of female sovereignty. His misogyny was of long duration. He had written of his own mother's inheritance of the Scottish throne as a 'double curse', she being a 'woman of sex and a new born babe of age'. He also blamed the corruption of the Scottish nobles on 'the fact that for forty years or more they had only had for governors in this kingdom women, little children, and traitorous and avaricious regents'.[10]

Elizabeth was no fool. She knew that her Scottish cousin was only paying lip service to her maxims. On one occasion, she sent the exasperated reprimand: 'I know not what to write, so little do I like to lose labour in vain; for if I saw counsel avail . . . I should think my time fortunately spent to make you reap the due fruit of right opportunity; but I see you have no like to help your state, nor to assure you from treason's leisure.'[11]

For the Queen of England and the King of Scots to convey letters to each other so frequently and for so long required considerable effort on the part of their attendants. With a shared border, travel routes between their two countries were well established by the time their correspondence began. These routes were used by messengers, couriers, ambassadors and other emissaries to transport information (both written and oral) and occasionally money and gifts between the two countries.

The routes may have been well established but travel between the two countries could still be treacherous. Many of the most commonly used roads were little more than rough tracks dating back to Roman and medieval times. They had originally been made for people and animals travelling on foot and were ill-suited for the iron-wheeled coaches that were common during the Tudor period. Gravel was scattered over the most frequently used junctions to soak up the mud, but the vast majority of roads quickly turned into quagmires for many months of the year, as one contemporary bemoaned: 'In the clay or cledgy soil [the roads] are very deep and troublesome in the winter.'[12]

The messengers employed by Elizabeth and James would have travelled on horseback rather than by coach. The speed at which they could travel depended on a number of factors, notably the season and the length that they were able to stay in the saddle. Experienced riders could cover a hundred miles per day during the summer months, which meant that it would take at least four days (assuming no mishaps along the way) to cover the four hundred miles between London and Edinburgh.

Early maps were far too bulky to carry, so riders had to rely on asking directions from fellow travellers or at stations along the way. They could also use the moon to guide them at night. Of course, the messengers employed by Elizabeth and James would have been well used to the journey, so getting lost was less of an issue. But they did still run the gauntlet of treacherous roads and highwaymen. Vagrancy was a growing problem during Elizabeth's reign thanks to rising inflation and an increasing population. Driven by poverty and hunger, large numbers of thieves would lurk behind trees and bushes to take travellers by surprise.

Royal messengers might have been prey to the same perils of the road as other travellers, but they could rely on a system established in the fifteenth century that involved relays of couriers. Henry VIII had appointed his secretary, Brian Tuke, Master of the Posts in 1512, with responsibility for ensuring the efficient conveyance of royal correspondence. Five years later, Tuke was made Governor of the King's Posts, a precursor to the modern-day Postmaster General. He and his successors oversaw the appointment of couriers, a position that required both trustworthiness and stamina. In Scotland, a postal system of sorts had been established in the thirteenth century for the exclusive use of the crown and its nobility and clergy, and it was only towards the end of the sixteenth century that a more formal system was introduced.

The efforts that these royal couriers went to in maintaining the thirty-year correspondence between the Queen of England and the King of Scots have been largely lost to history. Even their names are not known. But they played a vital role in fostering and preserving one of the most profoundly important relationships in British history.

There was also a constant stream of ambassadors, envoys and messengers travelling between the two kingdoms. They included Thomas Randolph, who undertook numerous embassies to Scotland during the first three decades of Elizabeth's reign. Her secretary, William Davison, was a clever and able diplomat and spent time at James's court in the late 1560s and 1580s. Of Scottish descent, he was 'a Scotsman in his heart' according to Melville and favoured the King of Scots' claim to the English throne over that of James's mother Mary.

By the early 1580s, two opposing parties had formed north of the border: one favoured Protestantism and alliance with England; the other Catholicism, alliance with France and the partial restoration of Queen Mary. As a committed Protestant, James might have naturally favoured the former party, but Elizabeth knew that she could not take his professions of goodwill at face value. In one letter, written in the summer of 1585, she upbraided him for his 'contrarious dealings' and reminded him: 'Who seeks two strings to one bow, they may shoot strong, but never straight.' Always eager to assert the superiority of her age and experience, she added: 'We old foxes can find shifts to save ourselves by others' malice.'[13]

Elizabeth enjoyed the upper hand in another, more potent way. She knew that James was eager to be named her heir. She therefore used the succession as a bargaining tool, giving him just enough hope that her throne would one day be his without actually committing to anything. In so doing, she ensured that he remained loyal to her rather than throwing in his lot with Spain, France or even the Scottish Catholics. Her apparent superiority was confirmed by a Spaniard who spent six months in Scotland in 1589 and scoffed: 'The King of Scotland is nobody: nor does he possess the authority or position of a king: and he does not move a step, nor eat a mouthful, that is not by order of the Queen [Elizabeth].'[14]

For all the effort that the Queen of England applied to her relationship with the King of Scots, it was by no means her only focus. During the 1570s she began to realise her imperial ambitions overseas. English seafarers sought to establish alternative routes to the lucrative markets of China and the East Indies which were then dominated by Spain and Portugal. This was vital for England's economy because in the 1550s, the cloth trade, England's main trade for centuries, had collapsed due to a number of factors, including increased inflation and new legislation. Merchants therefore needed new markets for their goods and new goods to sell. When Elizabeth's adventurers discovered sea routes and opened up new markets, English produce could be traded for luxury goods, such as furs from Russia, dyes from the eastern Mediterranean and silk, cotton and spices from India and the Far East.

Elizabeth was quick to grasp the potential for profit and sponsored some of the voyages. More tacitly, she encouraged the privateering exploits of men such as Sir Francis Drake, Sir John Hawkins and Sir Walter Raleigh, who made successful careers out of plundering Spanish treasure ships. Drake became the first European to sail to and explore much of the Americas (or 'New World'). Hot on his heels was Martin Frobisher, a prolific explorer and privateer who also sailed to the Arctic, while in the early 1580s Raleigh established a settlement on Roanoke Island, dubbed 'Virginia' after his royal mistress. Drake's pre-eminence was established in 1580 when, in his ship the *Golden Hind*, he became the first English sailor to complete a circumnavigation of the globe.[15] Elizabeth, who had invested in the voyage, knighted him the following year to honour his extraordinary achievement.

The exploits of these adventurers greatly enhanced Elizabeth's reputation, both at home and abroad, and made England a player to be reckoned with on the world stage. But there was a darker side. The English queen's privateers stoked the already deep-seated hostility of Spain, while England's expansion into new trade routes made her the target of resentment and rivalry from other European powers. More ominous still, Hawkins was the first known English adventurer to transport and trade enslaved Africans. Elizabeth was fully aware of this and in 1564 gave him a royal ship in exchange for a share of the profits. From these beginnings a large-scale transatlantic slave trade would grow in the following century, the consequences of which were as devastating as profitable.

If the long-term impact of Elizabeth's overseas exploration was deeply problematic, the short-term was almost entirely positive. The arrival of luxury goods from overseas not only revived England's flagging economy but significantly enhanced the magnificence of the court. The 1570s saw the beginning of a golden age of court culture, with Elizabeth at its centre. All the elaborate entertainments and ceremonies had her as their focus. She was the peerless Virgin Queen, at once both aloof and alluring. As one of her most ardent admirers, Sir Christopher Hatton, observed: 'The Queen did fish for men's souls, and had so sweet a bait that no-one could escape her network.'[16] It was a brilliant piece of propaganda that transformed her unmarried state from a source of anxiety to a virtue – one that diverted attention from the increasing concern about the succession.

As an active patron of the arts and sciences, Elizabeth welcomed some of the greatest scholars, scientists, explorers, artists, poets, playwrights and performers from England and abroad – everyone from Sir Francis Bacon and Edmund Spenser to Sir Walter Raleigh and William Shakespeare. Having been educated by the humanist scholars Roger Ascham and William Grindal, she encouraged the growth of humanist thinking. As well as promoting the study and reform of the humanities (including history, law, languages and literature), humanism advocated the wisdom of ancient Greece and Rome. Elizabeth had been translating such texts since childhood and continued to do so throughout her reign.

The Queen's intellectual curiosity also extended to scientific discoveries, such as those of her court physician William Gilbert, who discovered that the earth is a dipole magnet and that magnetism is a property of all matter. Elizabeth's fluency in several languages enabled her to converse with foreign visitors, too, including the celebrated Flemish artists John de Critz and Marcus Gheeraerts the Elder. Music played a major part in court life. Elizabeth excelled at the lute and virginals, and often delighted visitors with a performance. She also employed such renowned composers as Thomas Tallis and William Byrd. All this amounted to a cultural revolution in England, a melting pot of new ideas, discoveries and accomplishment that marked the height of the English Renaissance.

Elizabeth fully appreciated the political importance of staging displays of wealth and ostentation at her court. 'She lives a life of magnificence and festivity such as can hardly be imagined and occupies a great portion of her time with balls, feasting, hunting and similar amusements with the utmost possible display,' observed a Venetian envoy.[17] Another foreign visitor concurred: 'They are intent on amusing themselves and on dancing till after midnight.'[18] But all the apparent decadence was carefully controlled by Elizabeth. As an unmarried queen, it was vital that her reputation remain unsullied so that she could command the respect of her people and preserve her place in the international marriage market. Thanks to her unwavering vigilance, merriment never descended into drunkenness or flirtatiousness into sexual transgression, so that one contemporary was able to observe: 'The court of Queen Elizabeth was at once gay, decent, and superb.'[19]

In contrast to her father, Elizabeth was not a great builder of palaces, but she ensured that they were lavishly appointed, often with luxury furnishings brought in by her trading ships. Her favourite palace was Richmond, where she let her taste for fanciful and sumptuous furnishings run wild. Among the many decorative features that she commissioned was a boat-shaped bed with 'curtains of sea water green'. Further up river was Hampton Court, 'the most splendid and magnificent royal palace of any that may be found in England – or, indeed, in any other kingdom', according to one foreign visitor. There, Elizabeth would sit in state in the so-called 'Paradise Chamber', which was hung with tapestries garnished with gold, pearls and precious stones. The centrepiece was her throne, which was studded with 'very large diamonds, rubies, sapphires, and the like, that glitter among other precious stones and pearls as the sun among the stars'.[20] The luxury continued at Greenwich, south-east of London, where the Queen's private dining room included a tablecloth made from peacock feathers sewn together.

When it came to impressing courtiers and visitors, the Queen knew that ceremony was as important as decoration. A Swiss visitor named Thomas Platter was invited to watch the preparation of Elizabeth's 'luncheon' in her presence chamber at Nonsuch Palace. He described how her guardsmen, 'wearing tabards, red, if I remember, with the royal arms on their backs embroidered in gold', carried in two tables and set them down in front of an empty throne, which represented the Queen. There followed a procession of other guards, gentlemen and 'a charming gentlewoman or lady-in-waiting, who bowed very gracefully . . . thrice to the empty table'. Then no fewer than forty of the Queen's guardsmen entered, 'tall, fine, strong men' with 'a weapon at their sides', each bearing a single covered dish of food. One by one, a gentleman removed the cover of each dish while the lady-in-waiting presented a small portion to the guard to taste for poison. The wine and beer were also tasted. Finally, after the long table had been fully laid out with food 'and honours performed as if the Queen herself had sat there, whatever dishes there were, were offered to the Queen in her apartment for her to make her choice'. The same performance was re-enacted for all three courses. Elizabeth's musicians then gave a brief recital to signal an end to the spectacle and Platter and the other guests withdrew.[21]

Such displays were both time-consuming and costly, but more than worth it. As well as impressing members of the court, visitors such as Platter would carry word of the English queen's incomparable splendour across Europe, thus enhancing her prestige. Elizabeth made sure that her ordinary subjects were aware of her magnificence, too. Her ostentatious summer 'progresses' became the stuff of legend. Although Elizabeth never ventured further west than Bristol or further north than Stafford, she made sure to be seen by as many of her people as possible on the way, as well as on her return to the capital. Her baggage train alone typically comprised about eighty wagons, laden with rich tapestries, furniture, clothes and accessories.

Elizabeth also established a series of set-pieces with her poorer subjects, notably the Maundy Thursday ceremony, when she washed the feet of as many poor women as the years of her age, and distributed clothing, food, wine and money. Occasions such as this greatly enhanced Elizabeth's popularity and reinforced her image as a Virgin Mary figure on earth.

As Elizabeth moved ever further from her childbearing years, so the yawning gap left by her refusal to name her successor was filled with increasingly frenzied gossip and speculation. But such talk could be deadly, as one of the Queen's heirs found to her cost. In 1579, Elizabeth hosted a visit by her latest suitor, François, Duke of Anjou and Alençon, the youngest son of Henry II and Catherine de Medici. More than twenty years younger than Elizabeth, who was now in her late forties, he represented her last throw of the dice in the international marriage market. She made much of her young suitor, giving him the playful nickname 'frog' and appearing so besotted that even hard-bitten courtiers who had witnessed numerous marriage prospects crumble into dust began to believe that the Queen might at last take a husband. But this match, too, had been born more of politics than passion; a means of threatening Philip II with an alliance with France and, perhaps, of reminding her would-be successors that she might yet pull the rug from under them.

The Anjou courtship excited a great deal of speculation at court. Margaret Stanley, Countess of Derby, had been a regular visitor throughout the reign and, as befitted her royal status, had served as trainbearer to the Queen at important occasions. However, when she was overheard gossiping about the young duke, Elizabeth immediately ordered that she be placed under house arrest. The Spanish ambassador explained this seemingly harsh treatment of idle gossip as resulting from Margaret's claim to the throne.

With the countess under arrest, Elizabeth ordered a further investigation into her activities. When Margaret summoned a healer and astrologer named Dr William Randall into her household, it was immediately viewed as suspicious, even though she had suffered from poor health for several years. After being treated by Randall from May to August 1579, the countess was summarily charged with witchcraft. The fact that the Queen herself regularly consulted an astrologer, Dr John Dee, was quietly ignored. Her government claimed that Randall had used witchcraft to predict when Elizabeth's reign would end, presumably with a view to letting Margaret know when she might inherit the throne. News of the controversy spread rapidly. By the time it reached the Venetian ambassador in France, it had been exaggerated into a plot to assassinate the Queen, with Margaret herself administering the poison.

Randall was condemned for conjuring and hanged the following year. The countess wrote in alarm to Elizabeth's spymaster Walsingham, assuring him that Randall had only been treating her various health complaints and she had no idea 'that he lived in great wickedness'. It was almost certainly in response to the controversy that in March 1581, the Act against Seditious Words and Rumours was passed. It forbade using witchcraft to prophesy 'how long her Majesty shall

live . . . or who shall reign . . . after her Highness's decease', as
well as speculation about the identity of her successor. Any
miscreants would be severely punished for a first offence; a
second would mean death. As Robert Cecil later reflected:
'The subject itself is so perilous to touch amongst us, as it sets
a mark upon his head forever that hatches such a bird.'[22]

No further action was taken against Margaret Stanley for
the time being, but she remained under house arrest and in
fear for her life. Only in 1584 did the Queen agree to her
release. But Walsingham and his spies continued to keep a
close watch on the countess and her family and Elizabeth
would not hear of her return to service. As one contemporary
noted: 'For jealousy [she] comes not at the Court.'[23]

Margaret Stanley's disgrace had seriously undermined her
claim to the throne, which was perhaps just as Elizabeth
intended. The Grey sisters had suffered an even harsher treatment at the Queen's hands. It was as if Elizabeth was picking
off the claimants to her throne one by one, destroying or at
least impeding their chances of succeeding her until only
James of Scotland was in the running. One anonymous
contemporary certainly believed this was the case: 'It has been
a point of great wisdom in mine opinion and of great safety to
her Highness' person, state, and dignity to preserve hitherto
the line of the next inheritors by the house of Scotland (I
mean both the mother and the son), whose deaths have been
so diligently sought by the other competitors and had been
long ere this achieved if her Majesty's own wisdom and royal
clemency (as is thought) had not placed special eye upon the
conservation thereof from time to time.'[24]

In 1581, one of the rival claimants to the Stuarts saved
Elizabeth the trouble of ruining his prospects. In that year,
Edward Seymour, Lord Beauchamp, the eldest son of
Katherine Grey, married Honora Rogers. The two families

were distantly connected: Honora's brother Andrew had married, as his second wife, Beauchamp's aunt, Lady Mary Seymour. But as merely the daughter of a knight, Honora was well beneath Beauchamp in status and was described by one source as 'notorious'. Lord Hertford vehemently opposed the marriage, knowing it would damage his son's claim to the throne. He sent an associate named George Ludlow to discuss the matter with the Rogers family. Ludlow reported that Honora was 'baggage', her father Sir Richard 'a fool', and that Beauchamp had only intended to have 'but a night's lodging with her'.[25]

But things had already progressed beyond the point of no return. The Spanish ambassador reported disapprovingly that the young man who might have been king had made an ill-considered match with a 'lady of much lower quality'.[26] Lord Hertford was so furious that he arranged to have his son seized and brought to one of his houses to keep him away from Honora. But in the end the matter was resolved by the Queen and her council, who ruled that Hertford must accept the marriage as valid. It suited Elizabeth perfectly that one of her potential heirs had undermined his claim by marrying so far beneath him. The couple went on to have three sons (Edward, William and Francis) and three daughters (Honora, Anne and Mary), but the royal blood of these offspring was too tainted for them to be considered serious contenders for the throne.

In 1582, a dramatic event north of the border almost snatched one of the frontrunners from the race. That August, the sixteen-year-old James VI visited Ruthven Castle near Perth, the ancestral home of William Ruthven, whom the young king had named Earl of Gowrie exactly a year earlier. The Ruthvens were one of the most powerful families in Scotland and had long proved troublesome to the crown. Together with his father, William had been involved in the murder of David Riccio in 1566 and he had been the custodian of Mary, Queen of Scots during her imprisonment at Lochleven the following year. At the time of James's visit to William's castle, the Scottish government was divided between two great parties: William and his confederates favoured alliance with England and Protestantism, while the other, led by Esmé Stewart, Duke of Lennox, were Francophiles and advocated the reascendancy of Roman Catholicism. Lennox was then high in favour with the young king so wielded considerable influence. Ruthven and his allies therefore resorted to desperate measures. They refused to let James leave the earl's castle and seized control of the government.

Elizabeth naturally favoured Ruthven's party and sent two emissaries, Sir George Carey and Robert Bowes, to persuade James to abandon his fondness for the now exiled Earl of Lennox. Young though he was, the King proved less tractable than she had expected. Her envoys having failed, she wrote to assure James of her 'sincere well meaning towards you'. With a healthy dose of condescension, she went on to advise him 'not to incline to make yourself a party of any faction within your own realm (an inconvenience most dangerous either for yourself or for any other prince to fall into), but to have a care, as prince and sovereign among your subjects, to minister justice indifferently unto them'.[27]

But Elizabeth was never one to back the wrong horse and when it became clear that the Ruthven regime was floundering, her councillors applied further pressure by threatening to release their nemesis, Mary, Queen of Scots, and allow her to become joint sovereign with her son. This was no idle threat. In 1583, the Queen and her council met to consider whether Mary should be released on certain conditions. The most

important was that she should at last ratify the Treaty of
Edinburgh and 'forbear to claim any right to the kingdom of
England during Queen Elizabeth's life; and afterwards be
content to refer the Title of Succession to the judgement of
the estates of England'. The notion of a joint sovereignty over
Scotland between Mary and her son – an idea that had been
floated two years earlier – was dismissed. When the proposal
was put to representatives of the Scottish government, they
rejected it outright.

In June 1583, after almost a year in captivity, James escaped
with the aid of Lennox's supporters. His ally the Earl of Arran
seized control of the government and Gowrie was arrested
and executed in May the following year. Most of his associates fled to exile in England or Ireland and were later pardoned
by the King of Scots.

By the time of her son's escape, Mary Stuart had been
Elizabeth's prisoner for fifteen years. Conspiracies and
rumours had continued to swirl about the captive queen after
the foiled Ridolfi Plot in 1572. But the years that followed had
been comparatively quiet and she had seemed more resigned
to her captivity. Despite being a prisoner, she lived a comfort-
able life, spending her days reading, embroidering, conversing
with her ladies, playing with her numerous pets and receiving
guests. Righteous indignation still burned within Mary. In her
letters to Elizabeth she complained bitterly of 'ma longe captiv-
ité'. She was also crushed with disappointment that James
showed no inclination to come to her rescue.[28] Mary's plight
excited sympathy in Catholic Europe. The Spanish ambassador reported the 'implacable vengeance with which this Queen
[Elizabeth] was treating her by depriving her of her liberty'.[29]

In November 1583, Walsingham's agents uncovered a plot
led by Sir Francis Throckmorton, the nephew of the Queen's

ambassador to Scotland. The spymaster himself was in
Scotland at the time, but such was the efficiency of his network
that his fellow councillor Burghley was able to supervise the
investigation in his absence. The latter learned that
Throckmorton had garnered support from Philip II for an
invasion by the French Duke of Guise. With the aid of
England's Catholics, he would dethrone Elizabeth, marry
Mary and rule England as joint sovereign. The plot was
quickly discovered and thwarted and Throckmorton was
executed in July 1584. Philip's ambassador, Mendoza, was
discovered to have been involved on his master's behalf and
was expelled from England. If Mary had been privy to it, she
was careful to cover her tracks, which left Elizabeth unable to
act against her – for the time being, at least.

Plots such as Francis Throckmorton's brought the succession back to the fore. In 1584, another controversial tract,
Leycester's Commonwealth, was published. Although it was
primarily an attack on the Queen's great favourite, it included
a lengthy debate on the succession. Its tone reflected the
general mood of anxiety and uncertainty at court: 'If her
Majesty should die tomorrow . . . what would you do? Which
way would you look? Or what head or part knew any good
subject in the realm to follow?' One of the more scurrilous
claims of the book was that Leicester had changed the wording of the statute of succession from 'lawful issue' to 'natural
issue', thereby enabling him to pass off one of his bastard
offspring as Elizabeth's and claim the throne for him in the
event of the Queen's death.

Leycester's Commonwealth went on to provide a detailed
legal argument in favour of the Stuart succession. It began
by citing the impediments to the claim of the Queen of Scots
and her son – 'foreign birth, King Henry's testament, and
religion' – before thoroughly dismantling them. The author

pointed to the Stuarts' 'continual mixture with English blood from the beginning (and especially of late, the Queen's grandmother [Margaret Tudor] and husband [Lord Darnley] being English, and so her son begotten of an English father)'. They also recycled the by now well-worn arguments that because Scotland owed allegiance to England, it was not a foreign country, and that Edward III's statute had specifically barred claimants 'born beyond the sea', which Mary and James were not.[30]

The book was influential enough for Walsingham to investigate who was responsible for it. Given its bias towards Mary Stuart, he believed it to be the work of her exiled agent, Thomas Morgan. Robert Dudley agreed. One of Mary's spies warned her: 'Leicester has lately told a friend that he will persecute you to the uttermost.'[31] Although they failed to identify the author (or authors), Elizabeth and her council took vigorous measures to suppress the book. But by the time it came to their attention, it had already been widely copied. Its circulation was so persistent that the Queen issued a letter denouncing it to the magistrates of Cheshire.

In August 1584, Walsingham scored a major intelligence coup. He had been keeping a close watch on the Jesuit William Crichton (or Creighton), whom he suspected of plotting with the captive Scottish queen. On 23 August, Crichton was caught on a secret voyage to Scotland by a routine Dutch naval patrol. He was found to be carrying various papers in English and Italian about a great enterprise against England. The Dutch commander sent the papers to Walsingham, who immediately ordered a warship to bring Crichton to England. The Jesuit was lodged in the spymaster's house and subjected to intense interrogation. Walsingham found the invasion plan that had been behind Throckmorton's plot the previous year.

He also learned that 'the Scottish Queen was made privy'. Lastly, and most importantly, Crichton confessed that the enterprise was merely suspended and would be put into action 'when the king of Spain shall be rid of his Low Countries troubles'.[32]

The latter referred to the conflict that was raging in the Netherlands. The country had been entirely under Philip II's control until a group of cities and provinces had rebelled against his rule in the mid-1560s. This resulted in the country being divided between the Spanish-controlled Netherlands and the Calvinist-dominated United Provinces (or Dutch Republic) which had declared their independence in 1579. Walsingham had long pressed for English intervention on behalf of the Dutch rebels and Crichton's confession gave him the ammunition he needed to convince Elizabeth that this was the best course of action to safeguard her kingdom. She signed the Treaty of Nonsuch in August 1585 and dispatched the Earl of Leicester to the Netherlands with a sizeable force of English men and munitions.

Oblivious to Crichton's confession, in September 1584 Mary renewed the proposal that she might be released to return to Scotland, where she would reign jointly with her son. As an incentive, she promised to openly support Elizabeth's right to rule and to oppose papal interference in both England and Scotland: 'Then none . . . will dare touch the one realm for religion without offending both.' Assuring Elizabeth that she would 'never find [me] false to her', Mary even offered to relinquish her claim to the English throne.[33] Surprisingly, given her deep-seated distrust of the Scottish queen, which Walsingham's discovery had intensified, Elizabeth seemed open to the idea. But the same was not true of James. When Mary had first raised the scheme in 1581, he had only just begun to exert his independent authority as king and had expressed polite enthusiasm. Now aged eighteen, he was a good deal less inclined to share power with a mother he barely knew. As one of his contemporaries observed: 'He would rather have her as she is, than himself to give her place.' James himself was quick to scorn the idea that 'I should seem to nourish in my mind, a vindictive resolution against England, or at the least, some principals there, for the Queen my mother's quarrel'.[34] In the spring of 1585, he finally rejected his mother's proposal outright.

This was a bitter blow for Mary. 'Alas! Was ever a sight so detestable and impious before God and man, as an only child despoiling his mother and her crown of royal estate?' she lamented in a letter to Elizabeth.[35] The latter hardly shared her disappointment. She might have shown herself willing to consider Mary's release, but the chances of her freeing the most deadly rival to her throne had surely always been remote. She was quick to take advantage of James's disregard for his mother by driving an even deeper wedge between them. 'If the half of that good nature had been in his mother that I imagine to be in himself he had not been so soon fatherless,' she told him. In another secret missive, she urged the King of Scots to help protect her from the 'bloody hand of a murderer, which some of your near of kin [Mary] did grant'. James replied by 'offering unto you my person, and all that is mine, to be used and employed by you as a loving mother would use her natural and devoted child'. He assured her: 'I swear on my part ever to prefer you to all kin and friendship I have in any country.'[36] This, and his regular use of 'mother' when addressing Elizabeth, must have been a source of intense satisfaction to a woman who had been widely criticised for rejecting marriage (and therefore childbirth) in contrast to her far more socially acceptable rival, who had embraced both and courted disaster.

On 19 October 1584, the privy council signed the Bond of Association. This was the work of Walsingham and Burghley and their draft made it clear that it was in response to Crichton's revelations. It began: 'The life of our gracious sovereign lady Queen Elizabeth has been most traitorously and devilishly sought.' The bond then called on all those who swore it to pursue anyone who tried to harm the Queen and 'never to allow, accept, or favour any such pretended successors, by whom or for whom any such detestable act shall be attempted or committed'.[37]

The bond was reshaped into a parliamentary Act ('The Act for the Queen's Safety') the following year. Before this became law, Elizabeth had it reworded so that the heir of any conspirator was protected, provided they were not involved in the conspiracy themselves. This was almost certainly intended for James's benefit. He had proved himself loyal to Elizabeth by rejecting his mother's scheme for joint sovereignty and this was his reward. The final Act stipulated that any attempted invasion, rebellion or plot by a 'pretender' to seize the throne must be investigated by a tribunal of peers and privy councillors. It also made it a capital offence to commit any act 'whereby the Queen's life shall be shortened'. Any person found guilty was to be barred from inheriting the throne and 'pursued to death by all the Queen's subjects'.[38] The latter provision was a direct attack on Mary – and a stark warning to her son. If he involved himself in any plots against Elizabeth, he would forever forfeit his right to her throne.

Before the new Act became law, Burghley drafted an addendum which stipulated that in the event of the Queen's untimely death, the powers of the crown would be exercised by an extraordinary 'great council' until such time as Parliament named a Protestant successor.[39] This revived the scheme that he had first proposed more than twenty years earlier, following Elizabeth's brush with death after contracting smallpox, whereby a monarchical republic would be established to govern the realm in the event of the Queen's death without an agreed heir. Now, as then, there is no record of how far Elizabeth was consulted in the scheme, but it did not make it into the final Act.

Elizabeth and James might have appeared on the best of terms throughout this time, but the endemic hostility between their two kingdoms continued to spark friction. On 28 July 1585, Lord Francis Russell, who was serving in Elizabeth's army on the borders, was mortally wounded in a quarrel which suddenly flared up during a truce-day. The Queen wrote at once to James, expressing her outrage 'that a Scot should dare violate his hands on any of our noble blood ... when our friendship should have sent out his hottest beams to the kindling of the entire affection of both realms'. James was quick to assure her of his 'honest innocence in this late mischief' and promised to punish the perpetrators severely. The controversy rumbled on for months, however, and Elizabeth was still demanding vengeance the following spring.[40]

At the end of 1585, the King of Scots sent an envoy to the English court with instructions to treat for a firm alliance and 'privately, to inform you [Elizabeth] of my secret intention in all things'. She returned a message with the same sentiments and dispatched an ambassador north to further the negotiations. Their mutual distrust showed through the overblown assurances of friendship, however, with James assuring Elizabeth 'that all my deeds shall correspond to my promises', while she urged him 'that no whispering treason shall have credit in your ears'.[41]

In January 1586, the Queen sent Thomas Randolph on what would be his last embassy to Scotland. A few months later, he was joined by the experienced diplomat Edward Wotton. Their task was to conclude an offensive and defensive alliance in response to the growing threat from Catholic France and Spain, and to persuade James to join Elizabeth in protecting the Protestant Dutch Republic. Wotton was also instructed to further a marriage between James and either Anne of Denmark or Arbella Stuart. But according to Melville, Wotton was 'a very ill instrument' who served his own interests above those of his royal mistress. He was one of a growing body of English courtiers who were working against James's succession to the English throne. Melville claimed: 'Those who at present have a chief management at the Court . . . make all the opposition they can to our King, because of their unmerciful dealing to his mother, for the which they fear some day to be punished, when he comes to be King of England.' Such 'double dealing' was becoming ever more prominent in Anglo-Scottish diplomacy.[42]

The Treaty of Berwick was concluded on 6 July 1586. As well as severing James's ties with his mother for good, this 'league of amity' provided that each kingdom would support the other in the event of an invasion. Elizabeth also granted James an annual pension of £4,000 (she had originally promised £5,000). For a king with a significantly smaller treasury than his English neighbour, this was very welcome. But its value went beyond the financial: the pension was taken by many to be a surety that Elizabeth considered James her heir. True to form, though, she made no specific mention of his right to her throne – a fact that caused him bitter disappointment. She was clearly determined to use the succession as bait to keep the King of Scots in line and prevent him from following policies or foreign alliances that would be prejudicial to English interests.

James could at least console himself with having secured a letter from the English queen in which she promised not to do anything that might damage his claim, adding the rider 'unless by any manifest ingratitude (which we hope shall never proceed from you) we should be justly moved and provoked to the contrary'. She also agreed to insert a clause conferring on him 'some special name of honour and dignity . . . with her Majesty's benevolence'. This probably referred to the English lands of the Earl and Countess of Lennox, his paternal grand-parents, which he had been trying to get his hands on for years. He judged that they would help counter the alien status that stood in the way of his claiming the English throne. But Elizabeth showed no more inclination to grant him the lands than she had before. Ten years later they were still battling it out, with James insisting that the lands had been 'promised under her hand' and the Queen firmly denying that the prom-ise referred to any such thing.[43]

James might have hoped that in forging a closer alliance with England, the people there might view him less as a foreigner and more as their monarch-in-waiting. For his captive mother, though, it signalled an end to her hopes that James might join her in ousting Elizabeth from the throne, or that he might convert to the Catholic faith. Bitterly disap-pointed by what she saw as her son's betrayal, she sent a message to Philip II that she was willing to give him her title to the English crown.

Mary's letters had formerly been sent through the French embassy, although from 1583 Walsingham had been reading them first. But in September 1585 the spymaster used the replacement of Mauvissière by Guillaume de l'Aubespeine, Baron de Châteauneuf, as ambassador as an excuse to order that all her correspondence should be sent straight to him. Mary's recent transfer to Chartley Manor in Staffordshire, where she was under the custody of Sir Amyas Paulet, a strict and austere man, had intensified her desperation to escape her long and increasingly suffocating imprisonment. She therefore began to lend an ever more willing ear to the Catholic conspirators who were working to destroy Elizabeth and make Mary Queen of England.

'So long as that devilish woman lives, neither Her Majesty must make account to continue in quiet possession of her crown, nor her faithful servants assure themselves of safety of their lives,' Walsingham wrote to Robert Dudley, Earl of Leicester.[44] The Catholic threat had increased sharply since the Pope had issued his bull of excommunication against Elizabeth in 1570 and even Walsingham's highly sophisticated spy network was struggling to keep his royal mistress safe. Elizabeth was fully aware of the threat but had doggedly refused to act against Mary. Walsingham and his fellow adviser Burghley therefore resolved to provide her with incontrovertible proof that Mary was plotting to assassinate her.

Walsingham devised a scheme to encourage the captive queen to re-establish the secret correspondence that she had formerly sent through Mauvissière. He enlisted a plausible double agent, Gilbert Gifford, who introduced himself to Mary and the French embassy. Gifford convinced them that he was able to provide a vehicle for Mary to communicate with the outside world. In January 1586, a complex intelligence operation began. Ciphered letters were smuggled in and out of Chartley in beer barrels, enabling Mary to read and reply to over a year's backlog of correspondence. All these passed through Walsingham's office, where they were unsealed and deciphered by his master cryptographer, Thomas Phelippes, before being resealed and carried to their intended addressee.

On the same day that the Treaty of Berwick was signed, Walsingham's agents took possession of a ciphered letter from a Catholic gentleman named Anthony Babington, who sought Mary's blessing for 'the dispatch of the usurper [Elizabeth] by six noble gentlemen, who for the zeal they bear to the Catholic cause and your Majesty's service will undertake that tragical execution'. Simultaneously with Elizabeth's assassination, a rebellion would break out with Spanish support and Mary would be crowned Queen of England. In her reply, written on 17 July 1586, Mary urged: 'Set the six gentlemen to work', and signed the letter. She added that she desired the overthrow of her son and 'some stirring in Ireland'.[45] After deciphering it, Phelippes drew a set of gallows on the address leaf. Mary had inadvertently sealed her doom.

Walsingham had added a postscript to Mary's letter in her handwriting, asking Babington to name the six gentlemen who would assassinate Elizabeth. There followed an ominous silence. On 2 August, Phelippes asked his master whether Babington should be arrested 'or otherwise played with'. Walsingham replied the following day, telling him to proceed with the arrest. But he added: 'You will not believe how much I am grieved with the event of this cause and fear the addition of the postscript hath bred the jealousy [suspicion]' of Babington.[46] To his relief, the plotters had not escaped and two weeks later they were arrested. Mary's secretaries were also arrested and interrogated. They confessed to writing the 'Gallows Letter' at her command. Her apartments at Chartley Manor were searched and all her papers seized. They included more than one hundred ciphers used in her correspondence.

Under torture, Babington and his fellow conspirators confessed the whole plot – and, crucially, Mary's complicity in it. They suffered the full horrors of a traitor's death the following month. But the question on everyone's lips was:

what would Elizabeth do to the woman whom they had conspired to put on her throne? After nineteen years of plots and conspiracies, Elizabeth finally had the proof she needed to put Mary to death. Throughout those years, her spymaster had been convinced that the captive queen was at the centre of the so-called 'Enterprise of England', whereby she would usurp Elizabeth's throne with the support of Spain and England's Catholics. His painstaking surveillance had uncovered numerous conspiracies, both rumoured and real, but there had never been conclusive proof against Mary. Now he had finally secured it and joined the rest of Elizabeth's council in urging her to order Mary's execution.

But Elizabeth, as ever, was slow to act against her Scottish cousin. Her first move was to instruct Sir Amyas Paulet to tighten the security around the former queen, whom she termed 'so dangerous and crafty a charge', and to deprive her of her former luxuries. 'Let your wicked murderess know how with hearty sorrow her vile deserts compel these orders,' she added, 'and bid her from me ask God forgiveness for her treacherous dealings.'[47]

Elizabeth also wrote a sharp letter of reprimand to Mary: 'You have in various ways and manners attempted to take my life and bring my kingdom to destruction by bloodshed . . . I have never proceeded so harshly against you, but have, on the contrary, protected and maintained you like myself.' She proceeded to rail against the captive queen to her Catholic supporters. 'Well, what do you think of your Queen of Scotland?' she demanded of the Venetian envoy. 'With black ingratitude and treachery she tries to kill me who so often saved her life. Now I am certain of her evil intent.'[48]

According to Melville, the King of Scots was in as much danger as his mother. He wrote of a plot by the English privy council to 'get the King her son in their hands, and to put him in hope, that he should obtain the Crown of England, the rather, that he was within their country'. Once they had lured James to England, they would not only ensure that he was unable to avenge his mother's death but would 'take his life also, after . . . they had laid their plots how to make him odious to the people'.[49] There is little evidence to support Melville's claim, but it speaks to the febrile atmosphere that existed between the two courts.

Elizabeth herself was at pains to show every courtesy towards Mary's son. He in turn was anxious to disassociate himself from his treacherous mother. His claim to the English throne came through her and the fact that she had committed high treason against the current incumbent dealt a sizeable blow to his chances of inheriting it: regardless of his innocence in the matter, he was tainted by association. James was quick to express his relief upon hearing that the Babington Plot had been foiled and sent an ambassador to offer his personal congratulations. Elizabeth's reply was just as effusive. '[I] do render you many loving thanks for the joy you take of my narrow escape from the jaws of death, to which I might easily have fallen but that the hand of the highest saved me from that snare.' She then urged the King of Scots to root out any Jesuits from his kingdom, since they were behind the plot, and ended with an assurance that he could trust her above all others.[50] The word 'trust' applied to James, but not to his mother.

Shortly after James received the letter, Mary was put on trial in the Great Hall of Fotheringhay Castle, Northamptonshire, where she had been moved after her arrest. A spirited remark she made during her defence inadvertently prejudiced her claim to the English throne – and therefore that of her son. She declared that she 'would not offend against her progenitors the kings of Scots by acknowledging herself a subject of the crown of England'.[51] This played into the hands of those who opposed her right to succeed Elizabeth on the basis that she was an alien according to the statute of Edward III.

One of the most dramatic moments of the trial came when Mary accused Walsingham of engineering her destruction by falsifying evidence. Rising to his feet, he made a stout denial:

> I call God to witness that as a private person I have done nothing unbeseeming an honest man, nor, as I bear the place of a public man, have I done anything unworthy of my place. I confess that being very careful for the safety of the Queen and the realm, I have curiously searched out all the practices against the same.[52]

On 16 October, the second and final day of the trial, Elizabeth wrote again to Mary's son. She referred only obliquely to the momentous proceedings that were taking place and told James: 'Matters of that weight ... cannot as yet receive a conclusion.' But in a postscript, she recommended the messenger who carried the letter to the Scottish court and confided: 'I have willed him tell you some things from me; I beseech you hear them favourably.'[53]

There are no other surviving letters between the two monarchs until January 1587. But the lack of correspondence disguised a frenzy of activity as messengers, ambassadors and spies hurried back and forth with news of the woman whom the whole of Christendom was talking about.

On 25 October, the trial was moved to Westminster Palace, while Mary remained at Fotheringhay. The 42-man commission, including her nemesis Walsingham, found Mary guilty of conspiring 'the hurt, death and destruction of the royal person of our sovereign lady the Queen'. Parliament was subsequently convened to decide the sentence, which on 4 December was confirmed as death.[54]

Immediately after the sentence had been passed, a document was drafted setting out a lengthy justification for Elizabeth's decision not to name her successor. It is not clear who wrote it or on whose orders, but the content was obviously not intended for public consumption. It argued that if Elizabeth had bowed to pressure and nominated Mary as her heir, then the Scottish queen's conviction would have thrown everything into disarray. Her instinct had always been that naming her heir would put her in grave danger and she had now been proven right: 'Had she declared Mary – who has just been sentenced to death – as her next heir, she would soon have created a great number of enemies ready to threaten her life, and she would have given them even more cause to plot against her.' It went on: 'As long as the Queen does not name her successor, it is certain that thanks to her supreme authority and to the love of her subjects, her choice will carry the greatest weight for her people: she keeps all the competitors calm and devoted to her, always hopeful that if they have well merited . . . they will manage to be adopted by her.' The author then explained that Elizabeth's silence also enabled her 'to test, day after day, the virtue and superiority of the persons who may succeed her'.

Of the various contenders for the throne, only James was mentioned in person. This was highly significant, but the author made it clear that though his lineage was 'powerful', the Queen might still decide 'to impose a foreign prince as heir'. Having set out the political justification for the Queen's policy, the text concluded with the personal: 'Usually princes are indeed prone to be jealous of their successors.'[55]

Whether it was commissioned or even written by Elizabeth, this document provides perhaps the frankest appraisal of her perspective on the matter. Mary's treachery might have thrown her into a dilemma, but it had also proved the wisdom of her persistent refusal to name her heir.

The white heat of the controversy lay not at Westminster, where both the verdict and sentence had been easily reached, nor even at Fotheringhay, where the fallen Queen awaited daily tidings of her fate. It was centred on the Queen of England, without whose sanction the execution could not be carried out and who was wracked by guilt, indecision and fear. She knew that as soon as she signed the warrant, her kingdom would face the very real threat of a backlash from Catholic Europe. Mary had already written to Philip of Spain, urging him to avenge her death by invading England and taking the crown for himself.

And then there was James. His kingdom might have been dwarfed by the might of Spain and France, but he caused Elizabeth more agonies of conscience than those two super-powers combined. All the diplomatic courtesies between her 'dearest brother' James and his 'dearest sister' Elizabeth, the unspoken agreement they had reached about the succession, might be utterly and forever destroyed if the English queen signed the warrant for Mary's execution. James had already let it be known via an envoy to Elizabeth's court that he would 'no ways keep friendship if his mother's life be touched'.[56] Was this just for form's sake, to play the part of a loving and dutiful son to a mother he neither knew nor respected? Or would Elizabeth find that Mary's blood, once spilt, would prove thicker than water?

The fact that Mary was a close relative of her own was not lost on Elizabeth either. She referred to it time and again as she agonised over her fate. 'What will they now say that for the safety of her life a maiden Queen could be content to spill the blood even of her own kinswoman?' she lamented. Mary herself was at pains to remind her English cousin of their connection and referred to Henry VII as 'your grandfather and mine' in a letter she sent to Elizabeth in December 1586.[57] She certainly had the strongest blood claim to the English throne of any person living – her son included. And Elizabeth was no longer awash with potential successors. Lady Margaret Douglas, Lady Katherine Grey and Lady Mary Grey were all dead. Katherine's sons bore the stain of illegitimacy, Henry Hastings was in his fifties with no children and Arbella Stuart was an untested girl of eleven. The King of Scots was still the frontrunner, but he too was unmarried and childless. Elizabeth knew all too well how fragile life could be. She also knew that she would be setting a dangerous precedent by putting a fellow anointed queen to death.

For all her inner turmoil, Elizabeth probably knew that Mary had to die. She had been convicted of treason by the highest court in the land, her sentence issued by Parliament itself. If Elizabeth allowed her to go on living, it would make a mockery of the entire English justice system, not to mention putting Elizabeth's life in great peril. It was only a matter of time before one of the Catholic plots to put Mary on her throne would succeed. 'I am not so void of judgement as not to see mine own peril; nor yet so ignorant as not to know it were in nature a foolish course to cherish a sword to cut mine own throat,' she protested to a delegation from Parliament that pressed her to have Mary executed. The Queen of Scots' blood must be spilt; Elizabeth just did not want it on her own hands. In desperation, she wrote to Sir Amyas Paulet, urging him to 'ease her of this burden' by secretly putting Mary to death with poison or some other means. Horrified at the suggestion, Paulet protested that he would not make 'a shipwreck of my conscience, or leave so great a blot on my poor posterity'.[58]

In December 1586, the King of Scots, whose stance towards his mother had always been ambiguous at best, fired off a volley of letters to his representatives and contacts in England, urging them to plead Mary's case to Elizabeth. Among them was the Earl of Leicester, to whom James offered the disingenuous assurance: 'I am honest, no changer of course, altogether in all things as I profess to be.' He went on to provide an unusually candid insight into his predicament: 'How fond and inconstant I were if I should prefer my mother to the title [as Elizabeth's heir] let all men judge. My religion ever moved me to hate her course, although my honour constrains me to insist for her life.'[59]

No sooner had he written this letter than he hurried off another, far less tactful one to William Keith, one of his representatives in England. 'I am sorry the Queen hath suffered this to proceed so far to my dishonour, and so contrary to her good fame as ... to condemn a sovereign prince descended on all hands of the best blood of Europe,' he protested. Warming to his theme, he drew a direct comparison between Mary's impending fate and that of the English queen's own mother: 'King Henry VIII's reputation was never prejudged in anything but in the beheading of his bedfellow. But yet that tragedy was far inferior to this.'[60] James could hardly have levied a worse insult at Elizabeth. The execution of her mother on the orders of her father had been the most traumatic event of her turbulent childhood and one to which she had never referred directly. James had also called Anne Boleyn merely Henry's 'bedfellow' rather than an anointed queen and had thrown in the additional slur that her fate was in any case far less significant than his mother's.

A private rant to a trusted envoy was one thing, but James made it clear that he wanted his representatives to show the letter to Elizabeth herself. This unenviable task fell to Patrick

Gray, the sixth Lord Gray – a curious choice, given Gray's known Anglocentrism and the fact that just a few months earlier he had urged Elizabeth to have Mary executed. 'If you look for the continuance of my favour, spare no pains nor plainness in this case, but read my letter written to William Keith and conform yourself wholly to the contents thereof,' he told Gray. 'Would God she might see the inward parts of my heart where she should see a great jewel of honesty toward her locked up in a coffer of perplexity.' Seasoned diplomat though he was, there was nothing Gray could do to soften the blow. When he relayed the contents of his master's letter to Elizabeth, she flew into a rage and, as he reported, took such 'chafe as ye would wonder'. James, who by now seemed to be regretting his outburst, was quick to offer an apology.[61]

On 26 January 1587, the King of Scots wrote directly to the English queen, begging her to spare his mother's life. Still treading carefully after the diplomatic fallout caused by his last letter, he began: 'I doubt greatly in what fashion to write . . . for you have already taken so evil with my plainness as I fear [if] I shall persist in that course you shall rather be exasperated to passions in reading the words than by the plainness thereof be persuaded to consider rightly the simple truth.' He then expressed a strong belief that executing Mary would be a flagrant violation of the Law of Divine Right, so dear to his heart, which made sovereigns accountable only to God. There were threats, too, lurking beneath the diplomatic niceties. 'What thing, madam, can greater touch me in honour that [am] a king and a son than that my nearest neighbour, being in straightest friendship with me, shall rigorously put to death a free sovereign prince and my natural mother, alike in estate and sex to her that so uses her.' James went on to remind the English queen that he and 'all other princes in Europe' would be 'eternally beholden' to her if she granted 'my so reasonable request'. He attempted to smooth over the fact that he had earlier condemned his mother's treason and urged: 'I pray you not to take me to be a chameleon.' The letter was signed: 'Your most loving and affectionate brother and cousin.'[62]

It was a half-hearted gesture, motivated more by the outrage of James's subjects that their former queen had been denied proper justice than a genuine attempt to save his mother's life. In fact, he was more interested in safeguarding his right to the English throne and tasked his representatives with pursuing this, even though it proved to be at the expense of their efforts for Mary. Their proposal that she should be transferred to the custody of 'some indifferent prince' on agreement that she would thenceforth renounce any involvement in English affairs was roundly rejected. 'Suppose you I am so mad to trust my life in another's hand and send it out of my own?' Elizabeth demanded in a letter to James. Having dismissed this 'absurdity', she stressed the justice of Mary's trial and rehearsed the reasons why she deserved to be put to death. She then begged James, 'Let no sinister whisperers, nor busy troublers of princes' states, persuade to leave your surest, and stick to unstable stays,' and ended by praying that God would 'make you see your true friends'.[63]

In reminding James why his mother had to die, it seems that Elizabeth reminded herself, too. Although the letter bears no date, it was likely written on 1 February 1587 – the same day that she finally signed Mary's execution warrant. This letter reached the court in Scotland exactly one week later – the same day that the erstwhile Queen of Scots was beheaded. What happened in between has been the subject of fierce debate ever since.

The controversy centres on whether Elizabeth, as she later claimed, signed the warrant but ordered her secretary William

Davison not to issue it until she gave the order. According to Davison's account, she had authorised the warrant without hesitation and 'with a smiling countenance' instructed him to dispatch it.[64] On the night of 1 February, Davison made a secret visit to his close ally Walsingham at his home on Seething Lane, close to the Tower of London. The spymaster had been recuperating there since mid-December 1586 when he had suffered a physical collapse, prompted by the intense stress that he had been labouring under for years. Walsingham arranged for Davison to meet his brother-in-law, Robert Beale, clerk of the privy council, at his house the following morning. There, they made arrangements for Beale to convey the warrant to Fotheringhay once it had been signed by the council. Walsingham also arranged for the executioner (whom he had kept in readiness) to be sent to Fotheringhay in secret.

On 3 February, the privy council, under Burghley's leadership, signed the order for dispatching the warrant. This was then sent to Walsingham for his signature and immediately afterwards conveyed to Fotheringhay. Having waited so long for the order, Sir Amyas Paulet wasted no time in making preparations for the execution.

Mary took the news of her imminent demise calmly, consoling her weeping ladies with the thought of 'how signal a mercy God was showing her in rescuing her from the power of so bad a woman as the Queen of England'.[65] Wearing a dress the colour of martyrs, 'borrowed hair' and a resolute countenance, on the morning of 8 February 1587 Mary mounted the scaffold in the Great Hall of Fotheringhay. Although she was only forty-four years old, her famously tall, slender frame had become stooped, her shoulders rounded and her figure fuller than when the world had last seen her. An eyewitness account, probably written by or for Thomas Andrewes, the sheriff of Northamptonshire who presided over the execution, tells of how Mary turned to one of her servants, a Scotsman named Melvin, and addressed him so that all those present could hear. She used this final opportunity to reiterate both her own claim to the English throne and that of her son: 'He that is the true judge of all secret thoughts knows my mind, how it has ever been my desire to have Scotland and England united together. And commend me to my son, and tell him that I have not done anything that may prejudice his kingdom of Scotland.' Mary then turned to the assembled lords and reminded them: 'I am cousin to your Queen and descended from the blood of Henry the VIIIth ... a married Queen of France and the anointed Queen of Scotland.'[66]

Having made all those present aware of just how royal was the blood that was about to be spilt, Mary told the waiting executioner that she was 'glad that the end of all her sorrows was so near'. She then lowered her head onto the block and gave the signal that she was ready for death. It was at this point that dignified solemnity turned to macabre farce. The eyewitnesses looked on aghast as Mary was 'cruelly handled' by the executioner, who 'struck at her neck' with his axe but missed and instead sliced into the side of her face. 'Lord Jesus, receive my soul,' she exclaimed, before another misplaced blow fell. Finally, at the third attempt, her head was severed. When the executioner stooped to pick it up, it came away in his hands and he was left holding only Mary's wig. Her little dog then scurried from where it had been hiding under her dress and 'laid itself down betwixt her head and body'.[67]

When the news of Mary's execution reached the court in London, Elizabeth seemed unable to comprehend it. 'Her words failed her,' claimed William Camden, 'she was in a manner astonished.' She remained that way for the rest of the evening, giving no indication of the gathering storm. The next morning, she flew into a terrifying 'heat and passion', screaming out against the execution 'as a thing she never commanded or intended'. She then set about 'casting the burden generally upon them all', but, as Davison lamented, 'chiefly upon my shoulders'. He was stripped of his office, sent to the Tower and fined the colossal sum of £10,000 (around £1.7 million today). Still the Queen's rage did not abate. She threatened to throw her entire council into the Tower and ordered ten of them to appear before the Lord Chancellor, the Lord Chief Justice and the Archbishop of Canterbury to justify their actions. Even her closest adviser, Lord Burghley, was said to be in 'deep disgrace' for many weeks after the event.[68] The Queen's furious reprimand of Davison and her councillors had another purpose than to deflect the blame from herself: it reminded them that she, not they, wielded ultimate authority in England. It was a lesson that they would remember until (almost) the end of her reign.

When, at length, the storm abated, it was followed by a show of intense sorrow. 'She gave herself over to grief, putting herself into mourning weeds, and shedding abundance of tears,' Camden noted. The Venetian envoy reported that Elizabeth had 'taken to her bed owing to the great grief she suffered through this untoward event'. Others were more sceptical. 'It is very fine for the Queen of England now to give out that it was done without her wish, the contrary being so clearly the case,' Philip II sneered. Whether crocodile tears or genuine anguish, Elizabeth had a strong political incentive for convincing the world that Mary's death – 'that ugly unkindly murder' – had been an unhappy accident. The execution of a woman who was already being hailed as a 'sweet saint and martyr' left England dangerously vulnerable to a revenge attack by the Catholic powers of Europe, not to mention her northerly neighbour.[69]

The King of Scots made the same show of grief as his English counterpart. He was reported to have taken the news of his mother's death 'very heavily', although another observed that he 'moved never his countenance on hearing of it, nor leaves not his pastime and hunting more than of before'. James immediately convened Scotland's Parliament and 'lamenting the mishandling of his mother by his enemies who were in England, he desired the assistance of his subjects to be avenged'. All those present 'cried out in a great rage, to set forward . . . to revenge that unkindly and unlawful murder'. Henry Scrope, Warden of the English West March, a region on the southern side of the Anglo-Scottish border, reported on 'the great brags given out by our opposite neighbours for revenge'. Another official warned: 'This March is very weak and unfit to resist any sudden invasion.'[70]

On 23 March 1587 an Act 'For the Surety of the Queen's Majesty's most Royal Person, and the Continuance of the Realm in Peace' received royal assent. It provided a retrospective justification of Mary's execution. While in theory it related to Elizabeth's subjects, it was more aimed at those beyond England's borders. There was widespread outrage in Scotland that their former queen had been so brutally put to death. Under pressure to avenge his mother, the King of Scots kept up the appearance of sharing their fury.

In alarm, Elizabeth sent Robert ('Robin') Carey, son of her cousin Henry and one of her most trusted courtiers, to Scotland in order both to offer her heartfelt condolences to James and profess her innocence in his mother's death. In the letter she sent with Carey, she referred to 'this kinsman of mine' whom she assured James would 'instruct you truly of that which is too irksome for my pen to tell you'.[71] Drawing attention to their kinship was perhaps deliberate: just as Carey's family had recovered from Anne Boleyn's fall and were now high in favour, so James might hope for better times after his mother's execution.

Given the intense hostility towards England north of the border, it was a dangerous mission and Carey admitted that there were 'few or none in the court being willing to undertake that journey'. When James heard of Carey's impending arrival, he advised him to divert to the English-held border town of Berwick and dispatched two of his councillors to receive the letters and messages that he carried. They included an impassioned missive from Elizabeth to James, full of 'extreme dolour' at Mary's execution – 'that miserable accident which, far contrary to my meaning, has befallen . . . I beseech you that as God and many more know how innocent I am in this case'.[72]

The succession was a powerful balm to James's outward grief. 'After his Majesty had ripely considered the best and worst of that deed [Mary's execution], remembered himself of the many friends he had in England, who had no hand in his mother's death, he thought it not just to trouble the peace and quiet of the kingdom for the deed of a few who guided the Queen and Court, he being thereof himself apparent heir,' Melville reflected. Shortly after receiving Elizabeth's letter, it was reported: 'The King shall love her [Elizabeth] and honour her before all other princes', that he had publicly excused her of all blame in 'the late execution of his mother, and lays the same upon her Council'. He also wrote directly to Elizabeth, acknowledging the letter she had sent via Carey, in which 'you purge yourself of yon unhappy fact'. He assured his 'dearest sister': 'I dare not wrong you so far as not to judge honourably of your unspotted part therein' and asked only that 'you will give me at this time such a full satisfaction, in all respects, as shall be a means to strengthen and unite this isle, establish and maintain the true religion, and oblige me to be, as of before I was, your most loving and dearest brother.'[73]

Lord Gray, who had unsuccessfully tried (in public at least) to dissuade the English queen from putting her Scottish cousin to death, told Archibald Douglas, eighth Earl of Angus: 'This news of his pardon did wonderfully content her Majesty, who desires nothing more than to have it generally conceived that she had least part in the action.' The swiftness with which James forgave Elizabeth sparked vociferous criticism, both in Scotland and abroad. Melville scornfully remarked that 'the blood was already fallen from his Majesty's heart'. But he also hinted that James had not entirely forgiven and forgotten. 'Because the Queen was of good years, and not like to live long, he was resolved to abide his time to be revenged upon his enemies.'[74]

It had been a tragedy worthy of Shakespeare himself, riddled with dark intrigue, violent retribution and fatal misunderstanding. And, just as in *Romeo and Juliet* untimely death unites the warring houses of Montague and Capulet, so the Stuart king, having been absolved from avenging his mother's demise, was reconciled with her mortal but repentant Tudor enemy. James had played his part and Elizabeth had played hers. Any threat of enmity would be forever vanquished by the prospect of the Stuart succession to the Tudor throne. The words that Mary had embroidered towards the end of her long captivity had proved strikingly prophetic: 'In my end is my beginning.'

But even a player of Elizabeth's skill could not maintain the pretence forever. By July 1587, some five months after the execution, Mary's corpse still lay rotting in Fotheringhay Castle. The 'noisome' stench became so intolerable in the summer heat that the remaining servants balked at the prospect of entering the room where the coffin was kept. At the end of that month, Elizabeth finally gave orders for her cousin's body to be moved to Peterborough Cathedral for burial. Although she made a show of ordering a lavish funeral, with full royal honours and great pomp, it fooled no one. The last queen to be buried there was Catherine of Aragon, the rejected first wife of Elizabeth's father, whom her mother Anne Boleyn had supplanted. While it was not customary for royalty to attend funerals, the representative sent by the Queen was not even the highest-ranking member of her entourage. The insult made a mockery of the 'extreme dolour' which she claimed had hung over her ever since Mary's death.

CHAPTER 7

'AN EAGLET OF HER OWN KIND'

In the summer of 1587, Arbella Stuart received an invitation to attend the Queen, who was staying at Theobalds House, Lord Burghley's Hertfordshire home, where the court was on progress. Coming so soon after Mary's execution, the invitation was taken by some of Elizabeth's courtiers as an indication that she meant to make the young woman her heir.

Now approaching her teenage years, Arbella felt increasingly suffocated by her domineering grandmother, who was determined to control every aspect of her life at Hardwick. She was even obliged to sleep in the same room as the countess – something that the latter would insist upon until her granddaughter was well into her twenties. If ever Arbella made any attempt to assert her independence, her grandmother reprimanded her 'in despiteful and disgraceful words ... which she could not endure'. She would regularly have her nose 'tweaked' in punishment.[1]

Being raised as a pampered but restricted royal heiress did not have a beneficial effect upon Arbella's character. To assert her claim and navigate the dangerous, often deadly world of Elizabethan politics and diplomacy would have taken shrewdness, nerves of steel and a healthy dose of luck. All these her grandmother Bess had in abundance but Arbella sadly lacked. The Queen's habit of showing her great favour one minute and snubbing her the next hardly improved the young woman's stability.

Elizabeth also used Arbella as a pawn in her political power games. As a potential heiress to the throne, she was an attractive prospect, one that the Queen exploited to the full. Now that she herself was no longer a player in the international marriage market, Arbella was a useful substitute. As early as 1585, she had seemed to consider marrying her to James, who had expressed 'an affectionate favour and good will' towards his young cousin. But the Queen had swiftly abandoned this plan because it would have made the succession too certain and carried the risk of the Stuart couple launching an invasion to claim their crown before Elizabeth was dead. Judging it better to keep the two main claimants on opposing sides, in 1587, the year of Arbella's first visit to court, Elizabeth changed tack by offering her as a bride to Rainutio Farnese, son of the Duke of Parma and great-nephew of Philip II, as a means of neutralising the threat then posed by Spain. Over the next fifteen years, Arbella's name would be linked to practically every eligible suitor in Europe. But Elizabeth knew that if a match was ever concluded, Arbella could turn from useful puppet to dangerous rival, particularly if the marriage produced children. She therefore never seriously entertained the idea of allowing her to take a husband.

The King of Scots kept an anxious eye on all of this, determined to prevent his chief rival from making a marriage that would give her the edge in the contest for Elizabeth's throne. When Farnese was first proposed as a husband for his Stuart cousin, he demanded 'that the Lady Arabella be not given in marriage without the King's special advice and consent' and made it clear that he wanted 'to have the bestowing of her'. Elizabeth reacted with fury, but James was not to be cowed on this occasion. He wrote to Arbella directly, emphasising their 'natural bond of blood' and praising her virtues. 'I cannot forbear to signify to you hereby what contentment I have received hearing of your so virtuous behaviour . . . it pleases [me] most to see so virtuous and honourable scions arise of that race whereof we have both our descent.' He also expressed a hope that 'a mutual intelligence . . . be entertained betwixt us' by the regular exchange of letters.[2] There is no evidence that such a correspondence was ever established.

Arbella was as powerless to influence the choice of her husband as she was the choice of her dress or what time she went to bed. Little wonder that she seized upon the invitation to Theobalds as a means of escaping her stifled existence at Hatfield. But her visit did not get off to the most promising start. The Countess of Shrewsbury and her son Charles were also present and the latter noted: 'Her Majesty spoke to her [Arbella] but not long.' Elizabeth's attitude then appeared to shift. She began to show Arbella great favour by inviting her to dine in the presence chamber and seating her next to herself. The Queen's host and principal minister Lord Burghley also 'made exceeding much of her', dining with Arbella and her uncle. At one point, Burghley was seen to whisper something to Sir Walter Raleigh. The latter responded: 'It would be a happy thing', which Charles took to mean that his niece would one day be queen. This impression was reinforced by Elizabeth, who shortly after Arbella's visit remarked to the French ambassador: 'Look to her well: she will one day be even as I am.'[3] But, as was her custom, she stopped short of formally acknowledging the young woman's claim.

Another claimant was preparing to launch an attempt to take Elizabeth's throne by force. The fact that Mary, Queen of Scots had bequeathed Philip II her claim to the English crown shortly before her execution helped justify his planned invasion of England, even though the legal basis for that gesture was highly dubious. It was bolstered by a treatise written by William Allen, an English Cardinal of the Roman Catholic Church. *An admonition to the nobility and people of England and Ireland* mounted a scathing attack on the English queen, 'an incestuous bastard, begotten and born in sin of an infamous courtesan'. It also promoted Philip's right to her throne. Although he had long cherished hopes of claiming the English crown that he had briefly enjoyed through marriage to Elizabeth's sister, Philip pretended that he was acting to avenge Mary Stuart's execution. 'It is very fine for the Queen of England now to give out that it was done without her wish,' he declared, 'the contrary being so clearly the case.'[4]

As he prepared a huge invasion fleet comprising 130 ships and 18,000 men, Philip made friendly overtures to the King of Scots. Elizabeth knew that an alliance between them would effectively place England in a stranglehold. She therefore went on a concerted charm offensive towards her northerly neighbour, sending messages of friendship, along with her cousin and favourite, Robert Carey, Lord Hunsdon, to conclude another Anglo-Scottish alliance. As well as the unspoken promise of the succession, Elizabeth had religion on her side and James eventually agreed to support England against their common 'papist' enemy.

In May 1588, the same month that the Spanish Armada set sail, Elizabeth wrote to thank James for rejecting Philip's overtures and for encouraging Carey's, 'which all doth make me ready to drink most willingly a large draught of the river of Lethe'.[5] In Greek mythology, the River of Lethe flowed through the underworld and anyone who drank from it experienced complete forgetfulness. The matter that she perhaps hoped James would forget was the part she had played in his mother's death. As well as reaffirming this in writing, she sent another messenger to present her case to James in person. If the Scottish king had not been so inclined to favour the woman whose throne he hoped one day to inherit, he might have reflected that she was protesting a little too much.

In early July, Elizabeth wrote again to James, expressing her joy at their newly reaffirmed friendship. 'Never was there in Christendom between two princes surer amity nor sounder dealing,' she gushed, promising James that she was 'one that never seeks more of you than that which shall be best for yourself'. The latter remark may have been an oblique reference to the succession, as well as the unity of their religious purpose. The spectre of Mary still loomed large, but by now James had resorted to his former belief in Elizabeth's innocence – in public, if not in private. 'I am greatly satisfied, my dear brother, that you believe the truth of my actions so manifestly openly proved,' she assured him.[6] It was the last time that either would refer to the woman whose bloody death might have forever divided them.

In August 1588, as the Armada bore down on England's shores, James wrote to offer Elizabeth 'my forces, my person, and all that I may command . . . as may best serve for the defence of your country. Wherein I promise to behave myself, not as a stranger and foreign prince, but as your natural son and compatriot of your country in all respects . . . whereby your adversaries may have ado not with England but with the whole isle of Britain'.[7] The Scottish king's offer of troops might have been a bit half-hearted (not to mention late in the day) but his evocation of a united isle was a powerful one that betrayed his hopes for the future, not just the immediate need to repel the Spanish enemy. And with the English queen in her mid-fifties and beyond childbearing years, those hopes were growing by the day.

On 9 August, Elizabeth travelled to Tilbury in Essex, where the Earl of Leicester had assembled a force of 4,500 militia to defend the Thames estuary against any incursion upriver towards London. War was the business of kings, not queens, and Elizabeth had spent the previous thirty years trying to avoid it. But the time for negotiation had passed, so she transformed herself from Virgin Queen to warrior queen. Dressed in a military-inspired outfit with a plumed helmet and steel breastplate over a white velvet gown, she rode on horseback, Leicester walking beside her, to address her troops. The speech that she gave has gone down in history as the most brilliant of all her public addresses. She famously assured her soldiers that although she had 'the body of a weak and feeble woman', she had 'the heart and stomach of a King, and a King of England too', and vowed to fight alongside them if Parma's troops reached her shores.

In fact, by the time the Queen delivered this famous speech, the Spanish fleet had been all but defeated. The Armada was supposed to have been merely an escort for the main invasion force, the Duke of Parma's army, which was stationed in the Netherlands. But they failed to rendezvous, which gave the English fleet the chance to seize the initiative. The day before Elizabeth addressed her troops at Tilbury, her naval commanders launched fire ships against the Spanish fleet, which was anchored off Calais, awaiting Parma's army. These small ships were filled with tar, brimstone, gunpowder and other flammable materials. This audacious move was inspired by Walsingham, who earlier had sent orders to Dover that fishing boats, faggots and tar should be collected for the purpose. However, the English commanders judged there was no time to wait for these to arrive in Calais so decided to sacrifice their own warships. Sir Francis Drake and John Hawkins each offered up a ship and, along with six other vessels, these were loaded with the flammable materials and set alight, then cast downwind among the closely anchored Armada ships.

Although no Spanish ships were burned, their captains ordered the anchors to be cut and the fleet scattered in confusion, breaking their formation. Seizing the advantage, the English closed in for battle and won a decisive victory close to Gravelines, off the Flanders coast. Pursued by an English fleet led by Lord High Admiral Charles Howard, the Spanish were driven northwards by adverse winds towards Scotland and a number of ships were lost in the Atlantic and on Irish coasts. Less than half of the original fleet made it home to Spain, and only 3,000 men.

Later that month, Elizabeth wrote to James in triumph that the Armada had been 'well-beaten in our narrow seas' and was heading north towards Scotland, 'where I doubt not they shall receive small succour and less welcome'. It was more a request than an observation and Elizabeth yet again hinted at the succession as an incentive, telling James: 'If, by leaving them [the Spanish ships] unhelped, you may increase the English hearts unto you, you shall not do the worst deed for your behalf.'[8] The Scottish king was quick to assure Elizabeth that the beleaguered Spanish fleet had not approached his shores. In the meantime, Cardinal Allen, who had failed to whip up England's Catholics into taking up arms against their queen, quietly consigned his treatise to the flames. 'She is only a woman, only the mistress of half an island, and yet she makes herself feared by Spain, by France, by Empire, by all!' exclaimed a dumbfounded Pope Sixtus V.[9] Elizabeth had apparently conquered not just Philip II's Armada but the widely held prejudices against female sovereignty.

The Earl of Leicester's loyal service during the Armada crisis would be one of the last duties he performed for his royal mistress. His health had been faltering for some time and he died, aged fifty-six, on 4 September 1588, on his way to take the waters in Buxton. Grief-stricken, Elizabeth locked herself away in her bedchamber for so many days that Lord Burghley ordered the door to be broken. The brief note that Leicester wrote her six days before his death, thanking her for the medicine she had sent him and enquiring after her own health, became her most treasured possession. She inscribed it 'his last letter' and kept it in a locked casket by her bed for the rest of her days.[10]

Leicester's death affected others, too. For thirty years he had been the chief advocate for the claim of his brother-in-law Henry Hastings, Earl of Huntingdon. Now there were few who would argue for the earl, who was in his early fifties with little chance of having any children. Huntingdon himself seemed no more inclined to press his claim than he had been for the previous thirty years. His sole focus remained his service to the Queen. When the Armada had been within sight of the south coast of England, he had moved to Newcastle to secure the Scottish border in the event of an invasion from the north. Even after the threat from Spain had diminished and James had protested his loyalty to the English crown, the earl had continued building up northern resources to withstand any fresh onslaughts.

In late summer 1588, Arbella Stuart, then thirteen, was invited to attend Elizabeth at the court in London, where the Armada celebrations were in full flow. She was accorded the privilege of attending the Queen in her privy chamber and was much fêted by other members of the court. Had she been more experienced in the ways of the court, Arbella might have responded with grace and discretion. Instead, as a Venetian envoy later recalled, she 'displayed such haughtiness that she soon began to claim the first place; and one day on going into chapel she herself took precedence of all the Princesses who were in her Majesty's suite; nor would she retire, though repeatedly told to do so by the Master of Ceremonies, for she said that by God's will that was the very lowest place that could possibly be given her'. Elizabeth was not impressed. 'In indignation [she] ordered her back to her private existence without so much as seeing her before she took her leave, or indeed ever afterwards,' a Venetian envoy reported.[11]

Arbella's own account of the visit, written some years later, suggests there may have been another reason for her expulsion from court. A portrait of her painted at around this time shows an attractive young woman with reddish fair hair, a heart-shaped face and large, dark-blue eyes. Her royal blood made her even more appealing to the ambitious men of the court, including Robert Devereux, Earl of Essex, described as being 'then in highest favour' with the Queen. When Elizabeth spied Arbella talking to Essex 'in a friendly fashion', she lashed out in a jealous rage. Arbella complained petulantly of having been 'disgraced in the presence at Greenwich and discouraged in the lobby at Whitehall'.[12] She was subsequently banished from court and would not return for three years.

The Queen's dismissal of Arbella was prompted by more than simple jealousy. For thirty years, Elizabeth had played one claimant off against another, showing them favour one moment and admonishing them the next. Ever since she had first invited Arbella to attend her at Theobalds, expectations had been raised that she was about to name her as heir to the throne. All those with an eye to the future had therefore clustered around her, eager to ingratiate themselves. Following her banishment, these so-called supporters dropped her like a hot stone. One foreign observer noted that 'small account' was made of Arbella in Scotland and Spain 'by reason she was not Catholic', while others thought she was the weaker claimant because of her sex. As one contemporary put it: 'A woman ought not to be preferred, before so many men.'[13]

A year after his rival's visit to court, James resolved to strengthen his position at home and abroad by taking a wife. He had hitherto shown little interest in women, preferring the company of male favourites, but he appreciated the political advantages that marriage could bring. Certainly, it would bolster his standing with the people of England if, in stark contrast to their queen, he filled the royal nursery with an heir and spares. His chosen bride was fourteen-year-old Anne of Denmark, the younger daughter of the Protestant King Frederick II. James's advisers urged him to seek the Queen of England's approval for the match. Even though Elizabeth had proposed the Danish princess as a potential bride some years before, she was rumoured to be against any marriage for the King of Scots because it would enhance his standing in England if his wife bore him an heir. When asked, she expressed her disapproval. Unlike Arbella, though, James did not require the Queen's permission. On the eve of his twenty-third birthday in June 1589, he sent his earl marshal to Copenhagen to arrange the contract.

The marriage was forged by proxy on 20 August, but shortly after the young bride had set sail for her new kingdom, her fleet was battered by a violent storm and took refuge off the coast of Norway. Upon hearing of this, James resolved to sail across the North Sea and escort Anne to Scotland in person. This uncharacteristic display of chivalry might have been prompted by rumours about his relationship with his new favourite, Alexander Lindsay, who was whispered to be the King's 'nightly bed-fellow'. James was determined to prove his manhood and eradicate what he termed 'a great jealousy [suspicion] of my inability, as if I were a barren stock'.[14] His choice of words might have been intended as a deliberate slight on Elizabeth, who had reportedly lamented that she was of 'barren stock' upon hearing of James's birth.

The Scottish king reached Norway on 19 November. Upon meeting his new wife for the first time, he made a show of kissing her full on the mouth 'after the Scots fashion' in front of the assembled courtiers.[15] The official marriage ceremony took place four days later. The newlyweds stayed in Norway until the following spring, then embarked for Scotland. But James's chivalrous gesture almost ended in disaster when the fleet sailed headlong into another tempest and one of the ships was lost. By the time the King and his new Queen finally made it back to Scotland, he was convinced that both storms had been the work of witchcraft. It was the beginning of a dangerous obsession that would find full and terrifying expression in the witch hunts that he spearheaded on both sides of the border.

'No one that lives thanks God more devoutly for all your escapes, nor is more joyful of your sure arrival than myself,' Elizabeth assured the King of Scots upon his return. She went on to denounce the various plots that had sprung up in his kingdom during his absence, something she had written to warn him about while he was abroad. James expressed his thanks and asked that Elizabeth might offer her advice 'for my particular behaviour in preparing myself and country as the necessity of the time shall require'.[16] It was a dance that they would perform many times: James playing the part of the naive young ruler craving the guidance of his superior in years and experience. Elizabeth relished her elevated role and took every opportunity to convey her wisdom and advice, while James suppressed any irritation at being patronised as he kept his eyes fixed on the prize ahead.

Not long after James's return to Scotland, Elizabeth lost the man to whom she had owed her life for the previous two decades. Sir Francis Walsingham's health had deteriorated sharply in the eighteen months after the Armada and he had been absent from the privy council from February to June 1589. It is not clear what he was suffering from, but his frequent complaints of pains in his head, stomach and back sparked diagnoses ranging from kidney stones to cancer. Nevertheless, Walsingham rallied in the latter half of the year and attended council meetings until a week before his death on 6 April 1590.

Although he had never been as close to the Queen as Burghley or Leicester, Walsingham had shared her suspicions of Mary, Queen of Scots and had kept a close eye on Scottish affairs ever since being appointed a principal secretary and privy councillor in 1573. His obsessive suspicion of Catholic plots both within and beyond England's shores had safe-guarded Elizabeth's throne on numerous occasions, not just the prominent conspiracies such as those led by the likes of Ridolfi, Throckmorton and Babington. Two days after his death, a Spanish spy in London wrote to Philip II: 'Secretary Walsingham has just expired, at which there is much sorrow.' On receiving the letter, the King scribbled in the margin: 'There, yes! But it is good news here.' By contrast, Burghley reflected: 'I am fully persuaded . . . the Queen's Majesty, and her realm, and I and others his particular friends have had a great loss, both for the public use of his good and painful long services, and for the private comfort I had by his mutual friendship.'[17]

The death of her great spymaster would have left Elizabeth dangerously vulnerable if he had not begun to train up a replacement a couple of years earlier. As well as shadowing his father, Lord Burghley, Robert Cecil had been a protégé of Walsingham. Although it is not clear when he entered the latter's service, he was certainly active after the defeat of the

Armada, when he kept a close watch for any hint of a renewed attack. Among his informants were two brothers who were based near Biarritz, from where they could keep watch on the Atlantic coast for a sizeable number of Spanish ships setting sail. To maintain their cover, the two men pretended to be shipping contraband goods between France and Spain, which enabled them to make frequent visits to nearby ports and report on naval or military activity.

Recent scholarship has proved that rather than taking over Walsingham's network, Cecil developed a new one of his own.[18] He preferred to rely on a small group of about twenty trusted individuals. This was considerably fewer than Walsingham had employed, but they covered a large area that included Amsterdam, Calais, Brussels, Seville, Lisbon and Sweden. Learning from Walsingham's example, Cecil mostly employed merchants because they travelled widely and could speak and write several languages. Neither did Scotland escape his notice. He had at least one merchant-cum-agent there, and in the years following Walsingham's death he gradually built up other contacts. Like his predecessor, Cecil instructed his agents to send their reports in code, which he decrypted using unique ciphers for each agent.

Impressive though Cecil's activities were, they never quite matched those of his mentor. There was no structure in place to maintain Walsingham's network, so much of his work was lost. Furthermore, Essex competed with Cecil for the honour of being Elizabeth's new spymaster. In the absence of a single person in charge, English agents often failed to collaborate and information fell through the gaps.

In December 1591, having received no reply to three previous letters regarding Elizabeth's failure to pay the much-needed pension she had agreed in the Treaty of Berwick, James complained: 'I weary to be so long time suitor, as one who was not born to be a beggar, but to be begged at ... Remember, that as I am your kinsman, so am I a true prince. The disdaining of me can be no honour to you.' Elizabeth was no less tetchy in reply, reproving James for ignoring her advice about some Catholic plots in Scotland and ending: 'I will pray for you, that God will unseal your eyes, that too long have been shut.' Her impatience was even more evident in January 1592 when she accused James of harbouring a conspirator against her throne. She reminded him of the great care she had taken of him 'since you first breathed' and upbraided him for repaying her in such a way. 'Suppose you, my dear brother, that these be not rather ensigns of an enemy than the taste of a friend?' she demanded. Her indignation turned to scorn a few months later when she roundly rejected James's request for advice: 'I find so many ways your state so unjointed, that it needs a skilfuler bone-setter than I to join each part in his right place.' The King of Scots sent a robust if rather delayed defence of his actions and thanked the Queen for 'your motherly care in all my adoes'.[19]

All the while, Elizabeth continued to keep Arbella in play. She invited her back to court in 1591, on the pretence of pursuing the marriage to Rainutio Farnese. She made much of the young woman and Arbella basked in the 'fair words' of courtiers who had an eye to the future. Arbella later recalled with pride: 'It pleased her Majesty to give me leave to gaze on her, and by trial pronounce me an eaglet of her own kind, as worthy . . . to carry her thunderbolt.' But the Duke of Parma's death in 1592 put an end to the scheme. Rainutio was his successor and therefore too powerful a consort for Arbella in Elizabeth's eyes. Another contender was Christian IV, who became King of Denmark in 1588. It was rumoured that the couple would inherit the throne as man and wife upon

Elizabeth's death. But this match had no greater chance of success than the many that had preceded it. Even the Countess of Shrewsbury began to lose patience. When she urged that it was high time her granddaughter was married, the Queen merely promised she 'would be careful of her'.[20]

CHAPTER 8

'BY SO MANY KNOTS
AM I LINKED UNTO YOU'

In 1593, the Queen celebrated her sixtieth birthday. She had outlived all her Tudor predecessors and had to stay on the throne for only another three years to surpass her father's reign. Already, though, she had defied all expectations for a queen regnant. She had seen off rival claimants, kept her rebellious Catholic subjects in tow and vanquished the might of Spain – all without a husband to guide her.

But there was no room for complacency. Elizabeth's advancing age lent a new intensity to the decades-old issue of the succession. The Queen herself seemed to feel it. The number of letters she wrote to James rose sharply during the 1590s. Moreover, almost all of them were written in her own hand, despite the fact that by now she was suffering from chronic rheumatism in her right wrist. The frequency of James's letters to Elizabeth also increased during the decade, but he continued to rely on secretaries to compose them. He was also occasionally slow to respond. In April 1593, he apologised to Elizabeth for what he feared she might judge to be his 'slothful arrogance', having received three letters from her without sending an answer.[1]

Three months later, the Queen wrote one of the most candid letters of their long correspondence: 'At large I have discoursed for your estate, and have thereof adjoined my advice and counsel, ever the very like as if my own case that touched, without malice, void of deceit, and clear from any faction, but only adhering to your safety, which being preserved, I have obtained the scope of my designs.' The inference was clear: the hundreds of hours she had spent 'scribbling' her letters of advice to him over the past two decades had all been aimed at safeguarding his position, not only as King of Scots but as a future King of England.[2]

The succession was increasingly on the minds of Elizabeth's subjects, too. A rash of succession tracts appeared during the early 1590s. A number were written by some of the country's most distinguished lawyers. Among them was Peter Wentworth, who as well as being related to two of Henry VIII's wives was the brother-in-law of Sir Francis Walsingham. His brother Paul, also a Member of Parliament, had previously sparked controversy by claiming that Elizabeth's refusal to let the succession be debated was a breach of freedom of speech. Peter's first protest about the succession in the Parliament of 1572 had earned him a spell in the Tower. Undeterred, in the late 1580s he composed a supplication urging Elizabeth to settle the matter once and for all. Having failed to secure an audience with her, he resorted to writing a series of essays about the succession. Although these were only circulated in clandestine scribal copies, they were discovered by the authorities and Wentworth was imprisoned for his pains.

Despite the privy council's attempts to silence him, Peter Wentworth persisted in his support of the Stuart claim. During his third and final stay in the Tower, which began in 1593, he wrote *A Pithie Exhortation to her Maiestie for Establishing her Successor to the Crowne*. While he acknowledged that 'men honour the sun rising, and withdraw it from the sun setting', he insisted that leaving the succession unresolved was too great a danger to be ignored and reminded

Elizabeth: 'Mark (gracious Queen) your dear father in his wisdom foresaw wonderful miseries immediately and directly arising, from his leaving of his subjects without succession known and established.' Setting aside his earlier indecision, he made clear his support for the King of Scots, who was 'by both his parents descended of English blood [so] will in England become English and a favourer chiefly of Englishmen'. The treatise ended with a prayer that the people of England 'may give the crown and realm with cheerfulness and peace to that man, to whom [God] has been pleased to give the right'.[3] Given his connections, Wentworth could have sought a reprieve, but he felt so passionately about the matter that he seemed resolved to make a martyr of himself. He remained a prisoner in the Tower and died there in 1596.

With the Queen ever more determined to stamp out any debate about the succession, her courtiers resorted to other means. The play *Gorboduc* had first been performed before the court in Whitehall by the Gentlemen of the Inner Temple at the Christmas celebrations of 1561. One of its authors was Thomas Sackville, who as well as being a poet and dramatist was a Member of Parliament and later Lord High Treasurer. The theme of his play was the disputed inheritance of Gorboduc, a mythical King of Britain. It drew discreet (and positive) parallels to the Suffolk claim and cast a Scot as the villain who attempted to seize the crown after the extinction of the direct royal line and to subject England to the 'unnatural thraldom of a stranger's reign'.[4] Its overarching message was that it was imperative for the succession to be settled by Parliament without further delay. The significance of the performance had not been lost on either Elizabeth or her assembled courtiers. The play was reprinted in the early 1590s, together with *The Serpent of Division*, a narrative on the same theme about the feud between the Roman Emperor

Caesar and his statesman Pompey. It is no small irony that Sackville was the judge who committed Wentworth to prison for writing about the succession.[5]

Gorboduc was by no means the only expression of anti-Stuart feeling. A telling remark by James Morice, a renowned Puritan lawyer, around the time of the February 1593 Parliament, suggests that the King of Scots was losing his position as the frontrunner in the race for Elizabeth's throne. When Wentworth approached Morice for advice on how to settle the matter in Parliament, the latter urged him to steer well clear, for 'if we should enter into dealing with titles of the Crown we had need (I think) hold a parliament a whole year long'. His implication that support for James was not strong enough to reach a consensus was reinforced by a further concern that if Parliament debated the issue, it would be a 'cause of grief' to James. Sir Walter Raleigh entered the fray by telling Elizabeth that the King of Scots' credentials were becoming more and more doubtful. He also mocked Members of Parliament and commentators such as Wentworth – 'these great patriots' – for their indecision over whether James or the Earl of Huntingdon ought to be preferred and argued that if it was put to the vote, the result would be both divisive and ineffectual.[6]

One reason for James's dwindling support in England in the early 1590s was that he was struggling to maintain order north of the border. As in England, religious differences were at the heart of the trouble. The Scottish reformed church (the Kirk) was attempting to rid the country of bishops, dioceses and parishes and to fully establish Presbyterianism, a Calvinist branch of Protestantism which emphasised the sovereignty of God, the authority of the scriptures and the importance of grace through faith in Christ. It also advocated a system of church government by representative assemblies of elders.

Although he was nominally leader of this church, James frequently clashed with the Presbyterians, most often because he saw the bishops as the natural allies of monarchy and was determined to reintroduce a more traditional church hierarchy, with the bishops as the chief local authorities. At the same time, there was a Jesuit mission under way in Scotland aimed at garnering help from Spain to reimpose Catholicism on both sides of the border and oust Elizabeth from her throne. The turbulent Scottish nobility was divided along religious lines and James was failing to exert control over them.

Then, towards the end of 1592, the so-called 'Spanish Blanks' plot was uncovered. Several prominent Scottish nobles were involved in this attempt to incite a Spanish invasion. The Scottish authorities got wind of the plans and a gentleman named George Kerr was arrested on an island off the west coast of Scotland as he prepared to set sail for Spain. In his possession was a chest containing documents that were blank except for the signatures of four Catholic Scottish nobles. Under torture, Kerr confessed that these blanks were to be filled in by the Scottish Jesuit, William Crichton, as a means of furthering a Spanish invasion of 30,000 troops from the Netherlands, 4,000 of which would establish Catholic control there and the rest would advance south to England. Worse still from James's perspective, Kerr was also carrying a copy of a position paper written by the Scottish king on the possible advantages to him of accepting Spanish help.

Among the nobles involved was William Douglas, tenth Earl of Angus, who was of Scottish royal blood and served as the King's lieutenant in the north of Scotland, as well as the earls of Erroll and Huntley. Rather than meting out the punishment that such treacherous actions merited, James was inclined to lenience. Angus was arrested but subsequently escaped from Edinburgh Castle, while Erroll and Huntley were merely given a date to appear before the authorities and explain themselves. Having failed to meet it, they went to ground in the north.

This was by no means the only time that the King had been more benevolent towards Catholics than his Presbyterian subjects expected. As early as 1584, *Leycester's Commonwealth* reported: 'Now of late ... there is begun in men's hearts a certain mislike or grudge against him [James], for that it is given out everywhere that he is inclined to be a Papist and an enemy to her Majesty's proceedings.' Although there was no proof of this, James's lax treatment of the Spanish Blanks plotters fuelled the long-held suspicions among Protestants on both sides of the border that his professed faith was not to be relied upon. In vain he protested: 'As for the particular points of Religion ... I am no hypocrite.' Even James's apologists such as Wentworth admitted that he had 'already showed himself too remiss in punishing so many of his own subjects of their profession [Catholicism]'. He had seemed friendly to Spain, too. In 1589, Francisco de Cuellar, a survivor from one of the wrecked Armada ships, had sought refuge in Scotland because he had heard that the Scottish king 'protected all the Spaniards who reached his kingdom, clothed them, and gave them passages to Spain'.[7]

The fact that James was closely associated with some of the Spanish Blanks plotters excited suspicion that he was at best indolent and at worst complicit in the whole affair. As well as sparking fierce criticism in Scotland, this caused grave misgivings among England's Protestants – Elizabeth included. In September 1593 she rushed off a furious letter to James, calling him 'the spectacle of a seduced king' and declaring: 'I doubt whether shame or sorrow have had the upper hand, when I read your last lines to me. Who of judgement that deemed me not simple, could suppose that any answers you have written me, should satisfy nay enter into the opinion of one not void of senses?' She went on to accuse James of being 'childish, foolish, and witless' and warned: 'If you tread the path you go in, I will pray for you, but leave you to your harms.'[8]

Meanwhile, events across the Channel heightened the tensions in England and served as a salutary reminder that for as long as Elizabeth prevaricated over the succession, one of her overseas rivals might try to decide the matter by force. In August 1589, Henry III of France had been assassinated by a Catholic fanatic. As he was childless, his death signalled the end of the House of Valois and the throne was claimed by Henry of Navarre, the first French king of the House of Bourbon. The Wars of Religion that had torn France apart for the previous three decades now became a war of succession. Philip II seized the opportunity to gain the advantage over his foremost rival by pushing the claim of his daughter, the Infanta Isabella, niece of the late King Henry III. He had already successfully intervened in the Portuguese succession crisis nine years earlier, stepping into the vacuum created by the demise of the so-called 'Cardinal King' Henry, who died childless, and taking the throne by force. But France was not so easily won. Henry IV had been baptised a Catholic but raised a Protestant, and for the next four years he battled fierce opposition from the Catholic League. In 1593, after a military stalemate, he converted to Catholicism, reportedly remarking: 'Paris is well worth a mass.'

The turbulence prompted by the French succession crisis sparked a new Catholic plot the same year as Henry IV's conversion. Hatched in Flanders, it sought to assassinate Elizabeth and raise Ferdinando Stanley, the newly created fifth Earl of Derby, to the throne. As the son of Lady Margaret Stanley and the great-grandson of Henry VIII's younger sister

Mary, the new earl had a blood claim, but it was his Catholic heritage that made him an appealing prospect. Ferdinando was no stranger to the court, having been summoned there by the Queen in his youth 'to be fashioned in good manners' and spending several of his teenage years as a squire in the royal household.[9] A noted patron of the arts, he was more interested in plays and poetry than politics. His company of players, Strange's Men, performed at court several times during the 1580s and by the early 1590s they were the leading company in England, with William Shakespeare one of their number.

The newly created earl might have been from a staunchly Catholic family but his own religious sympathies were more ambiguous. An influential Jesuit priest named Robert Persons (or Parsons), who expressed support for the Stanleys' right to the English throne, admitted: 'The Earl of Derby's religion is held to be doubtful, as some do think him to be of all three religions [Roman Catholic; Church of England; Puritan] and others of none.' He therefore concluded that 'no side will esteem or trust him'. This did not deter other 'papist' plotters from scheming to make the earl king. Burghley was informed of a priest in Rome who had said of Derby: 'Though he were of no religion, [he] should find friends to decide a nearer estate [to the throne].'[10]

The 1593 plot was facilitated by Richard Hesketh, who hailed from a family of Roman Catholics with close links to the late fourth Earl of Derby, Lady Margaret Stanley's husband. He met Cardinal Allen in Flanders and the two men agreed that Hesketh would travel back to England and persuade Ferdinando to seize the throne. The new earl held two private meetings with Hesketh and then took him to London for further discussions with his mother Margaret, who was still banished from court. But reason eventually won out over ambition. In fittingly theatrical style, Ferdinando rejected Hesketh's proposal with scorn and indignation as a thing utterly repugnant to him, then promptly turned him over to Burghley. Hesketh went to his death bitterly renouncing those who had sent him on the mission and denying that he was ever a Catholic. The earl, meanwhile, hoped that his dramatic condemnation of the plot would win him favour and promotion with the Queen. He was therefore dismayed when he was passed over for the position of Lord Chamberlain of Chester, complaining that he was 'crossed in court and crossed in his country'.[11]

Another of the Queen's blood relatives continued to be the subject of rumour and conspiracy during the early 1590s. For as long as Elizabeth used Arbella as pawn in the international marriage market while not committing to any of her prospective suitors, there was always the risk that an ambitious courtier or Catholic plotter would seize the initiative.

A plot had been uncovered in 1592, shortly after another brief visit by Arbella to court. Under interrogation, a captured priest revealed that two Catholic Scots had promised 'to convey her [Arbella] by stealth out of England into Flanders: which, if it be done, she shall shortly visit Spain'. Under torture, one of the conspirators confessed that a leader of the plot had told them: 'It is Arbella ... who they most certain would proclaim queen if her mistress [Elizabeth] should happen to die, the rather as they might still rule after their own designments under a woman's government.' Burghley wrote in alarm to Arbella's grandmother, Bess, who assured him: 'Arbella walks not late, at such time as she shall take the air, it shall be near the house, and well attended on; she goes not to anybody's house at all, I see her almost every hour in the day, she lies in my bedchamber.'[12]

For the next ten years Arbella was kept a virtual prisoner at Hardwick, which rendered her already fragile mental health dangerously unstable. She had viewed marriage as a means of escaping her overbearing grandmother and was worn down by years of false hopes and promises. 'What fair words I have had of courtiers and councillors, and so they are vanished into smoke,' she lamented. During her long exile from court, further Catholic plots swirled about her, particularly as she was perceived to be malleable in the matter of religion. Robert Persons referred to her as 'tender green and flexible . . . to be wrought hereafter and settled according to future events and times'. Even Robert Cecil, one of the best-informed members of Elizabeth's court, referred to her as being 'infected by Papistry'.[13] Arbella's ambiguous religious preferences made her a favoured candidate for Protestants and Catholics alike – and an equal threat to both. It was an ambiguity that James tried, but never quite succeeded, to emulate.

In the summer of 1593, a report appeared that 'Sir Robert Cecil intends to be king, by marrying Arabella, and now lacks only the name'. One of Cecil's agents in Rome reported a conversation with a priest in the staff of Cardinal Allen, who lamented: 'England is gone. We know of their secret proceedings; they expect a new queen and another Cecil.' In other words, Elizabeth would be succeeded by Arbella and her chief adviser Lord Burghley would be succeeded by his son Robert. It was all wildly untrue, but Robert Cecil's enemies were quick to make the most of it. The Earl of Essex gleefully encouraged the court gossip about the 'pretended wedlock between his honour's [Burghley's] little son [Robert Cecil] and dame Arbella'.[14]

Throughout this time, James took care to cultivate allies in the English court, notably the Cecils. The younger, Robert, seemed inclined to favour James's claim to Elizabeth's throne but remained non-committal for the time being. His father Lord Burghley was rumoured to back Arbella Stuart or Edward, Lord Beauchamp, elder son of Lady Katherine Grey. As Lord Treasurer, he was ultimately responsible for ensuring that the pension assigned to James by the Treaty of Berwick was paid annually, but the repeated failure to do so had led to tensions. Moreover, James placed much of the blame for his mother's execution on Burghley's shoulders.

Hedging his bets, the King of Scots made friendly overtures towards the Queen's young favourite, Essex. In 1592, James approached him for help with a minor matter of business, which he claimed he had previously petitioned Burghley about, but 'always without effect'.[15] Despite his protestations of devotion to Elizabeth, Essex had his eye firmly set on the future and was all too ready to cultivate her likely successor. But James knew that the earl could prove just as false a friend to him. Headstrong, arrogant and ambitious, Essex was rumoured to have designs on the throne himself. His supporters were reported to have 'made great boasts, that he was descended from the Royal Family of the Scots . . . and of the Blood Royal of England . . . and that for this reason he had a better title to the Sceptre of England than any other of his competitors'.[16]

The year 1594 brought more positive news for the Scottish king. On 19 February, Anne of Denmark gave birth to their first child – a son – at Stirling Castle. At a stroke, this significantly bolstered James's claim to the English throne. Now he could not only offer his Tudor blood, his experience as King of Scotland and his male gender: he had a dynasty. It was traditional for royal children to be named after their parents or grandparents, but James chose the name Henry after Elizabeth's father and grandfather, a clear signal of his ambition to succeed her. He also invited the English queen to act as godmother, in return for which honour he pressed her to name him publicly as 'second person to the crown of England'. Elizabeth ignored this latter request and merely sent an envoy to offer her congratulations 'for so great favour bestowed upon him by Almighty God in sending him a young prince'. After a long delay, she graciously agreed to stand as godmother, 'beholding my luck so fortunate as to be the baptiser of both father and son'.[17]

With plans for the baptism under way, one of James's rivals for the English throne was removed from the race. On the evening of 5 April 1594, a little over six months after becoming the fifth Earl of Derby, Ferdinando Stanley suddenly fell ill at his ancestral home, Knowsley Hall. He travelled to another of his properties, Lathom House, and was said to have taken bezoar stone and powdered unicorn's horn to try to cure his malady. Not surprisingly, they served no purpose and he died there on 16 April. He was in his mid-thirties and had been in good health until then, so his death naturally excited suspicion. The earl himself, as he lay dying, wailed that he had been bewitched, while others thought he had been poisoned in revenge for his part in Richard Hesketh's execution four months earlier. It was claimed that Hesketh had threatened Derby would soon die if he did not fall in with his plans. Having died with no sons, Ferdinando's earldom was inherited by his brother William. But this sparked a lengthy inheritance dispute which fatally undermined the family's status as royal heirs.[18]

James, now a step closer to the English throne, set the date of his new son's baptism for the end of August 1594. He asked the Queen to send a representative, but she demurred. He delayed the event for as long as he could, but when there was still no sign of an English ambassador, he ordered that it go ahead. He eventually received word that Elizabeth had finally dispatched the Earl of Sussex to attend the ceremony. She also sent 'a fair cupboard of silver overgilt . . . and some cups of massy gold'. It was a lavish enough gift but the damage had been done. The baby prince's mother, Queen Anne, wrote a pointed letter of thanks, reminding Elizabeth: 'It has pleased God to bless us in our son, so near in blood belonging to yourself.'[19]

James made the most of the christening by ensuring that the presiding bishop's hour-long oration drew attention to the 'proximity and nearness of blood' between the royal houses of Scotland and England. He also had a formal account of the event published for posterity and made sure a copy was sent to the English queen. The same theme was taken up in a set of celebratory verses, personally approved by James, which styled him 'King of all Britain in possession'. Elizabeth was furious and demanded an immediate apology, 'considering her portion is the greatest part of Britain and his the less'. Unrepentant, James retorted that given his descent, he 'could not but make claim to the crown of England after the decease of Her Majesty'.[20]

Another source of friction that year was a controversy involving James's illegitimate half-brother Francis Stewart, fifth Earl of Bothwell.[21] A notorious traitor, Stewart had been a thorn in the King's side for more than a decade, conspiring endlessly for power and being imprisoned numerous times for crimes that included witchcraft, murder and treason. He had planned an invasion of England in revenge for Mary, Queen of Scots' execution in 1587, and six years later he had forced himself, sword in hand, into James's bedchamber at Holyrood. In April 1594, having enlisted support on the English borders, Stewart marched on Edinburgh with several hundred men. They were easily defeated by the royal forces and the earl fled to sanctuary in England. James rushed off a

letter to Elizabeth, accusing her of being 'seduced' into shel-
tering such a traitor (a word that she had recently used against
him), or at the very least having committed an 'ignorant error'.
'I have ever been an enemy to all your enemies,' he insisted. 'It
is so far against all princely honour, as I protest I abhor the
least thought thereof.'[22]

Elizabeth replied with furious indignation. She began by
pointing out that if James had followed her advice and dealt
with Stewart on several previous occasions, the present
controversy would not have arisen. 'If I [have] been in abuse,
I claim you as the author of my deceit, in believing more
good than the sequel hath told me,' she ranted. 'My desserts
to you have been so sincere as shall never need a threat of hell
to her that hath ever procured your bliss.' As usual, the succession gave Elizabeth the upper hand in their exchanges and
James was immediately contrite. He humbly pleaded that the
offence she took from his words was 'far otherwise of my
meaning' and apologised for his 'homely rudeness'. He went
on to assure her: 'I ever bear that reverence to all virtuous
ladies, but above all to you, whose blood, long and trusty
friendship, and manifold virtues, require such loving and
kind reverence of [from] me.'[23]

In a relationship based solely on letters and messages
carried by others, Elizabeth's silence made James even more
uncomfortable than her reprimands. In October 1594 she
expressed her satisfaction that he had at last expelled the
Catholic earls involved in the Spanish Blanks plot. But if
James hoped that Elizabeth would reward his compliance by
naming him her heir, he was disappointed when instead what
followed were nine long months without any communication
from the English queen. In frustration, the King of Scots
ranted: 'How can I wonder enough that you . . . be fallen in so
lethargic a sleep, as you are so far from either advertising or

aiding, that you do not so much as once [write] to enquire what hath been here a-doing these nine months past? Use me as you list, you shall never shake [me] off, by so many knots am I linked unto you.'[24] Never before had James asserted his claim to Elizabeth's throne so strongly. She could use him as an eager supplicant, a compliant pupil, but she could never ignore him. He was a living reminder of the issue that she most wanted to forget.

Elizabeth was not prepared to let such disrespect go unnoticed. She told James that he ought to look to his own actions, notably the presence of Catholic rebels in his kingdom, before criticising hers. 'Who was then in deep lethargy,' she demanded, 'that gave so long a breath to so evil a cause ... I neglect your causes! Would God you cured as well your diseased state as I have narrowly watched to see it preserved.' She added the ominous warning: 'Suppose you that a reign as long as mine hath so few friends, or want so narrow intelligence, as that complaints and moans made to foreign estates, of straight dealings made by such as ought most have helped you, could be kept secret from my knowledge? ... There is no king, nor potentate, to whom, I thank God, I need yield account of my actions.'[25]

In the years after the Armada, the English Catholic exiles who favoured a Spanish takeover of the kingdom had shifted their focus from armed invasion to a war of words. In 1594, a book was published that sent shockwaves across England and Scotland. Entitled *A Conference about the next succession to the Crowne of Ingland*, the cited author was Robert Doleman, but this may have been a pseudonym for a Catholic group headed by Robert Persons. Its aim, in common with similar treatises published around this time, was to undermine the claim of the frontrunner, James, and garner support for a Catholic, ideally Spanish, claimant.

A Conference was dedicated to the Earl of Essex, which was less to compliment than to discredit him, seeing that he was forever pushing for aggressive action against Spain. Although the opening epistle was dripping with praise for the royal favourite, by giving him such prominence in a book concerning the succession – a subject that none of Elizabeth's subjects was permitted to discuss – the author clearly hoped to excite the suspicions of the Queen, the Scottish king and even Essex's supporters. Elizabeth's most trusted adviser, Lord Burghley, also came under fire. Persons claimed that he supported Arbella's claim above all others, which may have been inspired by the (unsubstantiated) rumours, three years earlier, that Burghley had considered marrying her to his son Robert.[26]

But the main target of *A Conference* was James. As well as citing the common law against aliens, it inaccurately claimed that a clause in the Act for the Queen's Safety barred anyone associated with a plot against Elizabeth from inheriting her throne. In fact, this was from the Bond of Association and had been removed from the Act before it became law in 1585, but Persons' mistake might have been deliberate. He also argued against the long-established (but never formally adopted) system of primogeniture and promoted the benefits of an elective rather than a hereditary monarchy. Other authors, both Catholic and Protestant, concurred with this, notably Peter Wentworth, who argued that it should not necessarily be the person closest in blood who succeeded. He also scorned James's capacity to rule his own kingdom, where he was 'tossed and tumbled by troublesome people'.

The book went on to list no fewer than fourteen possible heirs to Elizabeth's crown and analysed the claims of each. James's lineage was criticised because it was based on an illegitimate son of Edward III's eldest surviving son John of Gaunt and his mistress (later wife) Katherine Swynford. His

Stuart rival Arbella was dismissed as being inexperienced and, worse still: 'She is a woman, who ought not to be preferred, before so many men as at this time do or may stand for the crown . . . it were [too] much to have three women to reign in England one after the other, whereas in the space of above a thousand years before them, there hath not reigned so many of that sex.'[27]

Henry Hastings, third Earl of Huntingdon, was not descended from Henry VII but was related to Edward III on both his mother's and father's side. The tract singled him out as 'the person most favoured by the puritans hitherto in common voice and opinion of men', although Persons acknowledged that Edward Seymour, Lord Beauchamp, was hot on his heels.[28] Ferdinando Stanley, fifth Earl of Derby, also warranted a mention, as did the more distant claimants Charles Neville, sixth Earl of Westmorland, and Alexander Farnese, Duke of Parma, distant kin of Edward IV and John of Gaunt respectively.

At the same time as casting doubt on the mostly English or Scottish-born claimants to Elizabeth's throne, Persons promoted the idea of a Spanish successor. His preferred candidate could best be described as a rank outsider: Philip II's daughter, the Infanta Isabella Clara Eugenia, whom he described as being 'of the ancient blood royal of England'. Born in 1566 to Philip II's third wife, Elisabeth of Valois, the Infanta Isabella was a legitimate descendant of John of Gaunt, whereas the Tudors were descended from his illegitimate line. To strengthen the Infanta's claim, Persons suggested that she should marry another blood claimant: William Stanley, sixth Earl of Derby. Isabella's right to Elizabeth's throne was tenuous, to say the least, and a number of tracts refuting it appeared in the years that followed.[29] But the anti-Stuart and anti-Protestant sentiment that the *Conference* represented was very real.

Interestingly, one part of Persons' otherwise inflammatory tract was in complete agreement with the English queen. He argued that the succession ought not to be decided during her lifetime because it would imperil her personal safety and the peace of the realm. 'There is none to succeed that may be presumed by the nearness of blood to desire more the Queen's safety than their own commodity,' he opined in an obvious side-swipe at James. If she named her successor, then not only would the loyalties of her subjects shift to him or her as to the rising sun, but the disappointed candidates would take up arms. To keep the succession unresolved was therefore by far the lesser evil – something that Sir Walter Raleigh had also argued.[30]

Persons' tract – all two hundred and ninety-seven pages of it – might seem rambling and chaotic to modern eyes, as it did to many contemporaries, but in the courts of London and Edinburgh it was like the sudden pouncing of a cat among a flock of pigeons. The English queen, who had seen off the Armada with sang-froid and stirring speeches, was so rattled that she ordered the palace gates to be locked shut and her courtiers' lodgings searched by torchlight. Any copies of the treacherous book uncovered were immediately consigned to the flames. But the damage had been done. It was now open season for the subject that Elizabeth had striven to keep strictly taboo for more than thirty years.

Either to warn or to provoke the King of Scots, Lord Burghley had a copy sent to him. When James read it, he was both 'highly offended' and deeply unsettled by its contents. Its appearance brought his obsessive nature to the fore and he was seen pacing about his bedchamber clutching a copy. An English spy reported that the book 'is so charily kept by the King as that it cannot by no means be wanting from him'. The King's sensitivity to any threat to his claim had been heightened by his strained relations with Elizabeth in recent years and by his loss of support among England's Protestants sparked by his apparent favour towards prominent Scottish Catholics. Even Peter Wentworth, whose treatise argued in favour of the Scottish king, admitted that he 'fleeted and altered' in his view of the succession.[31]

In response to *A Conference*, and in an attempt to secure overseas support, the King of Scots sent a detailed outline of his claim to his brother-in-law, Christian IV of Denmark, as well as to various other Danish and German dukes. The English diplomat George Nicolson reported that James had also employed the Scottish writer and courtier Alexander Dickson to compose a treatise to counter Persons' arguments and promote his right to Elizabeth's throne. *Of the Right of the Crowne efter Hir Majesty* appeared shortly afterwards. At the heart of Dickson's thesis was a lengthy explanation of why the common law did not apply to the crown, with notable precedents cited in the form of Stephen of Blois and Henry of Anjou, both of whom had become king of England despite being born outside the allegiance of the English monarchy.[32] Dickson also launched a stinging attack on the English queen for not settling the succession, drawing a parallel with the eleventh-century king Edward the Confessor, whose ambiguous wishes for the succession had led to the Norman invasion of 1066.

During the years that followed, James encouraged other pamphlets vindicating his right to the English throne, although he was careful to do so discreetly for fear of offending the Queen. A notable example was *An apologie of the Scottische king*, published around 1600, which provided a laudatory justification of all his actions as King of Scots, as well as his hereditary right to the English throne. At the same time, James's ministers pronounced from the pulpit that Persons was a 'thief and traitor to both sovereigns and countries'. Most telling of all was the fact that two years after *A Conference* was published, an Act aimed at protecting James's ancestry was passed by the Scottish Parliament. This made it 'treasonable to slander the King's parents or progenitors'. The King of Scots himself declared: 'Although I would be silent, my blood and descent doth sufficiently proclaim it [his right to the English throne].' He also tried to quash the notion of his alien status by referring to 'my lawful future hopes'.[33]

James's bluff and bluster served more to remind people of Persons' arguments against his claim than to counter them. If he had paused to consider the matter, he would have realised that Persons had done him a favour. Until *A Conference* was published, most Catholic tracts regarding the succession had either ignored James altogether or levelled the occasional criticism of his claim. But by making the 'heretical' James his target, Persons had ensured that thereafter opposition to the Stuart succession would be explicitly associated with Spain and Catholicism, which in turn incited swathes of English Protestants who had hitherto wavered to come out in decisive support of the Scottish king. At the same time, the long-held fears of the Elizabethan regime that James would ally with Spain against England dissolved now that he was considered a declared enemy of Philip II and his Catholic subjects. But, as usual, the Scottish king was too sensitive to any attack on his credentials as Elizabeth's heir to see Persons' tract as the gift that it truly was.

CHAPTER 9

'FOR ALL THE CROWNS IN THE WORLD'

The year 1595 did not begin well for James. On 26 January, William Stanley, sixth Earl of Derby, married Lord Burghley's granddaughter Elizabeth de Vere, daughter of the seventeenth Earl of Oxford. Worse still, Queen Elizabeth herself attended the wedding, which was staged at her palace in Greenwich. Even though the Stanleys' claim had been damaged by the lengthy inheritance dispute that had followed the fifth Earl of Derby's demise, the fact that they appeared to enjoy the support of both the Queen and her chief minister was a source of concern north of the border.

But by late autumn, fortune's wheel had turned in James's favour. In October 1595 one of his surviving rivals for the throne was embroiled in a damaging scandal. Edward Seymour, Lord Hertford, had been careful to keep out of trouble ever since securing a fragile pardon from Elizabeth for his clandestine marriage to Katherine Grey thirty-five years earlier. But he had evidently raised his two sons with a keen awareness of their royal blood. In 1589 his younger son Thomas had tried to secure a notarial instrument declaring himself legitimate. Three years later, he initiated a legal appeal against the sentence that his parents' marriage had been invalid. Both these attempts were secretly supported by his father, who in 1595 initiated proceedings of his own, causing a record to be put into the Court of Arches to prove his former marriage had been lawful and his children therefore legitimate. He had taken care to be discreet, but his actions came to light in October 1595. The timing was unfortunate as Persons' book had recently been published, bringing the issue of the succession to the fore once again. The Queen therefore ordered Hertford to the Tower in November and stripped his elder son Edward of his title as Lord Beauchamp.

The following month, Henry Hastings, Earl of Huntingdon, died. He had served the Queen and her predecessors faithfully for more than forty years. As President of the Council in the North, he had ensured that the northern counties remained loyal to the crown and acted as a buffer against incursions by Scotland – fitting, given that as a fellow claimant to the English throne, he had effectively stood in the way of the King of Scots. Even on his deathbed, he was still drafting letters regarding the defence of the north and it was recorded that in his final hours: 'He held up his hands and said, God bless Queen Elizabeth, God save Queen Elizabeth'. The Queen went to comfort his widow Katherine in her 'unheard of sorrows' and showed her greater favour thereafter than she ever had before.[1]

Huntingdon's marriage to Katherine Dudley had produced no living children, so he had raised his eldest nephew, Francis, as his heir, but the latter outlived his uncle by only three days. Given that Huntingdon had died intestate, his brother George (Francis's father) tried to avoid taking on the administration of his impoverished estate. But the Queen insisted that the late earl was given a funeral befitting his rank and royal blood. He was buried with his nephew at St Helen's Church, Ashby-de-la-Zouch, in his native Leicestershire on 26 April 1596. Francis's son Henry eventually inherited the earldom of Huntingdon. Henry would marry another claimant, Elizabeth Stanley, youngest daughter of the late Ferdinando, fifth Earl of Derby, which technically strengthened his claim to the throne. But the disputed inheritance and the hints of treason by both Lady Margaret and her son Ferdinando had fatally undermined the Stanleys' prospects.

In the race for Elizabeth's throne, it was less a case of 'who dares wins' than 'survival of the fittest'. And despite years of frustrated hopes and bitter disappointments, the King of Scots was proving one of the most resilient candidates. Following Huntingdon's death, Peter Wentworth reflected: 'The removal of the most wise, heroical and popular competitors and their favourers which might have opposed, doth smooth and plane a way for him [James] to come in.'[2]

Before 1595 was out, a plot came to light involving Sir Michael Blount, lieutenant of the Tower, who had allegedly agreed to hold the fortress for Hertford in the event of Elizabeth's death. According to a witness testimony, Blount believed that the council would be powerless to take control when the Queen died, so he planned to settle the matter by force and 'arm 4 or 5 thousand [men] with all manner of munition and furniture, which he supposes sufficient to sway the diadem which way it please him'.[3] Blount's brother Richard, who was part of the harebrained scheme, was a close acquaintance of Peter Wentworth, then a prisoner in the Tower for speaking out about the succession. Wentworth was certainly aware of what was going on, even if he played no active part in it. He protested that he had never supported Hertford's claim to the throne, only that of his sons, Edward, Lord Beauchamp, and Thomas. After the investigation, Blount was stripped of his lieutenancy and imprisoned in the fortress that he had once commanded. He was not charged with treason though, and was released the following year. Many men had died for lesser crimes. The leniency shown to Blount has led to speculation that Hertford had some influential supporters in Elizabeth's council – notably Burghley, who had led the investigation.

Hertford was released in January 1596 and no further action was taken. Nevertheless, it had been an embarrassing episode for him and one which damaged his credibility as a claimant to the throne. He had barely recovered from it when, in the middle of the following year, Sir John Smythe, a distinguished military man and former ambassador to Spain, went on a drunken rampage during the Colchester musters. He urged the assembled troops to ignore their summons to any foreign war and instead to follow his nephew, Thomas Seymour, Hertford's younger son. When Lord Burghley heard of this, he immediately smelt a rat and ordered an investigation. This revealed that as well as uttering various libels against Burghley, Smythe had been stockpiling weapons. The chief minister wasted no time in having him sentenced and thrown into the Tower.

In September 1596, the 56-year-old Margaret Stanley, Countess of Derby, died. She was buried in St Edmund's Chapel, Westminster Abbey, as a nod to her royal blood. Her claim to the throne passed to her granddaughter Anne, future Countess of Castlehaven. Even though Burghley had aligned himself with the Stanleys, by now they were no longer considered serious contenders for the throne.

A short while later, what had been a halcyon period for James's campaign drew to a triumphant end when Matthew Hutton, Archbishop of York, delivered a sermon at court promoting the King of Scots' succession. The Queen passed no comment. She was in any case distracted by fears of another seaborne invasion attempt by Spain. Following the defeat of the Armada, Philip II had reorganised his navy and in 1593 he secured the port of Blavet in Brittany, from where he could launch a fresh invasion of England. There was also the ominous presence of the Duke of Parma and his huge army just across the North Sea. Two years later, the Spanish king put his plan into action, but as with the first enterprise, the Spanish ships were battered by storms and forced to retreat. Cecil, whose spy networks had failed to warn of the attempt, was no less relieved than his sovereign.

Elizabeth knew it was only a matter of time before Philip II tried again so she called on her allies for support. James was quick to respond with a proclamation in which he required all his Scottish subjects to unite with England against the common enemy of Spain. 'It hath set a deep impression of a cousin-like zeal, that mixes not his loss with her decay, and rejoices not that she should perish first, in hope of better fare,' a grateful Elizabeth wrote to James.[4] This was one of the clearest indications she had ever given that her throne (the 'better fare') might one day be his.

Although she preferred diplomacy over aggression, Elizabeth sanctioned a number of naval campaigns against Spain, notably to Cadiz in 1596 and the 'Islands Voyage' to the Azores in 1597. In the latter year, Philip II's third Armada reached the English Channel. It was almost as large as the 1588 fleet, but the weather once more played its part and those ships that were neither wrecked nor captured eventually retreated to Spain. This would be the Spanish king's last attempt to invade England. He died a little under a year later. Nevertheless, Cecil's spies, who again had failed to detect the details and timing of the third Amada, remained on high alert.

Perhaps hoping to be rewarded for his show of support during the ongoing hostilities with Spain, James stepped up his efforts to secure the English throne. In November 1596 he registered with the Scottish privy council a letter that Elizabeth had sent him ten years earlier, after the conclusion of the Treaty of Berwick, which promised not to hinder his claim to the throne.[5] He also invited the Queen to act as sole witness at the baptism of his new daughter, Elizabeth (the future queen of Bohemia). But the Queen rightly suspected that he intended to exploit the occasion for his own ends. At the same time as sending her the invitation, he once more asked her to declare him the second person in the realm. The significance of his choice of name for the infant princess was not lost on anyone either. Furious at having been used in this way, Elizabeth showed neither honour nor courtesy to the Scottish king at the baptism but merely sent her resident ambassador as proxy and supplied him with no christening gift, much to his embarrassment. James took this as the insult it was intended to be and pointedly excluded Elizabeth from the baptisms of his daughter Margaret in 1599 and son Charles in 1600.

James's sensitivity about the succession also found expression in his reaction to Edmund Spenser's epic poem *Faerie Queene*, an elaborate allegory dedicated to Elizabeth and published in 1596. He objected to the thinly veiled portrayal of his late mother as Duessa, an evil witch who represented the Catholic religion, conscious that this could prejudice his own suitability to inherit the English throne. He blamed Elizabeth (the inspiration for the title character) for its publication and ordered the Irish poet Walter Quinn to publish a rebuttal.

Towards the end of 1597, James became alarmed at reports that Elizabeth and her Parliament had acted disrespectfully towards the late Queen of Scots and had criticised his own claim to the throne. It was even said that the Spanish were on the verge of invading England and that the Queen had 'established the crown either by a second person or some other great office that might carry away the matter if God should call her Majesty'. The rumours were untrue, but James was too agitated to pause and verify them. He proceeded to deliver a furious speech in the Scottish Parliament that December, berating Elizabeth for her 'false and malicious envious dealing against his own person and state', for executing his mother and for failing to pay his pension. He also criticised the English Parliament for casting doubt on his claim to the crown.[6] For good measure, he made overtures towards Elizabeth's rebellious subjects in Ireland.

All this was reported to Elizabeth, with the embellishment that the King of Scots had expressed his intention to levy support from foreign rulers. Until now, the subject of the succession had been a well-practised dance between Elizabeth and James, each circling around it with careful and delicate steps. By pressing his claim so openly in front of his entire Parliament and hinting that he would enlist international allies to bolster it, James had at last exposed the searing ambition that he had taken such care to suppress for twenty years or more.

Incandescent with rage, the English queen fired off a 'very sharp' letter to the Scottish king. 'I do wonder what evil spirits have possessed you, to set forth so infamous devices, void of any show of truth . . . I see we two be of very different natures, for I vow to God I would not corrupt my tongue with an unknown report of the greatest foe I have, much less could I detract my best-deserving friend with a spot so foul as scarcely may ever be erased.' She ended with an ominous warning: 'Be assured, that you deal with such a king as will bear no wrongs and endure no infamy' and told James that she had instructed the bearer of her missive 'to signify such particulars as fit not a letter's talk'.[7]

In the past, such a reprimand would have thrown James into a flurry of apologies and assurances. But as Elizabeth's ambassador Sir William Bowes fearfully reported, the King's attitude had undergone a marked shift and he appeared to be increasingly alienated from England. James told the Queen that her accusations were unnecessarily sharp and that she was too ready to believe ill of him. He did not deny having spoken of the succession, but reasoned that he had been prompted to take action after being made aware of other claimants advancing their titles and making personal applications to the Queen. This much he verbally conveyed via Bowes. He also sent an envoy to England with a more polite, if deeply misogynistic, written response. Elizabeth's 'passionate' outburst had been entirely typical of her sex and: 'It becomes me not to strive with a lady'. Besides, he added: 'I perceive sparks of love to shine through the midst of the thickest clouds of passion.'[8]

At the same time as seeking home-grown allies to bolster his claim, the Scottish king began to cast his net wider. In May 1598 he launched a diplomatic campaign to garner support from the Protestant princes of Germany and Scandinavia, using his brother-in-law Christian IV of Denmark as an intermediary. He wanted them to put pressure on Elizabeth to name him her heir and was anxious to know if they would offer military assistance if he had to fight for the throne after her death. When they responded in non-committal form, James was driven to seek help from more unlikely sources. In the same year, he dispatched envoys to the courts of the newly crowned Philip III of Spain and Henry IV of France, and even engaged in a dialogue with the Pope, hoping to prevent him from supporting the Infanta Isabella's claim. Far from pressuring Elizabeth into naming him her heir, James's actions increased her irritation against him. She railed against his 'impertinence' and declared the succession 'a matter of so sour and distasteful nature' that she wished to hear no more about it.[9]

It may be no coincidence that around this time a rumour gathered ground which more than hinted at Elizabeth's plans to make Arbella her heir. The new French king was seeking a divorce from his barren wife Marguerite de Valois and James was alarmed by reports 'that the Queen of England would persuade the French king . . . either to divorce or kill his wife and to marry himself with the Lady Arbella to bring him into the succession of England'. Henry remarked that he would not 'refuse the princess Arbella of England, if, since as it is publicly said the crown of England really belongs to her, she were only declared presumptive heiress of it', but shrewdly added that he had no reason to believe such a thing would happen.[10]

James's rivals for the English throne were quick to take advantage of his disgrace with the Queen. A few months later he was obliged to defend himself against some 'slanders' which had been put about by a 'base villain'.[11] The villain in question was a suspected horse-thief and Catholic going by the name Valentine Thomas. He first appears in the records in connection with a Scotsman named Robert Crawforth of Wittsome, who was arrested on the English side of the border. Under examination by the Warden of the Middle Marches, Crawforth stated that he had met Thomas, then using what was probably his real name, Thomas Anderson, in October 1597. Together with a third man, they had travelled about stealing horses.

Then Crawforth's testimony took an unexpected turn. He claimed that he and his fellow thieves had stayed in Edinburgh and under cover of darkness gained admittance to the Palace of Holyrood with the help of the appropriately named John Steward, keeper of the King's chamber door. Steward 'brought the said Valentine presently to secret conference with the king so nightly for the space of 5 or 6 nights together to confer privately with the king'. Crawforth claimed that during these meetings Thomas promised James that he would do him such service 'that would deserve a thousand crowns at his Majesty's hands'. In short, he would tell the King 'how to conquer England without effusion of blood'. He had also given James a list of all the English nobles who favoured him, 'especially those about the court, to show him who were his friends and who were his foes'.[12] Crawforth parted company with Thomas and, following his arrest, agreed to help the English authorities to track down his former companion.

In 1598, Thomas was arrested near Morpeth in north-east England and transferred to custody in London. The English authorities seemed in no rush to deal with him – in August Dudley Carleton, later Secretary of State, observed that the matter was 'still put off'. But behind the scenes, the Elizabethan secret service was at work investigating Thomas's startling claim, made under interrogation, that he had been working hand in glove with the King of Scots, who had ordered him to 'take an occasion to deliver a petition to the Queen in manner as you shall think good, and so you may come near to stab her'. For this bloody errand, James promised to 'reward him thereafter'.[13] Elizabeth's officials concluded that Thomas was most likely a fantasist and posed little threat to their queen.

Elizabeth was informed of the matter. Not taking it any more seriously than her advisers, she decided to keep it secret and not inform James. Anglo-Scottish diplomacy was balanced on a knife edge at the best of times and this was exactly the sort of controversy that could throw it into confusion. Perhaps, too, she was trying to protect the candidate most likely to succeed her from any damaging slur to his reputation.

But it was not long before the King of Scots found out by other means. On 11 May 1598, George Nicolson reported to Lord Burghley that James had heard the rumours. His reaction was one of great alarm. Convinced that the accusation of 'vile murder', no matter how false, would damage his claim to

the English throne, he immediately insisted upon his innocence, 'protesting that for all the crowns in the world, he would
not be guilty' of committing such an act, 'especially to her
Majesty'. His already intense anxiety about the succession
now reached fever pitch. His primary concern was the Act for
the Queen's Safety, passed in 1585, which invalidated the
claim of any 'pretended successors' who caused the Queen's
life to be threatened in any way.[14]

Elizabeth instructed an agent named James Hudson to meet
with David Foulis, one of the King's officials, and provide a
report of their interview. Hudson recorded that Foulis had
assured him that his royal master had 'never apprehended
matter (whatsoever) in so high a degree, neither ever did or
will seek redress with greater earnestness than he will do in
this. For he says it cuts him off from all his hopes and possi-
bilities to come. It bereaves him of his princely reputation
with all princes. It buries his honour in the grave of oblivion
and blemishes his line and posterity forever'.[15]

At first, Elizabeth and her council tried to smooth the King
of Scots' ruffled feathers with assurances that Thomas's claims
would soon be forgotten. Lord Burghley scoffed that he
should be released as he 'is but a knave'.[16] On 1 July, Elizabeth
wrote to James for the first time in several months. 'Suppose
not that my silence has any other root than hating to make an
argument of my writing to you,' she assured him. Still determined to maintain her discretion, she was 'most desirous that
no mention might once be made of so villainous an act, especially that might but in word touch a sacred person'. Although
the Queen did not mention any details of the accusations, she
employed unusually forceful language in trying to convince
James that she gave them no credence: '[I] charge you in God's
name to believe, that I am not of so viperous a nature to
suppose or have thereof a thought against you.'[17]

Still hoping to contain the scandal, Elizabeth had Thomas placed in the Tower without trial. He would remain there for the rest of her reign. In response, James rushed off a letter full of furious condemnations against the 'vile and treacherous lies', 'shameless fictions' and 'groundless calumnies'. He also implored the Queen 'to delay the fellow's execution if he be yet alive to the effect that by some honourable means, wherein I am to deal with you, my undeserved slander may be removed from the minds of all men'.[18]

James would not rest until he was formally cleared of all involvement. Shortly after sending this letter, he dispatched an embassy to the English court, led by David Foulis. In his instructions to Foulis, James Elphinstone, the Scottish Secretary of State, made it clear that the King would be satisfied with nothing less than a 'public declaration of his innocence' and that his name must be removed from any records concerning Thomas's confession. At the same time, Foulis was to demand that a printed refutation of Thomas's 'slanderous speeches' be published across England.[19] Ironically, this would draw more attention to the controversy than if James had been content to let it fade into the same obscurity as the numerous other plots and rumours that routinely filled the dispatches of officials and agents on both sides of the border.

By now beset with anxiety and paranoia, James sent another letter to Elizabeth with his embassy. 'On my honour, I would wish that all the direct or indirect dealings that ever I had, that might concern your person or state, were in a book laid open before you,' he told her, 'and then you would see, that no subject of England hath kept himself clearer of any guilt against you than I have done, ever since I was born.'[20]

At the heart of the whole controversy lies a paradox. Thomas had posed little real threat to Elizabeth and neither she nor her councillors ever seriously believed that the King of Scots was involved. But in James's mind, the plot was of the greatest possible significance because of the threat he believed it posed to his chances of succeeding to Elizabeth's throne.

In the midst of the affair, the English queen received the devastating news that the man she affectionately called her 'spirit' had died. Lord Burghley had served her faithfully for more than forty years and she had trusted his advice above all others. He was still in active service when he suddenly collapsed in early August 1598, either from a heart attack or stroke, and died shortly afterwards. Elizabeth was grief-stricken for months. 'The Queen's highness doth often speak of him in tears, and turns aside when he is discoursed of,' reported her godson, Harington. '[She] even forbids any mention to be made of his name in the Council.'[21]

Burghley's son Robert was quick to fill his shoes. He had been appointed the Queen's secretary two years earlier and he now succeeded to his father's title as Lord Privy Seal. Cecil was a highly able and efficient successor, but never quite won the same level of trust or affection from the Queen, who disparagingly referred to him as 'little man' on account of his diminutive stature. Nevertheless, she recognised his considerable abilities and, with the rival claimants gathering ever closer to her throne, she was grateful for his vigilance. The 'Rainbow Portrait', which Cecil commissioned for his home, Hatfield House, shows the Queen wearing a cloak embroidered with eyes and ears, which is thought to refer to his role as her spymaster.

In November 1598, after six long months of desperate letters, furious denials and delicate negotiations, the English government decided on what they hoped was a solution to bring the Valentine Thomas controversy to a long overdue conclusion. Thomas was only indicted, rather than arraigned, and Elizabeth agreed not to execute him until some means could be found to honourably clear James of all involvement.

However, the King of Scots subsequently discovered that in a private letter to her agent in Scotland, she had made this promise conditional on James's 'good behaviour' towards her.

The government also drafted a declaration stating James's innocence in the plot, which was signed and sealed by the Queen. The wording was incontrovertible, if slightly irritable: 'Notwithstanding such satisfaction as we have given him [James] by our former private letters . . . he remains still much grieved with the scandal of such an imputation . . . [so] moved us to deliver some testimony in more public form . . . We do give no credit to such things as the said Valentine Thomas has affirmed against our good brother of any sort.' Elizabeth also declared: 'We consider him [James] to be a Christian Prince, of honour and religion.' But in setting out Thomas's alleged crimes – 'the taking away of life, for which he was promised great reward by the king' – she provided a fresh reminder of the whole controversy. Her declaration also made it clear that Thomas's confession had been secured 'without torture, menace or persuasion'.[22]

Throughout, Elizabeth had acted as the older, wiser states-person, which in turn had exposed James's naivety and impet-uousness. Of course, she had a far greater understanding of the English people whom she had ruled over for forty years. She also appreciated, as he did not, that keeping the contro-versy under wraps was the surest way to safeguard his claim to her throne. The Queen could not resist making the most of the superior position that she believed her actions had secured her, telling James that he might have asked the same of many kings and been refused. 'The best new year's gift that I can give you,' she averred, was her guidance – something that he had spurned in recent times.[23]

But the formal declaration was not at all what James had hoped for. He showed himself 'every way displeased with his servant Foulis' upon the latter's return to Scotland. He also rushed off an indignant letter to Elizabeth, complaining that she had made it clear that the declaration of his innocence had been wrought 'by importunity, and not willingly obtained by goodwill', and that the account it gave of James was based entirely on Elizabeth's opinion rather than his merits. 'I cannot find, in any point thereof, anything near to my just satisfaction,' he ranted. 'My expectation was, that by your patent you should have declared that . . . the bare and single allegiance of so infamous and base a villain, could bring forth no blemish to the honour and fame of one of my rank and calling.'[24]

The fact that Elizabeth chose not to send a reply suggests that she had reached the limits of her patience. She did, though, dispatch Sir William Bowes on an embassy to Scotland in the hope of finally bringing the affair to a conclusion. Anticipating that James would use the opportunity to press her envoy about the succession, she reminded Bowes of the promise she had made in 1586 not to prejudice the King of Scots' right to her throne, but added the ominous warning 'as long as he shall give us no just cause of exception'.[25]

Whether justified indignation or protesting too much, James's response to the Thomas Valentine affair – and in particular Elizabeth's handling of it – reveals just how desperate he was to be named her heir. His reputation in England mattered so much to him that any challenge to it, whether implied or, in the case of Thomas, explicitly stated, turned him from wily statesman to reckless ruler. Elizabeth's reaction is just as telling. She had gone to great lengths to keep the whole episode under wraps, aware of how damaging it could be to the lead claimant to her throne. When at last, worn down by James's insistent demands, she had agreed to publish a public declaration of his innocence, it had been worded in such a way as to raise more questions than it answered. This was no doubt Elizabeth's way of punishing her likely successor for so stubbornly refusing to listen to her advice.

There is also the possibility, however slight, that she genuinely suspected James of involvement in Thomas's plot. She knew all too well from their long-standing correspondence just how impatient he was to be named her heir. Beset by reports of Catholic plots and conspiracies on an almost daily basis, and coming to distrust even those closest to her, Elizabeth might have concluded that in the case of Valentine Thomas, there was no smoke without fire.

If so, she was not alone. The rumours that James had been behind Thomas's plot were slow to fade. In early 1601, he sent emissaries to England to urge that the Queen clear his name once and for all. But they failed to persuade her, as she explained to James: 'We would not stir anew that matter which now lies dead, and cannot be revived without some scandal how unjust soever.'[26]

By now, the King of Scots' paranoia about rival claimants was such that he even began to suspect his allies. In March 1599, the Earl of Essex embarked for Ireland at the head of a 17,000-strong English army (the largest ever sent there by the Tudors), charged with suppressing a rebellion against English rule led by the charismatic Hugh O'Neill, second Earl of Tyrone. Given that Essex's favour with the Queen now seemed unassailable, this raised hackles north of the border. The earl's friend Charles Blount, Lord Mountjoy, hurriedly dispatched a messenger to Scotland with the assurance that Essex would not exploit his powerful position and challenge James's claim.[27]

If the King of Scots did have concerns, they soon proved groundless. Presuming too much on Elizabeth's favour, Essex flouted his orders by making an ignominious truce with the Irish rebels before returning to England just six months into his posting. As soon as Essex arrived back in London, he was placed under house arrest. He drew comfort from the thought of his favour with James, whom he judged would soon inherit the English throne and restore his fortunes. At the same time, though, he feared that Elizabeth might live long enough to take drastic action against him. His ambition now mingled with desperation, he secretly urged the Scottish king to raise an army 'at a convenient time' and, together with forces mustered by Mountjoy in Ireland, march upon London and seize Elizabeth's throne. 'Such as I am, and all whatsoever I am . . . I consecrate unto your regal throne,' Essex assured James. 'Neither do I doubt, that the minds of all my countrymen . . . will jointly unite their hopes in your majesty's noble person, as the only centre, wherein our rest and happiness consist.'[28] Eager though he was to be King of England, James was not a man to back the wrong horse and gave only non-committal replies.

Essex was not alone in anticipating the Queen's death. As the sixteenth century drew to a close, a steady stream of English nobles and place-seekers made their way north of the border in the hope of ingratiating themselves with the man whom they felt certain would soon be their king. They included many Catholics, disaffected with the ageing queen. Among them was a gentleman named Edmund Ashfield. Before he set out for Scotland, he had written to James, urging him to publish a full account of his claim to Elizabeth's throne and offering advice on how he could gain support among the people of England. This had been prompted by the appearance of Persons' tract in 1594. Ashfield argued that if James would make a promise of future toleration towards English Catholics, they would rally behind his cause. He also warned that Elizabeth might allow James's arch-rival, Arbella Stuart, to marry an English husband, which would bolster her popularity enough to claim the throne and continue the 'sweet pleasing government' of England by a female ruler.[29]

In 1599, Ashfield obtained a pass to enter Scotland from Peregrine Bertie, Baron Willoughby d'Eresby, Governor of Berwick upon Tweed and Warden of the East March. He managed to secure two audiences with the King of Scots in Edinburgh. An agent of the Earl of Essex, who jealously guarded his favour with James, reported that Ashfield had discussed the possibility of the King's accession to the English throne over dinner with a group of noblemen. One of them had joked: 'Truly the Englishmen are good husbandmen, and have so well manured their grounds that we shall find a goodly and pleasant dwelling there when we come.'[30]

When word of Ashfield's activities reached William Bowes, Elizabeth's ambassador in Scotland, he and Willoughby arranged to have him apprehended and brought back to England. His papers were seized and taken to Berwick, from where Willoughby wrote to Cecil on 13 June 1599, explaining his actions. The following day, he received an order from the outraged Scottish king, demanding Ashfield's return, or at the very least an explanation for 'the taking away violently out of the heart of our country and in sight of our chief palace and eyes of our council, an English gentleman'.[31] In retaliation, he had Bowes placed under virtual house arrest and it was later reported that he had been imprisoned in Edinburgh Castle. Bowes escaped any further reprisals when Elizabeth had him recalled to England. Ashfield was not so fortunate. He was thrown into the Tower of London, where two Yeomen Warders stood guard to prevent any hopes of escape. Soon afterwards, James sent an ambassador to complain of Ashfield's arrest and demand his release. The council met to consider his request but concluded that the 'lewd fellow' should remain under lock and key.[32]

The King of Scots' bullishness over the Ashfield contro-versy belied his increasing anxiety that the throne which was now tantalisingly within his grasp might suddenly be snatched away. He was alarmed by rumours that Robert Cecil, intent upon an alliance with Spain, was trying to persuade Elizabeth to favour a candidate who would be acceptable to Philip III – namely his sister, the Infanta Isabella. He also heard that Cecil and Elizabeth were planning to arrange a marriage between Arbella Stuart and Matthias, the brother of the Holy Roman Emperor, to bolster her credentials as the Queen's successor. Twenty years of urging Elizabeth to name him her heir had brought him nothing but disappointment.

In August 1599, an associate of the Earl of Essex reported the arrogance of 'these Scots, who have, like that foolish hunter, promised the bear's skin before he be dead, cast lots upon offices, rooms, lands and earldoms to whom they shall be given, when the kingdom [England] shall be theirs'. Towards the end of that year, James encouraged his principal nobles to enter into a league, or 'band', to defend his right to the English crown. He followed this up in December by telling the Scottish Parliament that he would probably have to secure this right by force and solicited funds to do so. 'He was not certain how soon he should have to use arms,' reported Cecil's agent, 'but whenever it should be, he knew his right, and would venture crown and all for it.' This reckless approach had been encouraged by the Earl of Essex, who convinced James that if he did not take decisive action then his enemies on the English privy council would ruin his chances of ever inheriting the throne. In vain, Henry Percy, Earl of Northumberland, another of James's English correspondents, urged a gentler approach: 'No one can deny that you are so nigh to by right, and that it cannot be good for you, or us, that you should seek it sooner by force.'[33]

In the same year, a Swiss man named Thomas Platter visited England and wrote a detailed appraisal of what he encountered. The most fascinating of his observations concerned the Queen herself and how she was viewed by her people:

> The English esteem her not only as their queen but as their God, for which reason three things are prohibited on pain of death. Firstly none may enquire whether she is still a virgin, for they hold her too highly to admit of doubt. Secondly no one may question her government or estates, so completely is she trusted. And lastly it is forbidden on pain of death to make enquiries as to who is to succeed her on her decease, for fear that if it were known, this person in his lust for government might plot against the Queen's life. For they love their queen and fear her mightily, for she has ruled her kingdom for so long and kept the peace against all schemers; nor can she bear any other person besides herself to be popular with the people.[34]

With the objectivity of an outsider, Platter had got straight to the heart of the matter. Elizabeth might be feared and revered in equal measure, but she was also fundamentally insecure. She could not bear the thought of her popularity being eclipsed by anyone, most of all a successor. For as long as she refused to nominate one, and forbade her people from even discussing the possibility that the day would come when someone other than her would sit on the throne, she could safeguard her position as England's adored, unchallenged ruler.

But such was the anxiety about the future among the subjects of this ageing queen that even the threat of death would not silence them. The year after Platter's visit, the English government official and keeper of records Thomas Wilson, who also acted as an overseas agent for Robert Cecil, opined: 'This crown is not like to fall to the ground for want of heads that claim to wear it.' He claimed that the Queen and her Parliament had already named her successor in a document 'sealed up in 3 bales, and delivered to the King of France and 2 others, they having taken oath not to open it until the Queen's death'.[35] This far-fetched notion was given credibility by the widespread belief that Elizabeth would dispose of the crown in her will, just as her father had done.

Although Wilson admitted that it was 'straightly prohibited' to discuss the succession, he went on to give an account of at least twelve people with some kind of claim to the English throne who, in his words, 'gape for' Elizabeth's death.[36] 'The nearest in blood is James the Sixth, King of Scotland, as the heir of the eldest sister of King Henry 8, father to this Queen,' Wilson began. Second on his list was Arbella Stuart, 'the young damsel . . . who comes of the same line and by some thought more capable than he, for that she is English born. She is thought to be the likeliest next the King of Scotland if she [cannot] be proved to be daughter to a bastard, as they allege her father was'.

Wilson went on to list six English candidates in order: Edward Seymour, Lord Beauchamp, and his younger brother Thomas; William Stanley, sixth Earl of Derby; Henry Hastings, Earl of Huntingdon (Wilson evidently began his account while the earl was still alive); Charles Neville, Earl of Westmorland; and Henry Percy, ninth Earl of Northumberland. But as Wilson observed, all the home-grown claimants 'finding means to cut off each other and themselves also . . . open the conceits of foreign princes to claim this crown'. He named four such contenders.: Manuel of Portugal claimed descent from Philippa, the eldest daughter of John of Gaunt. The Duke of Parma was also descended through the Portuguese line. Philip III of Spain, 'whose claim is double', could claim

descent from John of Gaunt's daughter Katherine and his
mother Anna of Austria. And finally there was Philip's sister,
the Infanta Isabella, whose claim 'may well be the last because
it is the least to be reckoned of and furthest off'.

The account named various other, even more distant,
claimants, including King Henry IV of France. But the author
ruefully admitted: 'I am not so sharp sighted in pedigrees to
see how any of these would hold water ... but well I wot
[know] that a slender title oftentimes suffices for claiming and
gaining of a kingdom ... as has been seen often in that poor
island, first by William the Conqueror, and often since that in
the struggling of the houses of Lancaster and York, where
many times Might has overcome Right.' This last comment
betrays the deep-seated fear among many Englishmen that if
the succession was not settled, Elizabeth's death would plunge
the kingdom into civil war.

There was more hope than conviction in Wilson's concluding assessment: 'I do assure myself that the King of Scotland
will carry it [the crown], as very many Englishmen do know
assuredly.' He then reminded the reader of the fatal flaws of
the other claimants and provided a lengthy rebuttal of the
arguments that had been ranged against James. Foremost
among these was that he was technically an alien and therefore unable to inherit the crown. To this Wilson responded
that the law 'speaks only of aliens born out of the allegiance of
England beyond the sea, which Scotland is not: besides, the
King may by blood be said to be English, his father being an
Englishman and his grandmother an Englishwoman'. He also
called the legality of Henry VIII's will into question because it
was probably a forgery, and argued that it had not altogether
barred the Scottish line but had put it behind that of Henry's
younger sister Mary. His closing remark on the matter was
that the only reasons that Elizabeth had not named the King

of Scots' mother as her heir had been her religion 'and especially her bad behaviour towards the Queen'.[37]

In truth, however, James's Scottish birth was not the only obstacle to his succession in England. For several years now there had been a growing perception of him, even among his supporters, as weak and untrustworthy. He had proved slow to act against Catholic conspirators in Scotland and had failed to control the Kirk. His clandestine dealings with Spain and his ambiguous foreign policy had excited suspicion south of the border, as had his involvement in controversies such as the Spanish Blanks and the Thomas Valentine affair. Regular reports sent from Scotland to members of Elizabeth's government painted a picture of a king who often struggled to assert his authority and who was susceptible to favourites. The English ambassador in Scotland wrote of 'the fatal facility of this king' to be influenced by members of his chamber, while the Dean of Durham penned a scathing appraisal of James as 'a great dissembler, by all men's judgement that know him best'.[38] All this combined with the endemic distrust of the Scots to cast grave doubts on his suitability as a future King of England.

Two tracts that James wrote towards the close of the sixteenth century revealed the clash of cultures between the Stuart and Tudor monarchies that would become all too obvious in the years to come. *Basilikon Doron* and *The Trew Law of Free Monarchies* clearly articulated the Scottish king's vision of sovereignty. At the heart of James's theses was an unshakeable belief in the divine nature of kingship. He firmly rejected the ideas that were circulating in post-Reformation Europe that rather than simply asserting their God-given power, a monarch should foster a more contractual relationship with their subjects. If this contract was broken, the people had a right to oust their ruler from power – and, if necessary, kill them.

Basilikon Doron was written as a practical manual on king-ship for his eldest son and heir. In it, James told Henry that God 'made you a little God to sit on his throne, and rule over other men'. The 'glistering worldly glory of Kings' was bestowed on them so that they might become 'bright lamps of godliness and virtue', lighting their subjects' way towards similar good behaviour. He continued this theme in *Trew Law*: 'Kings are called Gods by the prophetical King David, because they sit upon God's throne in the earth.' James insisted that kings pre-dated parliaments and were therefore 'the authors & makers of the laws'. He also argued that removing even the most tyrannical sovereign would lead to greater disorder as their subjects struggled to find an alternative ruler and set up new laws – a prophetic observation.

The two books also cast light upon the Scottish king's deri-sory attitude towards the kingdom he hoped soon to inherit. He described England as 'reft by conquest from one to another', its laws subverted by William the Conqueror and his Norman regime.[39] By contrast, his native Scotland was a purer state that had resisted overseas invaders and could take pride in its independence. Such prose would have been hailed north of the border, but it made for uncomfortable reading in the south. If Elizabeth had read the books, as was likely, she must have had grave misgivings. They made it startlingly, disturb-ingly clear that James had heeded none of the advice on the nature of English monarchy that she had been steadily drip-feeding him for almost thirty years.

In February 1600, the King again called on his Scottish nobles to assist him in recruiting supporters south of the border by providing funds, promising to reimburse these when he at last succeeded Elizabeth. He pledged 'in the word of a prince that how soon it shall please God to possess us in the crown of

England according to our just and undoubted title, we shall, within the space of a year thereafter, thankfully pay and content every one of these persons that have advanced us at this time'. He also instructed his kinsman James Hamilton to offer assurance to English puritans that as soon as they were his subjects, 'I shall not only maintain and continue the profession of the Gospel there, but withal not suffer or permit any other religion to be professed and avowed within the bounds of that kingdom'. Cecil's agent in Scotland heard of all this and told his master that the King was resolved 'not to tarry upon her Majesty's death'.[40]

Neither did James let up in his appeals to Elizabeth. With the dawn of the new century, all subtlety was discarded as James pressed his claim time and again. He also frequently sent messengers south of the border on the pretence of carrying out errands when in fact they were cultivating the support of the English nobility. Likewise, he invented pretexts for dispatching ambassadors to Elizabeth's court, as well as some of his most trusted servants to act as spies.

But James had perhaps presumed too much on the Queen's advancing years and that her grip on state affairs must be loosening. She knew full well what all these missions and messages tended to. And her eyes were still sharp enough to catch even her closest advisers turning their own towards the north. Far from pressuring her to settle the succession at last, it strengthened her long-cherished policy of silence. The King of Scots might have lost patience, but the Queen of England had not.

CHAPTER 10

'DEAD BUT NOT YET BURIED'

On 5 August 1600, the King of Scots rose early to hunt in the beautiful parkland surrounding Falkland Palace, which he had gifted to his wife on their marriage eleven years earlier. It was smaller and more intimate than his other royal residences, such as Holyrood and Stirling, and had long been a favoured retreat because of the excellent hunting it offered. The 34-year-old king was accompanied by a retinue of high-ranking lords and attendants. They had only just set out when they were halted by the approach of a young man named Alexander Ruthven. He claimed that he and his brother John, third Earl of Gowrie, had detained a foreigner carrying a large quantity of money at Gowrie House in Perth, and urged the King to interrogate the man himself. After some hesitation, James agreed to ride there after the hunt. Alexander begged him to make haste, adding that he should keep the matter secret from his courtiers and bring as small a retinue as possible.

In agreeing to this unusual request, James was taking a considerable risk. The Ruthven family was steeped in treason and had been involved in several plots against the King. Notwithstanding this ominous history, James made his way to Gowrie House as soon as the hunt had finished. Having distracted the King's attendants and lured him, alone, to a turret room, Alexander threatened him with a dagger. During the ensuing struggle, the King's cries alerted his attendants, who rushed up to the turret and ran Alexander through with their swords. His brother John arrived shortly afterwards and, seeing Alexander's body, drew his sword. He, too, was killed by the King's men.

Whether or not this was truly, as it seemed, an assassination attempt by a notoriously treacherous family is shrouded in mystery. Some people willingly accepted that it was a revenge attack by the brothers for the execution of their father, while others claimed that the alleged plot was a cover-up by James, who had long wanted to get the Ruthvens out of the way. The fact that he apparently saw nothing amiss in accepting an invitation to visit their home, virtually unattended, provides reason to doubt the official version of events.

Whatever her private thoughts on the matter, the Queen of England sent Sir Henry Brouncker to the Scottish court, ostensibly to offer her congratulations on the King's 'escape'. But she also wrote a sharp reprimand to James for corresponding with her disgraced favourite, the Earl of Essex. Certain people, she noted, seemed to be preparing for her funeral, 'long ere, I suppose, their labours shall be needful'. She supposed this was intended as 'a good memorial that I am mortal' and added the pointed remark: 'So be they too that make such preparation beforehand.' The Scottish king wrote at once, expressing dismay that 'your ears should yet be so open to such as goes about, by all the means they can, to bury and abolish, by the force of lies and calumnies, that happy amity standing betwixt us'. He peevishly added that he merited 'more faith than all their knavish prattling' and that if Elizabeth were more 'acquainted with my disposition', she would have known the rumours to be false.[1]

James's peevishness increased as the English queen showed no more sign of bowing to pressure and resolving the succession than she had during the previous forty years. Instead, she continued to advise him as her heir, without naming him as such. Remaining true to her motto: *semper eadem* ('always the same'), she vaunted her constancy – symbolised by her mother's armillary sphere emblem, which she displayed on her portraiture, dress and jewellery – as a virtue to be celebrated, blithely ignoring the intense frustration that it sparked in others, James above all. In so doing, she drew a contrast to what she termed the 'variableness of Scottish affairs'. The political situation north of the border was certainly more volatile and turbulent than in England, and drawing attention to that now was almost certainly intended as a slur on James's abilities as ruler. 'Some you call traitors with proclaim,' she scornfully remarked, 'and, anon, there must be no proof allowed though never so apparent.'[2]

For all her bullishness, the dawn of the new century occasioned fear and suspicion rather than optimism in the ageing queen, who was now in her sixty-seventh year – well past the average life expectancy at the time. The loss of some of her closest advisers and favourites in recent years had sparked frequent bouts of depression. Elizabeth's own health was beginning to falter, too. Along with the migraines, stomach pains and insomnia that she had suffered throughout her life, she was so crippled with arthritis in her right hand and arm that she was often unable to write her own letters, while severe toothache prompted her to postpone audiences at short notice. 'She doth wax weak,' observed her frequent companion Robert Sidney, nephew of her late favourite, Leicester. Fully aware that the eyes of the court were trained on any sign of frailty, she wryly exclaimed: '*Mortua sed non sepulta!*' ('Dead but not yet buried!').[3]

In late 1600, a suspected conspiracy in the north of England came to light. Sir William Eure hailed from a family of aristocratic Catholic recusants and, despite having fallen foul of the law, he had been employed to help secure the border with Scotland. But the English authorities were keeping watch on him because in November 1600 they discovered that he had ventured north of the border to the house of Sir George Home, the King's chief adviser. James was staying with Sir George at the time and Robert Cecil received word that the King had held a private meeting with Eure 'in the dead time of night'. When questioned, Eure stoutly denied this at first, but then confessed to having had a 'long conference' with the Scottish king. His initial denial made Cecil even more suspicious, so even though he did not believe Eure capable of anything more than a 'very venial' cause, he had him arrested and imprisoned in the Tower.[4]

By the close of that year, the Earl of Essex, still languishing under house arrest, had cause to hope. The Queen, who had never liked to be deprived of his company for long, was beginning to speak well of his truce in Ireland. Emboldened, Essex stepped up his efforts with the man he was confident would succeed her. He now viewed the succession as his surest route to power and was determined to influence the outcome. At around this time his close friend Fulke Greville received an anonymous letter, which was almost certainly penned by Essex. It suggested that a scholar be commissioned to compile maxims on 'the uncertainty of the succession' as being one of the 'sufficient causes to ruin the greatest monarchy'.[5]

On Christmas Day 1600, Essex wrote James a long tirade against 'this reigning faction', by which he meant Robert Cecil's party, and warned of their 'devilish plots with your Majesty's own subjects against your person and life'. He went on to claim that the faction was spreading 'slanderous reports of your Majesty' and undermining his chances of claiming the throne by furthering the cause of the Spanish Infanta. Essex therefore urged James to send an ambassador to London, giving 1 February 1601 as a deadline, so that the earl could embark on 'this great work' – namely, the protection of James's prospects. He concluded: 'And when by God's favour your Majesty shall be secured from all practises here and against all competitions whatsoever, you shall be declared and acknowledged the certain and undoubted successor to this crown.'[6]

James's reply, in cipher, has not survived, but he evidently took Essex's advice to heart because shortly afterwards the Earl of Mar and Edward Bruce, Abbot of Kinloss, were told to prepare for an embassy to London. James instructed them to 'temper and frame all your dealing with the Queen or Council by the advice of my friends there'. Top of his list of instructions was 'to beseech her majesty to declare his [James's] right to the succession of this Crown . . . because he hath found by infallible proof that some very gracious with her majesty, being of extraordinary both power and malice, will not fail one day, if God prevent it not, to make their advantages of the uncertainty of succession, not only to the prejudice, but also to the evident hazard, and almost inevitable ruin, of the whole island'.[7] For good measure, he also ordered his ambassadors to revive their master's claim to the Lennox lands in England. Now more than ever the King needed the validity that these lands would provide. The two ambassadors were also to petition the Queen for the release of Sir William Eure and Edmund Ashfield.

But the embassy was delayed and by the time it was ready to leave in mid-February, the King of Scots received news that his English ally had taken matters into his own hands and staged a rebellion in London. Essex's aim was to overthrow his enemies on the council and force an audience with the Queen. He also tried to whip up fear among the citizens of London that the kingdom would soon be overrun by Spaniards,

Detail of the Treaty of Perpetual Peace between Henry VII and James IV, 1502, showing the rose of England intertwined with the thistle of Scotland.

This manuscript illustration of 1591 shows James IV of Scotland and Margaret Tudor, whose marriage formed the basis of their great-grandson James VI's claim to Elizabeth I's throne.

Mary, Queen of Scots with her first husband, the Dauphin Francis. He died the year after they became King and Queen of France, and Mary returned to Scotland.

Mary, Queen of Scots with her second husband Henry, Lord Darnley, whom she married in 1565. A year later their son, the future James VI, was born.

This idealised portrait shows Mary, Queen of Scots with her son, James VI. In fact, Mary saw her son for the last time when he was just ten months old.

Lady Katherine Grey with her elder son Edward, Lord Beauchamp, c.1562. He and his sons were viewed by many of Elizabeth I's subjects as having the strongest claim to her throne.

Lady Mary Grey, 1571. Although Katherine's younger sister never made a bid for the throne, Elizabeth's implacable suspicion of the Grey sisters blighted Mary's life.

Henry Hastings, third Earl of Huntingdon, 1588. A descendant of the Plantagenets, Huntingdon had strong support among Elizabeth I's council but always protested that he had no desire for her throne.

This little-known portrait of Elizabeth I was painted in around 1562, the year she almost died from smallpox, prompting a succession crisis.

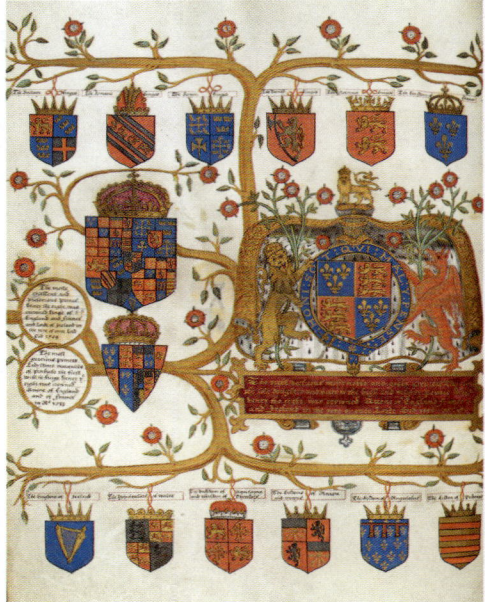

Detail of an exquisitely illustrated genealogical tree tracing Elizabeth I's descent all the way back to Count Rollo, who founded the Norman dynasty in the tenth century, c.1567.

This genealogical chart, made in around 1603 when James VI inherited Elizabeth I's throne, shows his Tudor ancestry. James is on the top row; at the bottom are his great-great-grandparents, Henry VII and Elizabeth of York.

William Cecil, Lord Burghley (shown here in c.1560s), was Elizabeth I's most trusted adviser and served her faithfully for more than forty years. She called him her 'spirit'.

Sir Francis Walsingham, c.1589. Elizabeth's spymaster (whom she nicknamed 'the Moor') spent two decades working feverishly to protect her from plots against her throne.

Robert Dudley, first Earl of Leicester, was Elizabeth I's greatest favourite and rumours about the nature of their relationship abounded. He failed to persuade her to marry him but they remained close until his death in 1588.

Embroidery made by Mary, Queen of Scots during her captivity in England. In the centre is a hand carrying a knife to prune a barren vine – a reference to her childless rival Elizabeth I.

Mary, Queen of Scots was a thorn in Elizabeth I's side for more than thirty years. Viewed by many as having the strongest claim to the English throne, she was the focus of numerous Catholic plots.

Thomas Howard, fourth Duke of Norfolk, was a kinsman of Elizabeth I. He was twice implicated for plotting to marry Mary, Queen of Scots and claim the throne. He was executed in 1572.

This portrait is thought to be Lady Margaret Stanley, Countess of Derby. A descendant of Henry VIII's younger sister Mary, she and her family had a strong claim to the throne.

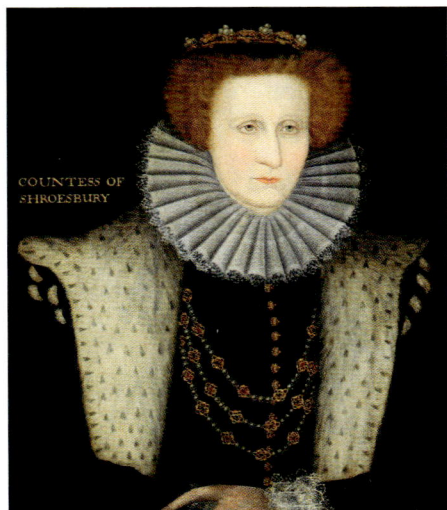

Elizabeth Talbot, Countess of Shrewsbury, better known as Bess of Hardwick, was one of the most formidable matriarchs of the Tudor age. She promoted the claim of her granddaughter, Arbella Stuart, to Elizabeth I's throne.

Henry VIII's niece, Lady Margaret Douglas, schemed relentlessly to claim the throne for herself or her family. Her ambitions were eventually realised through her grandson James VI, although she did not live to enjoy the triumph.

In this portrait, Arbella Stuart, just shy of two years old, wears a gold chain from which hangs a shield with a countess's coronet and the Lennox motto, *Pour parvenir, j'endure* [To achieve, I endure].

By the time this portrait was painted in 1589, Arbella Stuart was thirteen years old and had emerged as James VI's main competitor for Elizabeth I's crown.

This recently discovered miniature, painted in around 1592, is believed to be of Arbella. She bears a striking resemblance to Elizabeth I, both in appearance and dress, which may have been deliberate.

Arbella Stuart in 1605, when she was aged thirty and her cousin James VI had been King of England for two years.

Elizabeth I sent this miniature by Nicholas Hilliard to James VI's son, Henry, at Stirling Castle. Although she was Henry's godmother, she did not attend his baptism and caused offence by proving slow to send a representative.

Elizabeth I's 'frog', François, Duke of Anjou, was her last serious overseas suitor. Shown here in 1572 when he was aged seventeen, he was more than twenty years younger than the English queen.

Philip II of Spain was Elizabeth's former brother-in-law. After she spurned his marriage proposal early in her reign, he became an implacable enemy and strove relentlessly to seize the English throne by force.

Contemporary copy of the warrant for the execution of Mary, Queen of Scots, 1587. Although Elizabeth signed the original (which was later destroyed), she protested that she had not authorised it to be carried out.

The trial and execution of Mary, Queen of Scots in the Great Hall of Fotheringhay Castle, Northamptonshire, February 1587. Mary wore a scarlet dress, the colour of martyrs, and 'borrowed hair'.

Elizabeth's 'little man', Robert Cecil, stepped into his father Lord Burghley's shoes as the Queen's chief adviser. He was instrumental in smoothing the path for James VI's accession to her throne.

Detail of the 'Rainbow Portrait', c.1600–02. Commissioned by Robert Cecil, it carries numerous symbols and messages, including the eyes and ears embroidered on her cloak – a reference, perhaps, to his role in Elizabethan espionage.

Robert Devereux, second Earl of Essex, 1590. Cecil's rival Essex was Elizabeth I's last great favourite. More than thirty years younger than the Queen, he showered her with flattery while secretly courting her likely successor, James VI.

Ferdinando Stanley, fifth Earl of Derby. The son of Lady Margaret Stanley, Ferdinando was more interested in plays than politics. He died suddenly in 1594, the year that this portrait was painted.

Isabella Clara Eugenia, c.1599. The Spanish Infanta was the daughter of Philip II and emerged as a leading Catholic claimant to the English throne in the later years of Elizabeth I's reign.

James VI, 1595. This was painted when the King of Scots was just shy of his thirtieth birthday and rapidly losing patience with Elizabeth I, whom he had spent more than twenty years petitioning to name him heir.

Elizabeth I, c.1596. This portrait is highly unusual because it shows the Queen as she really appeared in her sixties, rather than employing the so-called 'mask of youth' that she insisted upon in most other portraits.

James VI's last letter to Elizabeth I, December 1602. Their thirty-year correspondence was the longest-running between two sovereigns in the early modern age. Elizabeth's letters are filled with advice on ruling England; James's with increasingly insistent pleas to make him her heir.

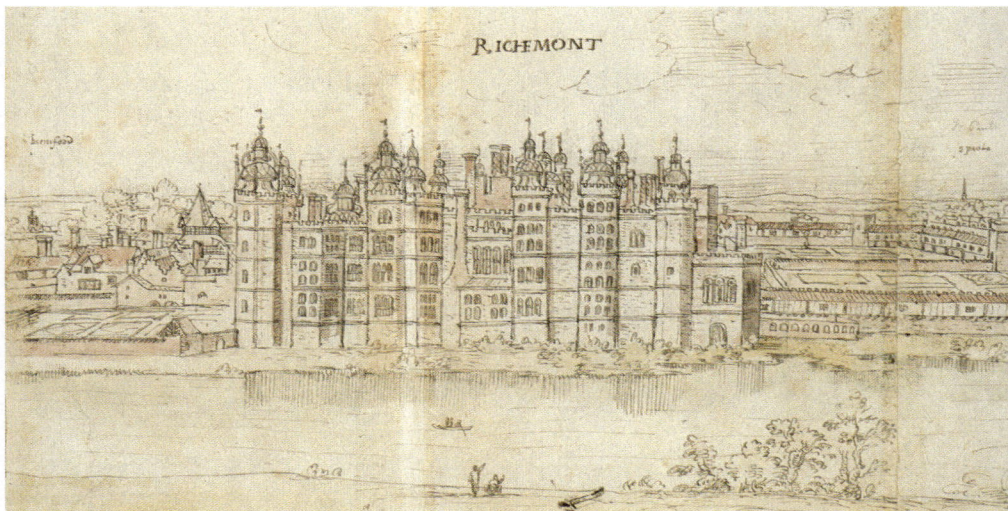

Richmond was Elizabeth I's favourite palace because of the comforts it offered – she called it her 'warm box', to which she could 'best trust her sickly old age'. She died there on 24 March 1603.

Allegorical painting by Paul Delaroche of the crown passing from Elizabeth I to James I, 1828. In fact, James was 400 miles north at the Palace of Holyrood when the Queen died.

Robert Carey, c.1591. Elizabeth I's kinsman 'Robin' was a cherished favourite but had his eyes set firmly on the future. As soon as the Queen was dead, he rode at record speed to break the news to James VI that he was now King of England.

The Masters of the Requests. Julius Cæsar & Roger Wilbram.

Agents for Venice And the Estates.

The Lord Cheiffe Justice of England Sr John Popham. The Chanuceler of y Excheqer. Sr John Fortescue.

The Principall Secretary. Sr Robt Cicell.

Controller of y Howshold. Sr Edward Wotton. Treasorer of y Howshold. Sr William Knowles.

Richard S George Windsor Herold of Armes.

A detail of the 1,000-strong funeral procession for Elizabeth I, April 1603. Robert Cecil, who was instrumental in James VI's accession, is shown just right of centre, walking alone.

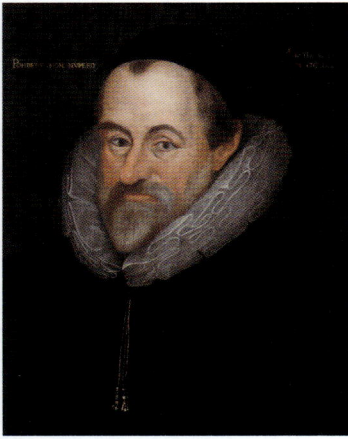

William Camden, 1609. This portrait was painted soon after he had resumed work on his *Annals* of Elizabeth's reign, on the orders of her successor.

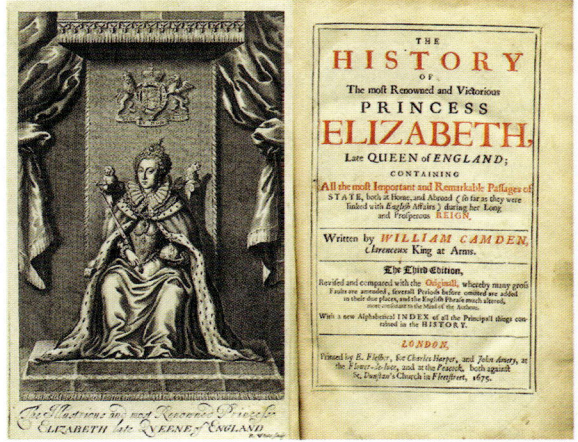

Title page of the 1675 edition of William Camden's *Annals*.

Extract from the original manuscript of Camden's *Annals* at the British Library, showing some of the previously hidden text that was revealed by enhanced imaging. Here, Camden has rewritten his earlier account of the Valentine Thomas controversy – a plot to assassinate Elizabeth I and put James on the throne.

claiming that 'the crown of England was offered to be sold to the infanta' by Sir Robert Cecil, Sir Walter Raleigh and Henry Brooke, Lord Cobham (who, conveniently, were his own enemies). 'Now or never is the time for you to pursue your liberties,' he declared, 'for you are sold for slaves to the Infanta of Spain.'[8] Such rhetoric was music to James's ears at a time when his anxiety about any rival claimants was at fever pitch and he was eager to present himself as the Protestant saviour of England against Spanish 'popery'. But his dealings with Essex excited suspicion that the real purpose of the earl's coup was to overthrow the Queen and put the King of Scots on the throne immediately. If this was the case, it failed miserably. Essex's pitiful rebellion was easily crushed by the authorities.

James hurriedly changed his instructions to Mar and Kinloss. If his 'friends' [Essex and his supporters] thought it beneficial for the ambassadors to intervene on the earl's behalf, they should do so. If, however, 'it be past redding [saving]', they should secure new allies for the King.[9] Even before Mar and Kinloss reached London, the executioner's axe had done its work and Essex had joined the ranks of beheaded traitors laid to rest in the Tower chapel.

After his ambassadors had left Scotland, James sent another, far lengthier set of instructions, telling them to find out whether the rebellion had been sparked by resentment against Elizabeth's council or against the Queen herself. If it was the latter, he was eager for the people of England to view him as their salvation, while at the same time not being seen to openly support the deposing of their queen. His greatest anxiety was: 'By suffering them to be overthrown for not declaring myself in time, they were forced to sue to other saints for shunning of their present overthrow.' If, as James liked to protest, he was part of England rather than an alien, then such talk was treason. But at the same time, he told Mar and Kinloss to persuade Elizabeth 'to renew her old promise that nothing shall be done by her in her time in prejudice of my future right'. In short, James was trying to make the most of the instability sparked by Essex's rebellion while safeguarding his future inheritance. 'Your whole commission was divided in two parts . . . to deal with the Queen and [her] present guiders, and to deal with the people – with the first publicly and for the present time, with the next privately and for the future time.' Even for the most seasoned of diplomats, it was a task fraught with danger to, as James put it, 'walk surely betwixt these two precipices of the Queen and the people'.

But that was not all. As the Scottish king warmed to his theme, so his desperation to secure the English throne became even more evident. He told the ambassadors to 'renew and confirm your acquaintance with the Lieutenant of the Tower', to secure the English fleet and seaports, to make sure his 'friends' in the shires were well armed, 'and generally to leave all things in such certainty and order as the enemies be not able in the meantime to lay such bars in my way as shall make things remediless when the time shall come'. James was fully prepared to seize the throne by force.[10]

Whether or not she heeded the rumours of James's involvement in Essex's rebellion, Elizabeth was immediately on her guard at the arrival of Mar and Kinloss, whom she termed 'so well a chosen couple'. George Nicolson, her agent in Scotland, had written to Cecil of the 'exceeding strange' embassy, the motive for which he reported was 'so secret [that] . . . the wisest are at a gaze to see what may follow it'. A week later, he was able to shed a little more light, telling Cecil that, among other things, the Scottish envoys had been instructed to discuss Sir William Eure 'and the rest', and to revive 'the Valentine Thomas matter'.[11]

Upon arriving at the court in London, Mar and Kinloss complained of Elizabeth's 'coldness' and reported that in a series of audiences, they received 'nothing but negative answers, the matters being of so sour nature to the Queen'. Cecil observed that she was suspicious of the King of Scots' connections with Essex and was 'infinitely distasted' that Mar and Kinloss 'were reserved in confessing the traffic between' them. She had good reason: it was said that at the time of Essex's arrest, he had been wearing James's most recent letter in a casket round his neck. Quite how far James had been involved in the rebellion will probably never be known, thanks to Essex's hurried burning of confidential papers. But it is telling that James later referred to the earl as his 'martyr'.[12]

Neither did the English queen have any patience for discussing the matter that James had 'insisted much upon'. Still, he was harping on the Valentine Thomas affair and 'a statute in England which defaults all persons from succession that shall be proved to have conspired any such matter as that knave is accused of'. Cecil reported that Elizabeth and the ambassadors had 'interchanged many words they thinking by argument to persuade her whose nature you know to be more unapt to yield even in trifles when she conceives they are challenged'.[13]

Elizabeth wrote to James that the business his ambassadors had been instructed to treat with her about had been settled by an embassy two years earlier. Exasperation made her set aside her customary discretion and name Valentine Thomas for the first time in her letters, telling James: 'We would not stir anew that matter which now lies dead, and cannot be revived without some scandal how unjust soever . . . . We hope to hear no more of any of these matters, which are so unworthy of our dispute.' Then came the condescending advice that had become a feature of her letters to the King of Scots: 'Let not shades deceive you, which may take away best substance from you, when they can turn but to dust or smoke. An upright demeanour bears ever more poise than all disguised shows of good can do. Remember, that a bird of the air, if no other instrument, to an honest king shall stand in [the] stead of many fained practises, to utter aught may any wise touch him.' She put an end to her 'scribbles' with a wish that James would realise 'what works [methods] becometh best a king, and what in the end will best avail him. Your loving sister, that longs to see you deal as kindly as I mean.'[14]

The Queen followed this up with a more formal response to the matters that James's ambassadors had been sent to deal with. She curtly dismissed his renewed appeal for the Lennox lands, telling him: 'Yourself cannot be ignorant that some consequences which depend thereupon have made us forbear to dispose of it one way or the other.' Elizabeth also refused to release Sir William Eure, citing his untrustworthiness in concealing the truth of his meeting with the Scottish king. Neither would she show clemency to Edmund Ashfield, but instead upbraided James for welcoming such disreputable characters into his realm. 'We think it strange that you do not better discern the merit of persons who seek access to you, than to esteem yourself in that respect interested in their good or evil usage, who, out of their own humour and busy natures, going beyond the duty of subjects, seek to shelter themselves against the danger of their own crimes by making you a cause, and so a party to their disgraces.'[15]

On 23 April 1601, the Queen appeared to send the King of Scots an even more ominous message by honouring two of his rivals for the throne. William Stanley, sixth Earl of Derby, was appointed to the Order of the Garter, filling the stall left vacant by Essex's execution, and Edward Seymour, Earl of Hertford, was promoted to the lord lieutenancies of Somerset and

Wiltshire. The French ambassador, Thuméry de Boissise, was quick to spot the significance. He told Henry IV: 'The said Derby and the children of the said Hertford are nearest in England to succeed to the crown.'[16] The previous year it had been reported that Cecil was secretly supporting the claim of Anne, daughter of the late fifth Earl of Derby. The fact that he had family ties with the Stanleys (his niece was married to the sixth earl) seemed to give this credence. Clearly, where James was concerned, this was no time for complacency.

CHAPTER 11

'SUPPRESSING ALL OTHER COMPETITORS'

Mar and Kinloss might have failed to win Elizabeth's good opinion, but they made the most of their time in London by following James's instructions to 'get me a party' there. There was an obvious choice: Robert Cecil, whose influence with the Queen was by now unrivalled. The Venetian envoy Giovanni Carlo Scaramelli observed: 'Through his hands pass all the affairs of the government.' James himself referred to Cecil as 'Master Secretary, who is king there in effect'.[1] After his ambassadors had paved the way, James wrote to Cecil, smoothing over the fact that until very recently he had been cultivating his disgraced arch-rival. He protested that though he 'loved him [Essex] for his virtues, he was no ways obliged to embrace his quarrels'. He called the secretary a 'fixed star', not a 'wavering planet', and claimed to place his entire trust in him to secure the succession.[2] James was pushing on an open door. Cecil was by far the shrewdest member of Elizabeth's council and seems to have already decided that the King of Scots had the greatest chance of inheriting her throne. It was almost certainly thanks to him that James's name had been kept out of Essex's trial.

Thus began a new correspondence that would endure for the rest of Elizabeth's reign, with Cecil helping to smooth James's path to the throne in return for the promise of favour when he was King of England. It was all conducted with the utmost secrecy. The King's letters were often closed by the seals of other Scottish courtiers with whom Cecil might legitimately have corresponded, while Cecil's were marked as being from the 'Duc de Bohan'. They used code numbers for each other and various other key members of their courts. James and Cecil also took the precaution of using intermediaries, notably Kinloss and Henry Howard.

The latter had formerly been one of Essex's closest followers but was now a member of Cecil's party. Thanks to Cecil, Howard had returned to court after years in the political wilderness following the execution of his traitorous brother Thomas, Duke of Norfolk. Henry Howard himself was once rumoured to have plotted to marry the Queen of Scots and had been imprisoned several times on suspicion of involvement in Catholic plots. In acting as Cecil's intermediary, he grasped the opportunity to begin cultivating James himself, sending long letters of advice, which the Scottish king termed 'Asiatic and endless volumes'. But James evidently held the earl in some esteem because he sent him a jewel with three precious stones, including a ruby.

At first, Cecil was neurotically concerned to keep his correspondence with the King of Scots a secret. When Henry Howard feared that a packet of letters had gone missing, he kept the news from Cecil because 'All the course of convoy and intelligence [would have been] ruined for ever . . . upon the multiplicity of doubts his mind would never have been at rest, nor he would have eaten or slept quietly; for nothing makes him confident, but experience of secret trust, and security of intelligence'. Cecil gradually relaxed his stance though. In one letter, he told James: 'If it should happen that the veil of secrecy were taken off by error or by destiny, the Queen herself (who were likeliest to resort to jealousy) should (notwithstanding) still discern clearly, that whatsoever has passed in this correspondence hath wholly tended to her own repose and safety.'[3]

The fact that the Scottish king needed such powerful Englishmen as Cecil and, earlier, Essex to champion his cause is compelling proof that his path to the throne was by no means assured. He had support in England, but clearly not enough of it to guarantee the crown. Rival claimants were not James's only concern. Some English Catholics believed that the Pope, as feudal overlord of England, had the right to choose Elizabeth's successor. Even as late as 1602, another report claimed that the crown would go to no one and that the Queen's subjects would decide 'to govern the kingdom by States, as they do in the Low Countries'.[4]

With his extensive network of spies and informants, Cecil was aware of such reports and did his utmost to steer the Scottish king through the troubled waters that they created. He recommended a 'softly, softly' approach to the succession and cautioned James against being 'too busy, to prepare the vulgar beforehand'. He also advised him to use 'clear and temperate courses' and to 'secure the heart of the highest [Elizabeth], to whose sex and quality nothing is so improper as either needless expostulations or over much curiosity in her own actions, the first showing unquietness in yourself, the second challenging some untimely interest in hers; both which are best foreborn'. In a more self-interested piece of advice, Cecil urged James to consult with a few choice individuals rather than seek 'any general acclamation of many'. The King of Scots sent a rather indignant reply that he was not 'so evil acquainted with the histories of all ages and nations' as to take such rash action, and assured Cecil that he would never give the Queen 'any just cause of jealousy, through my too busy behaviour'.[5]

For all his bluster, James would be deeply indebted to Cecil, whose sage advice dramatically improved the Scottish king's

relations with his English royal cousin. Setting aside his impatience, he penned letters filled with deferential affection and
avoided any further quarrels with the Queen. They hit their
mark. 'I trust that you will not doubt, but that your last letters
are so acceptably taken as my thanks cannot be lacking for the
same, but yield them you in grateful sort,' she told him. She
also increased James's pension and ensured the payments
were made promptly. And, crucially, while she persistently
refused to name him her heir – or, as she put it, to 'do any
public act that may enable your Majesty to future hopes' – she
continued to clear the path to his accession from any obstacles. The contemporary historian John Clapham concurred:
'Though in her lifetime she forbore to declare a successor . . .
yet by protecting him and suppressing all other competitors,
she manifested her inclination to uphold the right where God
himself had placed it.' At the same time, those who knew the
Queen best averred that, though she might never express it
publicly, her private preference was for the King of Scots. 'I
think her majesty in the secret of her heart wish it you before
any creature,' the Earl of Northumberland assured James.[6]

The influence that Cecil was able to exert over the two
monarchs, and thus the succession, cannot be overstated.
Neither can his dominance of the council, particularly now
that his chief rival Essex was out of the way for good. The
1590s had witnessed the steady rise of this council, with Cecil
taking his late father's place at its helm. As early as 1595, one
of Cecil's informants reported Scottish gossip that Elizabeth
'would never set Lady Arbella up [because of] her Majesty's
love of the now lords of her council', whom she feared would
be displaced if Arbella came to the throne.[7]

While her ministers busied themselves with the succession,
Elizabeth tightened the already strict laws forbidding any
debate about it. In 1601, a bill was drafted in Parliament

against the writing or publishing of books on the matter, which were said to breed faction and inspire treacherous acts against the Queen. But this did little to deter her subjects from discussing the most hotly contested issue of the day. A Lincolnshire minister named Henry Hooke, one of the foremost polemicists, admitted that the succession was now 'chatting and chapping matter for taverns and alehouses', rather than just being limited to whispered conversations between those closest to Elizabeth. Another observer concurred that the question of who would succeed the ageing queen was 'the common subject of all people's conversation'.[8]

In 1601, Shakespeare, whose cycle of plays about the Wars of the Roses had already warned of the dangers of a contested crown, wrote *The Phoenix and the Turtle*. This poem also reflected the growing anxiety about the succession. England's future seemed to depend on the miracle of the phoenix (Elizabeth), a bird that lives for many years, grows old, flies into a fire and is rejuvenated from its own ashes:

> Death is now the phoenix' nest,
> And the turtle's loyal breast
> To eternity doth rest,
>
> Leaving no posterity;
> 'Twas not their infirmity,
> It was married chastity.

The turtle dove was the symbol of faith and loyalty, and in Shakespeare's analogy its devotion to the phoenix created the heat of the flame that first consumed and then revived her. But the poem was written as a lament, rather than presaging a hopeful future, and Shakespeare concluded that the only loyalty that the phoenix could be sure of was his own.

In the same year, Henry Hooke wrote *Of succession to the Crown of England* – or, as he phrased it in the prologue, 'Touching the crown of England, who should take it up, when Elizabeth (long may she wear it) shall lay it down'. As well as extolling the peerless virtue of the 67-year-old queen, Hooke claimed that she had always shown such a clear preference for Mary, Queen of Scots and then her son James that the matter was already settled. Ignoring centuries of war, invasion and hostility, he asserted: 'It was the desire of many of our ancient kings to unite their two kingdoms of England and Scotland into one.' Warming to his theme, he continued:

When Elizabeth hath changed mortality for immortality . . . so at her departure, she will bequeath unto her people a legacy above all estimation, as namely herself dying revived in one of her own blood, her age renewed in his younger years; her aged infirmities repaired in the perfection of his strength, her virtues both of Christianity, and princely quality, doubled upon him, who shall arise and stand up, a man, instead of a woman, retaining in his life, the memory of her never dying honour.

The 'peaceable succession' of James would, Hooke argued, bring forth innumerable 'good effects'. He conjured up an image of a halcyon time when 'Queen Elizabeth is with God, and King James with us', comparing the former to 'the days of David' and the latter to 'the time of Solomon'. Peace, justice and 'pure religion' would reign supreme. Hooke concluded: 'Our expectation rests on him, who is the hope and comfort of our nation.'[9]

Even Sir John Harington risked his long-standing favour with his godmother by writing a lengthy essay in favour of the Stuart succession, though *A Tract on the Succession to the*

Crown was not published until two centuries after her death. Whether Harington sent a clandestine copy to James is unknown, but the tract contained a fulsome appraisal of the Scottish king's virtues, which was clearly intended to curry favour. Central to Harington's argument was Elizabeth's conference with the Scottish ambassador in 1561, during which he claimed she had made a clear promise of the throne to the Queen of Scots and her descendants. He twisted what in fact had been a non-committal remark ('When I am dead, they shall succeed that have most right') into the unequivocal promise: 'They were great fools that did not know that the line of Scotland must needs be next heirs.' Harington expressed a desire 'to put her Majesty so prettily in mind of her word, *Semper Eadem*, to signify to her how dishonourable it would be for her to change her mind.'[10]

In November 1601, Parliament assembled in London. It would be the last of Elizabeth's long reign. Of the thirteen held since 1558, the succession had dominated eight. Now, with the Queen in her sixty-ninth year, it was widely expected that the primary business would be to settle the matter once and for all. In anticipation of this, James dispatched yet another envoy to report on proceedings and promote his interests. Ludovic Stewart, Duke of Lennox, was the King's second cousin and a great favourite, but while Elizabeth showed him every courtesy, his presence at such a time was by no means welcome. She told James that Lennox had been at pains to persuade her to 'banish from mind any evil opinion or doubt of your sincerity to me'. The duke was heard to remark in private: 'His master doubted nothing more than that he should obtain what he desired so greatly and without resistance, so that he should neither have fit occasion to advance his friends and followers, nor to pull down our English pride and insolence.'[11]

When the Queen arrived for the opening of Parliament, the atmosphere was strained. Setting aside the question of her succession, she delivered the last, and perhaps the greatest, of all her speeches. 'To be a king and wear a crown is a thing more glorious to them that see it than it is pleasant to them that bear it,' she reflected. 'For myself, I was never so much enticed with the potent name of a king, or royal authority of a queen, as delighted that God hath made me his instrument to maintain his truth and glory and this kingdom from dishonour, damage, tyranny and oppression . . . And though you have had, and may have, many mightier and wiser princes sitting in this seat, yet you never had nor shall have any that will love you better.'[12] With these words, she neatly encapsulated the challenges of monarchy as she saw them. The air of resentment dissolved and many of those present were moved to tears.

It was less easy for the Queen to placate her ordinary subjects. The last fifteen years of her reign, following the defeat of the Armada in 1588, have often been viewed as a 'Golden Age', presided over by 'Good Queen Bess'. In fact, for much of this period the people of England were weighed down by the heavy burden of taxation, prompted by the protracted hostilities first with Spain, then with Ireland. The population rose sharply, from 2.8 million at the beginning of her reign to 4 million at the end. With greater demand for goods, prices rose, but wages fell because of the surplus workforce. During the 1590s, this was exacerbated by a succession of poor harvests, which led to a reduction in supply and, therefore, even higher prices. At the same time, many landlords enclosed their fields and farmed sheep instead of crops, which forced unemployment to even higher levels. Recurrent bouts of plague added to the already miserable plight of many of Elizabeth's subjects.

Not surprisingly, the later years of Elizabeth's reign witnessed a rise in social unrest, with crime and vagrancy becoming commonplace. For centuries, the monasteries had been the main source of charity at a local level, but after their destruction during the reign of Elizabeth's father there had been nothing to fill the void. In an attempt to address this, the 1601 Parliament passed the Poor Relief Act, which obliged each parish to collect taxes to support people who could not work. This led to some improvement for those at the bottom of the social ladder, but discontent rumbled on.

In a present afflicted by hardship, it was natural that many of Elizabeth's people should increasingly look to the future. In February 1602, a contemporary reported: 'Men speak freely of the King of Scots' title to the throne when it shall please God to take away her Majesty, nor is any man's ambition discovered stirring to work for power to oppose his right.' The same source also observed some apprehension 'among the better sort' that James would appoint Scotsmen to his council in England, but concluded: 'The King being half English is like to think the honour of being reputed a King of England greater than to be a King of Scots.'[13]

Confident that the Queen of England could not endure for much longer, James smoothed over the grudges and gripes that had beset their relationship during the previous few years and assumed the role of humble pupil to a superior master. Now at last, after a correspondence of some thirty years, he appeared ready to heed her advice. 'I protest to God, [you] shall ever be my only oracle,' he assured her in July 1602. He went on to praise Elizabeth as 'so wise a prince' and, on another occasion, 'right high and mighty princess'. He also promised to write privately to her in future, 'without the knowledge of any of my council; no, not my own secretary'.[14]

But while writing such deferential letters, James was busy strengthening his hand. One of his agents carried secret instructions to Henry Howard in anticipation of the Queen's death: 'If it shall please God to call her presently to his mercy, we think it shall be dangerous to leave the chair long empty, for the head being so far distant from the body may yield cause of distemper to the whole government.' The King urged that as soon as Elizabeth breathed her last, Howard should seek Cecil's advice 'in everything that may concern his [James's] entry and resort to that crown'.[15]

A witness reported that the Scottish king also tried to whip up more general support in England: '[He] labours by many agents to entertain affections here . . . It is said that he has in every part of the realm certain principal persons appointed immediately upon notice of the death of her Majesty to proclaim him, and to make what party they can for him.' Even now the matter was far from settled, as the same source admitted: 'Others are said to have an intention to marry the Earl of Hertford's younger son with the Lady Arbella and to carry it that way.'[16] This must refer to Hertford's elder son, Edward, because his younger son, Thomas, had died childless in 1600.

Not taking any chances with his would-be English subjects, James sought alliances with foreign powers in anticipation of inheriting the English throne. In the autumn of 1602, he staged negotiations with a French ambassador for a league between France, England and Scotland against Spain. The closer he crept to the English throne, the greater James's standing in Europe became. At the same time that he was treating with the French, Philip III of Spain proposed a marriage between his firstborn child Anna and James's eldest son and heir, Henry. Although the Scottish king dismissed the idea as a 'siren song', it must have been gratifying to be courted by the greatest potentates in Europe. He made sure to tell Elizabeth about all these approaches, pretending to submit himself to her guidance, while his real purpose was to prove his eminence on the international stage – and, thereby, his worthiness as her successor. She rewarded his deference with florid words, assuring her 'dear brother': '[I] think myself happy when either my warnings or counsels may in fittest time avail you.'[17]

There was one overseas correspondent whom the King of Scots omitted to mention, though – for good reason. A letter dated 31 July 1601, written in Latin and addressed to an influential Italian cardinal, was signed by James's wife Anne, who had close links with Rome. It claims to have been written with her husband's authority as a reply to letters he received from Pope Clement VIII. As part of a charm offensive towards the prospective King of England, Clement had suggested that Prince Henry be sent to Rome for his education. The gist of Anne's letter to the cardinal was that her husband was prepared to use her Catholic leanings for his own political ends – namely, to secure the throne of England.[18] The Pope wielded enormous influence in Europe, and the two 'superpowers', France and Spain, still owed allegiance to him. If Clement persuaded either to weigh in on the King of Scots' behalf, it would make him practically unbeatable. If this letter had been discovered at the time, it would have been explosive. At a stroke, the King of Scots would have lost the support of England's Protestants, his influential advocates on Elizabeth's council and even perhaps the Queen herself. It is a testament to James's desperation that he was willing to take such a risk.

At the same time as courting overseas allies, no matter their religious persuasion, James steadily built up his supporter base in England. 'All our greatest men nowadays make great show of affection to the Scottish King,' reported a contemporary, who added: 'The most part is thought rather of fear than love.

London undoubtedly is much addicted that way and a great part of the northern counties.'[19] One of the 'greatest men' was Henry Percy, Earl of Northumberland. In April 1602 he had written to pledge his allegiance to the Scottish king, whom he averred the Queen favoured 'in the secret of her heart'. An avowed Catholic, the earl had once declared that he would prefer to see James buried than crowned King of England, but he now offered his support on condition that the Scottish king would tolerate 'a mass in a corner'. This placed James in an awkward position because as well as Northumberland's Catholicism, the earl was no friend of Cecil or Howard. But he was too powerful a magnate to be rebuffed, so James wrote a cautious letter of thanks, urging Northumberland: 'Whenever it shall please God to call her [Elizabeth] to his mercy, you may be a chief instrument to assist my settling in that seat which I honour as the apparent heir, in all quietness, without the alteration or prejudice of any that will not wilfully resist to my right.' But he also cautioned the earl: 'Beware to offend the Queen with shadows and send no more messengers except [on] some great and urgent occasion.'[20]

One by one, the most influential of Elizabeth's courtiers threw in their lot with the man who looked most likely to succeed. By the summer of 1602, the King of Scots had recruited another supporter from within the Queen's inner sanctum. The identity of this person has never been established beyond doubt, but it is likely to have been Charles Howard, Earl of Nottingham, one of Elizabeth's closest advisers and kinsmen. The fact that James referred to him as his 'well-beloved cousin' gives weight to this theory. On 3 June, the Scottish king wrote to thank Cecil and his mystery colleague, who 'by your vigilant and judicious care so easily settled me in the only right course for my good, so happily preserved the Queen's mind from the poison of jealous prejudice'. James knew the risk that such courtiers were taking on his behalf, given Elizabeth's intense dislike of the succession being discussed: 'So dangerous is your state as subjects that, although your intention to your sovereign be never so upright, yet if the lion think your ears to be horns there will be no place admitted you for excuse.'[21]

It was not just Elizabeth's male courtiers whom James sought to cultivate. His correspondence reveals that he also made friendly overtures to Philadelphia Scrope, the sister of Robert Carey and one of the Queen's closest attendants, as well as to Charles Howard's daughter Frances, whose husband Henry Brooke, Lord Cobham, opposed James's claim and would later plot against him.

James kept an anxious eye, too, on the actions of Arbella Stuart, whom he referred to as 'the creature living nearest of kin to me, next my own children'. Protesting that 'nature enforces me to love her', he expressed concern at the rumours that she had converted to Catholicism and wished 'for her own weal that such order were taken as she might be preserved from evil company and that evil-inclined persons might not have access unto her to supplant [trick] her, abusing of the frailty of her youth and sex'. Although he claimed to be afraid for the damage that a Catholic conversion would inflict on Arbella's reputation in England, his real fear was that she would thereby attract the support of England's Catholics, as well as the might of Spain. There was little substance to these rumours, but such was the Scottish king's anxiety about a Catholic claimant stealing the crown at the last gasp that he instantly believed them. He was thrown into another panic in December 1602 upon hearing rumours of a planned treaty between England and Spain. The same rumours cited Arbella as 'successor to the throne' and 'heir to this kingdom'.[22]

The eyes of Europe were now sharply focused on the contenders for the English crown. In late 1602, Philip III of Spain decided not to back the claim of his sister Isabella. Partly this was because her marriage to the Archduke of Austria had produced no children and even Philip could see that the last thing the people of England would want was another childless queen. Furthermore, neither Isabella nor her husband showed any interest in pursuing her claim and instead urged Philip 'to lose no time in cultivating James and making peace with England'. Although Philip ordered his forces to be made ready the following spring, this was more for show because he knew full well that he lacked the resources to launch an invasion alone. But this did not mean that the Spanish king threw in his lot with James. Far from it: he was reported to have remarked that the King of Scots was 'personally to be distrusted' and had 'exhibited in all his actions a false and shifty inclination'.[23]

By the autumn and winter of 1602, the paranoid secrecy that had dominated the courts of England and Scotland for the previous few years had been abandoned and the succession was now openly discussed. 'Men talk freely of your Majesty's right,' the Earl of Northumberland told James. Even Cecil set aside his natural caution and admitted to the French ambassador that he supported the King of Scots as the heir to Elizabeth's throne. His remark was so unguarded that it was reported by other ambassadors.[24]

In February 1603, a young Scottish gentleman named Indernyty travelled through England and reported to James: 'Wherever I passed and lodged they think your Majesty their young lord, which within few years no man dared speak.' The King of Scots told Cecil that he looked forward to the day when he could travel south like 'St George . . . upon a towardly riding horse' rather than the 'wild unruly colt' that he was grappling with in Scotland.[25]

As the steady stream of English nobles and courtiers making their way north to the King in waiting turned into a torrent, Elizabeth seemed all but forgotten. 'The court was very much neglected, and in effect the people were generally weary of an old woman's government,' one contemporary recalled. Elizabeth was painfully aware of this and tormented by 'the question of the succession [which] every day rudely sounded in their ears'.[26]

The English queen was not the only woman who found herself overshadowed by the King of Scots. Arbella Stuart was unable to challenge the ascendancy of her rival claimant because she was labouring under ever more severe restrictions imposed by her grandmother. The Venetian ambassador to France had heard that she was 'never allowed to be alone or in any way mistress of her actions', while another envoy expressed his sympathy for 'the unhappy lady [who] has lived so many years buried'. Even James seemed moved to pity and later reflected on 'that unpleasant life which she hath led in the house of her grandmother with whose severity and age she, being a young lady, could hardly agree'. Even though Arbella was now in her late twenties, she was still treated like a child and complained of 'being bobbed and her nose played withal' if she disobeyed her grandmother. John Starkey, the chaplain at Hardwick, noted that the young woman's misery 'seemed not feigned, for often-times, being at her books, she would break forth into tears'.[27]

Eventually, it became too much to bear. In late 1602 Arbella hatched a plan to escape. Keenly aware of her value as a prospective bride, she resolved to marry her way out of captivity. Instead, she landed herself in even greater trouble because the man she had set her hopes upon was Edward Seymour, the grandson of his namesake, Lord Hertford, whose clandestine marriage to Lady Katherine Grey forty years earlier had been the source of such controversy. It is not certain that Arbella saw the marriage as a means of bolstering her claim to the throne. None of her letters suggests that she wanted anything other than to escape her miserable existence at Hardwick. But her choice of a man eleven years her junior and with no other connection to her than their shared royal blood surely only makes sense as a bid for the succession.

With the help of a servant named John Dodderidge, Arbella sent a message to Lord Hertford in London, telling him of her plan to marry his sixteen-year-old grandson. His horrified response was not at all what she had expected. Knowing that even to have received her message was damning enough, he chastised Dodderidge with 'many bitter reprehensions' for coming to him and immediately informed Sir Robert Cecil. The hapless messenger was duly placed under armed guard and questioned before being sent to the court for further interrogation by Cecil. In the meantime, he was somehow able to warn Arbella: 'My reception here is contrary to all expectation.'[28] This message was intercepted before it reached her.

News of the scandal rapidly spread from the court to the continent. Marin Cavalli, the Venetian ambassador in France, reported 'the uproar, which has happened in England recently, about Arabella'. In the Queen's mind, there was no doubt that Arbella's foolhardy scheme had been an attempt to bolster her claim to the throne. In vain, the young woman 'went down on her knees and implored pardon; declaring that she had taken this step to induce the Queen to change her prison, for she knew that any other must be much milder than the one she was in'.[29]

Elizabeth dispatched Sir Henry Brouncker to interrogate Arbella at Hardwick. He had undertaken a diplomatic mission to Scotland the previous year and had been judged 'true and wise' by the King, so perhaps Elizabeth wished to reassure James that the matter was in safe hands. She instructed him to talk to the young woman alone, without the overbearing presence of her grandmother. In truth, the countess was, as she assured Elizabeth, 'altogether ignorant of her [Arbella's] vain doings'. She was so 'wonderfully afflicted' when she heard of the scheme and 'took it so ill' that Brouncker was hard-pressed to stop her beating her granddaughter.[30] The elderly countess might have long cherished ambitions for Arbella to inherit the throne, but not like this.

At first, Arbella was defiant. Brouncker complained of her 'obstinate and wilful' answers. Her composure soon crumbled, however, and she began to relate her version of events 'so confusedly with words so far from the purpose as I knew not what to make of it'. Getting nowhere with his questioning, Brouncker instructed Arbella to prepare a written confession instead. This was hardly more coherent, as he admitted to the Queen: 'When I read it, I perceived it to be confused obscure and in truth ridiculous. I told her it was not a letter fit for me to carry, nor for your Highness to read ... She wrote again and little better than before, which made me believe that her wits were somewhat distracted either with fear of her grandmother or conceit of her own folly.'[31]

Brouncker eventually concluded that there was no conspiracy and that the whole sorry episode had been a foolhardy attempt by Arbella to draw attention to her unhappy situation. Upon his departure from Hardwick, he told of how the countess 'fastened a purse full of gold on me in honour of your Majesty'. She also begged that Elizabeth might take 'this unadvised young woman' off her hands and insisted: 'For my own part, I should have little care how meanly soever she were bestowed so as it were not offensive to your Highness.'[32] But the Queen was satisfied that Bess had played no part in it and rightly judged that from now on she would keep her granddaughter under even stricter scrutiny than before. Elizabeth asked that the countess report anything untoward in Arbella's behaviour or actions, which in effect made her a spy as well as a guardian.

Bess was eager to comply. She had her granddaughter's correspondence intercepted and even feigned replies to some of the letters in the hope of garnering more information. Copies of the seized letters and their false answers were sent to Cecil at court. Within weeks, the countess was reporting her suspicions that Arbella 'had some other like matter in hand'. But the strain of keeping this volatile young woman in check quickly began to take its toll. Brouncker noted: 'The old lady grows exceedingly weary of her charge, begins to be weak and sickly by breaking her sleep, and cannot long continue this vexation.'[33]

Arbella's reckless quest for freedom had resulted in her being rendered entirely powerless, both politically and domestically. She was chaste, with no opportunity to be otherwise; her every action was closely monitored, her every word recorded. Now not merely her grandmother's wrath but the threat of the Tower cowed her into obedience.

CHAPTER 12

'WISHING NO MORE QUEENS'

Elizabeth had enjoyed robust health throughout her long life and reign. Even when she was well into her sixties, twice the average life expectancy of the period, she still rode in the hunt, joined in energetic court dances and went on brisk walks in the gardens of her palaces 'as if she had been only eighteen years old'. In January 1599, a Spanish visitor to court had been astonished to see the Queen 'in her old age dancing three or four gaillards', an athletic dance characterised by leaps, jumps and hops. The following year, she defied her council's advice by embarking on yet another long summer progress. 'Her Majesty bids the old stay behind, and the young and able to go along with her,' reported the contemporary letter-writer Rowland Whyte.[1]

But even this formidable woman could not defy time forever. Elizabeth's unwavering confidence in public was increasingly at odds with her private self. She had never quite recovered from the shock of the Earl of Essex's rebellion. 'These troubles waste her much,' reported Sir John Harington. 'Every new message from the city doth disturb her ... the many evil plots and designs have overcome all her Highness' sweet temper. She walks much in her privy chamber, and stamps with her feet at ill news, and thrusts her rusty sword at times into the arras in great rage ... the dangers are over, and yet she always keeps a sword by her table.' When he paid a visit to his royal godmother in 1602, he found her 'shut up in a chamber from her subjects and most of her servants, and seldom seen but on holy days'. The sharp-eyed Scaramelli concurred: 'She has suddenly withdrawn into herself, she who was wont to live so gaily, especially in these last years of her life.'[2]

Throughout her long reign, Elizabeth had revelled in the flattery of her adoring courtiers. Now, Harington reflected sadly that he seemed to be one of the few who felt any sorrow at the sudden decline of 'this state's natural mother': 'I find some less mindful of what they are soon to lose, than of what they may perchance hereafter get.' Seeing through the increasingly transparent veneer of compliments, Elizabeth was said to have called for a looking glass for the first time in twenty years. When she saw her face 'lean and full of wrinkles', she 'fell presently into exclaiming against those which had so much commended her, and took it so offensively, that some which before had flattered her, dared not come into her sight'. Thereafter, she was 'extreme oppressed' with a deep melancholy. Even her favourite kinsman, Sir Robert Carey, could not rouse her from her depression: 'I used the best words I could to persuade her from this melancholy humour; but I found by her it was too deep rooted in her heart, and hardly to be removed.' The Queen confided to the French ambassador that she was 'weary of life'.[3]

But to the end, Elizabeth was never predictable. Determined to prove that, as she put it, she was 'not yet buried', throughout the spring and summer of 1602 she threw herself into a punishing schedule that would have left a much younger, fitter monarch gasping for breath. Beginning with the May Day festivities at Richmond, she embarked upon one of her most lavish summer progresses to date, visiting the homes of more than twenty courtiers within a thirty-mile radius of London. The last stop on her tour was the palace of Oatlands in Surrey, where she staged spectacular entertainments for the new French envoy. 'Blessed be God,' an astonished Cecil reported. 'I saw not Her Majesty so well these dozen years!' Another eyewitness concurred: 'At Court it is noted that the Queen's health and disposition of body is excellent, she not being in every way better disposed these many years.'[4]

It would prove a last, dazzling blaze of glory for a woman whose court and queenship had been the envy of Europe for the past four decades. In November, a contemporary diarist noted that the Queen had travelled from Richmond to Whitehall, 'but whereas she ought to have come in great pomp, she was taken with some sudden distemper by the way and so went in her close barge, whereby the Lord Mayor and citizens that rode out to meet her lost their labour'.[5] The following month, she attended the Christmas celebrations as normal. It was noted that among the many gifts she bestowed, she gave the King of Scots £2,000 and proceeded to increase his annual pension by the same amount. It was a welcome gift for an impoverished king, but her promise of the crown would have been more welcome still.

Those closest to Elizabeth during the festivities saw the sad truth behind the glittering veneer. Harington confided to his wife that the Queen had eaten little from the array of festive delicacies laid out before her and that when she had tried to drink, 'her heart seems too full to lack more filling'. He concluded mournfully that his godmother was 'in most pitiable state'. Not long afterwards, Elizabeth noticed her godson scribbling some verses. Hoping 'to feed her humour', he read them to her. After listening carefully, she reflected sadly: 'When thou dost feel creeping time at thy gate, these fooleries will please thee less; I am past my relish for such matters.'[6]

As news of the Queen's imminent demise seeped out of the court, speculation about the succession reached fever pitch.

The Scottish jurist and poet Sir Thomas Craig rushed off a pamphlet entitled *The Right of Succession to the Kingdom of England*, which in contrast to most other succession tracts addressed the larger question of whether the Queen had the constitutional right to choose her own successor. 'There arises a new debate whether she on her Death-Bed, or even when she was in Health, could determine her Successor,' he reported. His answer to this question was a definitive 'no'. The crown could only pass by hereditary right, he argued, and on this basis it belonged to his king, James VI. He pointed to the chaos that could follow if this right was disrupted, as had happened when Elizabeth's half-brother Edward had diverted the succession from his closest blood relatives to Lady Jane Grey. As Craig noted, it had been to no avail, for after Edward's death 'the great men of the kingdom observed what Nature taught and not what the King commanded'. Neither had Henry VIII been able to permanently deprive his daughters of their rights and 'break the laws of nature or the common law of succession, for succession in hereditary kingdoms is so truly the right of the successor, that it is inseparable, and cannot by any means be severed from him'.[7]

What was more, a hereditary succession was synonymous with God's will. Sir John Harington had argued that by following the natural blood line, the realm would be certain 'not to oppose man's presumption against God's providence'.[8] In one of his secret letters to the Scottish king, Cecil told James that Elizabeth, too, respected the hereditary right and denied that she was inclined to 'cut off the natural branch, and graft upon some wild stock'. This was all very well, but what if James pre-deceased Elizabeth? Would his eight-year-old son and heir Henry naturally take his place as first in line for her throne? This was apparently not something that James had considered – perhaps understandably so, since he was more than thirty years Elizabeth's junior and in relatively good health. But one of his English correspondents forced him to confront the possibility. At around the same time as Craig's tract appeared, the Earl of Northumberland wrote to warn James not to take the throne prematurely by force because if he died in the attempt, he could not assume that the people of England would accept his young son in his place.[9]

On 5 January 1603, Elizabeth wrote to the man who by now was the favourite to succeed her. After all the storms and tumults that had beset their relationship during the previous three decades, this letter had a sense of calm and self-reflection. Among other things, Elizabeth provided a detailed justification of her foreign policy, in particular her defence of the independent Dutch provinces, which had thrown off the mantle of Spanish authority. It was a pointed remark: she knew James had recently responded enthusiastically to Spanish overtures for an alliance. Reproaching him, she complained bitterly that she had always known 'you had no particular love to me'. But as ever, the diplomatic won out over the personal and she went on to give her opinion about the overtures that James had received from France. Even now, with her life ebbing away rapidly, there was no mention of the succession. She concluded: 'Thus you see, how to fulfil your trust reposed in me, (which to infringe I never mind) I have sincerely made patent my sincerity. And though not fraught with much wisdom, yet stuffed with great goodwill. I hope you will bear with my molesting you too long, with my scratching hand, as proceeding from a heart, that shall be ever filled, with the sure affection of your loving and friendly sister Elizabeth R.'[10]

It would be the Queen's last letter to James. Shortly after writing it, she left the court in Whitehall and moved to Richmond Palace, her 'warm box', to which she could 'best trust her sickly old age'. She was recovering from a cold when her condition suddenly worsened. This time, it was more serious. 'She refused to eat anything, to receive any physic, or admit any rest in bed,' reported one of her attendants. John Clapham claimed that 'she sat up six days together without any sleep' and observed 'she desired rather to die than to live'.[11] When the ailing queen asked that the ring she had worn since her coronation should be filed off her finger because it had grown into the flesh, it was taken as a sign of her imminent death.

Elizabeth's attendants began to despair as day after day she turned away food and drink, 'holding her finger almost continually in her mouth, with her eyes open and fixed upon the ground, where she sat on cushions without rising or resting herself, and was greatly emaciated by her long watching and fasting'. It seemed that she had simply decided to die. 'The Queen grew worse, because she would be so, none about her being able to persuade her to go to bed,' recalled an exasperated Robert Carey. John Manningham, another visitor to the palace, observed: 'It seems she might have lived if she would have used means; but she would not be persuaded, and princes must not be forced.' When in late February Elizabeth received news of the death of her long-standing attendant and kinswoman, Catherine, Countess of Nottingham, it accelerated her decline. 'The Queen loved the Countess well, and hath much lamented her death, remaining ever since in deep melancholy that she must die herself,' observed one courtier. Scaramelli agreed: 'The Queen for many days has not left her chamber . . . they say that the reason for this is her sorrow for the death of the Countess.'[12]

As Elizabeth lapsed ever further into decline, she was tormented by more ill tidings. One hundred and fifty miles north of Richmond, Arbella Stuart was continuing to cause trouble. In January, she had written Elizabeth a letter, likely drafted under her grandmother's instruction, pleading: 'I humbly prostrate myself at your Majesty's feet, craving pardon for what is passed.' She referred to herself as 'Your Majesty's most humble and dutiful handmaid'. But just a few days later she rushed off another missive, declaring that she was betrothed in secret to 'someone near and in favour with Her Majesty', but refused to reveal his identity.[13] Elizabeth was taking no chances and sent Brouncker back to Hardwick to interrogate the young woman.

Arbella eventually confessed that her secret lover was the already married King of Scots, whom she had never met. It had all been a desperate attempt to force the court's attention to her plight. Her subsequent letter was both anguished and defiant: 'It was convenient her Majesty should see and believe what busy bodies, untrue rumours, unjust practices, colourable and cunning devices are in remote parts among those whom the world understands to be exiled from her Majesty's presence, undeservedly.'[14]

Soon, Arbella was either too ill to eat or deliberately began to starve herself. She hinted at her intention to commit suicide. Alarmed, her grandmother capitulated and allowed Arbella to move (temporarily) to Owlcotes, another of her homes, two miles from Hardwick. When Brouncker arrived to question Arbella again soon afterwards, he found her still insistent that the King of Scots was her lover. She wrote letter after letter, each repeating this fiction, prompting Brouncker to conclude that she was suffering from the 'distempering of her brains . . . by the multitude of her idle discourses'. As well as being a desperate attempt to sustain the attention that her plight had generated at court and to escape the 'tedious conversation I am bound to', as she put it, the letters seem to have been a form of therapy. In her longest missive, which ran to twelve pages, Arbella wrote of 'disburdening' her 'weak body and travelling mind', and vowed to continue her 'idle conceits . . . until it make you ashamed to see into what a scribbling melancholy (which is a kind of madness and there are several kinds of it) you have brought me and leave me, if you leave me til I be my own woman and then your trouble and mine too will cease'. Unmoved, an exasperated Brouncker told Arbella's servant George Chaworth that she was of 'a hundred minds'.[15]

Arbella continued to veer between desperation, 'melancholy' and downright fury. In one of her more lucid dispatches, she demanded: 'Have I stained her Majesty's blood with unworthy or doubtful marriage? Have I claimed my land these twenty years though I had her Majesty's promise I should have it and has my Lord of Hertford regarded her Majesty's express commandment and been threatened and felt indignation so much? Have I forborne so long to send to the King of Scots to expostulate his unkindness and declare my mind to him in many matters and have no more thanks for my labour?'[16] She went on to compare herself to the Earl of Essex, who had supported her claim to the throne and possibly corresponded with her for a while. To remind the dying queen of her connection to the executed favourite and to openly lament his demise was a dangerous strategy. Clearly, Arbella had thrown any vestige of caution to the wind.

Tormented by her confinement and goaded by her grandmother's constant reproofs, Arbella's mental state was hardly strong enough to withstand the shocking event that took place in February, when her old chaplain and tutor John Starkey was discovered with his throat cut. It was rumoured that he had killed himself because he was plagued with guilt about the part that he had played in his protégé's intrigues. Consumed by fear and grief, Arbella fired off a furious letter to Brouncker:

'If you think to make me weary of my life and so conclude it according to Mr Starkey's tragical example, you are deceived.'[17]

The more Arbella ranted, the less of a threat she appeared to the court back in London – and the less of a viable contender for the throne. Cecil, who was keeping a close eye on this would-be queen, wrote across the back of one of her letters: 'I think that she hath some vapours on her brain.' He surely knew, as did his fellow councillors, that the chances of her ever succeeding to Elizabeth's throne were now remote. 'We are very sorry to find by the strange style of the Lady Arbella's letters that she hath her thoughts no better quieted,' the council wrote to Brouncker on 14 March. A few days later, their agent confirmed that Arbella 'hath neither altered her speech nor behaviour. She is certain in nothing but in her uncertainty . . . All her words and actions are so contrary to reason as no man can divine aright of her'.[18]

Mentally unstable though she was, Arbella was lucid in one thought at least: her urgent desire to escape the overbearing countess. Brouncker noted that she 'desires liberty' and told his masters: 'I persuade her to patience and conformity, but nothing will satisfy her but her remove from her grandmother, so settled is her mislike of the old lady.' Shortly after he wrote this, Arbella made a desperate attempt to flee Bess's clutches. She had managed to send a message via one of her attendants to her uncle Henry Cavendish, a former soldier in the Low Countries. It was arranged that he would meet her at the gates of Hardwick with one or two men in sight, but forty or so others, armed and on horseback, hidden from view. On the day appointed, Arbella made it to the gates as planned, but her grandmother refused to allow them to be opened. Cavendish was permitted to enter but could not lead his men to attack the hall without inflicting injury or worse on family members and servants. He therefore gave up the attempt.

This caused considerable alarm at the court in London, where it was feared that it had been part of a more widespread Catholic conspiracy. 'The Queen has received information that some dangerous practices have been intended for the violent removing of the Lady Arabella out of the charge of her grandmother,' reported the lords of the council.[19] Rumours flew that Elizabeth intended to have Arbella imprisoned at Woodstock Palace, just as she herself had been during her half-sister's reign. Pouring oil on troubled waters, Brouncker soon established that the plot, such as it was, had involved only Arbella's uncle and his retainers. Even so, Arbella was subsequently removed from her grandmother's custody to that of Henry Grey, sixth Earl of Kent, at Wrest Park in Bedfordshire, whose family was connected to the countess's through marriage.

'The rumours of Arabella much afflict the Queen,' reported one courtier. The Venetian envoy to England concurred: 'It is well known that this unexpected event has greatly disturbed the Queen . . . as far as health was concerned, her days seemed numerous indeed but not now she allows grief to overcome her strength.' Soon, the rumours became even more insistent. It was whispered that Arbella had not just escaped but had married one of her suitors in a desperate bid to seize the crown. Brouncker confirmed that the young woman was more 'wilful' than ever and that this 'arises out of a hope of the Queen's death'.[20]

Such reports seemed to hasten Elizabeth's decline. 'She raves of . . . Arabella, and is infinitely discontented; it is feared she will not long continue,' reported one anonymous observer. Scaramelli told a similar tale: 'Her Majesty's mind was over-whelmed by a grief greater than she could bear. It reached such a pitch that she passed three days and three nights with-out sleep and with scarcely any food. Her attention was fixed . . . on the affairs of lady Arabella, who now is, or feigns herself to be, half mad.' He subsequently reported: 'Her conduct is thought to have killed the Queen,' and referred to Arbella as 'Omicida della Regina' ('Murderer of the Queen') in a dispatch to his masters.[21]

Arbella's own words excite greater sympathy. In a long and impassioned letter to Brouncker, written on 9 March 1603, her anguish at having been so long the instrument of others is painfully clear and she expressed a heartfelt plea to 'be my own woman'. She was lucid enough to know that this latest missive, heartfelt though it was, would be perceived as a 'kind of madness' by the sober male advisers at the court in London.[22]

Reports of Arbella's increasingly volatile behaviour may have prompted Scaramelli to write a lengthy dispatch to the Doge and Senate on 27 February 1603, setting out his views on who was likeliest to succeed the Queen, whom he falsely reported was 'in excellent health, as I hear on all sides, and in perfect possession of all her senses'. The envoy admitted that because it was 'absolutely forbidden' to discuss the succession, 'it is very difficult to arrive at any certain conclusions'. His assessment contained a number of flaws (notably the 'seven wives' of Henry VIII) but provided a valuable temperature check from the heart of Elizabeth's court.[23]

If Henry VIII's will had been followed, then Elizabeth would have been succeeded by Edward Seymour, Lord Beauchamp, or, if he was deemed illegitimate, then by William Stanley, sixth Earl of Derby. But Scaramelli dismissed these descendants of Henry's younger sister Mary as being 'neither of them of great account because of a doubt as to legitimacy'. By contrast, he asserted: 'James and Arbella are the real claimants to the crown of England, descendants in equal degree from Margaret, elder sister of Henry the Eighth.' The secretary also mentioned Henry Hastings, great-nephew of the third Earl of

Huntingdon, whom he erroneously described as being a descendant of Henry VII's brother, rather than Edward IV's. He admitted that Hastings enjoyed a great deal of support among the nobility and that 'some think he will be the first to attempt the royal throne, but to no purpose'. He concluded: 'It seems that it [Hastings' claim] has not so good a foundation in right, nor so lively a support among men, as this of James and Arbella.'

Scaramelli proceeded to give a character assessment of the two leading claimants. James, he said, was 'prudent, melancholy, literary, more lavish than his revenue will support . . . He follows the religion of Calvin, but allows everyone in his kingdom to follow their own sect; the Roman religion alone is forbidden. It is held for certain, however, that if he succeeds to the English throne he will permit the rights of the Roman Catholic Church, though he himself would continue a Calvinist, at least for some time.' The Venetian shrewdly added: 'King James aspired to the English crown from his youth, and they say that his ambition helps him to swallow the shedding of his mother's blood, and has caused him to avoid irritating the Queen of England by displaying the greatest regard and subservience towards her.' The two main obstacles in his path were still his Scottish birth and his mother's treachery, which Scaramelli claimed 'incapacitates her son'.

But the Venetian had no doubt that James's determination would overcome these obstacles. 'As he has ever aspired to the crown of England he has bound upwards of thirty thousand of his subjects . . . to arm and follow him at his slightest request, for six weeks; during which period, after the death of Elizabeth, he would cross the rivers Solway and Tweed and the mountains which divide Scotland from England, and march on London, a distance of two hundred miles [it is closer to 350 miles], where he would find his own party ready to do homage to him; while the Scottish fleet, supported by the King of Denmark, father of King James's wife, would be able to counterbalance the part of the English fleet which might reject him.'

Turning to James's rival, Scaramelli reported that Arbella was 'of great beauty, and remarkable qualities, being gifted with many accomplishments'. But she was held back by her 'very exalted ideas, having been brought up in the firm belief that she would succeed to the Crown'. Her arrogance had alienated the Queen and thereby hamstrung her claim. The fact that he believed Arbella to be a 'puritan' probably accounts for his rather disparaging description. But, as he reported, it was Arbella's sex that was the greatest impediment: 'It is . . . a fixed opinion that the Ministers, being convinced that this Kingdom is strong rather in reputation than in actual forces, are resolved among themselves not to be governed by a woman again, but to give the Crown to the King of Scotland.' In a letter to James written around the same time and appraising the mood of the country, the Earl of Northumberland concurred that his countrymen were 'wishing no more queens'.[24]

The same prejudice had been expressed almost twenty years earlier, when the author of Leycester's Commonwealth opined: 'Now her Majesty is past hope of childbirth and consequently seeing God hath given no better success that way in two women one after the other [Elizabeth and her half-sister Mary], it were not convenient (say they) that another of that sex should ensue.' Likewise, Persons had observed that it seemed to 'most men [too] much to have three women reign one after the other'. This was something with which James, who once declared 'women are the frailest sex', entirely concurred.[25] Elizabeth had reigned for longer and more successfully than any of her Tudor forebears, yet the misogyny of her court and kingdom was evidently so deeply ingrained that a male successor was still viewed as the ideal.

Scaramelli's final remark was perhaps the most perceptive. He recognised that for all the jostling for prime position among the potential heirs, the rumours of armed forces, invasion and rebellion, not to mention the unexpressed intentions of the dying queen, it was her chief minister, Robert Cecil, who held if not all the cards, then the ones that were most likely to win him the game: 'It is to be observed that Secretary Cecil, who is omnipotent in all the affairs of State, keeps a brother as governor on the frontiers of Scotland [Thomas Cecil, President of the Council in the North], and is placing people in the confidence of the Scottish King as governors of all the strong places in those parts.'[26]

At around the same time as Scaramelli was penning his lengthy assessment of the dying queen's potential successor, the council received a report that two unnamed noblemen had been overheard talking secretly after dinner about the prospects of Henry Hastings, future fifth Earl of Huntingdon, being sent to France from where he could build up a 'party' and challenge James's claim.[27] If such a scheme really had been discussed, its chances of success were slim. Hastings had no more political influence than his grandfather, whose own claim had been weakened by the impoverished estate he had inherited from the third earl.

It was the dead, as well as the living, who seemed to plague Elizabeth during her final days. She was said to have wailed out in torment at ordering the execution of Mary, Queen of Scots. Robert Carey described how she 'shed many tears and sighs, manifesting her innocence that she never gave consent to the death of that Queen'.[28] Whether her words betrayed genuine remorse or were uttered for the benefit of Mary's son, whom she probably knew was being informed of everything that passed at Richmond, must rest with conjecture. Perhaps it was a last attempt to pave the way for James's accession by casting doubt on the justice of his mother's fate.

'She rests ill at night,' a contemporary diarist noted, adding: 'She is, moreover, suspicious of some about her as ill-affected.'[29] The Queen was right to be suspicious. Close kin to Elizabeth though he was, Carey was typical of the courtiers who attended her as she lay dying. At the same time as professing his sorrow and 'wretched estate', he was anxious to protect his interests with whoever would succeed her. In his mind, there was no doubt that this would be the King of Scots. Carey had the edge over the many other English nobles who had been paying court to James over the preceding months and years, thanks to his appointment as Lord Warden of the Marches and the various diplomatic missions to Scotland that he had undertaken on Elizabeth's behalf. He was therefore better acquainted with James than most and had had ample opportunity to ingratiate himself. 'And hereupon I bethought myself with what grace and favour I was ever received by the King of Scots, whensoever I was sent to him,' Carey reflected. 'I wrote to him (knowing him to be the right heir to the crown of England) and certified him in what state her Majesty was. I desired him not to stir from Edinburgh; if of that sickness she should die, I would be the first man that should bring him news of it.'[30]

During her last illness, when Elizabeth sat motionless on cushions for hours on end, Cecil boldly told her that she must go to bed. Elizabeth roused herself one last time to snap at him: 'Little man, little man, "must" is not a word to use to princes. Your father were he here durst never speak to me so. Ah, but ye know that I must die, and it makes you presumptuous.' She did not know just how presumptuous. As she eked out her last days on earth, Cecil was busy drafting a proclamation announcing James's accession, which was sent up to

Scotland for approval. The recently appointed French ambassador, Christophe de Harlay, Comte de Beaumont, reported:
'It seemed the succession was amongst the lords and council
so assured to them' that they had a proclamation drawn up
and ready to be issued 'soudain après la mort de la Reine'
('suddenly after the death of the Queen'). Upon receiving it,
James declared that it 'sounded so sweetly' in his ears 'that he
can alter no notes in so agreeable a harmony'.[31]

As the dominant force in government, Cecil ensured that
his fellow advisers were working towards the same outcome.
'It is generally concluded that the Council are for the King of
Scots,' observed a witness. But the chief minister was leaving
nothing to chance. Strategic fortresses across England were
put on alert and the prominent English lawyer and Solicitor-
General for Ireland Sir Roger Wilbraham recorded in his
diary that the navy was braced 'in readiness against foreign
attempts'.[32] At the same time, the council banned unlawful
assemblies, suspended plays and set extra guards around pris-
ons and important buildings in London. As an extra precaution, Arbella Stuart was placed under close watch and
members of the nobility were summoned from their country
estates to court. Meanwhile, people living in areas immediately outside the capital began to move their valuables to more
secure places.

On 9 March, one courtier recorded: 'There is continual
posting between London and Scotland' and James 'is diligent
to have all in readiness and has reviewed his forces'. Even
now, with his royal mistress close to death, Cecil was secretive
to the point of paranoia: 'So subtle is Master Secretary that
hardly can it be judged which way he will take.' He was probably as anxious as the man whose path to the throne he was
trying to clear. As the Queen's spymaster, he was the first to
hear any whisperings of plots or uprisings. The same month,

he learned that Sir Edward Baynham, a disaffected Catholic described as 'a wild and free speaking young man', 'had protested that he will lose his life and so will forty thousand Catholics more ere the King of Scots shall come in'.[33] Baynham was promptly arrested and thrown into prison.

On 11 March, the Queen's symptoms suddenly worsened. Scaramelli reported that she had been seized by a 'defluxion [abscess] in the throat', which left her unable to speak and 'like a dead person'. 'Her attendants were alarmed lest the blood should suffocate her or cause her to break a blood vessel,' the Venetian noted. Neither of these calamities occurred, but the scare provides a clue to Elizabeth's illness. The abscess may have been a symptom of quinsy, a bacterial infection resulting from tonsilitis, which can be fatal without antibiotics. 'Her Majesty's life is absolutely despaired of, even if she be not already dead,' Scaramelli concluded. News of her imminent demise rapidly spread across Europe. Sir Francis Vere, commander of the Queen's troops in the Netherlands, heard from his agent at Richmond that 'between the coffer chamber and her bed chamber he saw great weep-ing and lamentation among the lords and ladies, as they passed to and fro, and perceived there was no hope that Her Majesty should escape . . . I never thought to live to see so dismal a day'.[34]

On 20 March, a 'conference' of councillors and nobles was held, straight after which letters were sent to 'sundry earls and barons' inviting them to join a 'Grand Counsel' as soon as the Queen breathed her last. Even though he had received the draft proclamation announcing his accession, James could not be sure that the only thing standing between himself and the English crown was the fragile thread that tethered Elizabeth to life. Letters written in cipher from Sir John

Peyton, lieutenant of the Tower of London, warned him of 'strong opposition' by the 'popish faction' with support from 'foreign ambassadors'.[35]

All this flies in the face of the established narrative about the Stuart succession, that James had steadily won such overwhelming support in England that his path to Elizabeth's throne was clear. In fact, he owed his position less to popular support and more to the machinations of Cecil and his faction, who had worked tirelessly for the previous two years to remove, or at least reduce, the obstacles that stood in his way. Even now, as their royal mistress's life slipped rapidly away, they feared that they had not done enough. 'The greater part of the realm are for the King of Scots, but many would oppose him had they any more potent competitor,' one courtier noted.[36]

At length, the Queen was persuaded by the Earl of Nottingham, widower of her late friend, to retire to bed. Thereafter, her life slipped away rapidly. In contrast to her father, she did not make a will as she lay on her deathbed; nor did she command her ministers to draft an Act of Parliament to decide the succession. Both could have overridden any of the issues with the potential claimants – notably James's alien status – just as Henry VIII's succession acts and will had overridden his daughters' illegitimacy. The author of a pro-Stuart tract was at pains to point this out: 'In the 28th and 35th years of King Henry's reign, upon some doubt, which then he himself seemed to have about the order of succession in his own children, and for taking away all occasion of controversy which after his death might arise thereupon, the Parliament gave authority to the king to debate and determine that matter himself.' The tract went on to question the legality of Henry's will though, and claimed it was 'forged, and the king's [dry] stamp set to by others'.[37] In the absence of either a will or an

Act of Parliament in March 1603, those who attended Elizabeth in her final days watched anxiously for any other sign of her intentions.

'She ended her life the twenty-fourth day of March, the last day of the year according to the English computation,' recorded John Clapham. 'The lineal descent of princes from Henry VII, having continued one hundred and seventeen years in one name and one family, was cut off with the thread of her life.'[38] Elizabeth's death fell on the eve of the Annunciation of the Virgin Mary (or Lady Day), which was fitting for the Queen who had made such a virtue of her unmarried state, especially as she had been born on the eve of the feast of the Virgin Mary. Lady Day was also considered the beginning of spring, which Jacobean propaganda made much of. The late queen's chaplain attested that her end had been peaceful: 'Her Majesty departed this life, mildly, like a lamb, easily like a ripe apple from the tree.'[39]

Robert Cecil had begun drafting a letter to his royal mistress's successor in her final hours, setting down his quill when he heard that her demise was imminent and taking it up again to congratulate the new King. The transition in his carefully crafted words from the present to the past tense was as smooth as from the Tudor to the Stuart dynasty.[40]

Robert Carey is a valuable source for Elizabeth's final hours as he was a witness to the dramatic events that unfolded. His memoirs were probably not compiled until 1627, however, by which time James was dead and his son sat on the English throne, so his version of the succession cannot be wholly relied upon. Carey recorded: 'On Wednesday, the twenty-third of March, she [Elizabeth] grew speechless. That afternoon, by signs, she called for her Council, and by putting her hand to her head, when the King of Scots was named to succeed her, they all knew he was the man she desired should reign after her.'[41]

If Elizabeth had made such a gesture, was it really so obvious what it meant? She had been plagued by headaches and migraines throughout her life, often brought on by stress. Two weeks before her death, it had been reported that 'she cannot abide discourses of government and state'.[42] As she lay battling for breath and her councillors urgently pressed her to name her successor, it was at least equally possible that the gesture was prompted by pain. Moreover, a few hours earlier, the Queen had made a similar movement with her hand and it had been interpreted as a sign of her piety: 'She took great delight in hearing prayers [and] would often at the name of Jesus lift up her hands and eyes to Heaven.' Then, shortly after having apparently made the same signal to indicate James's succession, 'she made signs for John Whitgift, Archbishop of Canterbury, and her chaplains to come to her ... The Archbishop kneeled down by her and examined her first of her faith, and she so punctually answered all his several questions by lifting up her eyes and holding up her hand ... After he had continued long in prayer till the old man's knees were weary, he blessed her and meant to rise and leave her. The Queen made a sign with her hand, which one of her ladies, knowing her meaning, told the Archbishop the Queen desired he would pray still.'[43]

Concluding his description of the Queen's final hours, Carey was at pains to point out: 'This that I heard with my ears, and did see with my eyes, I thought it my duty to set down, and to affirm it for a truth, upon the faith of a Christian, because I know there have been many false lies reported of the end and death of that good lady.'[44] By the time he wrote this, William Camden had published his version of the succession. Perhaps this was one of the false lies to which Carey referred. If so, then his own account had the same conclusion, even if it differed in detail.

During the days, weeks and years that followed, the dying queen's fragile raising of her hand was like a pebble dropped into a pond, sending ripples of increasingly distorted versions across England and Europe. The antiquarian Robert Cotton described how the Queen not only lifted her hand but raised herself in the bed 'and pulling her arms out of bed she held both her hands jointly together over her head in manner of a crown'.[45] By 1607, the gesture had become firmly established as a clear and decisive indication of her successor. Nicolo Molin, Venetian ambassador to England, recalled:

[The King of Scots] came to the throne by legitimate succession and right of blood. He was never named, however, as her successor by the late queen during her life; not that she had any objection to him as her heir, but because of that jealousy which Princes feel even towards their own children. It was only when she knew herself to be dying that she indicated rather than actually declared him as her successor. Her last moments approaching, the members of Council who were present asked her what might be her will in this matter, and she replied not to a 'rogue' – which in English means a low-born fellow – but to one who wore – and here her speech failing her she made with her hands the sign that signified a crown. Asked if she meant France she shook her head, as she did when Spain was named; when asked if she meant Scotland she assented. A few hours later she died.[46]

Carey was not the only one present at the Queen's bedside who left behind an account of what he witnessed. A document from the time describes how, on 22 March, her trusted kinsman and adviser Charles Howard, Earl of Nottingham, had finally insisted on knowing her plans for the succession. In reply, she gasped that the new king should be 'our cousin of Scotland'.[47] This is not corroborated by any other source. Indeed, one of those present at Richmond attested that Elizabeth was unable to speak for three days before her death. But Nottingham and Cecil had already prepared for James's accession well before their royal mistress breathed her last and they were quick to repeat this fabricated version to the foreign dignitaries at court who would then carry the news across Europe.

One of the first was Scaramelli, the sharp-tongued Venetian envoy. He described how 'with tears and sighs', Elizabeth begged her advisers to bestow the crown on the person they judged most deserving. She then confided 'in her secret thought' that this had always been James, for he had a greater claim to her throne than she did, 'both in right of birth and because he excelled her in merit having been born a king, while she was but a private person'. She apparently added that his claim was further strengthened because 'he brought with him a whole kingdom, while she had brought nothing but herself, a woman'.[48] It is hard to decide which is more far-fetched: that Elizabeth, who had been beyond speech and 'like a dead person' for days, should suddenly rally sufficiently to make a speech naming her successor, or that she who had defended her birthright so vigorously throughout her long reign should at the last admit that the King of Scots was her superior in blood as well as sex. But one element of Scaramelli's report is more plausible. He claimed that the council suppressed the Queen's nomination of James in order to make its own role in his succession more important.

Cecil and Nottingham also convinced the French ambassador of their tale. Beaumont had either been a guest at

Richmond or had travelled there frequently to garner news of the ailing queen for his master, Henry IV. Meticulous in his sources, his is one of the most reliable accounts of Elizabeth's final days. Late on the evening of 22 March, the same day she was purported to have told Nottingham and Cecil that she wished James to succeed her, Beaumont reported that there had been no 'public nomination' of James by the dying queen, either by word or will. He confirmed this on 25 March, the day after the Queen's death, in a letter to the French ambassador in Spain, describing how she had neither spoken to nor even seemed to notice anyone around her, and had been completely without speech for three days. Beaumont's enquiries had been exhaustive enough for him to confidently assert: 'En cet état je n'estime pas qu'elle fasse aucun testament ni qu'elle declare son successeur' ('In that state I don't see how she can have left a will or named her successor').[49]

But just ten days later, Beaumont had changed his tune – or had had it changed for him. Following a conference with Cecil and Nottingham, the ambassador reported that a few days before her death, the Queen had told those two advisers 'in confidence' that she recognised no other successor but James. She went on to insist that she did not 'want her kingdom to fall into the hands of scoundrels, that is to say of Rascals ("*Canailles*")', by whom she was understood to mean the descendants of her old rival Katherine Grey. When, later, Cecil and Nottingham asked her to repeat her wishes to the other privy councillors, she was beyond speech but signalled her intention by putting her hand to her head.[50]

On 28 March, 'all the council and divers of the nobility' sent a message to the King of France that on her sickbed Elizabeth had given 'her own princely allowance and wished recommendation' of James's title. A few months later, the man who had orchestrated the transition from the Tudor to the Stuart regime was still pedalling this fiction. Cecil insisted before the Star Chamber that 'her late Majesty in her last sickness devised' the crown 'by parolle [word]' to the Scottish king.[51] And so the narrative was established for the next four hundred years. The Stuart succession had been a foregone conclusion, not – as in reality it was – a hard-fought battle between rival claimants that had lasted throughout Elizabeth's long reign.

John Clapham summed up the mass of contradictory reports about Elizabeth's final days and hours. His conclusion was brief and circumspect: '[The] reports, whether they were true indeed or given out of purpose by such as would have them so believed, it is hard to say.' Ambassador Beaumont reflected: 'A few days before the death of the Queen all the nobility and commons of England prepared themselves for the immediate election and nomination of the King of Scotland as her successor.'[52]

Here, perhaps, was the most accurate judgement of all. What, in the end, had given James the edge had not been the quality of his royal blood or the advantage of his gender but a small minority of English statesmen working assiduously on his behalf. The 'monarchical republic' that Lord Burghley had envisaged early in Elizabeth's reign, with the council directing affairs of state before a new monarch was safely on the throne, had come to fruition forty years after it had first been envisaged.

CHAPTER 13

'THIS PEACEABLE COMING
IN OF THE KING'

According to legend, as soon as the Queen's last breath had left her body, Philadelphia Scrope, daughter of Elizabeth's late cousin Henry Carey, opened the window of the royal bedchamber and dropped a sapphire ring to her brother, Robert Carey, who was waiting below. The ring had been given to Philadelphia by James, who had instructed her to send it to him as a sign that the Queen was dead. The story goes that Carey rode with it at breakneck speed to Scotland, determined to be the first to carry the news to James that he was now King of England.

If this happened at all, it was not quite so straightforward. In his memoirs, Carey claimed that when Elizabeth died, her council forbade him from taking the news to the King of Scots 'till their pleasures were further known'. They then went to Robert Cecil's chamber for a private conference, 'and as they went they gave a special command to the porters [at Richmond Palace] that none should go out of the gates but such servants as they should send to prepare their coaches and horses for London'. Anxious not to lose his opportunity to be the first to tell James that the Queen was dead, Carey stole out of Richmond and rode to Whitehall, to await the arrival of the council. When he heard that they were gathered in the orchard there, he sent a message via the earl marshal of the privy council that he was ready to attend them. The earl marshal soon returned and told Carey that the lords of the council 'were very glad when they heard I was not gone' and summoned Carey so that they could order him to Scotland 'with all speed'. But before he went to them, the earl marshal received word that they would betray him and send another in his stead, so urged him to set out for Scotland without delay.[1]

Carey acted on the earl marshal's advice and tore off on a furious ride to Scotland. His haste almost proved fatal. He covered the first 347 miles in a staggering two days and three hours – almost half the usual time. He was within a stone's throw of the border when he fell heavily and his startled horse kicked out, striking a 'great blow' to his head. With blood pouring from the wound, Carey remounted and rode on to Edinburgh, reaching the palace of Holyrood after the King had gone to bed. 'I was quickly let in, and carried up to the King's chamber. I kneeled by him, and saluted him by the title of England, Scotland, France and Ireland.' After questioning Carey about the manner of the Queen's death, James asked if he carried letters from the council. Carey admitted he had none, but handed him 'a blue ring from a fair lady' – possibly his sister, Philadelphia, as the legend claimed. James examined it closely, then declared: 'It is enough: I know by this you are a true messenger.' The trouble that Carey had gone to in delivering the news had been worth it: before he took his leave, James assured him, 'I will be as good a master to you, and will requite this service with honour and reward.' The next day, Carey was appointed gentleman of the King's bedchamber, one of the most prized positions in the royal household. As he reflected: 'Now was I to begin a new world.'[2]

England's new king did not wait for an official communication from the council but hurried off a letter to Cecil, rejoicing that the 'whole state . . . [had] consented to proclaim us her lawful successor and to be their king, for the which we offer first our most hearty thanks to God'. He assured the secretary that he would not allow his efforts and those of the other English nobles who had paved the way for his accession 'to slide out of our memory without condign remuneration'. Shortly afterwards, the Earl of Montrose, Lord President of the Scottish privy council, wrote his own note of thanks to Cecil: 'It has pleased God . . . to bless our King and master with his due crown of England so happily without shed of blood or trouble to his Majesty . . . chiefly by the wisdom and assistance of your lordship.'[3]

Meanwhile, in Richmond, an hour or two after the Queen's breath had ceased, Cecil proclaimed James king in front of his fellow privy councillors. They then rode to the gates of Whitehall Palace and at ten o'clock in the morning made the same proclamation before the citizens of London. It was repeated at Temple Bar, St Paul's, Ludgate, Cheapside and Cornhill before being printed for general distribution throughout the kingdom. The proclamation declared:

> It hath pleased Almighty God to call to his mercy out of this transitory life our Sovereign Lady, the High and Mighty Prince, Elizabeth late Queen of England, France and Ireland, by whose death and dissolution, the Imperial Crown of these Realms aforesaid are now absolutely, wholly, and solely come to the High and Mighty Prince, James the Sixth King of Scotland.

The wording left no doubt that James VI and I was king 'by law, by lineal succession, and undoubted right' and that his accession was accepted 'with one full voice and consent of tongue and heart'. Interestingly, while the proclamation made much of the marriage of Henry VII and Elizabeth of York, which had brought to an end the 'bloody and Civil Wars . . . to the joy unspeakable of this Kingdom', it made no mention whatsoever of Margaret Tudor's marriage to James IV – the union upon which the new king's succession was entirely based. James's late mother, Mary, Queen of Scots, was also conspicuous by her absence. This was almost certainly to avoid any reminder that Henry VIII had barred Margaret and her descendants from inheriting his throne. By contrast, the proclamation that was issued in Scotland a week later fully recognised the union of the two crowns.

The English proclamation ended with an order to all the lieutenants, sheriffs, justices, mayors and other enforcers of the law to suppress any 'disorderly assemblies' or other activities 'prejudicial to . . . our only undoubted and dear Lord and Sovereign that now is, James the first King of all the said Kingdoms'.[4] This betrayed how deep-seated were the privy council's fears that the Scottish king's accession might provoke rebellion.

They were right to be cautious. In towns across England, some of the local officials charged with reading out the proclamation did not immediately comply, uncertain whether it was a genuine confirmation of James's right to the throne or a coup orchestrated at the heart of power, similar to that which had ushered Lady Jane Grey to the throne fifty years earlier. One Justice of the Peace in Norfolk insisted on waiting for a second proclamation, which was signed by three additional lords to the first, before he would declare it to his parish. When James was proclaimed in Northampton, there was 'no applause' and the town preacher opined that he should only be recognised as king if he proved 'sound in religion'.[5]

James's accession had introduced just as dangerously unstable an element to the succession as that of Henry IV, who had ousted his cousin Richard II from the throne in 1399. Now, as then, the notion of choice rather than simply hereditary right had muddied the waters. The eighteenth-century English jurist, William Blackstone, observed that although the crown was hereditary, 'the right of inheritance may from time to time be changed or limited by act of Parliament'. This idea had become so entrenched that in reflecting on the last year of Stuart rule in 1714, another author opined: 'In all ages, our constant custom and practice has been to limit the succession under conditions to a certain line, for avoiding all the contests and disturbances at frequent elections; and yet to reserve a power of excluding the next in blood, if under any incapacity of reigning, or, though capable, yet sometimes not so fit as a worthier in the same family; and, very often, for great and important reasons, quite to transfer the right of succession from one line to another.'[6]

As was often the case with a disputed succession, most people jumped on the bandwagon of the successful candidate, or at least kept any misgivings to themselves, which made James's accession appear more inevitable than it had actually been. 'It was an universal assent of all, that gave this speedy and dutiful passage unto your Majesty's rightful claim,' John Chamberlain, a wealthy Londoner who corresponded with some of the most prominent members of Stuart society, assured the new king in a letter dripping with sycophancy. All the preparations that had been made against civil unrest seemed needless. 'No tumult, no contradiction, no disorder in the city: every man went about his business as readily, as peaceably, as securely as though there had been no change, nor any news ever heard of competitors,' John Manningham recorded in his diary.[7]

Just two days after James's accession, Robert Cotton submitted a genealogy to the English authorities that proved

James's right to the English crown.[8] His close acquaintance Henry Howard also commissioned him to write a defence of James's claim. Cotton needed little persuasion: he had been a firm supporter of the Stuart succession for some time, not least because of his own Scottish heritage, which included direct descent from Robert the Bruce. He even added Bruce to his signature after James's accession. The new king knighted Cotton almost as soon as he arrived in England.

'This peaceable coming in of the King was unexpected of all parts of the people,' reflected Anne Clifford, one of the late queen's attendants at Richmond. There was hardly a dissenting view among the contemporary letters and reports. 'The change has been accomplished in this manner,' reported the French ambassador, 'though for years all Christendom held for certain that it must be attended with trouble and confusion.' Robert Cecil's brother Thomas wrote from York: 'The contentment of the people is unspeakable, seeing all things proceed so quietly, whereas they expected in the interim their houses should have been spoiled and sacked.' Sir Francis Bacon, who had been disappointed of office during Elizabeth's reign but hoped for better under James, opined that the transition from Tudor to Stuart rule had been so easy that no 'son could succeed his father with greater silence, or less danger or disturbance of estate'.[9]

But all was not quite as it appeared. Robert Carey reported that when the news travelled north, 'The East border broke forth into great unruliness, insomuch as many complaints came to the King thereof.' Too weak from his head wound to attend to them in person, Carey sent two deputies to 'appease the trouble and make them quiet'. Any consolation he took from his new position in the King's bedchamber was short-lived. Carey claimed that the appointment sparked envy

among the 'great ones' at court and the King 'deceived my
expectation' by depriving him of the new post.[10] But he
continued to frequent the court and was eventually rewarded
when his wife was given a position in the new queen's household and Carey himself was made governor of the King's
younger son, Charles, a weak and sickly child. He was later
promoted to chief gentleman of the prince's bedchamber and
master of the robes.

Barely had the echoes of James's proclamation faded than
rumours of Catholic plots abounded. It was said that the
Infanta Isabella and her husband Archduke Albert had been
proclaimed King and Queen of England in Brussels and that
Catholics across Europe were gathering to support them.
John Chamberlain and John Manningham both reported that
Edward, Lord Beauchamp, eldest son of Lady Katherine
Grey, was still being promoted as the late queen's heir, with
the support of some 'principal papists'. An even more damaging report held that James had turned Catholic and promised
the Pope that he would grant toleration to all those of that
faith in England and Ireland. Alarmed, the privy council
ordered local magistrates to arrest all suspicious persons,
rumour mongers and those 'tending to the disturbance of the
common peace'. Priests were instructed to preach sermons
admonishing their congregations to remember their allegiance
to the new king. James himself was at pains to point out that
he was 'successor to her [Elizabeth] in the kingdom, so near as
we are in blood'.[11]

Within days, scores of ambitious courtiers and officials
had hurried north, ostensibly to offer their congratulations to
the new king but in the unexpressed hope of feathering their
own nests. 'There is much posting that way,' Chamberlain
observed on 30 March, 'and many run thither of their own
errand, as if it were nothing else but first come first served.'

The new king himself expressed his satisfaction at how 'the people of all sorts rid and ran, nay rather flew to meet me . . . their gestures discovering a passionate longing, and earnestness to meet and embrace their new sovereign'. His effusive gratitude and bonhomie soon wore thin and on 2 April he issued a general letter urging these new English subjects to leave and those who had not yet ventured to Scotland to remain at home. 'For although it be very agreeable to us . . . yet it is no less acceptable to us to have a sufficient number of you together attending at London with your accustomed care upon our affairs.'[12] Elizabeth had spent much of her forty-four-year reign greeting, conversing with and travelling among her people and they had loved her for it. As the courtiers who returned to London with their tails firmly between their legs might have reflected, James had managed the same for less than a week.

In their haste to acknowledge King James, the late queen's subjects appeared to have forgotten her entirely. For days after her death, her corpse lay at Richmond, wrapped in a cerecloth in a 'very ill' fashion, with 'mean persons' having access to it. Her body was subsequently moved by night in a torchlit barge to Whitehall Palace. There, a small group of Elizabeth's former ladies in waiting kept watch over the coffin day and night. They included the Earl of Nottingham's granddaughter, Elizabeth Southwell. She is the source of a story that while she and her fellow attendants were 'all in our places about the corpse, which was fast nailed up in a board coffin, with leaves of lead covered with velvet, her body burst with such a crack that it split the wood, lead and cere-cloth, whereupon, the next day, she was fain to be new trimmed up'. This grisly story is unlikely to be true. Southwell was not the most reliable of sources and it was typical of tales that circulated after the death of the old monarch and were encouraged by the new, to prove that this semi-divine being had been just flesh and blood after all.[13]

'Such is the condition of great princes,' John Clapham lamented, 'more unhappy in this respect than their own subjects, in that, while they live, they are followed by all men, and at their death they are lamented of none.'[14]

CHAPTER 14

'PLAY THE KING'

'As God is my witness, it never was, is, nor shall be my intention to enter that kingdom in any other sort but as the son and righteous heir of England, with all peace and calmness, and without any kind of alteration in state or government as far as possible I can.' James had written these words at Holyroodhouse Palace on 24 March 1603, not then aware that early the same morning, Queen Elizabeth had died and he was now both King of Scotland and King of England.[1]

The sense of 'business as usual' was continued in the communications that followed. 'There is no more difference betwixt London and Edinburgh, yea, not so much, as betwixt Inverness or Aberdeen and Edinburgh,' James declared to the people of his northern capital on 3 April 1603, ten days after inheriting the English throne. 'And as God has joined the right of both the kingdoms in my person, so you may [be] joined in wealth, in religion, in hearts, and affections . . . Think not of me, as a king going from one part to another; but as a king lawfully called, going from one part of the isle to the other, so that your comfort may be the greater.'[2]

James went on to make the bold claim that he had effectively been running affairs south of the border for many months now. In June 1603, he boasted to the French ambassador that 'in Scotland, long before the death of [Elizabeth], he had directed her whole council, and governed her ministers, by whom he was better served and obeyed than herself'.[3] Certainly, many of the late queen's most influential advisers had been cultivating her likely successor for years before her demise. But she had maintained a vice-like grip on affairs of state almost to her last breath. If James truly believed otherwise, it was probably because Cecil had flattered him into this impression. He would soon realise that he was very far from either understanding or directing the English government.

While the privy council made sure that James's new subjects were in no doubt of his hereditary right to the throne, foreign observers were more circumspect. In general, they referred to him as an elected monarch rather than one who had succeeded by right of birth. The French ambassador noted the 'election and nomination of the king of Scotland', but was at pains to stress: 'His title is most legitimate and is supported by the good opinion the English have of his character, by the fact that he has sons, and because he is already versed in government.'[4]

On 5 April, James set out from Edinburgh, promising his Scottish subjects that he would return every three years.[5] Anxious to be kept fully informed of Scottish affairs once in England, the following month he ordered the establishment of a public postal route between Edinburgh and Berwick, on the English border. A short while later, a royal postal route was established between London and Edinburgh.

James took a deliberately slow and circuitous journey in the hope that by the time he reached London the sadness over Elizabeth's funeral, which was eventually scheduled for 28 April, might be forgotten. There was certainly no question of his attending. A long-standing royal tradition, laced with a healthy dose of superstition, stated that the new monarch should not attend the funeral of the old, as if they would somehow be tainted by their death. But Scaramelli was quick to ascribe a more sinister motive: 'His Majesty has ordered the funeral of the Queen to take place without waiting his arrival, and they say he wishes to see her neither alive nor dead, for he can never expel from his memory the fact that his mother was put to death at the hands of the public executioner, with great disgrace and cruelty, an indignity to a crowned head that has no parallel in history except the cases of . . . the two adulterous Queens of Henry VIII of England, Anne Boleyn and Catherine Howard, and Jane, who rebelled against Mary of England.' The Venetian ambassador added: 'Elizabeth's portrait is being hidden everywhere, and Mary Stuart's shown instead with declaration that she suffered for no other cause than for her religion.'[6]

It was one thing for a new monarch not to associate with his dead predecessor, but James extended the same stricture to his family, courtiers, ambassadors and their retinues. His wife Anne had written to ask if she should wear mourning, but he told her it was 'utterly impertinent at this time'. When Henry IV's envoy arrived in Edinburgh, decked out in mourning attire, to offer the French king's congratulations, he was roundly told that 'no one, whether ambassador, foreigner or English, was admitted . . . in black'. His rival for the throne showed no greater respect for the late queen. When James invited Arbella to act as principal mourner at the funeral, she declined, allegedly remarking that since she had not been permitted access to Elizabeth during her lifetime, she would not now be brought on stage as a public spectacle.[7]

Nevertheless, the late queen's funeral was conducted with the same ostentatious pomp and ceremony that had accompanied her public appearances in life. An estimated 200,000 people turned out to watch as more than a thousand nobles, bishops and courtiers processed through the streets of London to Westminster Abbey. At the head of the procession was the coffin surmounted by an effigy of the late queen dressed in royal robes – so lifelike that it made mourners gasp. The contemporary chronicler John Stow recorded the intense emotion of the occasion: 'There was such a general sighing, groaning, and weeping, as the like hath not been seen or known in the memory of man, neither does any history mention any people, time, or state, to make the like lamentation for the death of their sovereign.'[8]

The new king commissioned an opulent tomb for his predecessor at a cost of £1,485 (equivalent to around £205,000 today). Crafted from white marble by the renowned Flemish sculptor Maximilian Colt, it was erected in the north aisle of the Lady Chapel, built by Elizabeth's grandfather Henry VII. The inscription described the late queen as 'Mother of her country, a nursing-mother to religion and all liberal sciences, skilled in many languages, adorned with excellent endowments both of body and mind, and excellent for princely virtues beyond her sex'. Emphasising her gender was perhaps deliberate: it drew attention to one of the few advantages James had over the late queen. The inscription went on to hail him as 'King of Great Britain, France and Ireland [who] hath devoutly and justly erected this monument to her whose virtues and kingdoms he inherits'.

James also ordered the long overdue completion of his grandmother's tomb in the south aisle of the chapel. Lady Margaret Douglas had spent most of her life pursuing the dynastic ambitions of her family but died twenty-five years before they were finally realised through her grandson. For James, the expense was worth it: Margaret's magnificent tomb provided an extra reminder to his new subjects of the English royal blood that flowed through his veins.

Almost everywhere the new king went, he was greeted with cheering crowds, fireworks, bonfires, feasting and gifts. He used the journey south to show off both his largesse and his brutality. With one hand he doled out knighthoods and with the other he ordered the summary hanging of a thief without due process of law. On 3 May, James arrived at Theobalds House and met his host and long-term correspondent Robert Cecil for the first time. He also conducted his first English privy council meeting. Ten days later, as a reward for all that Cecil had done for him in the preceding years, he made him Baron Cecil of Essendon and Principal Secretary to the King's Majesty. Further promotions would follow in the years to come.

By the time James reached London, the capital had swelled by an extra 100,000 people. One of their number observed: 'In the highways, fields, meadows, closes, and on trees so great [were the crowds] that they covered the beauty of the fields; and so greedy were they to behold the King that they injured and hurt one another.' A staggering 40,000 eager well-wishers and place-seekers were reported trying to gain admission to court, and they 'swarmed . . . at every back gate and privy door'. Even James's former nemesis Robert Persons wrote to beg forgiveness for his notorious tract and offer his congratulations on the King's accession. Calling himself a 'poor worm of the earth', he praised James's 'great wisdom' and declared that 'all the world doth applaud' him.[9]

But the praise did not altogether drown out the dissenting voices. Doubts about the new king's religious stance combined with deep-seated xenophobia. A farm worker in Hertfordshire was indicted for declaring himself ready to take up arms to prevent a Scot from sitting on the English throne. In a similar vein, a Sussex labourer was hauled before the magistrates for reminding anyone who would listen that Henry VIII had decreed that 'no foreign prince should inherit the crown'.[10]

Such hostility aside, initial impressions of England's new king were favourable. 'The King is of the sharpest wit and invention, ready and pithy in speech, an exceeding good memory; of the sweetest, pleasantest and best nature that ever I knew,' pronounced the lawyer Roger Wilbraham. Scaramelli also praised the new king's intellectual abilities and his fondness for hunting, which qualities 'attract men to him and render him acceptable to the aristocracy'. When granted his first audience with the King at Greenwich, the ambassador described the 'attitude of adoration' that his councillors ('flattering parasites', as another contemporary termed them) displayed as they fanned out around the throne.

But Scaramelli soon ran out of positive things to say. 'From his dress he would have been taken for the meanest of his courtiers,' he sneered. How different from the vast array of gorgeous gowns encrusted with priceless gems and pearls that had so dazzled the late queen's courtiers. Sir Thomas Lake, later Secretary of State and a favourite of James, also admitted that he did not show 'great majesty nor solemnities in his accesses'. Sir Francis Bacon was ambitious for promotion so avoided speaking out against the King, but his praise was so faint as to be damning. He privately observed that James showed a lack of foresight in calling for advice about 'the time past [rather] than of the time to come' – just as he had disregard all the advice that the late Queen had drip-fed him during her reign. Another contemporary courtier, Sir Anthony Weldon, agreed that although 'crafty and cunning in petty things', the new king was slow to grasp 'weighty affairs' and coined the famous description of him as 'the wisest fool in Christendom'.[11]

James's own good opinion of his new subjects proved just as transient. He was cut from a very different cloth to his predecessor, who had revelled in public displays of majesty and lapped up the adoration of her subjects. After just a few days in London, the new king was reported to have taken 'great offence' against the eager supplicants for his favour.[12]

In a superstitious age, when crop failures, sudden deaths and natural disasters were taken to be the result of witchcraft or of God's disapproval, the onset of a terrible plague in London at around the same time as the new king's arrival seemed an evil omen. His state entry into the city was swiftly postponed and the royal party beat a hasty retreat to Winchester, while a quarter of London's population was wiped out in one of the worst epidemics for years.

The infection had abated enough for James's coronation to be held at Westminster Abbey as planned on 25 July, but attendance was strictly curtailed. Among the pageants prepared for the procession was a triumphal arch designed by the poet and playwright Thomas Middleton. It showed the ascent of the late queen to heaven in the form of Astraea, Greek goddess of justice, before she returned like the Holy Ghost to be locked in the breast of the new king. Elsewhere, James was depicted as a phoenix rising from the ashes of his glorious predecessor. Large crowds braved the risk of contagion to see such wonders and cheer the King's procession through the city. They were poorly rewarded for their pains. 'He was not like his predecessor, the late Queen of famous memory, that with a well-pleased affection met her people's acclamations,' the contemporary historian Arthur Wilson scathingly remarked. 'He endured the day's brunt with patience, being assured he should never have another.'[13]

But on other occasions James's forbearance quickly gave way to obvious irritation. 'Afterwards in his public appearances, the access of the people made him so impatient, that he often dispersed them with frowns,' Wilson noted. Things had hardly improved four years later when Nicolo Molin, the Venetian ambassador, reported: 'He does not caress the people nor make them that good cheer as the late Queen did, whereby she won their loves; for the English adore their Sovereigns, and if the King passed through the same street a hundred times a day the people would still run to see him; they like their King to show pleasure at their devotion, as the late Queen knew well how to do; but this King manifests no taste for them but rather contempt and dislike. The result is he is despised and almost hated.'[14]

Now that he was King of England, James was just as sensitive to any talk or even hint about his right to that title as he had been during the long years of waiting for Elizabeth's throne. A rash of pamphlets was printed after his accession in response to the propensity of some unnamed persons 'to dispute his Majesty's just and most lawful title'. Ambassador Beaumont made a thoughtless remark about Arbella Stuart being a suitable successor to the new King. James wrote at once to Henry IV demanding that Beaumont be replaced by Charles Cauchon de Maupas du Tour, who had pleased him as ambassador to Scotland.[15]

England's new king also put a swift and brutal end to a controversy that had vexed him for years. 'That King kept a severe memory of the accusation cast upon him by Valentine Thomas,' Thomas Birch later recorded, 'and within a month after his arrival in London, in the beginning of June 1603, ordered him to be brought to his trial, and executed.'[16] He might have been better advised to uphold his predecessor's policy of letting sleeping dogs lie. The execution did not so much rid James's English subjects of a traitor as remind them of the part their new king was accused of having played in the alleged assassination attempt.

In May 1603, the two rival Stuart claimants to the Tudor throne met for the first time at Greenwich. This was prompted by the ever-ambitious Countess of Shrewsbury, who had petitioned the new king to allow her to present her granddaughter to him. James had been gracious in victory: 'We shall be willing to confer [with] her and make her know how well we wish her in regard to her nearness of blood,' he told the countess. Scaramelli reported that Arbella, 'no longer mad', had been careful to express her loyalty to the new king. 'In all humility,' she offered assurance 'that she desires no other husband, no other state, no other life than that which King James, her cousin and Lord, in his goodness may assign her.'[17]

To the untrained eye, when the two finally met, all was civility and grace. But his private feelings towards the woman who had threatened his English inheritance were betrayed by his overheard remark that 'our cousin the Lady Arbella' should go back 'from wherein she came'. Even so, the meeting reignited the old rumours of a marriage between the two claimants. Scaramelli was quick to speculate: 'Lady Arbella, who is a regular termagant, came to visit the King on Sunday last with a suite of ladies and gentlemen. She has returned to favour, and they say that should the Queen [Anne] die she would be wedded and crowned at once.'[18]

Cecil, who had a greater understanding of the sensitivities involved than his royal master, persuaded James that Arbella should be allowed the freedom to choose where she lived. For a young woman who had spent most of her life in near-captivity, this was utopia. Rather than return to the Midlands, she opted to remain in London and took up residence in Sheen, west of the capital. James's concession had apparently bought his cousin's compliance. In December 1603, Arbella wrote to her aunt and godmother, Mary Talbot: 'When any great matter comes in question rest secure I beseech you, that I am not interested in it as an actor, howsoever the vanity of wicked men's vain designs have made my name pass through a gross and a subtle lawyer's lips of late, to the exercise [of] my patience, and not their credit.' She also expressed her gratitude to Sir Andrew Sinclair, a Scotsman who served on the Danish privy council and later joined the new King's bedchamber staff, for 'the patronage of so worthy a Prince, so interested in them of whom my fortune depends, and so graciously affected to me'. She had nothing but praise for her Stuart kinsman, 'whose gracious favour so many ways expressed is of itself a special comfort and honour to me [and] so precious to me' and concluded that she was sure that thanks to his protection, she would live safely and happily.[19]

The following year, the Scottish poet Alexander Craig published his *Poeticall Essayes*, which included a verse written as if by the ghost of Elizabeth:

Cease loving subjects, cease my death for to deplore . . .
So now my ghost is glad, that by my care his pain
My countries have their lawful King, the King his crowns
    again . . .
Learn to obey, and bathe no more thy blade in British
    blood:
All you my subjects dear, do homage due to him
And that shall make my blessed ghost in boundless joys to
    swim.[20]

In this piece of opportunist poetry, Craig had enabled the late queen to voice her retrospective approval of James's accession. The fact that it was necessary to publish such a verse is perhaps more telling than the rhetoric it proclaimed.

In one respect at least James won universal approval. Before his accession, there had been anxiety among the privy council that they would be replaced by his Scottish advisers.

There was thus a palpable sense of relief when he retained all thirteen of Elizabeth's privy councillors and promoted those who had smoothed his path to the throne. Principal among them was Robert Cecil, whom James made first Earl of Salisbury. Before his departure in November 1605, Ambassador Beaumont reported that Cecil 'begins to grow great with the King, staying alone with him shut up in the cabinet [James's personal closet] for three or four hours together'.[21] Others who were rewarded for supporting James's claim to the throne included Henry Howard, who was made Earl of Northampton, and Lord Mountjoy, who became Earl of Devonshire. The new king did appoint five Scots to the privy council, but their influence was negligible.

In other ways, though, the arrival of the Scottish king prompted a seismic shift in English court life. By the time of his accession, there was a well-established system of government structured around access to the king or queen. The privy chamber was the most intimate space in the royal household and positions within it were highly sought after because of the close and regular access they offered to the monarch's person. Even though they served in a private capacity, these officials therefore enjoyed considerable political influence. But when James came to the English throne, the focus shifted almost overnight from the privy chamber to the bedchamber. The former became more of a formal, ceremonial space, whereas the latter controlled the more intimate aspects of serving the King. And whereas there was a roughly equal number of English and Scottish attendants in the privy chamber, the bedchamber was comprised almost entirely of 'hungry Scots', in the words of one aggrieved contemporary. 'Every corner of the Court [was filled] with these beggarly bluecaps,' the politician and antiquarian Gervase Holles complained, in reference to the blue woollen bonnets that the Scots were reputed to wear. The situation had not improved a few years later, when his kinsman Sir John Holles resentfully noted: 'The Scottish monopolise his princely person, standing like mountains betwixt the beams of his grace and us.' He argued that posts in the bedchamber ought to be 'shared as well to those of our nation as to them'.[22]

In common with the late queen, James was a ruler of learning and intellect, and his court in Scotland had been deeply influenced by Renaissance traditions. He was interested in church music and literature, and had a particular passion for jewellery and fine clothes. His consort Anne of Denmark had also exerted a positive influence on Stuart court life, encouraging the patronage of artists, craftspeople, writers and performers from across Scotland and abroad. After James inherited Elizabeth's throne, William Shakespeare continued to enjoy royal patronage, as did his fellow poet and playwright Ben Jonson. The celebrated architect Inigo Jones built a new Banqueting House at Whitehall Palace in the fashionable Palladian style.

But a clash of cultures arose from the Stuart obsession with extravagant and often riotous masques, fuelled by the heavy drinking that was prevalent in James's court. This was at odds with the refined, strictly controlled pastimes of the late queen's time. Often, the players were so drunk that they could not remember their lines. 'I have much marvelled at these strange pageantries, and they do bring to my remembrance what passed of this sort in our Queen's days,' reflected her godson Sir John Harington. 'I never did see such lack of good order, discretion, and sobriety, as I have now done.' Lady Anne Clifford was just as disapproving: 'All the ladies about the court had gotten such ill names that it was grown a scandalous place.'[23]

The new queen also came under fire. The Venetian Secretary to England scornfully noted that Anne of Denmark lacked Elizabeth's sense of style and had even resorted to plundering the latter's wardrobe: 'Though she declared that she would never wear cast [off] clothes, still it was found that art could not devise anything more costly and gorgeous, and so the Court dressmakers are at work altering these old robes, for nothing new could surpass them.'[24]

Most scandalous of all was James's private life. In outward appearances, he was a model of conventionality with a wife and three children. But his marriage was one of politics rather than passion. He and Anne lived separate lives at court and it was noted that they did not 'converse' together. Instead, James surrounded himself with a succession of beautiful young men, each of whom was rapidly promoted to exalted positions at court.

'The King, in spite of all the heroic virtues ascribed to him when he left Scotland and inculcated by him in his books, seems to have sunk into a lethargy of pleasures, and will not take heed of matters of state,' Scaramelli reported. 'He seems to have forgotten that he is a King, except in his kingly pursuit of stags, to which he is quite foolishly devoted.' James protested to his council that hunting was 'the only means to maintain his health' and so 'desires them to take the charge and burden of affairs, and foresee that he be not interrupted or troubled with too much business'. All this was very different from what the English councillors had grown accustomed to in Elizabeth's time. She had been at the heart of her government and her court. No decision had been made without her, and she had skilfully played her advisers, courtiers and suitors off against each other to prevent any from gaining too much power. The queen bee in the hive, she had revelled in being the centre of attention at all times. This was anathema to the naturally reserved and reclusive King, who preferred the company of his dogs to that of his new courtiers. He had established very much the same routine as King of Scots, preferring to 'live retired with eight or ten of his favourites than openly' and ordering that 'none shall presume to come to him on hunting days'. He would have done well to heed his predecessor's advice and 'play the king'.[25]

In 1607, Ambassador Molin reported: 'The King has virtually given full and absolute authority to the Council. He is Sovereign in name and in appearance rather than in substance and effect.' For centuries, the monarch had been at the centre of patronage, using it as one of the most effective means to assert their power. Now, 'many who went to him with petitions and grievances have been told to go to the Council, for they are fully authorised to deal with all business public and private'.[26]

It was a strategy as dangerous as it was short-sighted. At first, James's privy councillors felt rudderless and uncertain, complaining of being overburdened with work. Even Cecil reflected wistfully on the days when he had served Elizabeth: 'I wish I waited now in her presence-chamber, with ease at my food, and rest in my bed. I am pushed from the shore of comfort, and know not where the winds and waves of a court will bear me.'[27] But in time, what had seemed a burden was seized as an opportunity by ambitious ministers hungry for power. They were also emboldened by the knowledge that they had been instrumental in James's accession to the English throne. Having played kingmaker, they proceeded to govern the kingdom while James indulged in hunting and other pastimes. And once the power vacuum left by the new king had been filled by his government, the latter was not likely to relinquish it, either for James or his successors.

At the same time as delegating the day-to-day business of government to the privy council, James showed a flagrant disregard for the English Parliament. Here, too, a clash of cultures was painfully evident. In Scotland, the King controlled Parliament (which he referred to as 'nothing else but the King's great council') through a committee that decided which legislation should be sent there for debate. Five years before inheriting Elizabeth's throne, he had instructed his son Henry to 'hold no Parliaments, but for necessity of new laws, which would be but seldom'.[28] He saw no reason to adopt a different system south of the border and therefore demanded that all proposals for laws should be submitted to him twenty days before the opening of Parliament. Only those that he chose to take forward would be debated and he would have the final approval of any that were passed by Parliament. This approach was entirely driven by his unshakeable belief in the divine right of kings. But it also betrayed either his ignorance or indifference to the fact that the English Parliament's power had grown steadily during the Tudor period. By the end of Elizabeth's reign it was not only the principal legislative authority in the kingdom but a forum for expressing and resolving grievances against the monarch. The new king's approach therefore soon sparked vociferous opposition.

Within an alarmingly short space of time, England's new king had courted deep-seated resentment. In June 1603, just three months after his accession, the 'Bye' Plot (so named because it was believed to be a minor component of the larger 'Main' Plot) came to light. It involved a group of Catholics who planned to kidnap the King and secure a number of concessions for the practice of their religion. But it lacked powerful supporters and soon collapsed in disarray. More serious was the Main Plot, which aimed to oust James from the throne and replace him with his cousin, Arbella Stuart. Its ringleaders, who had sought funding from Spain and Austria, were men of much greater influence. Foremost among them was Henry Brooke, Lord Cobham, who planned to marry Arbella to Thomas Grey, fifteenth Baron Grey de Wilton, a former member of the privy council who had made no secret of his aversion towards the King and his Scottish entourage. The late queen's favourite adventurer, Sir Walter Raleigh, was also suspected of involvement. James was already predisposed not to trust him because in the run-up to inheriting the English throne, he had been informed by Henry Howard that Raleigh opposed his claim.

When the conspiracy was uncovered, Raleigh and his fellow plotters were arrested and condemned. Arbella was present at their trial and heard the prosecutor, Edward Coke, pronounce to Raleigh: 'Your intent was to set up the Lady Arabella as a titular Queen and to depose our present rightful King.' Raleigh retorted that he had no acquaintance with her and that he liked her least of any woman he ever saw. Arbella herself had been careful to avoid being implicated in the plot. When Lord Cobham had written to tell her of his plans, she had 'laughed at' his letter and immediately sent it to the King. But to be on the safe side, she urged the Earl of Nottingham, seated next to her in the gallery, to speak in her defence. He promptly declared: 'The Lady doth here protest upon her salvation, that she never dealt in any of these things, and so she willed me to tell the Court.'[29] Although Lord Cobham was subsequently released, Raleigh would spend the next thirteen years in the Tower of London, becoming one of its longest-serving prisoners.

Arbella herself escaped any reprisals. James rewarded her loyalty by increasing her pension and inviting her to court. After meeting with her, he was confident that she posed no threat. He therefore ordered that she should be allowed greater freedom and treated more 'tenderly' than she had been during the reign of his predecessor.[30] She was accorded the honour of riding directly behind Queen Anne in the official state entry pageant. Arbella was subsequently appointed carver to the Queen and godmother to the royal couple's new daughter, Mary. She became a regular fixture at court plays and masques during the years that followed.

But the apparent harmony between the King and his Stuart cousin was only skin-deep. Honoured royal servant though she was, Arbella scorned the childish pastimes of her fellow court ladies and was privately cynical about the new king's government and his 'everlasting hunting'.[31] For his part, James did not entirely trust Arbella and found her company irksome, even though they shared an interest in intellectual matters, because he scorned learning in women. He also kept Arbella perpetually short of money – certainly not enough to fund the costly lifestyle required of a courtier. She even had to pawn some of her jewels to pay her creditors. In effect, she became as financially trapped at court as she had been physically trapped at Hardwick. It was not a predicament that she intended to suffer for long.

CHAPTER 15

'A GREAT QUANTITY OF GUNPOWDER'

As King James settled into life in England, the country accepted him as king not because his claim was beyond question or his virtues and accomplishments set him above all others. The reason was both simple and uninspiring: there had been no other single, strong competitor with the necessary support in government to succeed. James, for one, did not appreciate this. Taking the initial adulation he had received at face value, he cherished the mistaken belief that his new English subjects had forgotten their centuries-old enmity towards his native kingdom.

As a result, when the King convened his first English Parliament in 1604, he confidently expected it to pass his proposal for a formal union between his two kingdoms. This had been his expressed intention from the very day of his accession. On 24 March 1603, he had written to one of his English supporters that he hoped 'to have the means to knit that whole island in a happy and perpetual unity'.[1] Two days later, Robert Cotton had written a treatise in support of the idea. This highlighted examples from history of smaller kingdoms uniting to form a more powerful whole and made the union of England and Scotland seem both simple and logical.

In his opening speech, the new king reminded those present of his hereditary right to the throne, something that he had taken care to sketch out in a family tree that proved his descent all the way back to the Saxon kings of England.[2] He declared: 'By my descent lineally out of the loins of Henry the seventh, is reunited and confirmed in me the union of the two princely roses of the two Houses of Lancaster and York . . . But [this] is nothing comparable to the Union of two ancient and famous Kingdoms.' To conclude, he adapted a much-cherished metaphor of the late queen's: 'I am the husband, and all the whole isle is my lawful wife; I am the head, and it is my body; I am the shepherd, and it is my flock.'[3]

So far, so good. Parliament swiftly reaffirmed the hereditary justification for James's accession in the Succession to the Crown Act, or 'A most joyful and just recognition of the immediate, lawful and undoubted Succession, Descent and Right of the Crown'. The Act stressed that on Elizabeth's death her throne had passed to James 'by inherent birthright and lawful and undoubted succession, descend and come to your most excellent Majesty, as being lineally, justly and lawfully next and sole heir of the blood royal of this realm'.[4] In truth, hereditary right was by no means a long-established tradition in the English monarchy. One does not have to go back much further than the Tudor period to find examples that disprove the rule – notably Richard III's usurpation of his nephew in 1483. But given that James's English royal blood was the primary justification for his succession, he and the English Parliament made sure to promote it as an indefeasible right.

The new Act also made much of the idea of Anglo-Scottish unity, comparing it to the union of the Houses of York and Lancaster, which had brought an end to the Wars of the Roses when England had been 'torn and almost wasted with long and miserable dissension and bloody civil war'. With James's accession:

More inestimable and unspeakable Blessings are thereby poured upon us, because there is derived and grown from and out of that Union of those two princely Families, a more famous and greater Union (or rather a Re-uniting) of two mighty, famous and ancient Kingdoms (yet anciently but one) of *England* and *Scotland*, under one Imperial Crown, in your most Royal Person, who is lineally, rightfully and lawfully descended of the Body of the most excellent Lady *Margaret*, eldest Daughter of the most renowned King *Henry* the Seventh, and the High and Noble Princess Queen *Elizabeth* his Wife, eldest Daughter of King *Edward* the Fourth; the said Lady *Margaret* being eldest Sister of King *Henry* the Eighth, Father of the High and Mighty Princess of famous Memory, *Elizabeth* late Queen of *England*.[5]

But beneath the veneer of this rhetoric lurked deep-seated opposition to the idea of a formal union between England and Scotland. The fundamental issue was that the English thought Scotland should be incorporated into England, while the Scots believed the two kingdoms should be equal partners. The Scots were hardly encouraged by England's attempts to subjugate Wales and Ireland, which had caused a great deal of blood to be spilt in centuries past. South of the border, meanwhile, fears existed that giving up the 'sceptred isle' of Shakespeare, the 'ancient name of England', would lead to the loss of identity both at home and abroad.[6]

James paid little heed to such difficulties. Inspired by the Book of Isaiah, which states 'Kings shall be thy nursing father', he saw himself as a teacher-physician to his people who, like children, should meekly submit themselves to him and be cured of any ills or wrongful beliefs.[7] His writings and speeches were littered with this analogy, and he went into the first

English Parliament of his reign confident that its members would instantly fall in with his will. 'Hath not God first united these two kingdoms both in language, religion, and similitude of manners?' he declared. 'Yea, hath he not made us all in one island, compassed with one sea, and of itself by nature . . . indivisible? . . . What God hath conjoined then, let no man separate.'[8]

To his dismay, the new king's rhetoric was met not with adulation but 'amazement and silence'. In the long-running controversy over the succession, the prospect of a union between England and Scotland had been the elephant in the room – one that Elizabeth had pretended not to see and had barred her Parliaments from discussing openly. Having raised the issue head-on, James was not prepared for the onslaught that followed. Months of ill-tempered debate followed, the result of which was that Parliament utterly rejected both the name and the idea of Britain.

James was furious. He ranted that in stark contrast to Scotland, where his word was as good as law, in England there was 'nothing but curiosity from morning to evening, to find fault with my propositions'. Having lost patience, he pressed ahead regardless. On 20 October 1604, he was 'in most solemn manner proclaimed King of Great Britain, France and Ireland'. The following month, he announced that a shared currency would be issued: a twenty-shilling piece known as the 'unite'. He also commissioned a new flag (the 'Union Jack', for Jacobus, or James) and a coat of arms. All were empty gestures, supported by neither Parliament nor law. The Venetian ambassador noted: 'The question of the Union will, I am assured, be dropped; for His Majesty is now well aware that nothing can be effected, both sides displaying such obstinacy that an accommodation is impossible; and so his Majesty is resolved to abandon the question for the present, in hope that time may consume the ill-humours.' When Parliament was still unmoved three years later, James turned to open threats: 'I pray you, do not too far move me to do that which my Power may tempt me unto,' he warned the assembled members.[9]

The King was courting ominous disapproval from his ordinary subjects, too. This was expressed as early as December 1604, when one of his hounds went missing. It reappeared the following day with a note tied around its neck, begging him to 'speak to the King (for he hears you every day, and so doth he not us) that it will please His Majesty to go back to London, for else the country will be undone'. The Venetian ambassador Nicolo Molin recorded that James's hunting trips were 'the cause of indescribable ill-humour among the King's subjects, who in their needs and troubles find themselves cut off from their natural sovereign, and forced to go before the Council, which is full of rivalry and discord, and frequently is more guided by personal interest than by justice and duty'.[10]

But their king was too distracted by his passions to notice or care. As the 'nursing father', appointed by God, he would cure all ills in his new kingdom. And there was one malady in particular that he was determined to root out. In the same year that the Succession to the Crown Act was passed, James introduced harsh new measures against witches. His obsession with witch hunting was well known, both at home and abroad, and was a product of his misogyny. In 1597, he had earned the dubious distinction of becoming the only monarch in history to publish a book on the subject. *Daemonologie* was a global bestseller of its day, republished several times and later translated into Latin, French and Dutch. It served as a manual for witch hunters everywhere and fanned the flames (literally) of the witch hunts in his native Scotland, where there was a huge surge in the number of witchcraft trials during the years following publication.

James brought his witch-hunting fervour to England. In his view, the English law was by no means strict enough in prosecuting what he saw as the greatest menace to society. He therefore ordered that the Elizabethan statute on witchcraft be replaced with a much harsher version. The new Act Against Witchcraft of 1604 stipulated: 'If any person ... shall use practise or exercise any invocation or conjuration of any evil or wicked spirit, or shall consult, covenant with, entertain, employ, feed, or reward any evil and wicked spirit to or for any intent or purpose ... [they] shall suffer pains of death.'[11] The definition of witchcraft was significantly broadened so that now even harmless practices such as the use of charms were punishable by death.

At first, James's new subjects were eager to demonstrate their compliance. In the same year that the Act was passed, Christopher Marlowe's dark morality play, *The Tragicall History of the Life and Death of Doctor Faustus*, was published, sixteen years after it had first been performed. It was one of the most shocking portrayals of witchcraft ever to appear on stage and had been a little strong for Elizabethan tastes, but it enjoyed a renaissance under James. As well as terrifying people into avoiding any dabbling in the dark arts, the play intensified their hatred and fear of witches.

But the most famous of all the literary works inspired by the King's obsession with witchcraft was Shakespeare's *Macbeth*. Deliberately short in length (he was aware James had little patience for the theatre), it was first performed at court in 1606 during a visit by Queen Anne's brother, the King of Denmark, where witch hunting was even more rife than in Scotland. Shakespeare wove in several references to the tempest that had almost cost James and his wife their lives when they had crossed the North Sea in 1589. The storms were believed to have been the work of witchcraft and had led James to hunt down the perpetrators in the North Berwick witch trials, one of the largest such cases in history.

All this whipped up a climate of fear and suspicion. 'Wise women' or healers, who for centuries had tended to the sick and vulnerable in their local communities, were now in the frame for witchcraft, as were the old, poor, unmarried or any other people considered dispensable to society. Witchcraft accusations also became a convenient way of getting rid of a troublesome neighbour or rival.

At the same time, unease spread about the King's religious policy. In attempting to resolve the deep divisions that had existed since Henry VIII's reformation, James faced a greater challenge than his Tudor predecessors. He belonged to one church in England and another in Scotland, and somehow he had to reconcile the two. He decided that the differing opinions should be aired at a religious conference held at Hampton Court in January 1604. Although the hard-line Puritans and Catholics left disappointed, the King did achieve a broader consensus than his predecessor, whose religious settlement had proved an unsatisfactory compromise.

A few months later, James held another conference, at Somerset House, its purpose to end the hostilities with Spain that had endured ever since the Armada in 1588. The negotiations were successful and the ensuing Treaty of London established peace between the two countries for the first time in almost half a century. As part of the terms, Spain recognised the Protestant monarchy of England and renounced its intentions to restore the Roman Catholic Church there. In return, James agreed to withdraw military and financial support to the Dutch rebels, which had been in place ever since Elizabeth had signed the Treaty of Nonsuch with the United Provinces in 1585. This was a direct reversal of the late queen's policy and rode roughshod over the wishes she had expressed in her last ever letter to James. Caring nothing for that, he crowed that 'this was a happy day for him'. He could not resist adding that he hoped to preserve 'the kingdoms of Spain and England in friendship and union, unlike that other hostile Elizabeth who had caused so much mischief'.

Few of the King's Protestant subjects shared his satisfaction that England was now allied with the most potent Catholic power in Europe. Noel Caron, the Dutch ambassador to England, recorded: 'No promulgation was ever received in London with more coolness, yes – with more sadness.'[12] Disregarding public opinion, a few years later James sought to strengthen his alliance with Spain by proposing a marriage between his son Charles, and Philip III's daughter Maria Anna. In 1623, the prince went to meet his intended bride in Madrid, but the match was subsequently abandoned because the Infanta did not wish to marry a Protestant and Charles refused to convert to Catholicism.

Neither were the Catholics appeased. Before becoming King of England, James had offered reassurance that he would not persecute any Catholics who were 'quiet and give but an outward obedience to the law'.[13] But his ambivalent stance towards those of that faith, coupled with his being the son of a celebrated Catholic martyr, had offered hope that they would enjoy greater freedom under his rule than they had under Elizabeth. They were soon brutally disabused of this impression. While the late queen had turned a blind eye to private Catholic practices, James insisted upon a much stricter observance of the reformed faith, declaring: 'Who can't pray with me, can't love me.' Early in his reign, he and his councillors began drafting new legislation for the persecution of Catholics.

The Jesuit priest John Gerard summed up the sense of fear and disillusionment among that community: 'A flash of lightning, giving for the time a pale light unto those that sit in darkness, doth afterwards leave them in more desolation.'[14]

Soon desolation gave way to rebellion. In 1605, a group of Catholic gentlemen fanatics led by the charismatic Robert Catesby hatched a plot to blow up the House of Lords during the state opening of Parliament on 5 November. The King, his eldest son and heir Henry and the entire government would have been 'blown up all at a clap', as Robert Cecil later recorded.[15] This was to be the prelude to a popular revolt in the plotters' native Midland counties. But they did not intend to destroy the Stuart monarchy altogether. The plan was to place James's nine-year-old daughter Elizabeth on the throne, bypassing her brother Charles. This was no sentimental desire to return England to female monarchy: Elizabeth would be a puppet queen ruled by the Catholic husband she would be forced to marry.

Over a series of weeks and months, the plotters moved 'by a secret conveyance . . . a great quantity of gunpowder' into a cellar they had rented directly underneath Westminster Hall, where Parliament would convene. If ignited, it would have reduced to rubble not just the hall but an entire hundred metre radius around it. This audacious plot came perilously close to success. Thanks only to an anonymous tip-off to the authorities, received in late October, the King ordered a thorough search of Westminster. At around midnight on 4 November, 'even some twelve hours before the matter should have been put in execution', Guy Fawkes was found in the cellar with thirty-six barrels of gunpowder.[16]

The discovery of the Gunpowder Plot, as it has since become known, sent shockwaves across the kingdom and abroad. Sir Edward Hoby, who had been due to attend

Parliament, reported in alarm to his fellow diplomat in Brussels that 'at one instant and blast' the plot would have 'ruined the whole State and Kingdom of England'.[17] All the conspirators were eventually rounded up and those who were not killed in their attempt to flee met the full horrors of a traitor's death and were hanged, drawn and quartered.

The thwarting of the plot became a cause of national celebration. In January 1606, the Parliament in London passed the Observance of the Fifth of November Act, which ensured that James's English subjects would never forget how he had vanquished his enemies. Every year, special sermons were preached, church bells rung and bonfires lit. When rumours began to circulate that the plot had been a devilish conspiracy, it inspired James to introduce much harsher legislation against suspected witches, prompting a resurgence of the so-called 'witchcraze' that he had brought with him from Scotland.

Although it had been foiled, the Gunpowder Plot had seriously destabilised the Jacobean regime, ushering in a period of intense paranoia and suspicion, particularly towards Catholics. In March 1606, it was rumoured that James had been murdered on a hunting trip. 'The news spread to the city and the uproar was amazing,' reported the Venetian ambassador. 'Everyone flew to arms, the shops were shut, and cries began to be heard against Papists, foreigners and Spaniards.' Shortly afterwards, Parliament passed the 'Act for the better discovery of Popish Recusants', whereby Catholics became liable to imprisonment and forfeiture of property for refusing an oath of allegiance to the King. The plot left a deep impression on James himself. 'The King is in terror,' reported the Venetian ambassador. 'He does not appear nor does he take his meals in public as usual. He lives in the innermost rooms with only Scotsmen about him. The Lords of the Council also are alarmed and confused by the plot itself and by the King's suspicions.'[18] It had been the most salutary reminder possible that the brief flare of popularity James had enjoyed at his accession had now been all but extinguished.

By May 1606, the 'ill-humour' had soured into bitter resentment. Another Venetian envoy reported: 'The discontent has reached such a pitch that the other day there was affixed to the door of the Privy Council a general complaint of the King.' Rather than taking this as a warning to alter his behaviour, James reacted 'with some annoyance' and dismissed the complaints as 'foolish'. He had earlier baited his detractors by using hunting as a metaphor for his actions. In March 1605, he defined his kingship as the hunting of 'witches, prophets, puritans, dead cats and hares'. He gave Cecil the nickname 'my little beagle', continuing the metaphor with phrases such as the 'King's best beagle if he hunt well now in the hard ways' and 'the little beagle that lies at home by the fire'. Only Queen Anne provided anything like the glamour that had been the stock in trade of Elizabeth's magnificent court. She made Greenwich Palace and Somerset House a focus of court life, but it was one that did not include the King. By the time of her tenth and final pregnancy in 1606, she and the King were virtual strangers, occupying separate palaces and lives. One courtier observed that James 'was ever best when furthest from the Queen'.[19]

Neither did James play any significant role in the burgeoning new world of culture, science and exploration that had opened up during Elizabeth's reign. While she had patronised the likes of Shakespeare and Spenser, encouraged Raleigh, Hawkins and other 'adventurers' in their voyages and established a court that was at the forefront of artistic and scientific discovery, her successor showed no such interest. He was at best indifferent to the architectural innovations of Inigo Jones, spurned the insights of Sir Francis Bacon and William Harvey, mocked colonial exploration and fell asleep during England's most celebrated plays. In short, he was 'at heart a sixteenth-century King of Scots, ill-equipped to be a seventeenth-century King of England'.[20] The xenophobic English had been prepared to overlook James's foreignness when he came to the throne, believing he would adapt to their courtly customs. Now it was all they could see.

In a direct reversal of events leading up to his accession, Elizabeth's sun shone brightest, eclipsing that of the new king. Upon her death, there had been a palpable sense of relief that after fifty years of female sovereignty, the natural order of things had been restored and a king was on the throne once more. Now, those who had lived through her reign increasingly harked back to a halcyon time when England had enjoyed decades of peace and prosperity, triumphed over the might of Spain and had been presided over by a glorious queen and her court. A contemporary reflected that a few short years after Elizabeth's death, 'when we had experience of the Scottish government, then . . . in hate and detestation of them, the Queen did seem to revive. Then was her memory much magnified.'[21]

Soon praising the last Tudor queen became a powerful weapon for attacking the new Stuart regime. A popular saying ran: 'Rex fuit Elizabeth: nunc est regina Jacobus' ('Elizabeth was King: now James is Queen'). The origin of the epigram has never been identified but it was the most damning of all the comparisons between the two sovereigns – not to mention the most overt reference to the King's sexuality.[22] It is ironic that the greatest perceived advantage James had enjoyed over Elizabeth was his masculine gender; now even that had been called into question.

Determined to stamp out such reverence for the late queen, James brought to an abrupt end the long-standing celebration of Elizabeth's accession day. As Camden later recorded, in every year of her reign, 'all good men, throughout England, on November 17th, joyfully triumphed, with thanksgivings, sermons in churches, multiplied prayers, joyful ringing of bells, running at tilt, and festival mirth . . . which, in testimony of their affectionate love towards her, they never ceased to observe as long as she lived'. The King ordered that such festivities be replaced with services of thanksgiving, tournaments and banquets to mark his own accession. But the new monarch could not eclipse the hallowed memory of the old for long. By 1610, Elizabeth's accession day celebrations had been revived.[23]

In March 1608, James completed his fifth year as King of England, long enough to bring the kingdom firmly under his control. Elizabeth had faced far greater obstacles when establishing her sovereignty half a century earlier, not least the widespread prejudice against female rulers and the fact that she was, technically, illegitimate. By contrast, in 1603 England had rejoiced at the natural order of things being restored by having a king on the throne at last. James had cultivated many friends south of the border during his years as heir presumptive and they had helped smooth the path for his succession. Yet in a bewilderingly short space of time, a seismic shift had occurred in both the kingdom and the monarchy of England, which in turn had bred opposition. The Gunpowder Plot was far from an isolated scheme by a gang of harebrained radicals; it betrayed a deep-seated resentment against a king who was struggling to hold on to his throne.

More ominous still for the new king was that people were beginning to question his right to Gloriana's crown. Throughout her reign, Elizabeth had been deliberately vague about the succession. It had suited those in favour of the

Stuarts to post-rationalise James's accession as a foregone conclusion, but now even they were beginning to wonder whether in fact the Tudor queen had had someone else in mind. There were even whispers that the King was the bastard son of Mary, Queen of Scots and her lover, David Riccio, and that his own son and heir Prince Henry was the result of an adulterous affair by Queen Anne. James was swift to take action against such 'villainous speeches'.[24]

James was now served an uncomfortable reminder of the fundamental fragility of his claim. Edward Seymour, first Earl of Hertford, had declared his recognition of the new king as soon as Elizabeth died. He had been rewarded with offices, lands and even a diplomatic post as ambassador-extraordinary to Brussels, where he had responsibility for ratifying the 1604 Anglo-Spanish treaty. But James's generosity towards his former rival reached its limits when in 1607 Hertford began legal proceedings to have his eldest son Edward, Lord Beauchamp, declared legitimate. Although the King agreed to give Beauchamp and his heirs the right to inherit the title Earl of Hertford, he steadfastly refused to overturn the bastardy judgment. Even as late as 1621, the year of Hertford's death, James was reported to have attempted to obtain a parliamentary declaration that the earl's two sons were illegitimate. By then, both were dead.

James found that, in the words of Shakespeare, his head lay 'uneasy' now that it bore the crown of England. Driven by the need to reinforce his kingship, in 1608 he published *An Apologie for the Oath of Allegiance*. This sought to justify his recent controversial decision to force all his subjects, Catholic and Protestant alike, to take an oath recognising him as their rightful king and denying the power of the Pope. It achieved little but to draw attention to a controversy that was best forgotten, and even the King's supporters in government 'wished that he had not printed' the book. They quickly dissuaded him from embarking on another that he was planning, to refute the tract of Robert Persons that had been published in Elizabeth's reign, calling into question his right to her throne.[25] He did, though, give his assent to an important legal measure, passed the same year as his *Apologie* was published, which established that a child born in Scotland after James's accession to the throne of England in 1603 was considered under the common law to be an English subject and therefore entitled to own or inherit lands there.[26] This was a significant move, given that one of the prickliest objections to James's accession had been his alien status.

Before 1608 was out, James made one further attempt to ensure that England would at last come to view him as the rightful king. If his new subjects would not believe his words, then perhaps they would give more credence to those of an Englishman. William Camden was an esteemed scholar and antiquarian, widely regarded as the founder of modern historical research and writing. His first major work, *Britannia*, a topographical and historical survey of Great Britain and Ireland, had been published to great acclaim in 1586. As headmaster of Westminster School and Clarenceux King of Arms (a distinguished ceremonial office which included responsibility for heraldic and genealogical records), Camden was a prominent public figure and a product of the Elizabethan age. He had been educated in institutions shaped by the late queen's conception of reform and by influential patrons close to her who embodied the same religious, political and humanist vision as their royal mistress.

Principal among them had been Elizabeth's longest-serving and most trusted adviser, Lord Burghley. In 1596, two years before his death, he asked Camden to write a history of Elizabeth's reign, expressing 'a desire to eternise the memory of that renowned queen' before it was too late.[27] But, great statesman that he was, Burghley wanted a true record rather than a mere propaganda piece. He therefore provided Camden with many of his own private papers and records from the Queen's archives, as well as access to the unparalleled library of Sir Robert Cotton, a close acquaintance and former pupil of Camden, whose collection included numerous priceless manuscripts dating back to the eighth century. All of this, together with Camden's personal experience of Elizabeth's court, made him ideally placed to write a history of her reign.

However, it was not a commission that Camden had embraced with any enthusiasm. Such a task was 'far from my thought', as he admitted in his prefatory note to the reader. He was daunted by what he described as the 'piles and heaps of papers and writings of all sorts' that had been placed at his disposal and made only a faltering start during Elizabeth's lifetime. 'I laboured till I sweat again, covered all over with dust, to gather fit matter together . . . my industry began to flag and wax cold in the business.'[28] Her death gave him the perfect excuse to put it aside, hoping that someone else might take over or that the project would be quietly forgotten. Aside from the herculean task of sifting through the voluminous archival material, writing a history of the late queen now that a new king – a new dynasty – occupied the English throne was fraught with political sensitivities. As Clarenceux, he was a servant to this king, which presented a challenge to his integrity as a historian.

When he heard about Camden's *Annales*, the King spied an opportunity. To have a published account of Elizabeth's reign – and in particular the succession – written by one of the most esteemed historians of the age would help silence any whispers of usurpation, if of course the author was prepared to write it to the King's satisfaction. James had no scruple in

censoring his people and had sent writers to prison for offending him. Even his most powerful advisers self-censored their
writing for fear of angering him. Henry Howard, Earl of
Northampton, who wrote an account of the Gunpowder Plot
a few months after it was foiled, took care to show a copy to
the King before it was published. James had seemed pleased
with it at first, but just as it was about to go to the printer,
Howard received an order to make some amendments. He
became so panic-stricken that in a letter to his friend Robert
Cotton, he urged: 'Copy the words but burn this paper.'[29]

Camden thus had good reason to express reluctance when
James approached him to restart his history of Elizabeth. It
was the very definition of a poisoned chalice and Camden
tried everything to avoid drinking from it. But the King gave
him no choice. At his command work on the book was resumed
in 1608. Camden was his subject to command and the succession was his to rewrite.

CHAPTER 16

'WITHOUT MATE AND WITHOUT ESTATE'

In 1607, the Venetian envoy provided an appraisal of the woman who might have been Queen of England:

> The nearest relative the King has is Madame Arabella, descended from Margaret, daughter of Henry VII, which makes her cousin to the King. She is twenty-eight [she was actually thirty-two]; not very beautiful, but highly accomplished, for besides being of most refined manners she speaks fluently Latin, Italian, French, Spanish, reads Greek and Hebrew, and is always studying. She is not very rich, for the late Queen was jealous of everyone, and especially of those who had a claim on the throne, and so she took from her the larger part of her income, and the poor lady cannot live as magnificently nor reward her attendants as liberally as she would. The King professes to love her and to hold her in high esteem. She is allowed to come to Court, and the King promised, when he ascended the throne, that he would restore her property, but he has not done so yet, saying that she shall have it all and more on her marriage, but so far the husband has not been found, and she remains without mate and without estate.[1]

In 1608, Arbella's indomitable grandmother Bess died. Although she had removed Arbella from her will after her failed escape from Hardwick, the countess relented at the end

and left her a thousand pounds. Arbella went back to the place
of her former confinement in early 1609 and spent time with
her Talbot relations. She subsequently used some of her inheritance to purchase a house for herself in London's Blackfriars,
away from the prying eyes of the court. At Christmas, she was
struck down with smallpox, the disease that had almost
claimed the life of the late queen. Like Elizabeth, she survived,
but it served as a salutary reminder of her mortality. Now
aged thirty-four, she was resolved to settle the issue of her
marriage once and for all. The bitter realisation that the King
was no more minded to find her a husband than his predecessor spurred Arbella on to secure one for herself. By now, she
was deeply embittered against her Stuart cousin for treating
her less as the second lady of England and more as a poor
relation.

At the same time, the old rumours that Arbella had
converted to Catholicism resurfaced. To these were added
new ones, including that she planned to cross the seas and
marry a Scot named Douglas or Stephano Janiculo, the
pretender to the throne of Moldavia. Such was James's suspicion of his 'near kinswoman' that in early 1610 Arbella was
ordered by the King and his council to answer the rumours, in
particular that she planned to marry a foreign royal 'who
might in her name lay claim to the crown of England'. 'She
would neither affirm nor deny that she had thought of leaving
the kingdom,' reported the Venetian ambassador. 'She merely
said that, ill-treated as she was by all, it was only natural that
she should think of going.' To appease his troublesome cousin,
James gave her a gift of plate and money that New Year and
increased her pension. But it was a fraction of the huge sums
that he lavished on his favourites and hardly enough to secure
Arbella's loyalty. In one of her letters to the court, Arbella later
made the unlikely claim that at this time the King had given

her something altogether more valuable: permission to choose as husband any subject in the realm.[2]

Arbella returned once more to the idea of marrying a member of the Seymour family. This time her choice was William, the grandson of Lady Katherine Grey, whose elder brother Edward she had plotted to marry in the closing months of Elizabeth's reign. Aged twenty-two, he was thirteen years younger than Arbella. He was also impressionable and eager for advancement, so ignored King James's specific command that he and Arbella must have nothing to do with each other. According to William's own testimony, given when the privy council's suspicions were alerted, he 'boldly intruded' himself into Arbella's chamber and announced that he desired to marry her, claiming that he believed the King had given her permission to marry any subject in the land. Besides, he was merely 'a younger brother . . . unknown to the world, of mean estate, not born to challenge anything by my birthright . . . and she a lady of great honour and virtue and as I thought of great means'.[3] The idea of securing what he falsely assumed to be a considerable fortune evidently made marriage to a much older woman more enticing. They met twice a week after William declared his intentions and agreed to marry, but Seymour insisted in his testimony that he had intended to seek James's permission. Although the specific dates are not mentioned, it is possible that their union had been planned for several months, given that Arbella had been making a concerted effort to pay her debts and had been looking for a country home away from court.

News of the intended nuptials soon reached the King's ears and he ordered the couple to appear before the privy council, where they were instructed to abandon their marriage plans. Arbella protested 'that seeing herself deserted she had imagined that she could not be accused if she sought a husband of her own rank', to which James responded that she could marry anyone of whom he approved.[4] As an assurance of his continued favour, he invited her to the reception of the Prince of Württemberg, where she was seated under the golden cloth canopy with the royal family. She was given a similarly prominent position at the installation of the King's eldest son Henry as Prince of Wales in early June and danced in a celebratory masque.

But Arbella's compliance would not be so easily bought. At midnight on 21 June 1610, she and Seymour slipped out of the royal court and into a waiting boat. A servant then rowed them down the Thames to Greenwich Palace. There, at four o'clock the following morning, they were married in Arbella's apartments at Greenwich Palace. Despite the hour, not to mention the risks since an unauthorised marriage between blood claimants was treason, they had enlisted enough friends and attendants to witness the ceremony so that the legitimacy of their marriage could not be challenged, as that of Seymour's grandparents had been.

Their union was discovered a little over two weeks later. The timing could not have been worse. The King was still smarting from his Parliament's intractability. In a two-hour speech delivered on 21 March, he had berated the assembled dignitaries: 'The state of monarchy is the supremist thing upon earth . . . Kings are justly called gods, for that they exercise a manner of resemblance of divine power upon earth . . . They make and unmake their subjects, they have power of raising and casting down, of life and death, judges over all their subjects and in all causes and yet accountable to none but God only.'[5] His speech had been coldly received and weeks of protracted and increasingly ill-tempered debates had followed. James was also badly shaken by news of the French king Henry IV's assassination in May that year, when he was stabbed by a Catholic zealot while riding in a carriage through the streets of Paris. In early June, just days before Arbella's secret marriage, James had ordered his subjects to take the oath of allegiance. Clearly no mercy would be shown for the newlyweds.

On 8 and 9 July, the couple were interrogated and swiftly imprisoned. Seymour was sent to the Tower, while Arbella was confined at the Lambeth home of Sir Thomas Parry, a member of the King's privy council. Whilst there, in September she suffered what seems to have been a miscarriage. Upon hearing of this, James told Arbella that her husband would be imprisoned in the Tower for life and that she would be exiled to Durham. He wrote to the bishop there: 'Our cousin the Lady Arbella hath highly offended us in seeking to match herself without our knowledge (to whom she had the honour to be so near in blood) and in proceeding afterwards to a full conclusion of a marriage with the self same person whom, for many just causes, we had expressly forbidden to marry.' This 'indignity' had made him resolved to 'make others know, by her example, that no respect of personal affection can make us neglect those considerations wherein both the honour and order of our government is interested'. He therefore asked the bishop to take custody of Arbella – which, he added, was a far more lenient punishment than her 'disobedience and ingratitude' deserved.[6]

The King's choice of Durham was deliberate: not only did it get Arbella well away from London, but he clearly hoped that the bishop would instruct her in 'religion and virtue', eradicating any hint of the Catholicism with which she had dallied. The Venetian ambassador shrewdly observed that this exile was also born of the King's fear that his rival might attract dangerous supporters and wished 'to secure himself against dissatisfaction settling around her'. Dudley Carleton's response was typical of the misogynistic judgements on the controversy. 'I should tell you some news of a secret marriage

betwixt my Lord Beauchamp's younger son and the Lady
Arbella,' he told the English ambassador in Paris, 'for which
the poor gentleman does penance in the Tower, and the lady's
hot blood that could not live without a husband must be
cooled in some remote place in the country.'[7]

But illness – feigned or genuine – delayed Arbella's departure, and when she and her entourage finally set out in mid-
March 1611, they only reached as far as Barnet, just north of
London, before Arbella again pleaded ill health and the journey was halted. The records suggest that her husband was
able to join her there: a document dated 21 March was jointly
signed and sealed by them. Irritated by the further delay, the
King sent a physician to examine his cousin. The prognosis
was that while Arbella showed no physical signs of illness, she
was too weak to travel, so James reluctantly granted her a
month's rest. This was subsequently extended to early June.

On 3 June 1611, two days before she was due to set out for
the north, Arbella disguised herself in men's clothes, complete
with wig, hat, boots and rapier, and escaped her captors. At
the same time, her husband donned a disguise and once more
slipped out of the Tower. Arbella's aunt, Mary Talbot, Countess
of Shrewsbury, had helped fund the enterprise by purchasing
from Arbella the needlework panels stitched by Mary, Queen
of Scots during her imprisonment in the north. Arbella had
arranged to meet her husband at Blackwall, a port on the
Thames east of London, from where they would board a ship
bound for France. But when he failed to appear, her servants
persuaded her to set sail without him. Still hoping that William
might catch up with them, she insisted on lingering in the
Channel. The delay proved fatal: her ship was intercepted by
an English naval vessel. In a cruel twist of fate, her husband,
who had managed to escape and board another ship, made it
safely across the Channel to Ostend.

While Seymour was allowed his liberty, there would be no such clemency for Arbella. She was taken straight to the Tower. Although she was never formally charged with a crime, James issued a proclamation that referred to her 'divers great and heinous offences'. These were later defined by Francis Bacon as having married 'without acquainting his Majesty', choosing an inappropriate partner and fleeing the King's power. He opined: 'Being to our Sovereign, and she standing so near to his Majesty as she does, and then choosing such a condition as it pleased her to choose . . . it was not unlike the case of Mr Seymour's grandmother [Katherine Grey] . . . For although my lady [Arbella] should have put on a mind to continue her loyalty, as nature and duty did bind her; yet when she was in another sphere, she must have moved in the motion of that orb, and not of the planet itself.' James himself hammered home the point: 'She did match with one of the blood royal who was descended from Henry the Seventh, so that by this match there was a combination of titles, which princes have ever been jealous of.'[8]

The King ordered that his cousin should not 'rule her life after her own caprice' and privately replied to her petition for mercy with a sharp reprimand for having 'eaten of the forbidden tree'. The Venetian ambassador reported that Arbella's marriage was tantamount to 'rebellion', but most other commentators shared the King's view that she was an unruly woman who had 'touched pleasures in order to transgress'.[9]

While James's Scottish attendants 'aggravate the offence in so strange a manner, as that it might be compared to the [Gun] Powder Treason', his English advisers saw little danger in the mésalliance. One foreign diplomat claimed: 'There are many in this city of London who heartily deplore her unhappy case.' Another agreed: 'From the least to the greatest, everyone rejoiced over this escape and showed so great an affection to the Lady

Arbella that it nearly surpassed convenience.' Even Queen Anne
was sympathetic. But an anonymous treatise published in
Hanover the following year defended the King's harsh treatment
of his cousin. It asserted that he had merely upheld the policy of
the late queen, who had 'a womanish fear' of seeing her power
diminished if Arbella married and had children.[10]

Arbella sent a flurry of appeals to the King, declaring herself
'the most wretched and unfortunate creature that ever lived
[who] prostrates itself at the feet of the most merciful King
that ever was, desiring nothing but mercy and favour, not
being more afflicted for anything than for the loss of that
which hath been this long time the only comfort it had in the
world'. In a letter to her brother-in-law, Francis Seymour, she
lamented their royal blood: 'I must confess I fear the destiny
of your house and my own, both which have fared the worse
for being subject to that star.' Arbella's husband, who lived
mainly in Paris, converted to Roman Catholicism in 1611,
perhaps in the hope of attracting Catholic support for their
cause. In response, the King sent him an allowance of £400
per year, together with instructions to stay away from Catholic
strongholds. There were reports that, far from being appeased,
Seymour complained that such a sum was hardly enough to
sustain a prince of England.[11] There were rumours, too, that
he was plotting to help his wife escape from the Tower and
that she was scheming to smuggle him into it so that they
could live as man and wife, in a disturbing echo of Seymour's
grandparents, who had conceived a child in the fortress. At
the same time, Arbella's aunt, Mary Talbot, was accused by
the King's officials of planning to free her from the Tower.
There was also talk of a Roman Catholic plot to break Arbella
out. Such rumours probably owed more to the febrile atmosphere in the court than to any real danger.

Perhaps to distract himself or his subjects from the controversy, James decided to make a public (if rather belated) show of filial duty to his late mother. On 28 September 1612 he wrote to the Dean and Chapter of Peterborough Cathedral, explaining that 'the duty we owe to our dearest mother that like honour should be done to her body and like monument be extant of her as to others her and our progenitors have been used to be done, and ourselves have already performed to our dear sister, the late Queen Elizabeth'. He instructed the Dean to make arrangements for his mother's body to be removed from Peterborough 'in as decent and respectful manner as is fitting' and taken to Westminster Abbey, 'the place where the kings and queens of this realm are usually interred'.[12] Six years earlier, he had commissioned a magnificent tomb for the fallen Queen of Scots, which was now ready to receive her mortal remains.

On 11 October, Mary's coffin was interred in the new tomb, which was situated in the south aisle of the Lady Chapel. On top was a fine white marble effigy showing the Queen of Scots in a close-fitting coif, laced ruff and long mantle fastened with a brooch. At her feet was a crowned Scottish lion and above her stretched an elaborate marble canopy. The striking composition outshone the tomb that James had commissioned for her rival Elizabeth and also stood taller – which was, of course, the point. A lengthy Latin inscription celebrated the life and lineage of 'the best and greatest' of queens, 'sure and certain heiress to the crown of England while she lived: mother of James, most puissant sovereign of Great Britain'. The point was made again later in the inscription, when Mary was described as 'Mistress of Scotland by law, of France by marriage, of England by expectation, thus blest, by a three-fold right, with a three-fold crown'. Elizabeth, of course, had been queen of England alone.[13] The inscription went on to lambast the 'faint-hearted and crafty devices of her mortal enemies', whom she had fought 'courageously and vigorously' before being 'struck down by the axe (an unheard-of precedent, outrageous to royalty)'. Her son James, it declared, was 'the hope of a kingdom and posterity'.

Barely a month after this ostentatious show of grief for his long-dead mother, James was plunged into more sincere mourning by the sudden death of his eldest son. Prince Henry was just eighteen when he died from typhoid fever on 6 November 1612. A popular and accomplished young man, he had been the hope of the nation and even those who resented the Stuart king had looked forward to seeing his son on the throne. Now James's only male heir was his son Charles, who at almost ten years old lacked the physical prowess and princely accomplishments of his elder brother. Wasting no time, the King immediately began to instruct his new heir in every aspect of monarchy. Francis Bacon enthused that he was 'the best tutor in Europe'.[14] Charles later gained practical experience, too, accompanying his father on state visits and progresses, and playing an active role in government.

But what James pointedly omitted from his son's training as a future king was any of the advice that Elizabeth had given him during their thirty-year correspondence. Her numerous letters had served as a manual on English monarchy, encompassing everything from how to work with Parliament to the art of courting the people's love and respect through magnificent public appearances. James himself had paid only lip service to such invaluable insights and clearly had no intention of passing them on to his son. Charles would be a king in the mould of his Stuart father, not his Tudor predecessor.

A year after Prince Henry's death, Shakespeare published his history play: *Henry VIII*. As well as charting the tumultuous reign of the late queen's father, it presented James's accession as a natural and peaceful transfer of power. In the final act, Thomas Cranmer, Henry's Archbishop of Canterbury, prophesied the Elizabethan succession:

> ... as when
> The bird of wonder dies, the maiden phoenix,
> Her ashes new create another heir
> As great in admiration as herself,
> So shall she leave her blessedness to one –
> When heaven shall call her from this cloud of darkness –
> Who from the sacred ashes of her honour
> Shall star-like rise, as great in fame as she was,
> And so stand fix'd. Peace, plenty, love, truth, terror,
> That were the servants of this chosen infant,
> Shall then be his, and like a vine grow to him;
> Wherever the bright sun of heaven shall shine,
> His honour and the greatness of his name
> Shall be and make new nations.[15]

With this optimistic speech, Shakespeare tried to convince his audience that their king would equal the achievements of his predecessor. But during the ten years since Elizabeth's death, James's rise had been far from 'star-like', his 'fame' a poor imitation of hers. Not even the playwright's eloquent prose could make them believe this would ever change.

By 1614, the King was facing mounting opposition. Parliament objected to his persistent infringement upon its authority and some of its members dared to argue that he was a king by 'election' rather than 'blood' 'because in passing from Scotland to England he was called and to some extent chosen'.[16] The implication was clear: a ruler who had been selected might just as easily be unselected.

CHAPTER 17

'FACTS ARE FACTS'

In 1615, seven years after the King had ordered him to take up his quill again, the first instalment of William Camden's *Annales Rerum Anglicarum et Hibernicarum Regnante Elizabetha* (*Annales of English and Irish Affairs in the Reign of Elizabeth*) was published in Latin. The original commission had been daunting enough, but it seems that shortly after resuming work at the King's command, Camden had been presented with the unenviable task of rewriting history not just for James's subjects but for an international audience.

In 1604, a French historian named Jacques Auguste de Thou had published a critical account of Mary, Queen of Scots in his *Universal History*. It was heavily based on the *History of Scotland* by James's old tutor, George Buchanan, who had pilloried Mary as a murderous, immoral tyrant. De Thou had begun corresponding with Camden in 1605 and had confided to him the difficulty he faced in writing a history of Scotland during the 1560s, when James's mother had held and lost the throne before fleeing to England. James had been so affronted upon reading de Thou's finished work that he had persuaded him, via an intermediary (Isaac Casaubon, a French scholar who moved to England in 1610) to change it. De Thou protested that he could only write history based on the sources available to him. As he told Camden: 'Facts are facts and an honest man cannot conceal them.'¹ Those words would come back to haunt Camden in the years that followed.

Undeterred by de Thou's initial resistance, James promised to provide him with a more accurate historical account than Buchanan's so that he could set to work. In February 1611, he enlisted Sir Robert Cotton to arrange this, aware that he had been supplying material for Camden's *Annales* for a number of years. In a letter to an acquaintance, John Chamberlain made it clear just how closely the two men collaborated: '[A] good part of Queen Elizabeth's life, collected with the help of Sir Robert Cotton and written by Clarenceux [Camden]' had been completed in the space of just three months.²

The King demanded to see the draft account before a copy was sent to France. It was with great reluctance that Camden handed it over, protesting that it was still rough and unfinished. Clearly it was not complimentary enough to Mary for her son's liking. When the manuscript was returned, Camden was aghast to see it 'full of mutilations and gaps and certain words had been effaced by the effrontery of the copyist'. James's hand can clearly be seen in the work: a set of notes he dictated relating to events in 1564 were among the first ten volumes that were sent to Paris. Reluctant to bow to this political pressure, de Thou protested that he could not revise his history until he received the rest of Camden's notes. Later, when he tried to contact Camden directly, James stepped in to prevent it. A further ten volumes, heavily corrected by the King, were dispatched to the French historian in December 1611.³

With the King breathing down his neck, Camden might have been forgiven for writing a sanitised version of events, bending the truth to suit the new regime without discrediting the old. But having cut his teeth at Oxford before being appointed Master of Westminster School, one of the most prestigious academic institutions in the country, he was a historian of integrity and utterly meticulous in his research. He had spent years travelling extensively in pursuit of topographical and antiquarian information for *Britannia*, determined to base it on primary materials rather than his own pontifications.

Much of the seven years it took Camden to complete the first instalment of the *Annales* was taken up with sifting through the voluminous papers to which he had exclusive access. But he was also distracted by his duties as Clarenceux and by other literary projects, including persistent requests to supply the outstanding material for de Thou. Camden was also slowed down by bouts of ill health. He had only recently begun work on the book when he was taken seriously ill on his birthday, 2 May 1609, an illness that laid him low until the following October. Stress may have been a contributory factor. It is clear from Camden's correspondence how keenly he felt the difficulty of his position.[4]

While Camden wrote numerous drafts for almost every year of Elizabeth's reign, his original manuscript contains only one version of 1587, the year of Mary's execution. Given how he agonised over even the most trivial of details, it is likely that he made a significant number of drafts of this most highly sensitive of events and that they were quietly destroyed, either by Camden himself or perhaps at the King's orders.

Not surprisingly, the *Annales*, in contrast to almost all the contemporary sources, depicted James's reaction to his mother's downfall in an entirely positive light. Whereas at the time he had been criticised for his lukewarm efforts to save the doomed queen, Camden cast him as 'a most dutiful and pious son, and a prudent king', who 'laboured all that possibly he could . . . to save her life'. He laid the blame for James's failure to achieve this on the faction-ridden Scots, most of whom 'favoured Queen Elizabeth [rather] than the captive Queen', as well as the Scottish ministers, who ignored the King's command 'to recommend his mother's preservation to God in their prayers'.[5]

As well as exonerating the King of blame for his mother's downfall, Camden's account clearly tried to eradicate any doubt that her treason invalidated James's claim to the English throne. He told how on the same day that a guilty verdict was returned against Mary, a declaration was published by the commissioners and judges at her trial: 'That the sentence did nothing to derogate from the King of Scots in his title or honour, but that he was in the same place, degree and right, as if the said sentence had never been pronounced.' To hammer home the point that James's mother might have been a traitor to the English throne but his claim to it still stood, Camden quoted from one of the numerous letters and messages that he claimed James had sent to England: 'That it was a great injustice and indignity, that the nobility, council and subject of England should give sentence against a Queen of Scots, that was also descended of the Blood Royal of England: and no less injustice to think that the Estates of England can by authority of Parliament exclude the true and undoubted heirs from their reign of succession and lawful inheritance.'[6]

The *Annales* blamed Elizabeth's part in Mary's execution on her sex. 'She, being a woman naturally slow in her resolutions, began to consider in her mind, whether it were better to put her to death or to spare her.' The book went on to claim that she was panicked by scaremongers at court who spread rumours that the Spanish or Scottish were about to invade, that the Queen of Scots had escaped and raised an army, that the north of England had risen in rebellion, and that there was a new conspiracy to murder Elizabeth and set London ablaze. The Queen's courtiers, the *Annales* said, piled on the pressure, arguing that if she flinched from putting Mary to death, then she herself would be destroyed. Camden then took up Elizabeth's own version of events, whereby she signed Mary's death warrant but it was carried out without her authorisation.

Having thus excused Elizabeth for the part she played in Mary's death, Camden praised the latter's courage as she faced her execution. Omitting any reference to 'borrowed hair' or rounded shoulders, his account described her 'state, countenance and presence' as 'majestically composed, a cheerful look, and matron-like and modest habit'. Camden then recorded the speech that Mary gave before she met her death. It is similar to the contemporary account made by or for the official who presided over the execution, but with some notable embellishments. Camden put these words into her mouth: 'Admonish him [James] to hold in amity and friendship with the Queen of England.' The idea that James was so quick to forgive Elizabeth because he was obeying his mother's dying wish was a clever way of explaining away something for which he had been heavily criticised on both sides of the Scottish border. Camden also made sure to ramp up the King of Scots' anguish and fury upon hearing of Mary's execution. For good measure, he added that, to help secure James's forgiveness, Elizabeth affirmed: 'That the said sentence against his mother would not in the least hurt or prejudice his title to the succession.'[7]

Glossing over the horribly botched beheading, Camden went on to remind his readers of Mary's virtues – and, more to the point, how closely bound she was by blood to the English throne: 'Daughter to James the Fifth King of Scots, great-grand-daughter to Henry the Seventh King of England by his eldest Daughter' – this last point a deliberate sideswipe at the Greys, who were descended from Henry VII's younger daughter. Camden quoted in full an epitaph that he claimed had been set up close to her tomb in Peterborough but 'soon after taken away'. This was similar to the epitaph that James ordered when he moved his mother's remains to the new tomb in Westminster Abbey, but as that did not happen until long after Elizabeth's reign, Camden could not include it in his history. Camden therefore might have invented the Peterborough epitaph as a way of reminding his readers of Mary's lineage. It described her as: 'A King's daughter, the King of France his widow, the Queen of England's kinswoman and next heir'.[8]

Camden concluded his account of the King's mother by stressing the virtues and hopes she had in common with her cousin Elizabeth, most notably the succession of Mary's son to the English throne:

> Those things which both the Queens, Elizabeth and Mary, most of all desired, and in all their councils propounded to themselves, were hereby attained. Queen Mary (as she said just before her death) desired nothing more ardently, than that the divided kingdoms of England and Scotland might be united in the person of her dear son: and there was nothing which Queen Elizabeth wished for more earnestly, than that the true religion might be preserved in England together with the safety and security of the people. And that the high and great God granted them both their prayers England now seeth with unexpected felicity, and most joyfully acknowledge the same.[9]

It was a masterly reworking of history that swept away the bitter rivalry between two queens whose personalities, ideology and outlook could not have been more different. With the deft stroke of Camden's quill, they were forever united in their shared, posthumous joy at James's accession.

The 4,000 or so pages of Camden's original handwritten draft of his *Annales* were bound in ten volumes and still survive in the collections of the British Library.[10] It is immediately obvious how much they were amended prior to publication: almost every page is littered with crossings-out and interlineations as Camden tried to walk the precarious line between historical truth and kingly approval. Historians have known about the manuscript for many years, but until recently little research has been done on it. This is in marked contrast to the published *Annales*, which formed the bedrock of the historiography of Elizabeth's reign and has been widely quoted ever since it appeared in 1615.

But recent research led by the British Library has uncovered some startling revelations about Camden's original work. In addition to the numerous amendments that can be read with the naked eye, no fewer than two hundred pages have been pasted in, sixty-five of which replaced original text with a new version. Imaging technology has been used to reveal the words that lie beneath.[11] Most of the concealed text concerns only the tiniest points of detail – the number of horses in a battle, for example. But a small number of the original pages hide material that challenges the version of Elizabeth's history – and the succession – that has endured for the past four centuries.

The first passage that was pasted over concerns Elizabeth's excommunication by Pope Pius V in 1570. The bull had revived the doubts over Elizabeth's legitimacy that had been voiced at her accession by calling her 'the pretended Queen of England' and encouraging her Catholic subjects to rise up against her. The timing was significant: Pius was trying to capitalise on the discontent caused by the arrival of Mary, Queen of Scots into England, as well as the rebellion led by a group of Catholic lords in 1569. In his original text, Camden had planned to merely summarise the bull of excommunication, but the later addition provides a full transcript. It also stated that Pius was creating 'secret plots' and waging 'spiritual warfare' against Elizabeth. The revised version might have been prompted by James's wish to revive fears of papist conspiracies, which had begun to wane during the years following his narrow escape from a Catholic plot to blow him and his Parliament to the heavens.

There are two important changes to Camden's original text for the year 1598. The first concerns the death of Philip II of Spain. He had been a thorn in Elizabeth's side for forty years. Previously married to her half-sister Mary, he had proposed marriage to Elizabeth shortly after her accession. When she refused, he swiftly turned from appeasement to aggression and tried repeatedly to wrest the throne from Elizabeth's grasp, either by supporting plots against her or by launching invasions – notably the Armada of 1588. Again, Camden's prejudice against Elizabeth's enemies shows through in his original draft, which scorned her arch-rival as having 'no imperial skills'. He also claimed that Philip died of phthiriasis, a gruesome disease where parasites multiply in the human body, which was seen as a divine punishment from God. Having made peace with Spain a year after coming to the English throne, James was anxious not to cause offence, so it is no surprise that Camden's original text was replaced with a less damning assessment of Philip.

Not wishing to upset the King's Spanish ally was one thing, but the new analysis of Camden's original manuscript reveals that he was also obliged to conceal the truth behind a much darker chapter of Elizabeth's reign. The Valentine Thomas controversy, which implicated James in a plot to assassinate Elizabeth, had finally died down after the King ordered his execution shortly after inheriting the English crown. But with access to the late queen's secret correspondence, Camden seemed determined to reignite it. He recorded every detail of the assassination plot in characteristically meticulous detail. Although he stopped short of accusing James of involvement, merely presenting such detail would have been enough to set tongues wagging. Under pressure from James, however, he was obliged to paste over his original draft. The final version contains no mention of assassination, only that Thomas 'had accused the King of Scots with ill affection towards the Queen'. The fact that James went to such trouble to recast one of the most damaging episodes of his reign in a more favour-able light invites greater suspicion than Camden's original draft could ever have done.

Camden noted that in the wake of the controversy, James tried to 'disperse the rumour' by encouraging 'many men' in England and Ireland 'to preach his constancy in religion, his wisdom, his justice, his mercy, and the rest of his princely virtues; thereby to draw the minds of the commonalty to better persuasion of him'. The King also encouraged his supporters to write and distribute books 'that maintained his right of succession to the realm of England; and also to inform them, that the admittance of him would be beneficial to both kingdoms, and far more good than any other's intrusion'. Camden then quoted the reasons that James gave for his supe-rior claim, notably: 'That he relies upon excellent right thereto; that he is a King; that by joining both kingdoms, which hath been so long desired, he will much increase the glory of both.'[12] All this made it into the published version of the book. James evidently did not realise that instead of defending his position, it read as protesting too much.

No doubt at the King's prompting, Camden also dismissed the rumours that had abounded in the white heat of the Valentine Thomas controversy that James was secretly plotting with Catholics. 'About this time [1598] certain idle lewd fellows there were, I know not of what shop, to whom it was as good as a reward to disrupt the quiet peace. These men, to the end to break off by secret and wicked practices the amity betwixt the Queen and the King of Scots, spread rumours abroad that he inclined to the Papist's faction, and was of a most averse mind from the Queen.' Camden would have had access to ample material that supported these rumours, including letters from Robert Cecil's agents abroad. In May 1599, for example, John Petit had reported that 'for a kingdom' the Scottish king would 'become a counterfeit Catholic, like the King of France'. Three months later, another informant relayed a rumour 'that the King of Scots is in arms with 40,000 men to invade England, and the Spaniard comes to settle the King of Scots in this realm'.[13] All this, Camden was obliged to quietly ignore.

The most significant rewriting of all, though, concerned the succession. Here, Camden was not simply softening or rephrasing his original language; he invented an entirely fictional account. There is no pasting over: Camden's narrative of how Elizabeth named James her heir is written – and rewritten – in plain sight, albeit with numerous crossings-out and interlineations. Although he scribbled a few amendments, the draft is in a different hand to Camden's, which suggests that he could not bring himself to falsify such a pivotal moment in Elizabeth's reign – one that would have far-reaching consequences in the years that followed. It was almost certainly written by his friend Cotton, who had penned a near-identical account of his own.[14]

The *Annales* puts the lie that Elizabeth had appointed James as her successor onto the lips of her close kinsman and adviser, Charles Howard, Earl of Nottingham. It states that shortly before setting out for Richmond Palace in late January 1603,

Elizabeth told the earl: 'My throne is a throne of kings, neither ought any but my next heir to succeed me.' Nottingham wasted no time in relaying this to his fellow ministers. 'The Lord Admiral telling the rest of the Council what the Queen departing from Westminster spoke by the way concerning her Successor: it seemed good to them that he, the Lord Keeper, and the Secretary should go to her, and recall it to her mind again, signifying that the intent of their coming was to understand her pleasure for her Successor.'

The account goes on to say that on 22 March 1603, as the Queen lay close to death, Nottingham urged her to avoid any ambiguity from her 'dark speech' and to repeat to Cecil and Thomas Egerton, the Lord High Chancellor, what she had told him at Westminster. 'I told you my seat had been the seat of kings,' she declared. 'I do not want a lowly one to succeed me.' This is similar to Ambassador Beaumont's report, written a few days after Elizabeth's death, that she had declared she would have no 'rascals' to succeed her, which was understood to be a reference to the Grey descendants. Camden related how Elizabeth then insisted: 'I will that a King succeed me, and what King, but my nearest Kinsman the King of Scots?' Wanting to make completely sure of the case, Cecil asked whether that was her 'absolute resolution', to which she irritably retorted: 'I pray you trouble me no more, I'll have none but him.'[15]

Upon these few fabricated words the entire Stuart succession would rest – and, thereby, that of every related British royal dynasty that followed: the Hanoverians, the Saxe-Coburgs, all the way up to the modern-day Windsors. Camden's lie, likely supplied by his friend Cotton, would cast a web so tangled that it would only be unpicked four hundred years later.

The *Annales* went on to describe how, seeing herself deserted by courtiers who before had pledged undying devotion but now 'curried favour already with the King of Scotland', Elizabeth lapsed into a deep melancholy. 'These things so grieved the Queen, that she accounted herself a wretch forsaken, and the indignation of her sickness, wracked out such words from her. "They have yoked my neck; I have none now to trust: my estate is turned topside turvey."'[16] For all Elizabeth's grief at being neglected as her subjects turned to James, though, Camden asserted that she had intended him as her successor all along: 'Although, in policy, she forbore in public to speak of it, yet in her heart she always favoured; even as all men of all sorts, who had cast their affections and eyes upon him, the apparent Heir of the Crown; for all that false rumour of the marriage of the Lady Arbella the daughter of his uncle; for all the French ambassador thought to hinder the uniting of both kingdoms into one dominion, in one King.'[17]

Camden's book also painted a much more celebratory accession than James had in fact experienced: 'The sad desire of her [Elizabeth], which her death bequeathed to all England, was amply paralleled with the hopes conceived of the virtues of her famous Successor, who within a few hours of her death was (with the acclamations and joyful shouts of the people) proclaimed King.' This is contradicted by numerous witness accounts of the time, one of which records that the announcement of James's accession was greeted with 'silent joy' but 'no great shouting'. The contemporary dramatist Thomas Dekker observed the sense of shock at the passing of such a long-reigning queen and noted that everyone seemed 'so pitifully distracted by the horror of a change'.[18]

One final section of the *Annales* seemed to cause Camden more trouble than any other: how to end it. Multiple drafts, crossings-out and interlined text testify to his struggle. One word proved particularly bothersome. The antiquarian was determined to stay true to the original purpose of his book by

ending with a line celebrating 'the most happy memory' of a
queen whose legacy would endure in the hearts of men 'without jealousy'. The implication was clear: Elizabeth might be
the very definition of a hard act to follow, but her successors
should honour rather than envy her. When he read the draft,
James took great exception to that word 'jealousy'. In one of
his drafts, Camden crossed it out; in another, he put it in
brackets.[19] It was a battle of wills that the author eventually
won: jealousy remained in the final printed version.

In his original text, Camden concluded that Elizabeth had
been more successful than any other of her sex, or of her
male contemporaries. Not only was this a slight on James, but
on his mother, whom he had been so concerned to see
presented in a positive light. It is perhaps not surprising that
this sentence was struck through in the final draft and never
made it into print. Instead, Camden ended with a quote from
the King's own book, *Basilikon Doron*: 'Being that she was a
Queen, *who hath so long, and with so great wisdom governed her
kingdoms* (to use the words of her Successor, who in sincerity
confessed so much) *the like hath not been read or heard of,
either in our time, or since the days of the Roman Emperor
Augustus.*' He rightly judged that James would not object to
his own words being used.[20]

The newly discovered original manuscript shows that
Camden intended to close the book by expressing a hope that
others would write Elizabeth's history after him. Although it
was customary for authors to humbly plead the inadequacy of
their labours, this was no false modesty on his part. It was the
closest he came to admitting that the *Annales* ought not to be
relied upon as an accurate source for Elizabeth's reign – the
succession in particular. Meticulous historian that he was,
Camden had not held up a mirror to the past: he had distorted
it. But this line, too, never made it into the published book.

With almost all his attempts to tell the truth, or at least admit the falsehoods, having been foiled by James, Camden might have deliberately left one clue for future generations that the *Annales* should not be taken at face value. It is unusual that ten volumes of his original text should still be preserved. Most authors disposed of their drafts and notes, the scribbles and crossings-out that show the process of crafting a polished manuscript from imperfect beginnings. Also notable is the fact that Camden did not just hide these volumes away in an attic or chest, where they risked being discarded by his descendants. Instead, they ended up in the collection of Sir Robert Cotton, the most renowned collector and antiquarian of the age. Although there is no record of whether Camden himself gave his manuscript to Cotton, their correspondence reveals that they were friends, not just collaborators. Moreover, as Camden attested, Cotton had been his 'light and direction' in the making of the *Annales*, so knew exactly what the author had intended to convey – and what he was forced to conceal.[21]

King James had demanded regular access to Camden's drafts during the seven years that he had taken to complete the *Annales*. His impatience for it to be published was such that Camden feared his royal master would seize the drafts and order a pirated edition be printed. He therefore completed the first instalment, covering the first thirty years of Elizabeth's reign and, on the King's orders, rushed it to print in 1615. A fragment of a letter he sent to a friend hints at James's impatience to have the book in circulation. 'It pleased His Majesty . . . to give a warrant for the printing and publishing so much of my Annales as he had perused.'[22]

This first instalment was dedicated to Cotton, whose library and advice had been so indispensable to Camden. He included

a prefatory address to Truth, which acknowledged the sensitivity of the project, as well as the strength of his feelings about
historical integrity. He declared that to remove truth from
history was 'to pluck out the eyes of the beautifullest creature in
the world; and, instead of wholesome liquor, to offer a draught
of poison to the readers' minds'. The following passage can be
read as an apology for the part of Elizabeth's reign that Camden
knew he had deliberately misled the reader on:

> Things manifest and evident I have not concealed; Things
> doubtful I have interpreted favourably; things secret and
> abstruse I have not pried into. 'The hidden meanings of
> princes (saith that great master of history) and what they
> secretly design to search out, it is unlawful, it is doubtful
> and dangerous: pursue not therefore the search thereof.'

The master of history Camden referred to was the Roman
historian, Tacitus, many of whose works Elizabeth had read
and translated. The phrase 'doubtful and dangerous' had also
been used in a late Elizabethan succession tract, which had
cast doubt on James's claim to the English throne. This might
not have been a coincidence.

Camden went on to express a wish to be remembered only
as 'a smaller writer in the great affairs of history'. This was
more than false modesty. He made another apology at the
very end of the book, craving 'remission of my errors past'
and insisting: 'Far be such a philautia [pride] from me, to say
that none, faults in this work can see.' He ended with a final
plea: 'Then stay (rash censurer) and forbear to condemn all,
though some mistake be there.'[23]

As soon as he had ordered the first instalment of the *Annales*
to be published in 1615, James sent a representative to Paris
with the final instalment of Camden's manuscript for de Thou

to consult. Camden himself wrote to his French counterpart, gloomily predicting that he would incur as much trouble with his new book as de Thou had with his own, 'for we live in an age of lying and intolerance'. In a more defiant tone, he added that a good conscience fears nothing. 'We struggle in the same sea,' de Thou sympathised in a return letter, 'the same baleful stars look down on us, the same tides and storms drive us up and down, towards rock and reef.' He also asked Camden to send him the next instalment of the *Annales*: 'If he who can command will not allow it to be published, you can still share it with your friends.'[24]

Writing in 1687, the Scottish theologian and historian Bishop Gilbert Burnet claimed that when de Thou received the published *Annales*, he immediately noticed a discrepancy between the work and Camden's private letters to him. He 'writ severely' to Camden, demanding an explanation. The latter 'told him in truth, that King James would need revise it himself . . . and that many things were struck out and many things altered'.[25]

De Thou was evidently determined not to fall into the same trap. After receiving the *Annales*, he assured James's agent that he had already made numerous corrections to his *Universal History* and would continue working until it was completely revised. In fact, he intended to do no such thing. He had had enough of the King's pestering and resolved never to publish his revised work. It was only after his death in 1617 that his executors seized the manuscript and sent it to Geneva to be printed.

CHAPTER 18

'THE OFFICE OF A KING IS UNNECESSARY'

In the same year that Camden's *Annales* first appeared, James was finally rid of his long-standing rival for the throne. On 25 September 1615, Arbella Stuart died in the Tower, shortly before her fortieth birthday. During the four years of her imprisonment, she had sent numerous pleas for release, but all had been quietly ignored. Although there had been rumours of escape plans, none had come to fruition. John Chamberlain reported in 1613 and 1614 that her imprisonment had sparked a mental breakdown and described Arbella as 'cracked in her brain'. Her health broke with her spirit and she suffered a long and chronic sickness, exacerbated by her impoverished state, which rendered her unable to pay for food and other necessaries. On 8 September 1614, the Privy Council ordered a clergyman to attend Arbella who, they said, has 'of late fallen into some indisposition of body and mind' and needs a 'person of gravity and learning' to offer spiritual comfort and 'visit her from time to time'.[1]

Arbella seemed resolved to end her 'miserable state'. She would not allow her physicians to attend her and refused to eat. '[Without] his Majesties favour . . . I desire not to live, and if you remember of old I dare die so I be not guilty of my own death,' she wrote to an acquaintance. While she would not commit suicide because of the threat of eternal damnation, she would nevertheless hasten her end by other means.

Public sympathy for the captive Stuart heiress mounted. Around 1613 the playwright John Webster had penned *The Duchess of Malfi*, a popular tragedy about a young duchess who defies her brother's wishes by marrying in secret and is imprisoned after trying to escape. She is then driven to despair and madness before being executed. Two years later, the Venetian ambassador reported that Arbella's death was 'much regretted by many of the chief persons here'.[2]

Two days after Arbella had departed a life that had brought little but sorrow and frustration, she was buried in Westminster Abbey, in a vault beneath the south aisle of the Lady Chapel. Her coffin was placed directly on top of that of the King's mother. It seemed that now Arbella was dead, James could at last acknowledge her royal blood. But he proceeded to seize what was left of her goods. He also remained so fearful of this unruly kinswoman that nearly three years after her death he ordered his privy council to investigate whether she had given birth to a child who had been secretly conveyed across the seas.

A little over three months after the death of the wife whom he had barely seen, William Seymour was permitted to return from exile. No longer a threat to James's throne, he was raised to the Order of the Bath in November 1615. This proved the high point of the King's generosity. Thereafter, any offices and honours that Seymour received were at best meagre. The King might have publicly forgiven his treacherous marriage, but he never forgot it.[3]

By 1617, James's popularity among his English subjects had plummeted even further than when he had first commanded William Camden to resume work on the *Annales* nine years earlier. His latest favourite, George Villiers (later Duke of Buckingham), was courting widespread resentment, as was

the King's dogged pursuit of a union between his two kingdoms. His authority was also slipping in Scotland. In the same
year, he was obliged to journey north of the border for the first
time in the fourteen years since inheriting Elizabeth's throne.
He therefore judged it imperative that Camden's justification
of his succession be published without delay. With the late
queen's memory rapidly reaching cult status, James desperately needed her posthumous approval of his accession.

Upon receiving the King's request, Camden agreed to send
him the second and final instalment of the *Annales*, covering
the period 1589–1603. By now, he seemed no longer to care
what became of the manuscript that had been the bane of his
life for more than three decades. He submitted it to 'his
Majesty's censure, whether it please him that they should be
suppressed or published, for I am indifferent'. He warned
that some passages might offend his royal master, such as the
eulogy to Elizabeth's spymaster, Sir Francis Walsingham,
who had been the strongest advocate for the execution of
James's mother.

But there was an even more inflammatory passage:

I have not feared danger, no not from them, who by their
present power think the memory of the succeeding age may
be extinguished ... When all was done, I was much
perplexed and irresolute, whether I should publish it or not.
But censures, prejudice, hatred, obtrectation, which I foresaw to display their colours, and bid battle against me, have
not so much deterred me, as the desire of Truth, the love of
my country, and the memory of that Princess (which
deserves to be dear and sacred amongst Englishmen).[4]

This was the closest Camden had come to revealing just how
much pressure James had put him under throughout the long

and laborious process of compiling the work. Worn down by years of trying to strike a delicate balance between historical integrity and royal approval, he seemed to have grown genuinely indifferent to the latter. But his professed indifference to the fate of the final instalment was false. Camden begged that the manuscript be published in Latin to limit the readership: 'As I do not dislike, that they should be published in my lifetime, so I do not desire that they should be set forth in *English* until after my death, knowing how unjust carpers the unlearned Readers are.'[5] He knew, of course, the 'carping' that would ensue from this falsification of history was far from unjust. Eager though James was to justify his accession, after receiving the new instalment he seemed to lose enthusiasm for the project and made no immediate move to publish it.

'The king . . . seems dissatisfied with his people, stays as little as possible in London, never shows himself in the city, and in entering and leaving always takes the least frequented routes,' observed the Venetian ambassador on a visit to court in 1618. 'In short in all his actions he does not conceal his dislike.' Now in his fifties, James was 'somewhat heavy in person' and his hair was 'beginning to turn white'. Sir Anthony Weldon remarked that James was 'more corpulent through his clothes than in his body, yet fat enough, his clothes ever being made large and easy'. Still preferring the hunt to state business, one contemporary noted that the King 'avoids difficult affairs and listens to troublesome news with impatience'.[6]

In October 1618, the King ordered the execution of the Elizabethan court favourite and adventurer, Sir Walter Raleigh. Two years earlier, Raleigh had been released from his long imprisonment in the Tower to lead an expedition to Venezuela in search of the fabled El Dorado (City of Gold). Despite his initial reticence, James had soon proved just as

enthusiastic a supporter of overseas exploration as his predecessor. His reign saw the founding of the first British colonies
on the North American continent: Jamestown, Virginia, in
1607, Newfoundland in 1610 and Plymouth Colony,
Massachusetts in 1620. This laid the foundation for future
British settlement and the eventual formation of both Canada
and the United States of America. The notion of an overseas
empire appealed to a king who cherished his divine right, and
he appreciated the commercial advantages of Britain's trade
in goods and slaves.

In sharp contrast to Elizabeth, James stipulated that his
adventurers must avoid hostilities with Spanish colonies or
shipping. Unfortunately, during Raleigh's expedition a
detachment of his men attacked the Spanish outpost of St
Thomé, off the coast of Central Africa. Even though this
flouted Raleigh's explicit orders and those of King James, the
Spanish ambassador, Count Gondomar, demanded that
Raleigh be put to death on his return. More concerned for his
alliance with Spain than the wishes of his people in England,
James complied. In response to the strong public reaction
against Raleigh's execution, James published a 72-page
pamphlet, *The Declaration*, justifying his decision and refuting
the notion that the King was merely a puppet of Spain.

The appearance of a comet early the following year was
seen by many as an evil portent. As if to confirm their superstitious dread, Queen Anne died shortly afterwards, on 2
March 1619. The King's health also began to falter and it was
widely believed that he would soon follow her to the grave. He
rallied on this occasion, but the loss of his consort of thirty
years served as a salutary reminder of his own mortality.

Frustrated with his intractable English government, James
continued to take refuge in the hunt and the company of his
favourites. Foremost among the latter was George Villiers,

who now dominated king and court alike. The two men grew so close that they frequently shared a bed and James declared he wanted Buckingham to become his 'wife'. 'I desire only to live in this world for your sake,' he told the duke. 'I had rather live banished in any part of the earth with you, than live a sorrowful widow-life without you.' They had pet names for each other: 'dear Dad' and 'sow' for the King and 'Steenie' for the duke, after St Stephen, who was said to have the face of an angel.[7] But Buckingham had the heart of a devil and his overweening ambition and arrogance made him deeply resented by almost everyone except the King.

In a tract published in 1620, James reflected that he was a king 'being grown in years ... weary of controversies' and lamented: 'the crown of thorns went never out of my mind, remembering the thorny cares, which a King ... must be subject unto.' For years, James had suffered from kidney problems and arthritis, and both became more acute in the last five years of his life. Although he went to Whitehall for the usual festivities in December 1624, he 'kept his chamber all this Christmas, not coming once to the chapel or to any of the plays'.[8]

Shortly afterwards, James moved to Theobalds House in Hertfordshire, which he had acquired from Robert Cecil, the man who had smoothed his path to the throne. In his weakened state, the 58-year-old King fell prey to a fever, stroke and severe dysentery. On 27 March 1625, he slipped from a life beset with anxiety, frustration and rejection. His end had been as tranquil as his predecessor's: 'As he lived in peace, so did he die in peace,' remarked Sir Thomas Erskine, one of his many favourites.[9]

In the year of James's death, the final instalment of Camden's *Annales* was published, eight years after James had ordered

Camden to submit it. In a small but satisfying act of defiance, Camden had succeeded in delaying publication during his own lifetime and that of the King who had made his life such a misery. In 1621, he had written to de Thou's executor, Pierre Dupuy: 'You need not despair of seeing the rest of my *Annales*. God willing, you will read them in due course, even if times change.' Lamenting how dangerous was the historian's trade, he asked Dupuy if he might commit the manuscript to his 'safe keeping', to be published after Camden's death.[10] The Frenchman was as good as his word. The final instalment of the *Annales* was published in Latin at Leiden in 1625.

The book only appeared in London two years later – too late for the King who had gone to such lengths to have it published, but of use to his son and successor and to the monarchs who followed. It was an instant success, in part because of the extensive use of hitherto unpublished letters and other original sources. But it also coincided with a revival of all things Elizabethan, offering disgruntled Englishmen a nostalgic escape to a happier, more glorious time.

Camden's account would go on to become the single most important source in shaping the image of Elizabeth and her reign, influencing the interpretations of countless historians all the way up to the present day. It is largely thanks to him that she is still celebrated as 'Gloriana' and 'Good Queen Bess', a shining example of female monarchy that would inspire generations to come. James had paid a high price for rewriting the succession in his favour. Forever after, his reign would be overshadowed by that of his celebrated predecessor.

Almost to his last breath, Camden had been making notes on state affairs. A historian to the core, while he was working on his history of Elizabeth's reign he could not resist keeping detailed notes about the current one. By the time of his death, these notes had expanded into a chronicle of the domestic and international events that he had been witness to since the King of Scots inherited the throne of England twenty years earlier. He kept this new project a secret, anxious to avoid having to censor it, too. But when Camden died in November 1623 at the age of seventy-two, James's chaplain, John Hacket, who claimed to be a friend, 'did privately convey [the manuscript] out of the library'. The next record of it is in Trinity College Library, Cambridge, and it was printed in Latin, along with a selection of Camden's correspondence, as the 'Epistles' in 1691.[11] No English translation ever appeared, which meant that its readership was limited.

James had accorded his apologist a funeral in Westminster Abbey so opulent that it was well beyond his rank. As well as reflecting the esteem in which Camden had been held by his contemporaries, it was perhaps also a mark of gratitude by the King whose right to the throne he had established for both present and future generations. James's royal arms were displayed in the funeral procession, which called to mind that of the late queen's twenty years earlier. Fittingly, Camden's monument was placed between that of Isaac Casaubon, who had helped convey his draft manuscripts to de Thou, and Geoffrey Chaucer, who represented the poetic imagination. As if to further prove the fallibility of the historical record, Camden's epitaph incorrectly cited his age as seventy-four. In the white marble effigy above, his hand rests on the work of which he was most proud: *Britannia*. No mention is made of the *Annales*.

In contrast to the fearful populace, the frenzied scheming of councillors and the fabricated deathbed speeches and gestures that had accompanied Elizabeth's demise, James died safe in the knowledge that his 24-year-old son and heir would inherit the crown without question or competitor. Charles I was instantly proclaimed 'our only lawful, lineal and rightful liege lord' upon his father's death. He was, simply, the late king's 'only son and undoubted heir', so there was no need to mention his lineage or right, as Elizabeth's councillors had gone to such lengths to do for James. Charles was the first adult male to succeed as the direct heir to the English throne since Henry VIII in 1509. He would also be the last Stuart monarch to do so.[12]

'The King shows himself every way very gracious and affable,' enthused John Chamberlain. 'There is great hope conceived that the world will every way amend.' The Venetian ambassador agreed: 'The King's reputation increases day by day. He professes constancy in religion, sincerity in action and that he will not have recourse to subterfuges in his dealings. His attention to those things renders him more popular, and he conducts himself with every propriety.'[13] The same optimism had been expressed when James ascended the throne twenty-two years earlier. It would prove just as transient.

Charles's court underwent an immediate transformation from the informality of his father's day. 'The king observes a rule of great decorum,' reported the Venetian ambassador a few days after Charles's accession. 'The nobles do not enter his apartments in confusion as heretofore, but each rank has its appointed place and he has declared that he desires the rules and maxims of the late Queen Elizabeth, whose rule was so popular and who is so vastly famous.'[14] The bawdy decadence of James's court was swiftly replaced with strictly regulated ceremony and decorum.

But any hope that the new King would succeed where his father had failed by absorbing, rather than ignoring, the lessons of his Tudor predecessor, was soon extinguished. Elizabeth had once told his father to 'play the king' by letting his subjects see him in all his magisterial splendour, just as she had done to such dazzling effect.[15] But while Charles remodelled the court along Elizabethan lines, this did not extend to his own personal appearances. In contrast to Elizabeth's glorious public displays and progresses, the new king was obsessed with privacy and distance. He literally retreated behind closed doors, ordering treble locks to replace the old double locks and admitting only a handful of attendants.

More ominously, it was soon all too obvious that James had passed to his successor none of the lessons that Elizabeth had spent more than thirty years trying to teach him about the government of her kingdom. Abiding by the terms of Magna Carta, which had curtailed the tyranny of King John in 1215, she had always taken care not to infringe the civil rights or liberties of her people. Even at her most dominant, the late queen had worked with, not against, her Parliaments. In almost every Parliament of her reign, she had faced intense pressure to resolve the succession by marrying or naming her heir. For the most part, she had been willing to debate the issue. On the few occasions when she had lost patience and upbraided its members, she had never taken such a drastic step as to dissolve the assembly. If Charles had learned from her example, rather than abiding by the divine right of kings instilled in him by his father, the history of the British monarchy might have turned out very differently.

In preparation for the first Parliament of his reign, which was convened in June 1625, Charles summoned the late king's faithful courtier and apologist Sir Robert Cotton to prove that 'the kings of England have used to be present in the time of the debates and examples of causes and questions in Parliament as well as at other times'. It was clear that the new king intended to take the divine right principle to even greater extremes than his father had. Encouraged by his supporters, who pointed out that all his continental peers had overthrown their 'turbulent' Parliaments, he rode roughshod over parliamentary privileges and dismissed members whenever they proved intractable.[16] This was precisely what happened with the first session – dubbed the 'Useless Parliament' – which was brought to an abrupt end in August, having offended the King by refusing to grant the revenue he had requested.

Rather than taking this as a warning to change his approach for future Parliaments, Charles was encouraged by his favourites, the Duke of Buckingham among them. They bolstered his belief in the divine right and urged him to bypass the constitutional means of raising revenue and resort to arbitrary measures of uncertain legality. 'Remember that parliaments are altogether in my power for the calling, sitting, and continuance of them,' Charles told the next Parliament when it met early the following year.[17]

The new king's popularity was further damaged when, against the wishes of his advisers and subjects, he married the French princess Henrietta Maria, whose Roman Catholic faith caused grave misgivings in Parliament. Charles assured its members that he would do nothing to undermine the Church of England, but he had already pledged to ease anti-Catholic restrictions in a secret treaty with his new brother-in-law, Louis XIII.

'An incredible concourse of people' turned out to celebrate the new king's coronation at Westminster Abbey on 2 February 1626. But beneath the cheers there was profound unease. Charles's ceremonial entry into the city of London had to be postponed because of the plague, but he was averse to the idea anyway and eventually cancelled it altogether. His ill-tempered outburst at the royal goldsmith, whom he ordered to craft a new dove for the sceptre despite the lack of time, was noted by those present. The crowning ceremony itself proceeded without incident, but the text chosen for the sermon was later viewed as prophetic. 'Be faithful unto death,' declared the Bishop of Carlisle, 'and I will give you the crown of life.'[18]

With Parliament continuing to refuse Charles the subsidy he needed, he changed tack and imposed a forced loan upon his subjects. This generated in excess of £250,000 (around £30 million today) but dealt a fatal blow to Charles's relations with the people of England. Descending into tyranny, in November 1627 he had a test case heard in the King's Bench which found that the King had a prerogative right to imprison without trial any subject who refused to pay the loan. Parliament retaliated by invoking the terms of Magna Carta and adopting a Petition of Right to prevent Charles from levying taxes without its consent and imprisoning his subjects without due process. He initially assented, but then prorogued Parliament and ignored the petition.

The resentment towards the Stuart dynasty that had been gathering ground since 1603 now found full and devastating expression. In August 1628, the King's detested favourite, the Duke of Buckingham, was assassinated at Portsmouth, where he had gone to organise a campaign to aid French Catholics. Twice, Parliament had tried to have the duke impeached, but on both occasions the King had dissolved it. With Buckingham out of the way, its hostility towards Charles was unleashed. The first Parliament to meet after the duke's death attacked the King's religious policy. He responded by bringing the session to an immediate close and declared that he would call no future Parliaments 'until our people shall see more clearly our intents and actions . . . [and] shall come to a better understanding of us and themselves'. A remark made by the Venetian ambassador Anzolo Correr was prescient: 'As he [Charles] has given up governing by Parliament, as his predecessors did, it remains to be seen if he will go on and if he will be able to do by the royal authority what former kings did by the authority of the realm . . . [He] will be very fortunate if he does not fall into some great upheaval.'[19]

As Charles's turbulent reign wore on, so the spectre of uncertainty over the Stuarts' right to the Tudor throne was thrown into sharp relief. In 1629, he commissioned the celebrated Flemish artist Peter Rubens to produce *The Glorification of King James I*, a series of paintings for the Banqueting House ceiling which promoted the glory of the Stuart dynasty, mixing Christian images with those of Roman emperors. The finished piece was one of the most dazzling artworks in England but did little to appease the growing discontent with the Stuart monarchy.

The English were not alone in feeling hostile towards the Stuarts. Charles was just as unpopular in his native kingdom. Even though he had been born in Scotland, he had shown little interest in the country since moving to England as a child. It was not until 1633 that he finally travelled to Scotland for his coronation. By then he was widely viewed as an outsider, just as the English had viewed his father in 1603.

When Charles attempted to establish a new prayer book in Scotland in 1637, it was seen as an English imposition, even though it had been drafted by Scottish bishops. There was rioting in the streets and attacks on senior clerics and politicians, and before long Scotland had been whipped up into a full-scale rebellion. Having failed to bring order, the King raised an army and led it north. It was the first time in three hundred years that a monarch had gone to war without calling a Parliament in advance.[20] The Scottish rebels quickly seized the initiative and countered the King's advance with 30,000 troops. Having reached Berwick-upon-Tweed on the Scottish border, Charles was forced to conclude a truce that satisfied neither side.

As the King desperately tried to muster new troops, the Scottish rebels marched south into England and occupied Newcastle. Rather than grant Charles the money he needed to fight them, in February 1641 the so-called Long Parliament in London passed a bill that took away his right to dissolve the assembly. It also stipulated that Charles and his successors must assemble Parliament at least every three years. With the King caught in a pincer movement between his enemies in England and Scotland, the kingdom was plunged into a series of bitterly fought civil wars which eventually forced Charles from his throne.

Seized by the parliamentary forces in 1646, the King was held captive for more than two years before being tried for treason against his people. The proceedings opened in Westminster Hall on 20 January 1649. Charles was charged with 'wicked designs, wars, and evil practices ... for the advancement and upholding of a personal interest ... against the public interest, common right, liberty, justice, and peace of the people of this nation'.[21] Even now, he clung to the divine right so beloved of the Stuart monarchs. 'No earthly power can justly call me (who am your King) in question as a delinquent,' he told the assembled parliamentarians. 'The authority of obedience unto Kings is clearly warranted, and strictly commanded in both the Old and New Testament ... The King can do no wrong.'[22] His words were met with stony silence. A week later, he was condemned and sentenced to death.

On 30 January 1649, Charles was led out of the Banqueting House into the bitterly cold afternoon. One of his last sights on earth, before he mounted the steps to the scaffold built for his execution, was the painted ceiling he had commissioned from Rubens, glorifying the divine right of the Stuart monarchy.

When drafting his addendum to the Bill for the Queen's Safety in 1584, Lord Burghley had proposed that in the event of Elizabeth dying without naming her heir, a 'great council' should assume full royal powers until the succession was settled. But he made it clear that this was to be merely a temporary expedient, for 'It is likely and very probable that the state of both realms [England and Ireland] cannot long endure without a person that by justice ought to be the successor of the Crown shall be known'. Sixty-five years later, in March 1649, the House of Commons passed an Act abolishing the monarchy. It declared: 'The office of a King [is] unnecessary, burdensome, and dangerous to the liberty, safety, and public interest of the people.'[23]

In the space of a generation, the crown that had glittered so brightly on Elizabeth's head had been consigned to the flames.

'SURPRISED HER SEX'

On 14 January 1559, Elizabeth I set out from the Tower of London and processed in magnificent style through streets festooned with her banners and emblems and thronged with thousands of her subjects, eager for a glimpse of their new queen. Her stately progress was punctuated by a series of spectacular pageants along the processional route. When the royal entourage reached Cheapside, close to St Paul's Cathedral, Elizabeth stopped and gazed at the two enormous artificial hills that had been built, one barren and wasted and the other green and fertile. As she watched, an old man representing 'Time' emerged from a cave that had been constructed between them, followed by his daughter 'Truth' – a reference to her late sister Mary's motto, 'Truth the Daughter of Time'. In Truth's hands was an English translation of the Bible that had been banned during Mary's reign. When she presented this to the new queen, Elizabeth kissed it reverently and thanked the city for its gift. The symbolism was as profound as it was unsubtle: the new faith had triumphed over the old.

'Truth' and 'time' had also worked their effect on the succession. Throughout her forty-four-year reign, Elizabeth had resisted intense pressure from her privy council and parliaments and had turned a deaf ear to the pleadings of James to name him her heir. She had been the only monarch in English history not to make provision for the succession. Even more than her staggering achievements – her dazzling court, the defeat of the Armada, the beginnings of empire – this had defined her queenship. To the end, she had refused to name the person who would succeed her – or at least, not directly. Instead, she had left it to time. During those four and a half decades when England, Scotland and Europe held their breath, watching for who would succeed the self-proclaimed Virgin Queen, almost every would-be heir fell (or was pushed) by the wayside. As Elizabeth's life ebbed away, time delivered the truth: her successor would be the King of Scots.

For all the anxiety, intrigue and rivalry that Elizabeth's refusal to settle the succession had engendered, the wisdom of her policy was proved by the fact that to her last breath, her personal power in England had not been challenged by any 'rising sun'. True, scores of her subjects had turned their faces to that sun, but they had never relinquished their allegiance to their queen or tried to force her from the throne. The smoothness of James's accession had been a further testament to the wisdom of her approach. It had been a risky strategy though, and its success had owed much to the Queen's longevity. If her reign had been cut short by death or usurpation like those of her three immediate predecessors, it could have plunged the kingdom into civil war.

But Elizabeth had not left the matter to time and chance alone. From the outset of her reign, even when James's mother had directly challenged her rule, she had sought friendship with Scotland, bringing to an end centuries of hostility between the thistle and the rose. This had been enshrined in the Treaty of Berwick of 1586 and the accompanying pension that she granted to James.

More importantly, while the Queen had stopped short of naming James her heir, she had removed most, if not all, of the major obstacles that stood between him and her throne.

Arbella Stuart had been driven half mad by the long years of virtual house arrest, the rapid succession of glittering suitors who had been first offered then snatched away, the bestowing and sudden withdrawing of royal favour. Elizabeth had persecuted the Suffolk line just as relentlessly, imprisoning Katherine Grey and ordering her marriage to be declared invalid, thereby fatally undermining the claim of her descendants, destroying Mary Grey's marriage and life, and imprisoning and slandering Lady Margaret Stanley and her family. She had kept Henry Hastings, Earl of Huntingdon, in the political wilderness for years and appointed him to public office only when she was certain that he harboured no ambitions for her crown.

At the same time, the Queen had maintained a regular correspondence with the Scottish king for more than thirty years. In part, this had been aimed at preserving Anglo-Scottish amity, but the vast majority of her letters had tended towards educating him in what it took to succeed as a monarch of England. Such attention was not something that she bestowed on any of the other claimants to her throne.

Elizabeth seems to have set her mind on James almost from the moment of his birth, and certainly from 1567, when she proposed to Mary, Queen of Scots that she send her infant son to be raised in England. But, as was so often the case with this most pragmatic of queens, her decision had been made with the head rather than the heart. She knew full well that James was her closest blood relative and therefore had the most right, regardless of Henry VIII's will. Elizabeth herself had once been disinherited by her father, even though her blood had made her his rightful heir. She was evidently resolved not to do the same to James. Perhaps, too, like her grandfather Henry VII she appreciated the advantages of uniting England and Scotland into one realm.

But the fact that of all the claimants for her throne, James had the most right and, perhaps, the greatest chance of success, must have been a bitter pill for Elizabeth to swallow. He was, after all, the son of her greatest rival, Mary, Queen of Scots, the woman who had plagued her for almost thirty years. There was something else about the King of Scots that might have made him personally abhorrent to Elizabeth. He was a product of Scottish society, where women were derided for their weakness and the notion of female authority was abhorrent. As well as declaring it 'repugnant' that a woman should 'bear rule ... above any nation', John Knox had argued that female sovereigns had no right to appoint justices or officials – and, by extension, their heirs.[1] James had made little attempt to hide the fact that such views were entirely in line with his own. But he had gravely misjudged the situation in England by assuming that Elizabeth was able to rule so successfully only because her privy council had been running the show behind the scenes.

In a commemorative verse about Elizabeth, written shortly after he inherited her throne, James described her as having had 'A King's heart in a maid' and concluded that to forestall the adulation of her, 'Heaven hence by death did summon/To show she was a woman'. In a similar vein, Robert Cecil reflected that his former mistress had been 'more than a man, and, in truth, sometimes less than a woman'. Even Camden, who never tired of lauding the late queen's virtues, remarked that she 'surprised her sex'.

The last Tudor monarch might have pretended to regret being merely 'a weak and feeble woman', but at the very end of her reign, her true feelings were revealed. In February 1603, an envoy from the Doge and Senate of Venice visited the dying Queen at Richmond and said something that caused offence. Roused by furious indignation, she dismissed him with the admonishment: 'My sex cannot diminish my prestige.'[2]

Elizabeth is not a woman to be underestimated, either in her own lifetime or now, more than four hundred years after her death. If, as the newly exposed drafts of Camden's original manuscript suggest, she never named her successor, it was a masterstroke of statecraft rather than an example of womanly indecision. Deeds, as she had often told James, speak louder than words. The King of Scots might have stolen her crown, but it was a theft in which she had been almost entirely complicit.

ACKNOWLEDGEMENTS

The greatest thanks are due to the British Library, the source of the momentous discovery about the Elizabethan succession and the place where I wrote most of this book. I am particularly indebted to Helena Rutkowska, whose meticulous research brought to light William Camden's enforced falsehoods about James's accession, and to Julian Harrison and Andrea Clarke for being so generous with their time and expertise.

I have once more enjoyed the immeasurable support and guidance of my wonderful editors on both sides of the Atlantic: Rupert Lancaster at Hodder & Stoughton and George Gibson at Grove Atlantic, who came up with the idea for this book. I am also hugely grateful to Lucy Buxton for her editorial insights and attention to detail, to Juliet Brightmore for her inspired picture research and to Niamh Anderson, Alice Morley, George Biggs and Jenny Choi for everything they have done to bring the book to people's attention. I am thrilled with the jacket design, which was the creation of Sofia Hericson, and with the beautiful illustrations, courtesy of Joanna Boyle. Thank you, too, to Viv Church for the copyedit, Ian Allen for the proofread and Geraldine Beare for once more producing a meticulous index.

The Soho Agency has been with me throughout my writing career and words will never be sufficient to express how grateful I am to Julian Alexander, Ben Clark and Sarah Stamp for their endless wisdom, encouragement and good humour. I also owe a debt of thanks to my colleagues at Historic Royal Palaces, in particular Magda Muskala for her unflinching enthusiasm and support for my books, for all the signings (including the 'tower of books' she created at the Tower of London) and for supplying the delicious anecdote about Oliver Cromwell seeing Mary, Queen of Scots' coffin when it was moved from Peterborough to Westminster Abbey. I also have the enormous good fortune to work with Claudia Strange, the creator and director of the HRP podcast, and Charlotte Gunnell, digital producer, both of whom have enriched my time at the palaces more than I can say. Finally, my thanks go to the wonderful Development, Membership, Publishing and Curatorial teams for enabling me to share the dramatic story of the Elizabethan succession with HRP's visitors and supporters.

I am greatly indebted to the expertise and generosity of my fellow historians, notably Alison Weir who despite being the busiest woman in the world of history agreed to read an early draft of the manuscript and provided a wonderful endorsement. Gareth Russell has been the source of invaluable insights into Elizabeth's successor and very kindly shared with me an advance copy of his stunning new book, *Queen James*. On the other side of the globe, Dr Elizabeth Tunstall's research into the succession in general and the Valentine Thomas controversy in particular has been profoundly enlightening, and I relished the opportunity to continue our discussions in person at the British Library.

I am so grateful to Marnie Harris for her assiduous research, which unearthed some truly inspirational finds in the National Records of Scotland, the British Library and elsewhere. I have no doubt that a glittering career in history awaits her. Likewise to Phoebe Boffey for compiling a list of the letters that passed between the English and Scottish courts. Daniel Watkins of Alnwick Castle very kindly supplied me with details of Margaret Tudor's stay there in 1503, on her journey north to marry James IV of Scotland. He was also the first person to sign me up for an event on the book! My thanks also go to Mike Berlin of the Victoria & Albert Museum for sharing evidence of how portraits of Elizabeth were covered over when she died.

This is the seventeenth book that my family and friends have seen me through and their patience, encouragement and forbearance have never wavered. It is not something I take for granted. Thank you.

NOTES

When citing original manuscripts, I have modernised the spelling and grammar for ease of reference.

I have cited three different editions of Camden's *Annales*, as there are slight variations between them which are sometimes significant. The editions are as follows:

Camden, W, *The True and Royall Historie of the Famous Empresse Elizabeth, Queene of England, France and Ireland*, 3 vols. (London, 1625–9)

Camden, W, *The Historie of the Most Renowned and Victorious Princesse Elizabeth, late Queene of England* (London, 1630)

MacCaffrey, WT (ed.), *William Camden, The History of the Most Renowned and Victorious Princess Elizabeth, Late Queen of England*. Selected Chapters (Chicago and London, 1970)

Introduction: 'A drop of doubtful royal blood'

1. *CSPS* I no.249, pp.213–14
2. Bruce, J (ed), *Correspondence of King James VI of Scotland with Sir Robert Cecil and others in England, during the reign of Queen Elizabeth* (London, 1861); Harington, J, *A Tract on the Succession to the Crown* [1602], edited by Markham, CR (London, 1880), p.51; Camden, W, *Annales: The True and Royall History of the Famous Empresse Elizabeth* (London, 1625), III, p.381
3. BL Cotton MS Faustina F III, f. 215v–216r; Camden, *Annales: The True and Royall History*, III, pp.380–3

Chapter 1. The Thistle and the Rose

1. The beautifully illuminated copies of the treaty that each king commissioned still survive in the National Archives in London and the National Records of Scotland in Edinburgh.

2. TNA E39/58 and NRS SP 6/31 Treaty of Perpetual Peace, 1502; Dickinson, WC, Donaldson, G and Milne, IA (eds), *A Source Book of Scottish History*, II (1953), p. 59–61

3. Hays, D (ed and transl.), *The Anglica Historia of Polydore Vergil, A.D. 1485–1537*, Camden Series, LXXIV (London, 1950), p.114

4. *CSPS* I, no.210, p.176

5. BL Cotton MS Vespasian F XIII fo.135 Margaret, Queen of Scotland to her father Henry VII, following her marriage to James IV of Scotland, 1503

6. Mackay Mackenzie, W (ed), *The Poems of William Dunbar* (Edinburgh, 1990), pp.107–112

7. *LP Henry VIII*, I, no.2157, p. 972

8. Margaret had fallen pregnant shortly before the Battle of Flodden and gave birth to a son, Alexander, on 30 April 1514. He died in December 1515.

9. *LP Henry VIII*, XII part ii, no.1285; Fraser, A, *Mary, Queen of Scots* (London, 1994), p.7

10. James V's deathbed prophecy came true, but perhaps not as he expected. The Stuart dynasty would endure long after the execution of his daughter, Mary, Queen of Scots, in 1587, but it did end with another 'lass', Queen Anne, in 1714. Stuart luck, like Tudor luck before it, ran out when Prince William, Duke of Gloucester, Anne's only surviving child from seventeen pregnancies, died in 1700.

11. James V would be the last monarch to die in Scotland until 8 September 2022, when Queen Elizabeth II died at Balmoral Castle after reigning for longer than any of her English and Scottish predecessors.

12. Francis Steuart, A (ed), *Sir James Melville: Memoirs of His Own Life, 1549–93* (London, 1929), p.20

13. Clifford, A (ed), *The State Papers and Letters of Sir Ralph Sadler. To which is added, a memoir of the life of Sir Ralph Sadler, with historical notes by Walter Scott*, 2 vols. (Edinburgh, 1809), pp.559–60

14. TNA E23/4 Will of Henry VIII [30 December 1546]
15. *The Statutes of the Realm*, 11 vols. (London, 1820–28), III, pp.955–8

Chapter 2. 'I am resolved never to marry'

1. Inner Temple, London, Petyt MS 538, 47, fo.317
2. Brewer, JS (ed), Fuller, T, *The church history of Britain*, 6 vols. (London, 1845), IV, pp.138–9
3. Stone, JM, *The History of Mary I, Queen of England, as found in the Public Records, Despatches of Ambassadors, in original private letters, and other contemporary documents* (London, 1901), pp.497–8
4. Camden, W, *The Historie of the Most Renowned and Victorious Princesse Elizabeth, late Queene of England* (London, 1630), p.8
5. *CSPV* VI ii, pp.1058, 1549
6. Camden, *Historie*, p.10; *CSPV* VI iii, p.1538; Tytler, PF, *England under the Reigns of Edward VI and Mary, Illustrated in a Series of Original Letters*, 2 vols. (London, 1839), II, p.497; Adams, *Feria's Despatch*, p.335
7. *CSPV* VI iii, p.1538; Harington, *Nugae Antiquae*, p.312
8. Only when James I came to the throne was this rectified. Elizabeth's coffin was placed in the same vault as her half-sister's and James ordered a magnificent monument to be erected above them both. This bore the inscription: 'Partners both in throne and grave, here rest we, two sisters, Elizabeth and Mary, in the hope of resurrection.'
9. Knox, J, *The First Blast of the Trumpet against the monstrous regiment of women* (London, 1558), pp.9, 47v
10. Camden, *Historie*, p.34
11. Dunn, J, *Elizabeth and Mary: Cousins, Rivals, Queens* (New York, 2004), p.175; *CSPF Elizabeth 1561–2*, p.357
12. *CSPF Elizabeth 1560–1*, p.291
13. *CSPF Elizabeth* II, p.251; Reid, C (ed), *The Bardon Papers: Documents Relating to the Imprisonment and Trial of Mary Queen of Scots* (London, 1909), p.13
14. *CSP Scotland 1547–62* I, p.609
15. Plowden, A, *Two Queens in One Isle: The Deadly Relationship of Elizabeth I and Mary, Queen of Scots* (Sutton, 1999), p.61

16. Melville, *Memoirs*, p.65
17. *Elizabeth I: CollectedWorks*, p.59
18. Klarwill, V von, *Queen Elizabeth and Some Foreigners*, transl. Nash, TH (London, 1928), p.94
19. Pryor, F, *Elizabeth I: her life in letters* (California, 2003), p.31; HMC *Salisbury* I, p.158; *CSPS* I, no.69, p.107; Nenner, H, *The Right to be King: The Succession to the Crown of England, 1603–1714* (London, 1995), p.18
20. TNA SP 12/27 f.143r–144v: Answer of the Queen to the addresses of both Houses of Parliament delivered to Mr Speaker Thomas Williams, 28 January 1563; *CSPS* III, no.189, p.252; Weir, A, *Elizabeth the Queen* (London, 1999), p.46; Somerset, A, *Elizabeth I* (London, 1991), p.96
21. Melville, *Memoirs*, p.94; *CSPV* VII, p.594; Levin, C, *The Heart and Stomach of a King: Elizabeth I and the Politics of Sex and Power* (Philadelphia, 1994), p.172; Nenner, *The Right to be King*, p.19
22. The present-day monarch still carries this title.
23. *CSPS* XIII, pp.2–3; *CSPS* I, no.69, p.107
24. Falkus, *Private Lives*, p.98
25. *CSPS* I, no.336, p.518; *CSPF Elizabeth 1562*, pp.217–24
26. Robert Dudley was Elizabeth's Master of Horse.
27. Wilson, VA, *Queen Elizabeth's Maids of Honour and Ladies of the Privy Chamber* (London, 1922), p.25; Watkins, S, *In Public and Private: Elizabeth I and her World* (London, 1998), p.162; Arthur's age placed his conception at 1561, when the rumours about Elizabeth and Dudley had reached fever pitch. There is no firm evidence to corroborate the story, but it suited Philip's interests to discredit the English queen, whom he had abandoned any hope of marrying, so he made sure that it was repeated far and wide.
28. Weir, *Elizabeth the Queen*, p.51

Chapter 3. 'No queen in England but I'

1. *CSPF Elizabeth 1558–9*, p.443; *CSPS* I, no.21, p.45; no.315, p.468
2. *CSPS* I, no.75, p.116; no.120, p.176; no.305, p.443. See also: HMC *Salisbury* I, p.197
3. Camden, *Historie*, p.122

4. Kervyn de Lettenhove, JMBC, *Relations politiques de Pays-Bas et de l'Angleterre sous le règne de Philippe II*, 11 volumes (Brussels, 1892–1900), II, p.609
5. *CSP Rome* I, pp.51–2
6. Huntingdon also had five sisters. He was responsible for all ten of his siblings, and his mother, when his father Francis, the second earl, died in June 1561.
7. BL Harleian MS 787 fo.16: Henry Hastings, Earl of Huntingdon, to Robert Dudley [1563]
8. Cross, C, *The Puritan Earl: The Life of Henry Hastings, Third Earl of Huntingdon, 1536–1595* (London, 1966), p.3
9. *CSPF Elizabeth 1562*, p.14
10. *CSPF Elizabeth 1562*, p.15
11. *CSPF Elizabeth 1562*, p.13
12. *Elizabeth I: Collected Works*, p.61
13. *Elizabeth I: Collected Works*, pp.61–2; Plowden, *Two Queens*, p.69
14. *Elizabeth I: Collected Works*, pp.62–7
15. *Elizabeth I: Collected Works*, pp.65–6
16. *Elizabeth I: Collected Works*, pp.66–7
17. *CSPF Elizabeth 1561–2*, p.477; *CSP Scotland 1547–62* I, p.587
18. *CSP Scotland 1547–62* I, p.639
19. BL Harleian MS 6286 – Records of the Commission appointed to investigate the marriage of Katherine Grey and Edward Seymour
20. BL Additional MS 48023, fo.361v – A Journal of Matters of State ... From and Before the Death of King Edward the 6th Until the Year 1562
21. BL Additional MS 48023, fo.361v – A Journal of Matters of State ... From and Before the Death of King Edward the 6th Until the Year 1562
22. *CSPF Elizabeth 1562*, no.846, p.368
23. *CSPS* I, nos.187, 188, p.262
24. TNA SP 12/27 f.143r–144v: Answer of the Queen to the addresses of both Houses of Parliament delivered to Mr Speaker Thomas Williams, 28 January 1563. In ancient Greek mythology, Clotho is the youngest goddess of the Three Fates and spins the thread of human life.
25. *CSPS* I, no.190, p.263
26. *CSPS* I, no.189, p.262
27. *CSPS* I, no.189, p.262
28. 'A Statute for Those Who Are Born in Parts Beyond the Sea', *Statutes of the Realm*, I, p.310

29. *CSPV* VI, p.1077
30. *CSPS* I, no.190, p.263; *CSPF Elizabeth* 1563, p.100
31. *CSPF Elizabeth 1562*, no.1053, p.458; *CSPS* I, no.190, p.263
32. *CSPS* I, no.190, p.263; *CSPF Elizabeth 1562*, no.914, pp.397–8
33. *CSPS* I, no.190, p.263; no.211, p.296
34. Another of Elizabeth's close attendants, Lady Mary Sidney, sister of Robert Dudley, also fell prey to the disease. Although she survived, she was left horribly disfigured, as her husband lamented more than two decades later: 'I left her a full fair lady, in mine eye at least the fairest, and when I returned I found her as foul a lady as the smallpox could make her, which she did take by continual attendance of her majesty's most precious person (sick of the same disease) the scars of which (to her resolute discomfort) ever since hath done and doth remain in her face.' TNA SP 12/159 fo.38v
35. BL Harleian MS 787 fo.16: Henry Hastings, Earl of Huntingdon to Robert Dudley [1563]
36. *CSPS* I, no.192, p.265
37. BM Lansdowne MS 94 fo.30r
38. TNA SP 12/27 f.143r–144v: Answer of the Queen to the addresses of both Houses of Parliament delivered to Mr Speaker Thomas Williams, 28 January 1563
39. *CSPD Elizabeth* XXVIII, no.20
40. Nichols, JG (ed), *The Diary of Henry Machyn: citizen and Merchant-Taylor of London, from AD 1550 to AD 1563* (London, 1848), p.300
41. Seymour pleaded that he was unable to pay the fine and it was eventually commuted to £3,000.
42. Chapman, H, *Two Tudor Portraits: Henry Howard, Earl of Surrey and Lady Katherine Grey* (London, 1960), p.222
43. Hales, J, *A Declaration of the Succession of the Crowne Imperiall of Ingland* (London, 1713)
44. Bodleian Library Ashmolean MSS 829 fos.23–31
45. *CSPS* I, no.210, p.294

Chapter 4. 'Two women will not agree very long together'

1. Melville, *Memoirs*, pp.95–6
2. Melville, *Memoirs*, pp.94, 101

3. Melville, *Memoirs*, pp.78, 98, 101
4. *CSP Scotland 1547-62* I, p.559; *CSPS* II, no.26, p.36
5. *CSP Scotland Elizabeth*, II, p.49
6. Melville, *Memoirs*, p.81
7. Melville, *Memoirs*, pp.81, 91
8. Chamberlin, F, *Elizabeth and Leycester* (New York, 1939), p.158
9. Melville, *Memoirs*, p.107
10. Schutte, K, *A Biography of Margaret Douglas, Countess of Lennox* (Lampeter, c.2002), p.193
11. *CSP Scotland Elizabeth*, II, pp.81 225, 230
12. *Calendar of Border Papers*, I, no.5, pp.2–3; Melville, *Memoirs*, pp.114–19
13. *CSPS* I, no.315, p.468
14. Wright, T, *Queen Elizabeth and her Times, A Series of Original Letters, Selected from the Inedited Private Correspondence of the Lord Treasurer Burghley, the Earl of Leicester, the Secretaries Walsingham and Smith, Sir Christopher Hatton, etc*, 2 vols. (London,1838), I, p.207
15. Among them was Chequers House, which has been the country residence of British prime ministers since 1917.
16. *CSPF Elizabeth 1564–5*, p.428; *CSPF Elizabeth 1566–8*, p.17; *CSPS* II, no.140, p.192
17. Melville, *Memoirs*, p.92
18. Schutte, *Margaret Douglas*, p.199
19. Melville, *Memoirs*, pp.121–5
20. *CSPF Elizabeth 1566–68*, p.33
21. Weir, *Elizabeth the Queen*, p.174
22. Melville, *Memoirs*, p.126
23. Melville, Memoirs, p.126
24. Melville, *Memoirs*, p.130
25. Melville, *Memoirs*, p.130; *CSPS* I, no.365, p.562
26. Melville, *Memoirs*, p.131
27. Melville, *Memoirs*, pp.131–5
28. TNA SP 12/41/28; Neale, JE, *Elizabeth I and her Parliaments*, I 1559–1581 (London, 1958), pp.158–60; Hartley, TE (ed), *Proceedings in the Parliaments of Elizabeth I*, I 1558–1581, pp.121, 158–9, 163
29. BM Harleian MS 4627 no.2, fos.3–4, 26–7: Mary Queen of Scots' Claim to the English Succession Attacked on National and Religious Grounds
30. *CSPS* I, no.1, p.4

31. Williams, N, *Elizabeth the First, Queen of England* (London, 1968), p.50
32. *CSPS* I, no.390, p.597
33. *Elizabeth I: Collected Works*, pp.94–8; Neale, *Elizabeth I and her Parliaments*, I, p.136; Levine, M, *Tudor Dynastic Problems, 1460–1571* (London and New York, 2021), pp.116–17
34. The pamphlet was likely the work of the radical Protestant, Thomas Sampson. BL Egerton MS 2836 fos.37–71
35. *CSPS* I, no.381, p.580; Neale, *Elizabeth I and her Parliaments*, I, p.133
36. BL Cotton MS Caligula B IV fos.1–94; Harley MS 849 fo.1. See also: Axton, M, 'The Influence of Edmund Plowden's Succession Treatise', *Huntingdon Library Quarterly*, XXXVII (1974), pp.209–26
37. Melville, *Memoirs*, pp.139–40
38. Melville, *Memoirs*, p.145
39. *Elizabeth I: Collected Works*, pp.116–17
40. NRS RH15/23/16: Elizabeth I to Sir Nicholas Throckmorton, 14 July 1567 (copy). This later copy is taken from a hitherto unpublished original.
41. Kings MS 396: Genealogical tree of Elizabeth I [c.1567]. I am indebted to Dr Andrea Clark, Lead Curator of Medieval and Early Modern Manuscripts at the British Library, for bringing this to my attention.
42. Melville, *Memoirs*, p.149; Stevenson, J (ed), Selections From Unpublished Manuscripts in the College of Arms and the British Museum, illustrating the Reign of Mary, Queen of Scotland, *MDXLIII–MDLXVIII*, Maitland Club, 41 (Glasgow, 1837), p.177
43. *Elizabeth I: Collected Works*, p.117–19
44. BM Lansdowne MS 8 fos.67–8; Wilson, VA, *Queen Elizabeth's Maids of Honour and Ladies of the Privy Chamber* (London, 1922), p.69
45. Wilson, *Maids of Honour*, p.32
46. Two copies of this account survive in the British Library: Harleian MS 39 fo.380; Cotton Titus MS 107 fos.124 and 131
47. *CSPS* I, no.1, p.4
48. Hartley, TE (ed), *Proceedings in the parliaments of Elizabeth I*, 3 vols. (Leicester, 1981–95), I, p.138. For a similar statement made in 1572, see *CSPS* I, no.1, p.376

Chapter 5. 'Fair words and foul deeds'

1. Melville, *Memoirs*, pp.170–1
2. BL Cotton MS Caligula C I: Mary, Queen of Scots to Elizabeth I, announcing her arrival in England, 17 May 1568
3. *CSPF Elizabeth 1566-68*, pp.460–1
4. Weir, *Elizabeth the Queen*, p.201; *CSPS* II, no.26, p.36
5. *CSPS* II, no.39, p.57
6. *CSP Rome* I, p.289; *CSP Scotland Elizabeth*, II, p.428; Chamberlin, F, *The Sayings of Queen Elizabeth* (London, 1923), pp.233, 246
7. *CSPV* VII, p.427
8. *Elizabeth I: Collected Works*, pp.121–3
9. *CSPS* II, no.124, p.180
10. There is evidence to suggest that one of Walsingham's agents was the celebrated playwright Christopher Marlowe. He was frequently absent from his studies at Cambridge, yet when the university threatened to withhold his degree, the privy council intervened, commending his 'good service' to Queen Elizabeth. The threat was promptly withdrawn and Marlowe graduated with full honours. Further suspicion was aroused by the mysterious nature of his death in May 1593. He dined with Ingram Frizer, another secret government employee, in a lodging place in Deptford. A fight broke out between the two men over the bill and Marlowe was supposedly stabbed to death by Frizer. Other theories are that Elizabeth herself had ordered his assassination and even that Marlowe faked his own death and fled the country, later writing plays under the pseudonym William Shakespeare.
11. TNA SP 12/48/61, fol. 165r
12. Melville, *Memoirs*, p.181
13. *CSPV* VII, pp.468–9
14. The cushion was used in evidence at Norfolk's trial.
15. *CSP Rome* I, pp.401–2
16. *CSP Rome* II, p.3; *CSPS* II, no.281, p.340
17. *CSPS* II, no.281, p.342; McDiarmid, *Monarchical Republic*, p.165; *Elizabeth I: Collected Works*, p.130
18. BL Additional MS 48114 f.74
19. Cross, *The Puritan Earl*, p.280
20. Nicholson, W, (ed), *The remains of Edmund Grindal* (Cambridge, 1843), p.355

21. Cross, C (ed), *The letters of Sir Francis Hastings, 1574–1609* (Frome, 1969), p.59
22. Schutte, *Margaret Douglas*, p.230
23. Thomas Howard is sometimes confused with his elder half-brother of the same name, the third Duke of Norfolk. He was the second duke's son by his second marriage.
24. Schutte, *Margaret Douglas*, p.231; *CSP Scotland Elizabeth*, I, p.202
25. *Elizabeth I: Collected Works*, p.170
26. *CSPS* III, no.302, p.426
27. BM Lansdowne MS 34 fos.1, 53; *CSP Scotland Elizabeth*, I, p.119
28. BM Lansdowne MS 34 fo.53; *CSP Scotland Elizabeth*, I, p.119; Harington, *Tract on the* Succession, p.45; *CSP Scotland Elizabeth*, I, p.505
29. Borman, T, *Elizabeth's Women: The Hidden Story of the Virgin Queen* (London, 2008), p.310
30. Turnbull, W (ed and transl), *Letters of Mary Stuart, Queen of Scotland, selected from the 'Recueil des Lettres de Marie Stuart,' together with the chronological summary of events during the reign of the Queen of Scotland, by Prince A. Labanoff,* 8 vols. (London, 1845), V, 436. See also: Wilson, D, *Sweet Robin: a biography of Robert Dudley, Earl of Leicester, 1533–1588* (London, 1981) p.244; Lovell, MS, *Bess of Hardwick. First Lady of Chatsworth, 1527–1608* (London, 2005), p.307

Chapter 6. 'The bloody hand of a murderer'

1. Nichols, *The Progresses, Processions, and Magnificent Festivities of King James the First,* 4 vols. (London, 1828), I, p.129; Gilson, JP, *Catalogue of Western Manuscripts in the Old Royal and King's Collections* (London, 1921), p. xxviii
2. The first regent, James's illegitimate uncle, James Stewart, Earl of Moray, was assassinated after less than two years in post. He was succeeded by Matthew Stewart, Earl of Lennox, James's paternal grandfather, who was fatally wounded after a raid by Mary's supporters a year after being made regent. His successor, the Earl of Mar, 'took a vehement sickness' and died after a year in office. He was followed by James Douglas, fourth Earl of Morton, who had played a leading role in the murder of David

Riccio. He was the last and most successful of the regents and by the time of his violent death in 1581, James was old enough to rule in his own right.

3. His grandfather James V had been eighteen months old when he became king in 1513; his mother Mary only a week old in 1542.

4. BL Additional MS 19398 fo.44

5. Melville, *Memoirs*, p.297

6. *Letters of Queen Elizabeth and King James VI of Scotland*, pp.2–3. For James's poetry, see: Akrigg, GPV (ed), *Letters of King James VI & I* (Berkeley, University of California Press, 1984), pp.73–4; *CSP Scotland Elizabeth*, II, p.366

7. Harrison, GB, *The Letters of Queen Elizabeth* (London, 1935), p.166

8. *Letters of Queen Elizabeth and King James VI of Scotland*, pp.2–3; TNA SP 52/51 fo.75 Elizabeth I to James VI, 22 December 1593

9. McIlwain, CH (ed), *The Political Works of James I* (Cambridge, 1918), pp.11, 22

10. *Basilikon Doron*, in Somerville, JP (ed), *King James VI and I: Political Writings* (Cambridge, 1994), p.39; *CSP Scotland*, VII, p.271

11. *Letters of Queen Elizabeth and King James VI of Scotland*, pp.69–70

12. Mortimer, I, *The Time Traveller's Guide to Elizabethan England* (London, 2012), p.194. Elizabeth's Parliament passed several Acts to try to improve the situation, whereby surveyors were appointed in every parish to assess the state of the roads and corral the inhabitants into carrying out the necessary repairs. But most parishioners showed little interest in improving something that was mostly used by wealthy coach passengers. Instead, they simply walked around the quagmires in winter and picked their way over the hardened ruts in summer.

13. *Letters of Queen Elizabeth and King James VI of Scotland*, p.17

14. Allingham, H (ed), *Captain Cuellar's Adventures in Connacht & Ulster, A.D. 1588 . . . To which is added an introduction and complete translation of Captain Cuellar's Narrative of the Spanish Armada and his adventures in Ireland* (London, 1897), p.62

15. Drake's ship was originally called the *Pelican*, but he renamed her mid-voyage in honour of his patron, Sir Christopher Hatton, whose crest was a golden hind (a female red deer).

16. Haigh, *Elizabeth*, p.87
17. *CSPV* VII, p.659
18. Somerset, A, *Elizabeth I* (London, 1991), p.65; Nichols, JG (ed), *The diary of Henry Machyn: citizen and merchant taylor of London, from AD 1550 to AD 1563* (London, 1848), p.263
19. Boyle, J (ed), *Memoirs of the Life of Robert Carey ...Written by Himself* (London, 1759), p.73n
20. Watkins, S, *In Public and Private: Elizabeth I and her World* (London, 1998), p.59; Rye, WB (ed), *England as seen by Foreigners in the days of Elizabeth and James the First* (London, 1865) II, p.18
21. Williams, C (ed and transl), *Thomas Platter's Travels in England, 1599* (London, 1937), p.192
22. Nicolas, NH, *Memoirs of the life and times of Sir Christopher Hatton, K.G., Vice Chamberlain and Lord Chancellor to Queen Elizabeth. Including his correspondence with the Queen and other distinguished persons* (London, 1847), p.200; Bruce, *Correspondence*, pp.12–13
23. Nicolas, *Memoirs of Sir Christopher Hatton*, p.200; Smith, T, *The State of England, Anno Dom.1600*, edited by Fisher, FJ, Camden Miscellany, XVI, 3rd series, no.52 (London, 1936), pp.1–9
24. Burgoyne, FJ (ed), *Leycester's Commonwealth* (London, 1904), p.117
25. Hasler, PW, *The House of Commons, 1558–1603*, III (London, 1981), p.303
26. Gristwood, S, *Arbella: England's Lost Queen* (London, 2003), p.101
27. *Letters of Queen Elizabeth and King James VI of Scotland*, pp.1–4
28. BM Lansdowne MS 1236 fo.32
29. Williams, N, *Elizabeth I, Queen of England* (London, 1967), p.256; *CSPF Elizabeth 1581–82*, p.589; *CSPS* III, no.351, p.495
30. *Leycester's Commonwealth*, pp.94, 104, 107
31. Jenkins, E, *Elizabeth and Leicester* (London, 2002), pp.290, 298
32. Clifford, *Letters of Sir Ralph Sadler*, II, pp.400–1; TNA SP 12/173/13; BL Cotton MS Caligula C.ix, fo.133r
33. BL Add MSS 33594 ff.52v–53r
34. Laing, D et al (eds), *Original Letters of Mr John Colville, 1582–1603* (Edinburgh, 1858), p.315; McIlwain, *Political Works of James I*, p.6
35. Weir, *Elizabeth the Queen*, pp.355–6
36. HMC *Salisbury* XIII, pp.254–5, 309; *Letters of Queen Elizabeth*

and King James VI of Scotland, pp.11, 15; Akrigg, *Letters of King James VI & I*, p.67

37. TNA SP 12/174 fo.1. See also: 'The Bond of Association, 1584', in Archer, IW and Douglas Price, F (eds), *English Historical Documents*, V(A), 1558–1603 (London, 2011), p.961

38. 27 Eliz.1.c.1: An Act for Provision to be made for the Surety of the Queen's Majesty's most Royal Person, and the Continuance of the Realm in Peace

39. McDiarmid (ed), *The Monarchical Republic of Early Modern England: Essays in Response to Patrick Collinson* (Aldershot, 2007), p.37

40. *Letters of Queen Elizabeth and King James VI of Scotland*, pp.18–20, 29-30. In a tragic coincidence, Lord Russell had died on the very same day as his father, the second Earl of Bedford.

41. *Letters of Queen Elizabeth and King James VI of Scotland*, pp.24–5, 29–30

42. Melville, *Memoirs*, pp.298–9

43. *CSP Scotland Elizabeth*, II, pp.414–15

44. Read, C, *Mr Secretary Walsingham and the Policy of Queen Elizabeth*, 3 vols. (Oxford, 1925), II, p.342

45. TNA SP 53/19/12. Babington destroyed the so-called 'Gallows Letter' upon reading it, but Walsingham's agent made a copy of it, which still survives in The National Archives: SP 53/18/53

46. BL Cotton MS Appendix L fo.144*r*

47. *CSP Scotland Elizabeth*, II, p.657

48. Bassnett, S, *Elizabeth I: A Feminist Perspective* (Oxford and New York, 1988), p.113; *CSPV* VIII, p.206

49. Melville, *Memoirs*, pp.312-13

50. *Letters of Queen Elizabeth and King James*, pp.38–9

51. Cobbett, W and Howell, TB (eds), *A Complete Collection of State Trials*, 33 vols. (London, 1816–98), I, p.1171

52. Read, *Walsingham*, III, p.53

53. *Letters of Queen Elizabeth and King James*, pp.40–1

54. Fraser, *Mary, Queen of Scots*, pp.506–12

55. Cotton MS Julius F vi fo.248: Defence of the Queen's Silence on the Succession [1587?]

56. HMC *Salisbury* III, p.199

57. Perry, M, *The Word of a Prince* (London, 1990), p.273; Strickland, A, *The Life of Queen Elizabeth* (London, 1910), p.476

58. Perry, *Word of a Prince*, pp.272–3; Johnson, P, *Elizabeth I: A*

study in power and intellect (London, 1974), p.291; Fraser, *Mary, Queen of Scots*, p.529

59. Akrigg, *Letters of King James VI & I*, pp.77–8
60. *CSP Scotland*, X, p.249
61. Akrigg, *Letters of King James VI & I*, pp.80–1; TNA SP 52/41 fo.74
62. Cotton Caligula C IX, fos.192–3, James VI to Elizabeth I, 26 January 1587; Akrigg, *Letters of King James VI & I*, pp.81–3
63. *Letters of Queen Elizabeth and King James*, pp.43–5. 'Stays' refers to the position of a sailing vessel in relation to the wind.
64. BM Cotton MS Titus C VII ff.48–53
65. Camden, *Historie*, p.103; *CSPS* IV, p.35
66. 'A report of the manner of execution of the Scottish Queen performed the 8 day of February 1586 [1587]', cited in Hon. Mrs Maxwell Scott, *The Tragedy of Fotheringay* (Edinburgh, 1905)
67. Longford, E (ed), *The Oxford Book of Royal Anecdotes* (Oxford University Press, 1989), p.244; Melville, *Memoirs*, p.314. The dog died soon afterwards, apparently from pining for his dead mistress.
68. Camden, *Historie*, p.115; BM Lansdowne MS 1236 fo.32
69. Camden, *Historie*, p.115; *CSPV* VIII, p.256; Weir, *Elizabeth the Queen*, p.381; Melville, *Memoirs*, p.318; *CSP Scotland Elizabeth*, II, pp.274–5. See also: *CSPF Elizabeth 1586–7*, p.688
70. HMC *Salisbury* III, pp.230–1, p.334; Melville, *Memoirs*, pp.314–15; *Calendar of Border Papers*, I, no.484, p.245; no.485, p.245
71. Elizabeth, *Collected Works*, p. 296
72. Boyle, J (ed), *Memoirs of the Life of Robert Carey ...Written by Himself* (London, 1759), p.12; *Letters of Queen Elizabeth and King James*, p.45; *CSP Scotland Elizabeth*, II, p.285
73. Melville, *Memoirs*, p.318; *Letters of Queen Elizabeth and King James*, pp.45–6; Akrigg, *Letters of King James VI & I*, pp.84–5; HMC *Salisbury* III, p.230; *CSPF Elizabeth 1586–8*, p.276
74. Melville, *Memoirs*, pp.315–18; HMC *Salisbury* III, pp.230–1 or *CSPF Elizabeth 1586–8*, p.276

Chapter 7. 'An eaglet of her own kind'

1. Somerset, *Elizabeth*, p.561
2. HMC *Salisbury* III, p.268; *CSP Scotland Elizabeth*, II, pp.17, 605, 687
3. Durant, DN, *Arbella Stuart. A Rival to the Queen* (London,

1978), p.45; *Letters of Arbella Stuart*, p.20; Edwards, P, *Sir Walter Raleigh* (London, 1953), p.298

4. Allen, W, *An admonition to the nobility and people of England and Ireland concerninge the present vvarres made for the execution of his Holines sentence, by the highe and mightie Kinge Catholike of Spaine. By the Cardinal of Englande* (Antwerp, 1588), pp.8–9; Weir, *Elizabeth*, p.381

5. *Letters of Queen Elizabeth and King James*, pp.47–8

6. *Letters of Queen Elizabeth and King James*, p.50

7. *Letters of Queen Elizabeth and King James*, p.52; Akrigg, *Letters of King James VI & I*, pp.88–9

8. *Letters of Queen Elizabeth and King James*, p.53

9. Haigh, *Elizabeth*, p.173

10. This still survives in the collections of The National Archives: SP 12/215 fo.114

11. *CSPV* IX, p.541

12. Durant, *Arbella*, p.52

13. Gristwood, *Arbella*, p.130

14. Stewart, A, *The Cradle King: A Life of James VI & I* (London, 2003), p.111

15. Stewart, *Cradle King*, p.112

16. *Letters of Queen Elizabeth and King James*, pp.60–2

17. *CSPS* IV, p.578 BL Lansdowne MS 103, fol. 194r

18. Alford, S, *All His Spies: The Secret World of Robert Cecil* (London, 2024)

19. *Letters of Queen Elizabeth and King James*, pp.60–2, 68–9, 70, 72–3, 76, 90

20. *Letters of Arbella Stuart*, pp.21–2; Lewalski, Keifer B, 'Writing Resistance in Letters: Arbella Stuart and the Rhetoric of Disguise and Defiance', in *Letters of Queen Elizabeth and King James, Writing Women in Jacobean England* (Cambridge, 1993), p.70; *CSP Scotland Elizabeth*, II, p.413; 1587–8 IX, p.661. The Duke of Parma was himself put forward as a potential husband for Arbella in July 1590. *CSP Scotland Elizabeth* Vol.II, p.360

Chapter 8. 'By so many knots am I linked unto you'

1. BL Additional MS 23109, fols. 43r–44v

2. Harrison, *Letters of Queen Elizabeth*, p.83

3. Wentworth, P, *A Pithie Exhortation to her Maiestie for Establishing her Successor to the Crowne. Whereunto is added a Discourse Containing the Authors Opinion of the True and Lawfull Successor to Her Maiestie* [1598]

4. *Gorboduc*, quoted in *Minor Elizabethan Drama: I Pre-Shakespearean Tragedies* (London and New York, 1913), p.51

5. An excellent analysis of the dramatisation of the succession question is provided by Axton, M, *The Queen's Two Bodies: Drama and the Elizabethan Succession* (London, 1977)

6. BL Harley MS 6846 fo.108 – James Morice to Peter Wentworth [1593]; fo.88r – Oliver St John's deposition [1593]; Lefranc, P, 'Un Inédit de Raleigh sur la Succession', *Etudes anglaises*, 13 (1960), pp.44–5

7. *Leycester's Commonwealth*, p.112; McIlwain, *Political Works of James I*, p.12; Wentworth, *Pithie Exhortation*, p.66; Allingham, *Captain Cuellar's Adventures in Connacht & Ulster*, p.62

8. TNA SP 52/51 fo.75: Elizabeth I to James VI, 22 December 1593

9. Bagley, JJ, *The Earls of Derby 1485–1985* (London, 1985), p.53

10. Manley, L, 'From Strange's Men to Pembroke's Men: 2 "Henry VI" and The First Part of the Contention', *Shakespeare Quarterly*, 54 No.3 (Oxford, 2003), pp.253–87

11. Manley, 'Strange's Men', pp.253–87

12. BL Lansdowne MS 71 fo.3 Elizabeth, Countess of Shrewsbury to William Cecil, Lord Burghley, 21 September 1592; Gristwood, *Arbella*, p.124

13. Durant, *Arbella*, p.68; Persons, R, *A Conference About the Next Succession to the Crown of England* [Antwerp, 1594], pp.141, 249); HMC *Salisbury*, XII, p.658

14. Gristwood, *Arbella*, p.139; HMC *Salisbury* IV, p.335; *CSPD Elizabeth 1601–03*, p.37; Doran, S and Kewes, P (eds), *Doubtful and Dangerous: The Question of Succession in Late Elizabethan England* (Manchester, 2014), p.119

15. Stewart, *The Cradle King*, p.161

16. HMC *Salisbury*, IX, pp.307–10; Nenner, *The Right to be King*, p.265n

17. *CSP Scotland* XII, p.336; TNA SP 52/54 fo.1: Memorial for the Queen's envoy to the King of Scots [1594]; SP 52/54 fo.3: Elizabeth's acceptance of James VI's invitation to be godmother to his son, Henry [1594]; *CSP Scotland Elizabeth*, II, p.410

18. Ferdinando's daughters claimed their father's estates. The

complex and increasingly bitter legal battle eventually resulted in the lands being divided between William, his nieces and the Queen.

19. Melville, *Memoirs*, pp.366–9; TNA SP 52/54 fo.36: Anne of Denmark to Elizabeth I [August/September 1594]

20. *CSP Scotland Elizabeth*, II, pp.422, 431; TNA SP 52/54 fo.23: *A True Report of the Most Triumphant, and Royal Accomplishment of the Baptism of the most Excellent, right High, and mighty Prince, Frederik Henry, By the grace of God, Prince of Scotland, Solemnized the 30. day of August 1594*; Melville, A, *Principis Scoti-Britannorum Natalia* (Edinburgh, 1594); TNA SP 52/54 fo.34 James VI's response to Elizabeth I [1594]

21. Francis was a son of John Stewart, Prior of Coldingham, an illegitimate son of James V and his mistress Elizabeth Carmichael. Although he shared the same title, he was no relation of the even more notorious Lord Bothwell, James Hepburn, third husband of Mary, Queen of Scots.

22. *Letters of Queen Elizabeth and King James*, pp.100–03; Akrigg, *Letters of King James VI & I*, pp.128–30

23. *Letters of Queen Elizabeth and King James*, pp.105–8; Akrigg, *Letters of King James VI & I*, pp.132–4

24. *Letters of Queen Elizabeth and King James*, pp.110–12

25. *Letters of Queen Elizabeth and King James*, pp.169–70

26. Bailey, A, *The Succession to the English Crown: A historical sketch* (London, 1879), p.200

27. *Letters of Arbella Stuart*, p.29n

28. Doran and Kewes, *Doubtful and Dangerous*, pp.48, 65

29. See for example: Henry Hooke, *Of succession to the Crowne of England*, BL MS Royal 17 B XI fo.12v; Thomas Wilson, State of England, TNA SP 12/280 p.2

30. Persons, R, *A Conference about the next succession to the Crowne of Ingland* [Antwerp, 1594]

31. Guy, *Elizabeth*, p.252; Wentworth, *Pithie Exhortation*, p.6

32. A copy of Dickson's tract survives in the National Library of Scotland, Advocates' MS.31.4.8. The fact that both Stephen and Henry predated Edward III's statute about aliens, and were therefore poor examples, was later challenged by other commentators, notably Peter Wentworth.

33. Mayer, *Breaking the Silence on the Succession*, pp.16, 203–21; TNA SP 52/58 nos.3 and 10, 7 and 18 January 1596; McIlwain, *Political Works of James I*, p.11; Bruce, *Correspondence*, p.10

Chapter 9. 'For all the crowns in the world'

1. Cross, *The Puritan Earl*, pp.271–3
2. Wentworth, P, *A Pithie Exhortation to her Maiestie for Establishing her Successor to the Crowne. Whereunto is added a Discourse Containing the Authors Opinion of the True and Lawfull Successor to Her Maiestie* [1598], pp.66, 71
3. BL Lansdowne MS 79 fos.4 and 6: Testimony of Edmund Neville [November 1595]; Manning, R, 'The prosecution of Sir Michael Blount, Lieutenant of the Tower of London, 1595', *Bulletin of the Institute of Historical Research*, 57 (Oxford, 1984), pp.216–24
4. *Letters of Queen Elizabeth and King James*, p.113
5. *Register of the Privy Council of Scotland*, V, pp.324–5; Tunstall, E, 'The Paradox of the Valentine Thomas Affair: English Diplomacy, Royal Correspondence and the Elizabethan Succession', *Journal of the Australian and New Zealand Association of Medieval and Early Modern Studies*, 38, No.1 (Canberra, 2021), p.80
6. *CSP Scotland Elizabeth*, II, pp.744–6; Cameron, AI (ed), *The Warrender Papers*, I and II (Edinburgh, 1931–2), II, p.435
7. *Letters of Queen Elizabeth and King James*, pp.121–3
8. *Letters of Queen Elizabeth and King James*, pp.124–6
9. TNA SP 52/52 fo.234: A minute of Her Majesty's letter to George Nicholson, 25 April 1598
10. Gristwood, *Arbella*, p.152
11. *Letters of Queen Elizabeth and King James*, pp.126–7
12. TNA SP 59/37 fo.18: Examination of Robert Crawforth, 2 March 1598; *Calendar of Border Papers*, II, no.915, pp.520–2
13. TNA SP 12/268 fo.34: Dudley Carleton to John Chamberlain, 1 August 1598; SP 52/63 fo.81: *Confessions of Valentine Thomas*, 20 December 1598
14. TNA SP 52/62 fo.29: George Nicolson to Lord Burghley, 11 May 1598; *Calendar of Border Papers*, II, no.946, p.537; 'The Bond of Association, 1584', in Archer, IW and Douglas Price, F (eds), *English Historical Documents*, V(A), 1558–1603 (London, 2011), p.961
15. TNA SP 52/62 fo.38: James Hudson to Queen Elizabeth [c.June 1598]
16. *Calendar of Border Papers*, II, no.942, p.535

17. TNA SP 52/62 fo.44 Elizabeth to James, 1 July 1598
18. BL Cotton MS Titus C VII fo.19 James to Elizabeth, 30 July 1598
19. TNA SP 52/63 fos.30–1 David Foulis to Sir Robert Cecil, 9 October 1598
20. *Letters of Queen Elizabeth and King James*, pp.126–7
21. Guy, J, *Elizabeth: The Forgotten Years* (London, 2017), p.319
22. TNA SP 52/63 fo.82 Declaration of Queen Elizabeth Concerning Valentine Thomas, 20 December 1598; SP 52/52 fos.230r–231. See also: Harrison, GB, *The Elizabethan Journals: Being a record of those things most talked of during the years 1591– 1603* (London, 1955), p.325
23. *Letters of Queen Elizabeth and King James*, pp.127–8
24. TNA SP 52/64 fo.33 Sir James Elphinstone to Sir Robert Cecil, 28 February 1599; *Letters of Queen Elizabeth and King James*, pp.128–31
25. *CSP Scotland Elizabeth*, II, p.752, Elizabeth's instructions for one to be sent to Scotland, 1 July [1598]
26. *Letters of Queen Elizabeth and King James*, p.137
27. Birch, T, *Memoirs of the Reign of Queen Elizabeth from the year 1581 till her Death*, 2 vols. (London, 1754), II, pp.470–2
28. Birch, *Memoirs*, I, p.176; Spedding, J, *The Letters and Life of Francis Bacon*, II (London, 1874), pp.470–2
29. *Calendar State Papers Scotland*, XIII part ii (London, 1969), pp.1128–30
30. HMC *Salisbury*, IX (London, 1902), p.308
31. Bertie, G, *Five Generations of a Loyal House*, Part 1 (London, 1845), pp.338–49
32. Brennan, M, Kinnamon, N and Hannay, M (eds), *The Letters of Rowland Whyte to Sir Robert Sidney* (Philadelphia, 2013), p.378
33. HMC *Salisbury*, IX, p.308; Mayer, *Breaking the Silence on the Succession*, p.19; Bruce, J (ed), *Correspondence of King James VI of Scotland with Sir Robert Cecil and others in England, during the reign of Queen Elizabeth* (London, 1861), p.60
34. Williams, C (ed), *Thomas Platter's Travels in England, 1599* (London, 1937), p.228
35. Smith, T, *The State of England, Anno Dom.1600*, edited by Fisher, FJ, Camden Miscellany, XVI, 3rd series, no.52 (London, 1936), p.9
36. Smith, *The State of England*, pp.2, 5
37. Wilson, T, 'The State of England, Anno Dom.1600', *Camden Miscellany*, XVI (London, 1936) pp.1–9

38. Doran and Kewes, *Doubtful and Dangerous*, pp.224–5
39. Craigie, J (ed), *The Basilikon Doron of King James VI*, 2 vols, Scottish Text Society, 3rd series, 16, 18 (Edinburgh, 1944–50), I, pp.25, 175; Craigie, J (ed), *Minor Prose Works of King James VI and I* (Edinburgh, 1982), pp.70–1, 81
40. Akrigg, *Letters of King James VI & I*, pp.165–7; *CSP Scotland Elizabeth*, II, no.41 Nicolson to Cecil, 9 July 1600

Chapter 10. 'Dead but not yet buried'

1. *Letters of Queen Elizabeth and King James VI of Scotland*, pp.132–3
2. *Letters of Queen Elizabeth and King James VI of Scotland*, pp.90–3
3. *Letters of Queen Elizabeth and King James VI of Scotland*, pp.90–3
4. HMC *Salisbury*, XI, pp.15, 90
5. Hammer, PEJ, 'The Earl of Essex, Fulke Greville, and the employment of scholars', *Studies in Philology*, 91 (North Carolina, 1994), pp.167–80
6. Akrigg, *Letters of King James VI & I*, pp.214–15
7. Akrigg, *Letters of King James VI & I*, pp.169–70; Bruce, *Correspondence*, p.82
8. Doran and Kewes, *Doubtful and Dangerous*, p.115
9. Akrigg, *Letters of King James VI & I*, p.170
10. Akrigg, *Letters of King James VI & I*, pp.173–7. See also: Harrison, *Elizabethan Journals*, p.266
11. TNA SP 52/67 fo.14, George Nicolson to Sir Robert Cecil, 7 February 1601; Akrigg, *Letters of King James VI & I*, pp.173–7, fo.27, 14 February 1601
12. HMC *Salisbury*, X, pp.155–6, XIV, p.176; Stafford, HG, *James VI of Scotland and the Throne of England* (New York and London, 1940), p.251; Akrigg, *Letters of King James VI & I*, p.173
13. TNA SP 52/67 fo.92 Sir Robert Cecil to the Master of Grey, April 1601
14. BL Sloane MS 1786 fos.53–5, Elizabeth to James, 11 May 1601; *Letters of Queen Elizabeth and King James*, pp.134–5
15. *Letters of Queen Elizabeth and King James*, pp.137–8. Ashfield remained a prisoner in the Tower for the rest of Elizabeth's reign but was returned to favour in England when James became king. He was knighted at the Tower on 14 March 1604, given the lease of Whaddon Priory in his native Buckinghamshire and

admitted as one of his Majesty's pensioners in ordinary the following month.

16. TNA 31/3/32 fos.46–47, 55, Thuméry de Boissise to Henry IV, 14 and 30 April [O.S.] 1601

Chapter 11. 'Suppressing all other competitors'

1. *CSPV* IX, p.528; Akrigg, *Letters of King James VI & I*, p.175
2. Akrigg, *Letters of King James VI & I*, pp.178–81
3. Dalrymple, D, Lord Hailes (ed), *The Secret Correspondence of Sir Robert Cecil with James VI King of Scotland. Now First Published* (Edinburgh, 1766), pp.202–3; *Letters of Queen Elizabeth and King James*, p.17
4. Cheyney, EP, *A History of England from the Defeat of the Armada to the Death of Elizabeth*, 2 vols. (Gloucester, 1967), II, p.558
5. Bruce, *Correspondence*, p.7; *Letters of Queen Elizabeth and King James*, pp.3–8, 10–11
6. Wilson, *James VI & I*, p.155; TNA SP 52/62 fo.29; 52/52 fo.234, April 1598; Read and Read (eds), *Elizabeth of England*, p.101; Bruce, *Correspondence*, p.57
7. Gristwood, *Arbella*, p.147
8. BL MS Royal 17 B XI fos.1–19: Hooke, H, *Of succession to the Crown of England* [1601]; Craig, T, *The Right of Succession to the Kingdom of England*, in Nenner, H, *The Right to be King*, p.19
9. BL MS Royal 17 B XI fos.1–19
10. Harington, J, *A Tract on the Succession to the Crown* [1602], Chapter 2
11. *Letters of Queen Elizabeth and King James*, pp.140–1; Harrison, *Elizabethan Journals*, p.263
12. Hartley, *Proceedings*, III, pp.296–7
13. Collins, A (ed), *Letters and Memorials of State, in the reigns of Queen Mary, Queen Elizabeth, etc ...Written and collected by Sir Henry Sidney, etc*, 2 vols. (London, 1746) II, pp.200–3; Harrison, *Elizabethan Journals*, p.265
14. *Letters of Queen Elizabeth and King James*, pp.146, 147
15. Bruce, *Correspondence*, p.46
16. Harrison, *Elizabethan Journals*, p.290
17. *Letters of Queen Elizabeth and King James*, pp.149–50; TNA SP 52/68 f.75, Elizabeth I to James VI, 4 July 1602
18. Mayer, *Breaking the Silence on the Succession*, p.18

19. Harrison, *Elizabethan Journals*, p.263
20. Gristwood, *Arbella*, p.171; Akrigg, *Letters of King James VI & I*, pp.187, 189; Nenner, *The Right to be King*, p.29
21. Akrigg, *Letters of King James VI & I*, pp.192–5
22. Akrigg, *Letters of King James VI & I*, p.191; Gristwood, *Arbella*, pp.170–1
23. Houlbrooke, RA, *James VI and I: Ideas, Authority and Government* (Aldershot, 2006), p.42; *CSPS* IV, pp.720–9
24. Bruce, *Correspondence*, p.72; Teulet, A, *Relations politiques de la France et de l'Espagne avec l'Ecosse au 16e siècle*, 5 vols. (Paris, 1862), IV, p.165
25. Stafford, *James VI of Scotland*, p.288; Akrigg, *Letters of King James VI & I*, p.201
26. Brewer, JS (ed), Goodman, G, *The Court of King James I*, 2 vols. (London, 1839), I, pp.96–8; Camden, *Historie*, p.422; *CSPD Elizabeth 1580–1625* Addenda, p.407
27. *CSPV* VII, p.564; *CSPV* IX p.541; HMC *Salisbury* XIV, p.253; XV, p.65
28. Durant, *Arbella*, pp.95–6
29. *CSPV* VII, p.564
30. HMC *Salisbury* XII, pp.593–6
31. HMC *Salisbury* XII, pp.594–5
32. HMC *Salisbury* XII, pp.593–624, 626–7
33. HMC *Salisbury* XII, pp.682–3, 691, 693

Chapter 12. 'Wishing no more queens'

1. HMC *De L'Isle and Dudley* II, p.475
2. Harington, *Nugae Antiquae*, pp.90, 96; Weir, *Elizabeth*, p.480; Haigh, *Elizabeth*, p.166
3. Harington, Nugae Antiquae, pp.90, 96; Weir, *Elizabeth*, p.480; Haigh, *Elizabeth*, p.166.; Nichols, *Progresses of King James*, III, p.612; Birch, *Memoirs*, II, p.505; Carey, *Memoirs*, pp.137–8
4. Maclean, J (ed), *Letters from Sir Robert Cecil to Sir George Carew* (London, 1864), p.128; Harrison, *Elizabethan Journals*, p.300
5. Harrison, *Elizabethan Journals*, p.306
6. McClure, NE (ed), *The Letters and Epigrams of Sir John Harington* (London, 1930), pp.96–8
7. Craig, T, *The Right of Succession to the Kingdom of England* [1602] (London, 1703), pp.53, 127

8. Harington, *Tract on the Succession*, p.71
9. Bruce, *Correspondence*, pp.5, 58–60
10. TNA SP 52/69 f.53, Elizabeth I's last letter to James VI, 5 January 1603; *Letters of Queen Elizabeth and King James*, pp.154–6
11. Bassnett, *Feminist Perspective*, p.258; Read, EP and Read, C (eds), *Elizabeth of England*. [An edition of the manuscript entitled 'Certain Observations concerning the life and Reign of Queen Elizabeth' by John Clapham] (Philadelphia, 1951), p.98
12. Merton, C, 'The Women who served Queen Mary and Queen Elizabeth: Ladies, Gentlewomen and Maids of the Privy Chamber, 1553–1603', Cambridge PhD thesis (1992), p.90; Birch, *Memoirs* II, pp.506–7; Carey, *Memoirs*, p.140; Pasmore, S, *The Life and Times of Queen Elizabeth I at Richmond Palace* (Richmond Local History Society, 2003), p.65; *CSPD Elizabeth 1601–3*, pp.298, 301; *CSPV* IX, p.554. See also: HMC *Salisbury* XII, p.670
13. Pryor, *Elizabeth: Life in Letters*, p.131; HMC *Salisbury* XII, p.681; *CSPD Elizabeth 1601–03*, p.299
14. Gristwood, *Arbella*, p.156
15. HMC *Salisbury*, no.135, pp.139–45; *Letters of Arbella Stuart*, pp. 158–75, 278–81
16. *Letters of Arbella Stuart*, p.39
17. HMC *Salisbury* XII, pp.685–6
18. Durant, *Arbella*, p.108; HMC *Salisbury* XII, pp.690, 692, 693
19. *CSPD Elizabeth 1601–03*, p.301
20. *CSPD Elizabeth 1601–03*, p.301; Gristwood, *Arbella*, p.188; *CSPV* VII, p.554; HMC *Salisbury* XII, p.693
21. *CSPV* VII, pp.562, 564; *CSPD Elizabeth 1601–03*, p.302; Edwards, *Sir Walter Raleigh*, p.296
22. *Letters of Arbella Stuart*, pp.158–75
23. Somerset, *Elizabeth*, p.553; *CSPS* IV, p.650; HMC *De L'Isle and Dudley* II, p.475; *CSPV* IX, p.529, 539–42. Scaramelli includes Henry's mistress Elizabeth Blount as one of the wives.
24. *CSPV* IX, pp.539–42; Bruce, *Correspondence*, p.55
25. *Leycester's Commonwealth*, p.95; Persons, *A Conference*, p.266; McIlwain, *Political Works of James I*, p.37
26. *CSPV* IX, pp.539–42
27. TNA SP 14/3 fo.134; SP 14/4 fo.28v
28. Carey, *Memoirs*, p.137
29. Harrison, *Elizabethan Journals*, p.319
30. Carey, *Memoirs*, pp.139–40

31. BM Kings MS 123 fo.17 Christophe de Harlay, Comte de Beaumont to Villeroy [March 1603]; *CSPV* X, p.15; Nenner, *The Right to be King*, p.21; Mayer, *Breaking the Silence on the Succession*, p.27

32. Harrison, *Elizabethan Journals*, p.324; Spencer Scott, H (ed), Wilbraham, R, 'The Journal of Sir Roger Wilbraham', *The Camden Miscellany*, X (London, 1902), p.54

33. Harrison, *Elizabethan Journals*, pp.319, 324

34. *CSPV* IX no.1159, p.554; *CSPD Elizabeth 1601–03*, pp.302–3

35. Doran and Kewes, *Doubtful and Dangerous*, p.145

36. Harrison, *Elizabethan Journals*, p.319

37. Philodikaios, I [pseudonym], *A Treatise Declaring, And confirming against all objections the just title and right of the most excellent and worthie Prince, Iames the sixt, King of Scotland, to the succession of the crown of England* (Edinburgh, 1599), p.6

38. Read and Read (eds), *Elizabeth of England*, p.101. Originally, January 1 was the date of the new year in the Julian calendar, but after the fall of the Roman Empire, the date gradually changed in various parts of Europe to March 25, to conform with the Christian festival of the Annunciation. England adopted 25 March as New Year's Day in the twelfth century.

39. Bruce, J (ed), *The Diary of John Manningham Camden Society* (London, 1868), entry for 23 March 1603

40. SP 14/1 fo.2 Robert Cecil to James VI and I, 23/24 March 1603

41. Powell, GH (ed), *Memoirs of Robert Cary Earl of Monmouth* (London, 1905), p.74

42. Harrison, *Elizabethan Journals*, p.319

43. Harrison, *Elizabethan Journals*, p.327

44. Powell, Carey, *Memoirs*, p.74

45. BL Cotton MS Titus CVII fo.57r

46. *CSPV* X, pp.509–10. John Clapham provided a similar account: Read and Read (eds), *Elizabeth of England*, p.99

47. BL Cotton MS Titus C 107 fo.46; CVII fo.57r

48. *CSPV* IX, pp.564–6

49. BM Kings MS 123 fos.16r–17 Christophe de Harlay, Comte de Beaumont to Villeroy [March 1603]; *CSPV* X, p.15; Nenner, *The Right to be King*, p.21; BNF MS FF 3501 fos.275v–7v

50. BNF MS FF 3501 fos.275v–7v

51. BL Additional MS 38138 fo.27r ; Doran, S, *From Tudor to Stuart: The regime change from Elizabeth I to James I* (Oxford, 2024), p.13

52. Read and Read, *John Clapham*, p.101; Ellis, H (ed), *Original Letters Illustrative of English History, Including Numerous Royal Letters 3rd Series,Volumes III* (London, 1846), p.195; BM Kings MS 123 fo.17 Christophe de Harlay, Comte de Beaumont to Villeroy [March 1603]; *CSPV* X, p.15; Nenner, *The Right to be King*, p.21

Chapter 13. 'This peaceable coming in of the King'

1. Powell, Carey, *Memoirs*, pp.75–7
2. Powell, Carey, *Memoirs*, pp.77–80
3. Akrigg, *Letters of King James VI & I*, p.208; Alford, S, *All His Spies*, p.287
4. SP 14/1 fo.3 'A Proclamation, declaring the undoubted Right of our Soveraigne Lord King James, to the Crowne of the Realmes of England, Fraunce and Ireland', 24 March 1603; HMC *Salisbury*, XV, p.1; Larkin, F and Hughes, PL (eds), *Stuart Royal Proclamations*, 2 vols. (Oxford, 1973), I, vi, pp.2–3; *CSPD Elizabeth 1603–10*, p.1
5. Doran, *From Tudor to Stuart*, pp.124–5
6. Blackstone, W, *Commentaries on the Laws of England* (Oxford, 1765), I, p.184 ; [Anonymous], *Treason Unmask'd: Or the Queen's Title, The Revolution, And the Hanover Succession Vindicated Against the Treasonable Positions of a Book lately Publish'd, Intitled, The Hereditary Right of the Crown of England asserted; the History of the Succession since the Conquest clear'd, and the true English Constitution vindicated, from the Misrepresentations of Dr Higden's View and Defence* (London, 1713), p.228
7. SP 14/1 John Chamberlain to James VI and I, 25 March 1603; Bruce, *Diary of John Manningham*, p.147
8. TNA SP 14/1 fo.3: Sir Robert Cotton, 'A Discourse of ye Descent of the King's Majesty from the Saxons', 26 March 1603
9. Clifford, DJH (ed), *The Diaries of Lady Anne Clifford* (Stroud, 1992), p.21; *CSPV* X, p.15; Nenner, *The Right to be King*, p.17; HMC *Salisbury*, pp.10–11, 18, 28, 31–3; *CSPV* X, pp.3, 509; Bacon, F, *The felicity of Queen Elizabeth and her times, with other things* (London, 1651), p.21
10. Powell, Carey, *Memoirs*, p.80
11. McClure, NE (ed), *The Letters of John Chamberlain*

(Philadelphia, 1939), pp.188–9; *Diary of John Manningham*, pp.27–8; Guy, *Elizabeth*, p.387; Ellis, *Original Letters*, III, pp.64–7

12. *Chamberlain Letters*, p.189; Sommerville, *James VI and I: Political Writings*, pp.132–3; Akrigg, *Letters of King James VI & I*, p.210

13. Somerset, *Elizabeth*, p.569; Bruce, *Manningham Diary*, p.159; Nichols, *Progresses of King James*, III, p.613; Strickland, *Life of Elizabeth*, pp.704–5. Similar rumours had circulated after the death of Elizabeth's father, Henry VIII, and her ancestor William the Conqueror, both of whose corpses were said to have exploded from the build-up of noxious gases.

14. Read and Read (eds), *Elizabeth of England*, p.106

Chapter 14. 'Play the king'

1. Akrigg, *Letters of James VI & I*, pp.206 –7

2. Thomson, T (ed), Calderwood, D, *The History of the Kirk of Scotland*, 8 vols. (Edinburgh, 1842–49), VI, pp.215–16

3. Richards, JM, 'The English accession of James VI: "national" identity, gender and the personal monarchy of England', *English Historical Review*, 117 (Oxford, 2002), p.527

4. *CSPV* X, p.15

5. In fact, James only visited his native kingdom once (in 1617) after becoming King of England.

6. *CSPV* X, pp.2–16

7. Akrigg, *Letters of King James VI & I*, p.215; Guy, *Elizabeth*, p.389; *Letters of Arbella Stuart*, p.43

8. Stowe, J, *The Annales of England, faithfully collected out of the most autenticall authors, records and other monuments of antiquitie, lately collected, from the first habitation untill this present yeare 1605* (London, 1605), p.815

9. Nichols, *Progresses of King James*, I, pp.113–14, 139–40; Spencer Scott, H (ed), Wilbraham, R, 'The Journal of Sir Roger Wilbraham', *The Camden Miscellany*, X (London, 1902), p.56; Mayer, *Breaking the Silence on the Succession*, pp.315–22. Persons soon made it clear that he had an ulterior motive and hoped to win the new King of England over to the Catholic cause. His letter went unanswered.

10. Doran, *From Tudor to Stuart*, pp.124–5

11. Wilbraham, *Journal*, p.60; *CSPV*, X, pp.9, 39; Doran, *From Tudor to Stuart*, p.23; Stewart, A, *The Cradle King: A Life of James VI & I* (London, 2003), pp.171-2; Bacon, *Letters and Life*, III, p.77; Weldon, Sir A, *The Court and Character of King James* (London, 1650), pp.179, 186

12. Wilbraham, *Journal*, p.56

13. Wilson, A, *The History of Great Britain, being the Life and Reign of King James the First* (London, 1653), p.12–13

14. Wilson, *King James the First*, pp.12–13; *CSPV* X, p.513

15. Doran, *From Tudor to Stuart*, p.100; *CSPV* X, p.48; Teuelet, A, *Relations politiques de la France et de l'Espagne avec l'Ecosse au 16e siècle*, 5 vols. (Paris, 1862), IV, pp.375, 378–9

16. Birch, T, *An Historical View of the Negotiations between the Courts of England, France, and Brussels: From the Year 1592 to 1617* (London, 1749), p.179

17. *CSPV* X, pp.3, 42

18. Gristwood, *Arbella*, p.258

19. *Letters of Arbella Stuart*, pp.194, 212–13

20. Craig, A, *The Poeticall Essayes of Alexander Craige Scotobritaine* (London, 1604), sig.C4

21. TNA SP 31/3 fo.35 Christophe de Harlay, Count de Beaumont to Villeroy [1605]

22. Holles, G, *Memorials of the Holles Family 1493–1656*, Camden Society, 3rd series, LV (London, 1937), p.94; HMC Portland, IX, p.133; Cuddy, N, 'The Revival of the Entourage: The Bedchamber of James I, 1603–1625', in Starkey, D et al, *The English Court: From the Wars of the Roses to the Civil War* (London, 1987), pp.173–225

23. Harington, *Nugae Antiquae*, I, pp.348–52; Akrigg, GPV, *Jacobean Pageant or The Court of King James I* (London, 1962), p.242

24. *CSPV* X, pp. 58–72 (entry 91)

25. *CSPV* X, p.90; Nichols, *Progresses of King James*, p.491; *CSPV* X, p.513; Lodge, E (ed), *Illustrations of British History, Biography and Manners*, 3 vols. (London, 1838), pp.137–8; TNA SP 52/51 fo.75 Elizabeth I to James VI, 22 December 1593

26. *CSPV* X, pp.218, 510

27. Harington, *Nugae Antiquae*, I, p.345

28. Stewart, *Cradle King*, p.208

29. Lewalski, Keifer B, 'Writing Resistance in Letters: Arbella Stuart and the Rhetoric of Disguise and Defiance', in Stewart,

Cradle King, Writing Women in Jacobean England (Cambridge, 1993), pp.77–8

30. *Letters of Arbella Stuart*, pp.44–5
31. *Letters of Arbella Stuart*, p.186

Chapter 15. 'A great quantity of gunpowder'

1. Akrigg, *Letters of James VI & I*, p.207
2. TNA SP 14/1 fo.10 'The lineal descent of the Saxon Kings to James the King now living', 26 March 1603
3. Akrigg, *Letters of James VI & I*, p.207; Bruce, *Correspondence*, p.75; McIlwain, *Political Works of James I*, pp.271–3
4. 1 Jac.I, c.1 'A moste joyfull and juste Recognition of the immediate lawfull and undoubted Succession Descent and Righte of the Crowne, *The Statutes of the Realm*, 11 Vols (London 1820–28), IV, part ii, pp.1017–18
5. 'A Moste joyfull and juste Recognition of the immediate lawfull and undoubted Succession Descent and Righte of the Crowne', *The Statutes of the Realm*, 11 Vols (London, 1820–28), IV, part ii, pp.1017–18
6. Wright, CJ (ed), *Sir Robert Cotton as Collector: Essays on an Early Stuart Courtier and his Legacy* (London, 1997), p.18
7. Isaiah, Chapter 49, verse 23
8. Stewart, *Cradle King*, pp.206, 209
9. *CSPV* X, p.10; *Journal of the House of Commons* (London, 1802), pp.366–8; Stewart, *Cradle King*, p.213
10. Lodge, *Illustrations of British History*, III, p.108; *CSPV* X, p.353; BL Harley MS 677, ff.47v–48r
11. James I: 1603/4 Act of Parliament against conjuration and witchcraft and dealing with evil and wicked spirits
12. Rye, WB (ed), *England as seen by Foreigners in the days of Elizabeth and James the First* (London, 1865), p.121; Smout, TC, *Anglo-Scottish Relations from 1603 to 1900* (Oxford and London, 2005), p.17
13. Akrigg, *Letters of James VI & I*, p.207
14. Wormald, J, 'James VI and I', *New Oxford Dictionary of National Biography* (Oxford, 2004)
15. Nichols, *Progresses of King James*, I, p.578
16. Nichols, *Progresses of King James*, I, p.578
17. Nichols, *Progresses of King James*, I, p.584

18. *CSPV* X, pp.293, 333; Dalton, M, *The Countrey Justice, Containing the practise of the Justices of the Peace out of their Sessions* (London, 1622), p.317

19. HMC *Salisbury* XVII, no.66, p.134; Marcham, FG, 'James I of England and the Little Beagle Letters', in *Persecution and Liberty: Essays in Honor of George Lincoln Burr* (New York, 1860); Weldon, 'The Character of King James', in Scott, W, *Secret History of the Court of James the First*, 2 vols. (Edinburgh, 1811)

20. Stewart, *Cradle King*, p.184

21. Brewer, *The Court of King James*, I, pp.96–8

22. Gareth Russell provides an excellent assessment of James's sexuality in *Queen James: The Life and Loves of Britain's First King* (London, 2025)

23. Trevor-Roper, H, *Queen Elizabeth's First Historian: William Camden and the beginnings of English 'civil history'* (London, 1971), p.27. Elizabeth's Accession Day would continue to be honoured long into the eighteenth century.

24. Akrigg, *Letters of King James VI & I*, pp.286–7

25. Stewart, *Cradle King*, p.227

26. The measure was known as 'Calvin's Case' after Robert Calvin, the individual concerned. Born in Scotland in November 1605, he was granted estates in England, but his rights to those were challenged on the grounds that, as a Scot, he could not legally own English land. The courts found that he was an English subject and entitled to the benefits of English law. Calvin's Case would have far-reaching consequences. It was later adopted by courts in the United States and played an important role in shaping the American rule of birthright citizenship, which is still in place today.

27. MacCaffrey, WT (ed), *William Camden, The History of the Most Renowned and Victorious Princess Elizabeth, Late Queen of England. Selected Chapters* (Chicago and London, 1970), p.3

28. Camden, *Annales: The True and Royall History*, I, preface; MacCaffrey (ed), Camden, *Annales*, p.3

29. Howard, H, *A True and Perfect Relation of the Whole Proceedings Against the Late most Barbarous Traitors* (London, 1606); BL Cotton MS Titus C VI fo.16or Henry Howard, Earl of Northampton to Robert Cotton [1606]. I am grateful to Julian Harrison, Curator of Pre-1600 Historical Manuscripts at the British Library, for bringing this to my attention.

Chapter 16. 'Without mate and without estate'

1. *CSPV* X, p.514
2. *Chamberlain Letters*, p.292n; *CSPV* XI, p.410. The Privy Council records for this period were destroyed in the Great Fire of London in 1666, so Arbella's claim cannot be proven.
3. BL Harley MS 7003 fos.59–60 William Seymour to the Privy Council, 10 February 1610
4. *CSPV* XI, p.439
5. Ralph Lewis, B, *Monarchy: The History of an Idea* (Stroud, 2003), p.125
6. Akrigg, *Letters of King James VI & I*, pp.320–1
7. *CSPV* XII, p.110; *Letters of Arbella Stuart*, pp.70-2; BL Stowe MS 171 fo.292 Dudley Carleton to Thomas Edmondes, 13 July 1610
8. Spedding, J, et al (eds), *The Works of Francis Bacon*, 14 vols. (London, 1861–72), IX, pp.297–8
9. *Letters of Arbella Stuart*, pp.70–2; BL Stowe MS 171 fo.292 – Dudley Carleton to Thomas Edmondes, 13 July 1610
10. *Letters of Arbella Stuart*, pp.72–4
11. *Letters of Arbella Stuart*, pp.83–4, 250–1, 260, 263–6
12. Akrigg, *Letters of King James VI & I*, pp.326–7. Mary's empty tomb remained within the cathedral at Peterborough but was destroyed by Oliver Cromwell's forces in 1643. As a boy, Cromwell himself may have seen Mary's coffin when it was moved to Westminster in 1612 because the cortège passed close by his school. He would later play an instrumental role in the execution of her grandson, Charles I.
13. Elizabeth had inherited the title Queen of France but it was by then a meaningless carryover from her medieval ancestors.
14. Spedding, J, Ellis, RL and Heath, DD (eds), *The works of Francis Bacon*, 14 vols. (London, 1857–74), XIII, p.239
15. *Henry VIII*, Act V, scene V, lines 39–52
16. *CSPV* XIII, p.138

Chapter 17. 'Facts are facts'

1. Trevor-Roper, *Queen Elizabeth's First Historian*, p.13
2. *Chamberlain Letters*, pp.86–7. Much of Chamberlain's correspondence still survives and is one of the best sources for the early Stuart period.

3. Trevor-Roper, *Queen Elizabeth's First Historian*, p.16. An account of Cotton and Camden's input into de Thou's revision of his Universal History is provided by Botley, P and Vince, M (eds), *The Correspondence of Isaac Casaubon in England* (Geneva, 2018) I, pp.115–19

4. Smith, T, *V. CL. Gulielmi Camdeni et Illustrium Virorum ad G. Camdenum Epistolae* (London, 1691). See for example: no. 9, pp. 139–40

5. MacCaffrey (ed), Camden, *Annales*, p.272

6. MacCaffrey (ed), Camden, *Annales*, pp.259, 272

7. MacCaffrey (ed), Camden, *Annales*, pp.297, 300; Camden, *Annales: The True and Royall History*, I, p.207

8. MacCaffrey (ed), Camden, *Annales*, pp.280–9

9. MacCaffrey (ed), Camden, *Annales*, pp.289–90

10. BL Cotton MS Faustina F I-X

11. I am indebted to Helena Rutkowska, a collaborative DPhil student in partnership between the University of Oxford, Open University and the British Library, and to Julian Harrison and Andrea Clarke at the British Library, for being so generous with their time and expertise.

12. Camden, *Annales: The True and Royall History*, III, pp.229–30

13. Camden, *Annales: The True and Royall History*, IV, p.133; *CSPD Elizabeth* 1598–1601, pp.48–9; HMC *Salisbury* IX, pp.282–3

14. BL Cotton MS Titus CVII fos.57–57r

15. BL Cotton MS Faustina F III, f. 215v–216r; Camden, *Annales: The True and Royall History*, III, pp.380–3

16. Camden, *Annales: The True and Royall History*, III, pp.381–2; BL Cotton MS Titus C VII fo.57r

17. Camden, *Annales: The True and Royall History*, III, p.382

18. Camden, *Annales: The True and Royall History*, III, pp.384; Bruce, *Diary of John Manningham*, p.147; Dekker, T, *1603. The Wonderfull Yeare. Wherein is Shewed the Picture of London Lying Sicke of the Plague* (London, 1603), sig.B2v

19. BL Cotton MS Faustina F VII, f. 166r; IX, f. 129r

20. Camden, *Annales: The True and Royall History*, III, pp.384. The text in italics is a direct quote from *Basilikon Doron*. McIlwain, CH (ed), *The Political Works of James I* (Cambridge, 1918), p.11

21. MacCaffrey (ed), Camden, *Annales*, p.4

22. BL Additional MS 36294 fo.113 Camden to a friend [c.1615]

23. MacCaffrey (ed), Camden, *Annales*, pp.4–6; Persons, R, *Newes*

from Spayne and Holland (Antwerp, 1593); Camden, *Annales* (London, 1625), p.293

24. Trevor-Roper, *Queen Elizabeth's First Historian*, p.18
25. Burnet, G, *A defense of the reflections on the ninth book of the first volum [sic] of Mr. Varillas's History of heresies being a reply to his answer* (Amsterdam, 1687), p.52

Chapter 18. 'The office of a King is unnecessary'

1. *Chamberlain Letters*, p.443; *Letters of Arbella Stuart*, p.93
2. BL Harleian MS 7003 fo.87, Petition from Arbella Stuart to King James I [undated]; fo.146 Arbella Stuart to Viscount Fenton during her imprisonment in the Tower [?1614]; *Letters of Arbella Stuart*, p.101
3. Seymour later married Frances Devereux, the daughter of Arbella's friend, the Earl of Essex. He named his eldest daughter Arbella. Charles I showed greater favour towards William Seymour than his father had, appointing him governor of his eldest son, the future Charles II. It proved a valuable connection. When Charles came to the throne in 1660, he restored Seymour to his great-grandfather's dukedom of Somerset, thereby recognising the validity of the marriage of his grandparents, Katherine Grey and Lord Hertford. Seymour later ordered that Katherine's bones be removed from the humble churchyard of Yoxford and reinterred with those of her husband in a magnificent baroque monument in Salisbury Cathedral. The descendants of the newly created duke survive to this day.
4. Camden, *Annales: The True and Royall History*, I, preface
5. *Epistolae*, no.287, p.351
6. McElwee, W, *The Wisest Fool in Christendom: The Reign of James I and VI* (London, 1958), p.201; Weldon, Sir A, *The Court and Character of King James* (London, 1650), p.177; *CSPV* XV, p.420
7. Halliwell-Phillipps, *Letters of the Kings of England*, 2 vols. (London, 1846), II, p.236
8. Stewart, *Cradle King*, p.341
9. *King James VI and I: political writings*, pp.231–2; Stewart, *Cradle King*, p.341
10. Trevor-Roper, *Queen Elizabeth's First Historian*, pp.19–20
11. Wood, A, *Athenae Oxonienses: An Exact History of All the Writers*

and Bishops Who Have Had Their Education in the University of Oxford, 4 vols. (London, 1813–1820), II, p.347; Trinity College Library, Cambridge MS R.5.20 William Camden, *Annales* [of the reign of James VI and I]

12. Larkin, *Stuart Royal Proclamations*, II, pp.1–2. Charles I's son and eventual successor, Charles II, spent eleven years in exile during the Commonwealth and fought strenuously throughout that time to keep his claim alive. His brother and successor, James II, had to overcome significant opposition to his right to the throne in the so-called Exclusion Crisis. James II's daughter Mary and her husband William of Orange supplanted him in the 'Glorious Revolution' of 1688, but their right to the throne remained the subject of controversy for years to come. Their successor, Mary's sister Anne, the last of the Stuart monarchs, was opposed by the 'Jacobite' supporters of her ousted father.

13. Stewart, *Cradle King*, p.347
14. *CSPV* XIX, p.21
15. *Letters of Queen Elizabeth and King James VI of Scotland*, pp.2–3; TNA SP 52/51 fo.75 Elizabeth I to James VI, 22 December 1593
16. Cotton, R, *Cottoni Posthuma: divers choice pieces of that renowned antiquary Sir Robert Cotton ... preserved from the injury of time, and expos'd to public light, for the benefit of posterity* (London, 1651), pp.41–57; Cannon, J and Griffiths, R, *The Oxford Illustrated History of the British Monarchy* (Oxford, 1988), p.389
17. Jansson, M and Bidwell, WB (eds), *Proceedings in Parliament, 1625* (London and New Haven, 1987) II, p.395
18. Strong, *Coronation*, pp.246, 250; Revelation, Chapter 2, Verse 10
19. Larkin, JF (ed), *Stuart Royal Proclamations: Proclamations of Charles I, 1625–1646* (Oxford, 1983), II, pp.223, 228; *Oxford Illustrated History of the British Monarchy*, p.373
20. The last monarch to do so had been Edward II, who was deposed in 1327.
21. Gardiner, SR (ed), *The Constitutional Documents of the Puritan Revolution* (Oxford, 1903), pp.371–4
22. Gardiner, *Constitutional Documents*, pp.374–6
23. McDiarmid, *Monarchical Republic*, pp.166, 233

Epilogue. 'Surprised her sex'

1. Knox, J, *The First Blast of the Trumpet Against the Monstruous Regiment of Women* (Geneva, 1558), pp.9, 47v
2. Richards, JM, 'The English accession of James VI: "national" identity, gender and the personal monarchy of England', *English Historical Review*, 117 (Oxford, 2002), p.527; Haigh, C (ed), *Elizabeth I* (London and New York, 1988), p.22; *CSPV* IX, p.533

ABBREVIATIONS

BL	British Library
BNF	Bibliothèque Nationale de France
CSPD	*Calendar of State Papers, Domestic Series, of the Reign of Elizabeth*
CSPF	*Calendar of State Papers, Foreign Series, of the Reign of Elizabeth*
CSPS	*Calendar of State Papers, Spanish, Elizabeth*
CSPV	*Calendar of State Papers, Venice*
CSP Rome	*Calendar of State Papers, Relating to English Affairs, Preserved Principally at Rome*
CSP Scotland	*Calendar of the State Papers Relating to Scotland, Elizabeth and Mary, Queen of Scots*
LP Henry VIII	*Letters and Papers of Henry VIII*
HMC	Historical Manuscripts Commission
NRS	National Records of Scotland
TNA	The National Archives

BIBLIOGRAPHY

Archival sources (in date order)

The National Archives

E39/58, E39/59, E39/81 Treaty of Perpetual Peace, 1502 (another copy is held by the National Records of Scotland)

E23/4 Will of Henry VIII [30 December 1546]

SP 12/27 fo.143r–144v: Answer of the Queen to the addresses of both Houses of Parliament delivered to Mr Speaker Thomas Williams, 28 January 1563

SP 12/41/28 Controversy over Patrick Adamson's poem on James's birth, declaring him King of England, 1566

SP 12/48/61, fol. 165r Francis Walsingham to William Cecil, 20 December 1568

KB 8/45 Roll and file of court of the Lord High Steward and peers. Principal defendants and charges: Thomas Duke of Norfolk, high treason, conspiring to depose the Queen and marry Mary Queen of Scots, 17 November 1571–16 November 1572

SP 12/159 fo.38v Letter from Sir Henry Sidney lamenting his wife Mary's disfigurement from smallpox [1583?]

SP 12/173/13 Interrogation of William Crichton [August/September 1584]

SP 12/174 fo.1 The Bond of Association, 1584

SP 53/19/12 Anthony Babington to Mary, Queen of Scots, July 1586

SP 53/18/53 A contemporary copy of the 'Gallows Letter', the closest version to the original letter written by Mary, Queen of Scots to Anthony Babington on 17 July 1586

SP 52/41 fo.74 James VI to Patrick Gray, sixth Lord Gray [January 1587]

SP 12/215 f.114 Robert Dudley to Elizabeth I, 29 August 1588, inscribed by the Queen: 'his last letter'

SP 52/51 fo.75 Elizabeth I to James VI, 22 December 1593 regarding the 'Spanish Blanks' plot

SP 52/54 fo.1 Memorial for the Queen's envoy to the King of Scots upon the birth of Prince Henry [1594]

SP 52/54 fo.23 *A True Report of the Most Triumphant, and Royal Accomplishment of the Baptism of the most Excellent, right High, and mighty Prince, Frederik Henry, By the grace of God, Prince of Scotland, Solemnized the 30. day of August 1594*

SP 52/54 fo.3 Elizabeth's acceptance of James VI's invitation to be godmother to his son, Henry [1594]

SP 52/54 fo.34 James VI's response to Elizabeth I regarding the title 'King of all Britain' [1594]

SP 52/54 fo.36 Anne of Denmark to Elizabeth I [August/September 1594]

SP 52/58 fos.3 and 10 James VI's ministers preach against Robert Persons' tract, 7 and 18 January 1596

SP 59/37 fos.16 and 18 Examination of Robert Crawforth regarding the Thomas Valentine affair, 2 March 1598

SP 52/52 fo.234 A minute of Her Majesty's letter to George Nicholson expressing her irritation that James should press the issue of the succession, 25 April 1598

SP 52/62 fo.29 George Nicolson to Lord Burghley, 11 May 1598, regarding the Thomas Valentine affair

SP 52/62 fo.38 James Hudson to Elizabeth I regarding the Valentine Thomas affair [c.June 1598]

SP 52/62 fo.46 Instructions for One to be Sent into Scotland, 1 July 1598

SP 52/62 fo.44 Elizabeth I to James VI, 1 July 1598

SP 52/63 fo.16 James VI to Elizabeth I, 26 September 1598

SP 52/63 fo.17 Sir James Elphinstone to David Foulis, 26 September 1598

SP 52/63 fos.30 and 31 David Foulis to Sir Robert Cecil, 9 October 1598

SP 52/52 fo.227 Robert Cecil to George Nicolson, 7 November 1598

KB 8/54 Special oyer and terminer roll and file. Principal defendants and charges: Valentine Thomas, high treason, conspiring with the Scots to levy war against the Queen, 17 November 1597–16 November 1598

SP 52/63 fo.81 Confessions of Valentine Thomas, 20 December 1598

SP 52/63 fo.82 Declaration of Queen Elizabeth concerning Valentine Thomas, 20 December 1598. Another copy is in SP 52/52 fos.230r–231

SP 52/52 fo.233 Elizabeth I to George Nicolson, end December 1598

SP 52/64 fo.16 George Nicolson to Robert Cecil, 2 February 1599

SP 52/64 fo.33 Sir James Elphinstone to Robert Cecil, 28 February 1599

SP 12/280: An Account of the State of England in Anno Domini 1600 by Thomas Wilson

SP 52/67 fo.14 George Nicolson to Robert Cecil, 7 February 1601

SP 52/67 fo.27 George Nicolson to Robert Cecil, 14 February 1601

SP 31/3/32 fos.46–47, 55 Thuméry de Boissise to Henry IV, 14 and 30 April [O.S.] 1601

SP 52/67 fo.92 Robert Cecil to the Master of Grey, April 1601

SP 31/3 fo.35 Christophe de Harlay, Count de Beaumont to Villeroy [1605]

SP 52/68 fo.75, Elizabeth I to James VI, 4 July 1602

SP 52/69 fo.44 James VI's last letter to Elizabeth I, 8 December 1602

SP 52/69 fo.53 Elizabeth I's last letter to James VI, 5 January 1603

TNA SP 14/3 fo.134; SP 14/4 fo.28v Rumours about the Earl of Huntingdon's grandson challenging James VI's claim

SP 14/1 fo.2 Robert Cecil to James VI and I, 23/24 March 1603

SP 14/1 fo.6 John Chamberlain to James VI and I, professing his allegiance 25 March 1603

SP 14/1 fo.3 'A Proclamation, declaring the undoubted Right of our Soveraigne Lord King James, to the Crowne of the Realmes of England, Fraunce and Ireland,' 24 March 1603 (see fos.1–2 for a draft of the same)

SP 14/1 fo.10 'The lineal descent of the Saxon Kings to James the King now living,' 26 March 1603

SP 14/1 fo.3 Sir Robert Cotton, 'A Discourse of ye Descent of the King's Majesty from the Saxons,' 26 March 1603

British Library

Cotton MS Vespasian F XIII fo.135 Margaret, Queen of Scotland to her father Henry VII, following her marriage to James IV of Scotland, 1503

Additional MS 19398 fo.44 Henry VIII to Cardinal Thomas Wolsey [1519]

Additional MS 48023, fo.361v A Journal of Matters of State ... From and Before the Death of King Edward the 6th Until the Year 1562

Harleian MS 6286 Records of the Commission appointed to investigate the marriage of Katherine Grey and Edward Seymour [1562]

Lansdowne MS 94 fo.30r Draft of Elizabeth I's speech to Parliament, remonstrating with them over the succession [1563]

Harley MS 787 fo.16 Henry Hastings, Earl of Huntingdon to Robert Dudley [1563]

Harley MS 4627 no.2, fos.3–4, 26–7 Mary Queen of Scots' Claim to the English Succession Attacked on National and Religious Grounds [1560s?]

Cotton Caligula B IV fos.1–94; Harley 849 fos.1–38 Edmund Plowden's *A Treatise on Succession* [1566]

Egerton MS 2836 fos.37–71 'The Common Cry of Englishmen,' 1566

Cotton MS Caligula C I Mary, Queen of Scots to Elizabeth I, 17 May 1568

Kings MS 396 Genealogical tree of Elizabeth I [c.1567]

Additional MS 48114 f.74 'Cista Pacis Anglie' by Roger Edwardes, 1576

Cotton Caligula C IX, fos.139v–140, Elizabeth I to James VI, 26 April 1584

Cotton MS Caligula C.ix, fo.133r Interrogation of William Crichton [August/September 1584]

Additional MS 33594 ff.52v–53r Mary, Queen of Scots' proposal to be freed so that she could rule jointly with her son, 1584

Cotton MS Appendix L fo.144r Thomas Phelippes to Sir Francis Walsingham, regarding the arrest of Anthony Babington, 3 August 1586

Cotton Caligula C IX, fos.192–3 James VI to Elizabeth I, 26 January 1587

Cotton MS Julius F vi fo.248 Defence of the Queen's Silence on the Succession [1587?]

Lansdowne MS 103, fol. 194r Lord Burghley's reflection on Walsingham's death, 30 June 1590

Lansdowne MS 71 fo.3 Elizabeth, Countess of Shrewsbury to William Cecil, Lord Burghley, 21 September 1592

Additional MS 23109, fols. 43r–44v James VI to Elizabeth I, April 1593

Harley MS 6846 fo.108 James Morice to Peter Wentworth [1593]

Harley MS 6846 fo.88r Oliver St John's deposition [1593]

Lansdowne MS 79 fos.4 and 6 Testimony of Edmund Neville [November 1595]

Lansdowne MS 512 ff.12r–33v *A Discourse Concerning a Successor to Queen Elizabeth Written in her Life time* [c.1598]

Cotton MS Titus C VII fo.19 James VI to Elizabeth I, 30 July 1598

Cotton Julius F vi 75 fos.139r–141r Sir Edmund Ashfield to the King of Scots, advising him on preparing the ground for taking the English throne [c.1599]

Cotton MS Caligula D II fos.381–2 Sir William Bowes to Elizabeth I, 31 May 1599

Sloane MS 1786 fos.53–55 Elizabeth I to James VI, 11 May 1601

BL Kings MS 123 fo.16r Christophe de Harlay, Comte de Beaumont to Villeroy [March 1603]

Cotton MS Titus C VII fos.57–57r Sir Robert Cotton's account of Elizabeth's death [after 1603]

Harley MS 677, ff.47v–48r Matthew Hutton, Archbishop of York, to Cecil, complaining of King James's neglect of state affairs, December 1604

Cotton MS Titus C VI fo.16or Henry Howard, Earl of Northampton to Robert Cotton [1606]

Camden's draft *Annales* Cotton MS Faustina F I–X [1608–c.1615]

Harley MS 7003 fos.59–60 William Seymour to the Privy Council, 10 February 1610

Stowe MS 171 fo.292 Dudley Carleton to Thomas Edmondes, 13 July 1610

Harleian MS 7003 fo.87 Petition from Arbella Stuart to King James I [undated]

Harleian MS 7003 fo.146 Arbella Stuart to Viscount Fenton during her imprisonment in the Tower [1614?]

Additional MS 36294 fo.113 Camden to a friend [c.1615]

National Records of Scotland

SP 6/31 Treaty of Perpetual Peace, October 1502
RH15/23/16 Elizabeth I to Sir Nicholas Throckmorton, 14 July 1567 (copy)

National Library of Scotland

Advocates' MS 35.4.2 fos.640r-v 'Johnston's' History' of James VI's accession in England
Advocates' MS 31.4.8 Dickson, A, *Of the Right of the Crowne efter Hir Majesty, Three books where be occasione is refuted a treacherous libel intitling the house of Spagne to the succession therof* [1598]

University of Edinburgh Library

Laing MS III, 245 [Anonymous], *An apologie of the Scottische King* [c.1600]

Bodleian Library

Ashmolean MS 829 fos.23–31 Allegations Against the Surmised title of the Quine of Scots [1565]

Trinity College, Cambridge

R.5.20 William Camden, *Annales* [of the reign of James VI and I]

Bibliothèque Nationale de France

MS FF 3501 Letter book of Christophe de Harlay, French ambassador to England, 1602–05

Printed primary sources

Adams, S and Rodríguez-Salgado, MJ, 'The Count of Feria's Dispatch to Philip II of 14 November 1558', *Camden Miscellany* XXVIII (London, 1984)

Akrigg, GPV (ed), *Letters of King James VI & I* (Berkeley, University of California Press, 1984)

Allen, W, *An admonition to the nobility and people of England and Ireland concerninge the present vvarres made for the execution of his Holines sentence, by the highe and mightie Kinge Catholike of Spaine. By the Cardinal of Englande* (Antwerp, 1588)

Allingham, H (ed), *Captain Cuellar's Adventures in Connacht & Ulster, A.D. 1588 . . . To which is added an introduction and complete translation of Captain Cuellar's Narrative of the Spanish Armada and his adventures in Ireland* (London, 1897)

[Anonymous], *Leycester's Commonwealth* (London, 1584)

[Anonymous], *Treason Unmask'd: Or the Queen's Title, The Revolution, And the Hanover Succession Vindicated Against the Treasonable Positions of a Book lately Publish'd, Intitled, The Hereditary Right of the Crown of England asserted; the History of the Succession since the Conquest clear'd, and the true English Constitution vindicated, from the Misrepresentations of Dr Higden's View and Defence* (London, 1713)

Arber, E (ed), *John Knoxe, First Blast of the Trumpet against the Monstrous Regiment of Women* (London, 1878)

Bacon, F, *The felicity of Queen Elizabeth and her times, with other things* (London, 1651)

Bain, J (ed), *Calendar of the State Papers Relating to Scotland, 1357–1509*, IV (Edinburgh, 1888)

Bain, J (ed), *Calendar of Letters and Papers Relating to the Affairs of the Borders of England and Scotland*, 2 vols. (Edinburgh, 1894, 1896)

Bain, J, Mackie, JD, et al (eds), *Calendar of the State Papers Relating to Scotland and Mary, Queen of Scots, 1547–1603*, I–XIII part ii (Edinburgh, 1898–1969)

Beale, R, *The Order and Manner of the Execution of Mary Queen of Scots, Feb. 8, 1587* [1587]

Birch, T, *An Historical View of the Negotiations between the Courts of England, France, and Brussels: From the Year 1592 to 1617* (London, 1749)

Birch, T, *Memoirs of the Reign of Queen Elizabeth from the year 1581 till her Death*, 2 vols. (London, 1754)

Botley, P and Vince, M (eds), *The Correspondence of Isaac Casaubon in England*, I (Geneva, 2018)

Bowes, P (ed), D'Ewes, S, *The Journals of all the Parliaments during the reign of Queen Elizabeth, both in the House of Lords and the House of Commons* (London, 1682)

Boyle, J (ed), *Memoirs of the Life of Robert Carey ... Written by Himself* (London, 1759)

Brennan, M, Kinnamon, N and Hannay, M (eds), *The Letters of Rowland Whyte to Sir Robert Sidney* (Philadelphia, 2013)

Brewer, JS (ed), Goodman, G, *The Court of King James I*, 2 vols. (London, 1839)

Brown, R et al (eds), *Calendar of State Papers Relating To English Affairs in the Archives of Venice*, I–X (London, 1864–1947)

Bruce, J (ed), *Correspondence of King James VI of Scotland with Sir Robert Cecil and others in England, during the reign of Queen Elizabeth* (London, 1861)

Bruce, J (ed), *Letters of Queen Elizabeth and King James VI of Scotland: Some of them printed from originals in the possession of the Rev. Edward Ryder, and others from a MS which formerly belonged to Sir Peter Thompson, KT.*, Camden Society, 46 (London, 1849)

Bruce, J (ed), *The Diary of John Manningham*, Camden Society (London, 1868)

Burgoyne, FJ (ed), *Leycester's Commonwealth* (London, 1904)

Burnet, G, *A defense of the reflections on the ninth book of the first volum [sic] of Mr. Varillas's History of heresies being a reply to his answer* (Amsterdam, 1687)

Burton, JH and Masson, D (eds), *The register of the Privy Council of Scotland* (Edinburgh, 1877–98)

Camden, W, *The Historie of the Most Renowned and Victorious Princesse Elizabeth, late Queene of England* (London, 1630)

Camden, W, *The True and Royall Historie of the Famous Empresse Elizabeth, Queene of England, France and Ireland*, 3 vols. (London, 1625–9)

Cameron, AI (ed), *The Warrender Papers*, I and II (Edinburgh, 1931–2)

Cerovski, JS (ed), *Sir Robert Naunton, Fragmentia Regalia or Observations on Queen Elizabeth Her Times and Favourites* (London and Toronto, 1985)

Clifford, A (ed), *The State Papers and Letters of Sir Ralph Sadler. To which is added, a memoir of the life of Sir Ralph Sadler, with historical notes by Walter Scott*, 2 vols. (Edinburgh, 1809)

Clifford, DJH (ed), *The Diaries of Lady Anne Clifford* (Stroud, 1992)

Cobbett, W and Howell, TB (eds), *A Complete Collection of State Trials*, 33 vols. (London, 1816–98)

Collins, A (ed), *Letters and Memorials of State, in the reigns of Queen Mary, Queen Elizabeth, etc ...Written and collected by Sir Henry Sidney, etc*, 2 vols. (London, 1746)

Cooper, E (ed), *The life and letters of Lady Arabella Stuart*, 2 vols. (London, 1866)

Craig, A, *The Poeticall Essayes of Alexander Craige Scotobritaine* (London, 1604)

Craigie, J (ed), *Minor Prose Works of King James VI and I* (Edinburgh, 1982)

Craigie, J (ed), *The Basilikon Doron of King James VI*, 2 vols., Scottish Text Society, 3rd series, 16, 18 (Edinburgh, 1944–50)

Cross, C (ed), *The letters of Sir Francis Hastings, 1574–1609* (Frome, 1969)

Dalrymple, D, Lord Hailes (ed), *The Secret Correspondence of Sir Robert Cecil with James VI King of Scotland. Now First Published* (Edinburgh, 1766)

Dekker, T, *1603. The Wonderfull Yeare. Wherein is Shewed the Picture of London Lying Sicke of the Plague* (London, 1603)

Dickens, AG (ed), *Clifford Letters of the Sixteenth Century* (Durham, 1962)

Dickinson, WC, Donaldson, G and Milne, IA (eds), *A Source Book of Scottish History*, II (Edinburgh, 1953)

Dickson, T, Balfour, TJ et al (eds), *Compota Thesaurariorum Regum Scotorum. Accounts of the Lord High Treasurer of Scotland*, 5 vols. (Edinburgh, 1877–1978)

Dunbar, W, *The Thissil and the Rois*, in Mackay Mackenzie, W (ed), *The Poems of William Dunbar* (Edinburgh, 1990)

Ellis, H (ed), *Original Letters Illustrative of English History, Including Numerous Royal Letters*, 3rd Series, II–IV (London, 1846)

Falkus, C, *The Private Lives of the Tudor Monarchs* (London, 1974)

Francis Steuart, A (ed), *Sir James Melville: Memoirs of His Own Life, 1549–93* (London, 1929)

Gorboduc, in *Minor Elizabethan Drama: I Pre-Shakespearean Tragedies* (London and New York, 1913)

Green, MAE (ed), *Calendar of State Papers, Domestic series, of the reigns of Edward VI., Mary, Elizabeth, (James I) 1547–1580 (1581–1625)*, 12 vols. (London, 1856–72)

Halliwell-Phillipps, *Letters of the Kings of England*, 2 vols. (London, 1846)

Harbin, G, *The Hereditary Right of the Crown of England Asserted* (London, 1713)

Harington, Sir J, *A briefe view of the state of the Church of England as it stood in Q. Elizabeths and King James his reigne* (London, 1653)

Harington, Sir J, *Nugae Antiquae: Being a Miscellaneous Collection of Original Papers in Prose and Verse: Written in the Reigns of Henry VIII, Queen Mary, Elizabeth, King James, etc* (London, 1779)

Harrison, GB, *The Elizabethan Journals: Being a record of those things most talked about during the years 1591–1603* (London, 1955)

Harrison, GB, *The Letters of Queen Elizabeth* (London, 1935)

Harrison, GB and Jones, RA, *Andre Hurault de Maisse, A Journal of all that was accomplished by Monsieur de Maisse, ambassador in England from King Henri IV to Queen Elizabeth, 1597* (London, 1931)

Hays, D (ed and transl.), *The Anglica Historia of Polydore Vergil, A.D. 1485–1537*, Camden Series, LXXIV (London, 1950)

Hentzner, P, *Travels in England during the Reign of Queen Elizabeth* (London, 1889)

Historical Manuscripts Commission, *Calendar of the Manuscripts of the Marquis of Salisbury, Preserved at Hatfield House, Herts*, I–XV (London, 1883–1930)

Historical Manuscripts Commission, *Calendar of the Manuscripts of the Most Honourable the Marquess of Bath, preserved at Longleat, Wiltshire, 1533–1659*, V (London, 1980)

Historical Manuscripts Commission, *Report on the Manuscripts of Lord De L'Isle & Dudley, preserved at Penshurst Place*, I and II (London, 1925)

Historical Manuscripts Commission, *The Manuscripts of His Grace the Duke of Rutland, preserved at Belvoir Castle*, I (London, 1888)

Holles, G, *Memorials of the Holles Family 1493–1656*, Camden Society, 3rd Series, LV (London, 1937)

Hume, MAS, *Calendar of Letters and State Papers Relating to English Affairs, Preserved Principally in the Archives of Simancas, Elizabeth*, 4 vols. (London, 1892–99)

James VI of Scotland, *The Trew Law of Free Monarchies* (Edinburgh, 1598)

Knox, J, *The First Blast of the Trumpet Against the Monstruous Regiment of Women* (Geneva, 1558)

Lababnoff, A (ed), *Lettres, Instructions et Memoires de Marie Stuart, Reine d'Ecosse*, 7 vols. (London, 1844)

Laing, D et al (eds), *Original Letters of Mr John Colville, 1582–1603* (Edinburgh, 1858)

Larkin, F and Hughes, PL (eds), *Stuart Royal Proclamations*, 2 vols. (Oxford, 1973)

Loades, DM (ed), *Elizabeth I: The Golden Reign of Gloriana. English Monarchs: Treasures from the Archives* (Richmond, 2003)

Lodge, E (ed), *Illustrations of British History, Biography and Manners*, 3 vols. (London, 1838)

MacCaffrey, WT (ed), *William Camden, The History of the Most Renowned and Victorious Princess Elizabeth, Late Queen of England. Selected Chapters* (Chicago and London, 1970)

Maclean, J (ed), *Letters from Sir Robert Cecil to Sir George Carew* (London, 1864)

Marcus, LS, Mueller, J and Rose, MB (eds), *Elizabeth I: Collected Works* (Chicago and London, 2002)

Mayer, JC, *Breaking the Silence on the Succession: A sourcebook of manuscripts and rare texts* (Montpelier, 2003)

McClure, NE (ed), *The Letters and Epigrams of Sir John Harington* (London, 1930)

McClure, NE (ed), *The Letters of John Chamberlain* (Philadelphia, 1939)

McIlwain, CH (ed), *The Political Works of James I* (Cambridge, 1918)

Murdin, W, *A Collection of State Papers Relating to Affairs in the Reign of Queen Elizabeth, 1571-96 ... Left by William Cecil Lord Burghley ... at Hatfield House* (London, 1759)

Nichols, J (ed), *The Progresses, Processions, and Magnificent Festivities of King James the First*, 4 vols. (London, 1828)

Nichols, JG (ed), *The Diary of Henry Machyn: citizen and Merchant-Taylor of London, from AD 1550 to AD 1563* (London, 1848)

Nicolas, NH, *Memoirs of the life and times of Sir Christopher Hatton, K.G., Vice Chamberlain and Lord Chancellor to Queen Elizabeth. Including his correspondence with the Queen and other distinguished persons* (London, 1847)

Perry, M, *The Word of a Prince* (London, 1990)

Powell, GH (ed), *Memoirs of Robert Cary Earl of Monmouth* (London, 1905)

Pryor, F, *Elizabeth I: Her life in letters* (California, 2003)

Puttenham, G (ed) *The Art of English Poesie* (London, 1589)

Rait, RS and Dunlop, AI (eds), *King James's Secret: negotiations between Elizabeth and James VI relating to the execution of Mary Queen of Scots, from the Warrender papers* (London, 1927)

Read, EP and Read, C (eds), *Elizabeth of England. An edition of the manuscript entitled 'Certain Observations concerning the life and Reign of Queen Elizabeth' by John Clapham* (Philadelphia, 1951)

Rigg, JM (ed), *Calendar of State Papers, Relating to English Affairs, Preserved Principally at Rome, in the Vatican Archives and Library, 1558–71 and 1572–78*, 2 vols. (London, 1916, 1926)

Rye, WB (ed), *England as seen by Foreigners in the days of Elizabeth and James the First* (London, 1865)

Sanderson, W, *A Compleat History of the lives and reigns of Mary Queen of Scotland, and of her son . . . James the Sixth; . . . reconciling several opinions, in . . . testimony of her, and confuting others, in vindication of him against two scandalous authors. 1. The Court and Character of King James [by Sir Anthony Weldon]. 2. The History of Great Britain [by A. Wilson]* (London, 1656)

Sawyer, E (ed), *Memorials of Affairs of State in the Reigns of Queen Elizabeth and King James I, Collected (chiefly) from the Original Papers of the Right Honourable Sir Ralph Winwood*, I (London, 1725)

Smith, T, *The State of England, Anno Dom. 1600*, edited by Fisher, FJ, *Camden Miscellany*, XVI, 3rd Series, No. 52 (London, 1936)

Smith, T, *V. CL. Gulielmi Camdeni et Illustrium Virorum ad G. Camdenum Epistolae* (London, 1691)

Somerville, JP (ed), *King James VI and I: Political Writings* (Cambridge, 1994)

Spedding, J, *The Letters and Life of Francis Bacon*, 7 vols. (London, 1861–74)

Spedding, J, et al (eds), *The Works of Francis Bacon*, 14 vols. (London, 1861–72)

Spencer Scott, H (ed), Wilbraham, R, 'The Journal of Sir Roger Wilbraham,' *The Camden Miscellany*, X (London, 1902)

Steen, SJ, *The Letters of Lady Arbella Stuart* (Oxford, 1994)

Steven, MW (ed), *Queen Elizabeth I: Selected Works* (New York, 2004)

Stevenson, J (ed), *Selections From Unpublished Manuscripts in the College of Arms and the British Museum, illustrating the Reign of Mary, Queen of Scotland, MDXLIII–MDLXVIII*, Maitland Club, 41 (Glasgow, 1837)

Stevenson, J, Wernham, RB et al (eds), *Calendar of State Papers, Foreign Series, of the Reign of Elizabeth, 1558–1591* (London, 1863–1969)

Stowe, J, *The Annales of England, faithfully collected out of the most autenticall authors, records and other monuments of antiquitie, lately collected, from the first habitation untill this present yeare 1605* (London, 1605)

Strype, J (ed), Stow, J, *Survey of the Cities of London and Westminster*, 2 vols. (London, 1720)

Teuelet, A, *Relations politiques de la France et de l'Espagne avec l'Ecosse au 16e siècle, 5 vols* (Paris, 1862)

The Statutes of the Realm, 11 vols. (London, 1820–28)

The Workes Of The Most High And Mightie Prince, Iames By The Grace of God, King of Great Britaine, France And Ireland, Defender of the Faith, &c. (London, 1616)

Turnbull, W (ed and transl), *Letters of Mary Stuart, Queen of Scotland, selected from the 'Recueil des Lettres de Marie Stuart,' together with the chronological summary of events during the reign of the Queen of Scotland, by Prince A. Labanoff*, 8 vols. (London, 1845)

Tytler, PF, *England under the Reigns of Edward VI and Mary, Illustrated in a Series of Original Letters*, 2 vols. (London, 1839)

Weldon, Sir A, *The Court and Character of King James* (London, 1650)

Wernham, RB (ed), *List and Analysis of State Papers Foreign Series, Elizabeth I, Preserved in the Public Record Office, June 1591–December 1596*, 6 vols. (London, 1980–2000)

Williams, C (ed), *Thomas Platter's Travels in England, 1599* (London, 1937)

Wilson, A, *The History of Great Britain, being the Life and Reign of King James the First* (London, 1653)

Wilson, T, 'The State of England, Anno Dom.1600', *Camden Miscellany*, XVI (London, 1936)

Wright, T, *Queen Elizabeth and her Times, A Series of Original Letters, Selected from the Inedited Private Correspondence of the Lord Treasurer Burghley, the Earl of Leicester, the Secretaries Walsingham and Smith, Sir Christopher Hatton, etc*, 2 vols. (London, 1838)

Succession tracts (in date order)

Hales, J, *A Declaration of the Succession of the Crowne Imperiall of Ingland* [1563, printed London, 1713]

[Anonymous], *Allegations against the svrmisid title of the Qvine of Scotts* (London, 1565)

Plowden, E, *A Treatise on Succession* [1566]

[Anonymous] *The Common Cry of Englishmen* (London, 1566)

Leslie, J, *A Defence of the Honor of Marie, Queene of Scotland, by Eusebius Dicaeophile* (London, 1569)

Edwardes, R, *Castra Regia* (London, 1569)

Edwardes, R, *Cista Pacis Anglie* (London, 1576)

Puttenham, G, [*Justificacion*] [c.1587]

Wentworth, P, *Treatise Containing M. Wentworth's Judgment Concerning the Person of the True and lawful successor to these Realmes of England and Ireland* [1587]

Persons, R, *Newes from Spayne and Holland* (Antwerp, 1593)

[Persons, R] Doleman, R, *A Conference about the next Succession to the Crowne of Inglande* [Antwerp, 1594]

[Anonymous], *A Discourse Concerning a Successor to Queen Elizabeth Written in her Life time* [c.1598]

Wentworth, P, *A Pithie Exhortation to her Maiestie for Establishing her Successor to the Crowne.Whereunto is added a Discourse Containing the Authors Opinion of the True and Lawfull Successor to Her Maiestie* [1598]

Dickson, A, *Of the Right of the Crowne efter Hir Majesty, Three books where be occasione is refuted a treacherous libel intitling the house of Spagne to the succession therof* [1598]

Philodikaios, I [pseudonym], *A Treatise Declaring, And confirming against all objections the just title and right of the most excellent and worthie Prince, Iames the sixt, King of Scotland, to the succession of the crown of England* (Edinburgh, 1599)

[Anonymous], *An apologie of the Scottische King* [?1600]

[?Constable, H], *A Discoverye of a counterfecte conference helde at a counterfecte place, by counterfecte travellers, for thadvancement of a counterfecte tytle, and invented, printed, and published by one (PERSON) that dare not avowe his name* (Paris, 1600)

Hooke, H, *Of succession to the Crowne of England* [1601]

Harington, J, *A Tract on the Succession to the Crown* [1602] (London, 1880)

Craig, T, *The Right of Succession to the Kingdom of England* [1602] (London, 1703)

Hayward, J, *Answer To the First Part of a Certaine Conference Concerning Succession* (London, 1603)

Secondary sources

Alford, S, *All His Spies: The Secret World of Robert Cecil* (London, 2024)

Alford, S, *The Early Elizabethan Polity: William Cecil and the British Succession Crisis of the 1560s* (Cambridge, 1998)

Alford, S, *The Watchers: A Secret History of the Reign of Elizabeth I* (London, 2012)

Allinson, R, 'Conversations on Kingship: The Letters of Queen Elizabeth I and King James VI,' in Oakley Brown, L and Wilkinson, LJ (eds), *The Rituals and Rhetoric of Queenship: Medieval to Early Modern* (Dublin, 2009), pp.131–44

Allinson, R, 'These Latter Days of the World': The Correspondence of Elizabeth I and King James VI, 1590–1603', *Early Modern Literary Studies*, Special Issue, 16 (2007), 2.1-27(3)

Archer, IW, *Religion, Politics and Society in Sixteenth Century England* (Cambridge, 2003)

Ashdown, D.M., *Tudor Cousins: Rivals for the Throne* (Sutton, 2000)

Aveling, JC, *Northern Catholics: The Catholic recusants of the North Riding of Yorkshire* (London, 1966)

Axton, M, *The Queen's Two Bodies: Drama and the Elizabethan Succession* (London, 1977)

Axton, M, 'The Influence of Edmund Plowden's Succession Treatise,' *Huntingdon Library Quarterly*, XXXVII (1974), pp.209–26

Bailey, A, *The Succession to the English Crown: A historical sketch* (London, 1879)

Bassnett, S, *Elizabeth I: A Feminist Perspective* (Oxford and New York, 1988)

Bell, I, *Elizabeth I: The Voice of a Monarch* (London, 2010)

Bertie, G, *Five Generations of a Loyal House, Part 1* (London, 1845)

Black, JB, *The Reign of Elizabeth 1558–1603* (Oxford, 1936)

Borman, T, *Elizabeth's Women: The Hidden Story of the Virgin Queen* (London, 2008)

Bradley, ET, *Life of the Lady Arabella Stuart*, 2 vols. (London, 1889)

Brooks, CW, *Law, Politics and Society in Early Modern England* (Cambridge, 2009)

Cannon, J and Griffiths, R, *The Oxford Illustrated History of the British Monarchy* (Oxford, 1988)

Chamberlin, F, *Elizabeth and Leycester* (New York, 1939)

Chamberlin, F, *The Sayings of Queen Elizabeth* (London, 1923)

Chapman, H, *Two Tudor Portraits: Henry Howard, Earl of Surrey and Lady Katherine Grey* (London, 1960)

Cheyney, EP, *A History of England from the Defeat of the Armada to the Death of Elizabeth*, 2 volumes (Gloucester, 1967)

Collinson, P, *Elizabethan Essays* (London, 1994)

Collinson, P, 'The Elizabethan exclusion crisis and the Elizabethan polity', *Proceedings of the British Academy*, 84 (1994), pp.51–92

Collinson, P, *The Elizabethan Puritan Movement* (Oxford, 1988)

Cooper, E, *The Life and Letters of Lady Arbella Stuart*, 2 vols. (London, 1866)

Courtney, A, *James VI: Britannic Prince: King of Scots and Elizabeth's Heir, 1566–1603* (Abingdon, 2024)

Coward, B, *The Stanleys, Lord Stanley and Earls of Derby, 1385–1672: the origins, wealth and power of a landowning family* (Manchester, 1983)

Cross, C, *The Puritan Earl: The Life of Henry Hastings, Third Earl of Huntingdon, 1536–1595* (London, 1966)

Cruickshanks, E (ed), *The Stuart Courts* (Stroud, 2009)

Davey, R, *The Sisters of Lady Jane Grey and their wicked Grandfather* (London, 1911)

Doran, S, *Elizabeth. The Exhibition at the National Maritime Museum* (London, 2003)

Doran, S, *From Tudor to Stuart: The regime change from Elizabeth I to James I* (Oxford, 2024)

Doran, S, 'Loving and Affectionate Cousins? The Relationship between Elizabeth I and James VI of Scotland 1586–1603', in Doran, S and Richardson, G, *Tudor England and its Neighbours* (New York, 2005), pp.203–34

Doran, S, *Monarchy and Matrimony: The Courtships of Elizabeth I* (London, 1996)

Doran, S, 'Revenge her Foul and Most Unnatural Murder? The Impact of Mary Stuart's Execution on Anglo-Scottish Relations,' *History*, 85 (2000), pp.589–612

Doran, S and Kewes, P (eds), *Doubtful and Dangerous: The Question of Succession in Late Elizabethan England* (Manchester, 2014)

Dunlop, I, *Palaces and Progresses of Elizabeth I* (London, 1962)

Dunn, J, *Elizabeth and Mary: Cousins, Rivals, Queens* (New York, 2004)

Durant, DN, *Arbella Stuart. A Rival to the Queen* (London, 1978)

Durant, DN, *Bess of Hardwick: Portrait of an Elizabethan Dynast* (London, 1999)

Dutton, R, *English Court Life: From Henry VII to George II* (London, 1963)

Edwards, P, *Sir Walter Raleigh* (London, 1953)

Emmett, RJ, 'Anglo-Scottish Succession Tracts During the Late Elizabethan Period, 1595–1603,' unpublished MPhil thesis, University of Birmingham (2010)

Fraser, A, *Mary, Queen of Scots* (London, 1994)

Frye, S, *Maids and Mistresses, Cousins and Queens. Women's Alliances in Early Modern England* (New York and Oxford University Press, 1999)

Gajda, A, *The Earl of Essex and Late Elizabethan Political Culture* (Oxford, 2012)

Gilson, JP, *Lives of Lady Anne Clifford, Countess of Dorset, Pembroke and Montgomery, 1590–1676, And of Her Parents* (London, 1916)

Gristwood, S, *Arbella: England's Lost Queen* (London, 2003)

Guy, J, *Elizabeth: The Forgotten Years* (London, 2015)

Guy, J, *'My Heart is My Own': The Life of Mary, Queen of Scots* (London, 2004)

Guy, J (ed), *The Reign of Elizabeth I: court and culture in the last decade* (Cambridge, 1995)

Haigh, C (ed), *Elizabeth I* (London and New York, 1988)

Hammer, PEJ, 'The Earl of Essex, Fulke Greville, and the employment of scholars', *Studies in Philology*, 91 (North Carolina, 1994), pp.167–80

Handover, PM, *Arbella Stuart. Royal Lady of Hardwick and Cousin to King James* (London, 1957)

Hartley, TE (ed), *Proceedings in the Parliaments of Elizabeth I* (Leicester and London, 1981–1995)

Hasler, PW, *The House of Commons, 1558-1603*, III (London, 1981)

Head, DM, 'Henry VIII's Scottish Policy', *Scottish Historical Review*, 61:171 (April 1982)

Hicks, L, 'Sir Robert Cecil, Father Persons and the succession, 1600–1601', *Archivum Historicum Societatis Iesu*, 24 (1955), pp.95–139

Hopkins, L, *Drama and the Succession to the Crown, 1561–1663* (Routledge, 2011)

Hopkins, L, *Queen Elizabeth I and her Court* (London and New York, 1990)

Houlbrooke, RA, *James VI and I: Ideas, Authority and Government* (Aldershot, 2006)

Hume, M, *The Courtships of Queen Elizabeth. A History of the Various Negotiations for her Marriage* (London, 1904)

Hurstfield, J, 'The succession struggle in late Elizabethan England,' in Bindoff, ST, Hurstfield, J and Williams, CH (eds), *Elizabethan Government and Society. Essays presented to Sir John Neale* (London, 1961), pp.369–96

Innes, MJM, 'Robert Persons, Popular Sovereignty, and the Late Elizabethan Succession Debate,' *Historical Journal*, 62 Part 1 (2019)

Ives, E, 'Tudor dynastic problems revisited,' *Historical Research*, 81 (2008), pp.255–79

Jenkins, E, *Elizabeth and Leicester* (London, 2002)

Jensen, DL, 'The phantom will of Mary Queen of Scots,' *Scotia*, IV (Vancouver, 1980), pp.1–15

Johnson, P, *Elizabeth I: A study in power and intellect* (London, 1974)

Keechang, K, *Aliens in Medieval Law: The origins of modern citizenship* (Cambridge, 2000)

Kenny, RW, *Elizabeth's Admiral: The Political Career of Charles Howard, Earl of Nottingham, 1536–1624* (Baltimore, 1970)

Kervyn de Lettenhove, JMBC, *Relations politiques de Pays-Bas et de l'Angleterre sous le règne de Philippe II*, 11 vols. (Brussels, 1892–1900)

King, A and Etty, C, *England and Scotland, 1286–1603* (London, 2016)

Klarwill, V von, *Queen Elizabeth and Some Foreigners*, transl. Nash, TH (London, 1928)

Lake, P, *How Shakespeare put Politics on the Stage: Power and Succession in the History Plays* (New Haven, 2017)

Lee, M, *Great Britain's Solomon: James VI and I in his Three Kingdoms* (Illinois, 1990)

Lefranc, P, 'Un Inédit de Raleigh sur la Succession', *Etudes anglaises*, 13 (1960), pp.44–5

Levin, C, *The Heart and Stomach of a King: Elizabeth I and the Politics of Sex and Power* (Philadelphia, 1994)

Levin, C, *The Reign and Life of Elizabeth I: Politics, culture and society* (Basingstoke, 2022)

Levine, M, *The Early Elizabethan Succession Question* (California, 1966)

Levine, M, *Tudor Dynastic Problems, 1460-1571* (London and New York, 2021)

Lewalski, Keifer B, 'Writing Resistance in Letters: Arbella Stuart and the Rhetoric of Disguise and Defiance,' in *Tudor Dynastic Problems, Writing Women in Jacobean England* (Cambridge, 1993), pp.71–92

Loades, D, *The Tudor Court* (Oxford, 2003)

Longford, E (ed), *The Oxford Book of Royal Anecdotes* (Oxford University Press, 1989)

Loomie, AJ, 'Philip III and the Stuart succession in England, 1600–1603,' *Revue Belge de Philologie et d'Histoire*, 43 (1965), pp.492–514

Lovell, MS, *Bess of Hardwick. First Lady of Chatsworth, 1527–1608* (London, 2005)

Macauley, S, 'The Lennox Crisis, 1558–1563,' in *Northern History*, 41 Part 2 (Leeds, 2004), pp.267–87

Manley, L, 'From Strange's Men to Pembroke's Men: 2 "Henry VI" and The First Part of the Contention,' *Shakespeare Quarterly*, 54 No.3 (Oxford, 2003), pp.253–87

Manning, R, 'The prosecution of Sir Michael Blount, Lieutenant of the Tower of London, 1595,' *Bulletin of the Institute of Historical Research*, 57 (Oxford, 1984), pp.216–24

Marcham, FG, 'James I of England and the Little Beagle Letters,' in *Persecution and Liberty: Essays in Honor of George Lincoln Burr* (New York, 1860)

Mayer, JC, *The Struggle for the Succession in Late Elizabethan England: Politics, polemics and cultural representations* (Montpellier, 2004)

McDiarmid, JF, *The Monarchical Republic of Early Modern England: Essays in Response to Patrick Collinson* (Aldershot, 2007)

McInnes, I, *Arabella: The Life and Times of Lady Arabella Seymour, 1575–1615* (London, 1968)

McLaren, A, 'The quest for a king: gender, marriage, and succession in Elizabethan England,' *Journal of British Studies*, 41 (2002), pp.259–90

Merton, C, 'The Women who served Queen Mary and Queen Elizabeth: Ladies, Gentlewomen and Maids of the Privy Chamber, 1553–1603', Cambridge PhD thesis (1992)

Mortimer, I, *The Time Traveller's Guide to Elizabethan England* (London, 2012)

Mueller, J, '"To My Very Good Brother the King of Scots": Elizabeth I's Correspondence with James VI and the Question of the Succession', *PMLA*, 115, No.5 (Columbia, 2000)

Neale, JE, *Elizabeth I and her Parliaments*, 2 vols. (London, 1958)

Neale, JE, 'Parliament and the Succession Question in 1562/3 and 1566,' *English Historical Review*, 36, No.144, (London, 1921), pp. 497–520

Neale, JE, 'Peter Wentworth,' *English Historical Review*, XXXIX (1924), pp.184–205

Nenner, H, *The Right to be King: The Succession to the Crown of England, 1603–1714* (London, 1995)

Parry, G, 'The monarchical republic and magic: William Cecil and the exclusion of Mary Queen of Scots,' *Reformation*, XVII (2012), pp.29–47

Pasmore, S, *The Life and Times of Queen Elizabeth I at Richmond Palace* (Richmond Local History Society, 2003)

Peck, LL, *Northampton: patronage and policy at the court of James I* (London, 1982)

Percival, R and A, *The Court of Elizabeth the First* (London, 1976)

Plowden, A, *Marriage with my Kingdom: The Courtships of Elizabeth I* (London, 1977)

Plowden, A, *Two Queens in One Isle: The Deadly Relationship of Elizabeth I and Mary, Queen of Scots* (Sutton, 1999)

Pollard, AF, *Political History of England*, VI: 1547–1603 (London, 1910)

Pollen, JH, 'The Accession of King James I,' *The Month* (London, 1903), pp.572–85

Pollen, JH, 'The Question of Queen Elizabeth's Successor', *The Month* (London, 1903), pp.517–32

Porter, L, *The Thistle and the Rose* (London, 2024)

Questier, M, *Dynastic Politics and the British Reformation, 1558–1630* (Oxford, 2019)

Ralph Lewis, B, *Monarchy: The History of an Idea* (Stroud, 2003), p.125

Read, C, *Mr Secretary Walsingham and the Policy of Queen Elizabeth*, 3 vols. (Oxford, 1925)

Richards, JM, 'The English accession of James VI: "national" identity, gender and the personal monarchy of England,' *English Historical Review*, 117 (Oxford, 2002), pp.513–35

Riehl, A, *The Face of Queenship: Early Modern Representations of Elizabeth I* (London, 2010)

Russell, G, *Queen James: The Life and Loves of Britain's First King* (London, 2025)

Schutte, K, *A Biography of Margaret Douglas, Countess of Lennox, 1515–1578, Niece of Henry VIII and Mother-in-law of Mary, Queen of Scots* (Lampeter, 2000)

Schutte, V, *Unexpected Heirs in Early Modern Europe: Potential kings and queens* (Cham, Switzerland, 2017)

Scott, W, *Secret History of the Court of James the First*, 2 vols. (Edinburgh, 1811)

Seymour, W, *Ordeal by Ambition. An English family in the shadow of the Tudors* (London, 1972)

Sharpe, K, *Sir Robert Cotton, 1586–1631: history and politics in early modern England* (Oxford, 1979)

Smout, TC (ed), *Anglo-Scottish Relations from 1603 to 1900* (Oxford, 2005)

Somerset, A, *Elizabeth I* (London, 1991)

Stafford, HG, *James VI of Scotland and the Throne of England* (New York and London, 1940)

Starkey, D (ed), *The English Court: from the Wars of the Roses to the Civil War* (Longman, 1987)

Stewart, A, *The Cradle King: A Life of James VI & I* (London, 2004)

Strickland, A, *The Life of Queen Elizabeth* (London, 1910)

Strong, R, *The Cult of Elizabeth. Elizabethan Portraiture and Pageantry* (London, 1977)

Tallis, N, *Elizabeth's Rival: The Tumultuous Tale of Lettice Knollys, Countess of Leicester* (London, 2017)

Thomson, T (ed), Calderwood, D, *The History of the Kirk of Scotland*, 8 vols. (Edinburgh, 1842–49)

Thurley, S, *Hampton Court: A Social and Architectural History* (New Haven and London, 2003)

Thurley, S, *The Royal Palaces of Tudor England. Architecture and Court Life, 1460–1547* (New Haven and London, 1993)

Trevor-Roper, H, *Queen Elizabeth's First Historian: William Camden and the beginnings of English 'civil history'* (London, 1971)

Tunstall, E, 'Of Honour and Innocence: Royal Correspondence and the Execution of Mary, Queen of Scots,' *Melbourne Historical Journal*, 47 (2019/20), pp.57–72

Tunstall, E, 'The Correspondence of Elizabeth I and James VI in the context of Anglo-Scottish Relations, 1572–1603,' unpublished Master of Philosophy thesis, University of Adelaide, September 2015

Tunstall, E, 'The Paradox of the Valentine Thomas Affair: English Diplomacy, Royal Correspondence and the Elizabethan Succession,' *Journal of the Australian and New Zealand Association of Medieval and Early Modern Studies*, 38, No.1 (Canberra, 2021), pp.65–87

Tunstall, E, *The Succession Debate and Contested Authority in Elizabethan England, 1558–1603* (Cham, 2024)

Tyacke, N, 'Puritan politicians and King James VI and I, 1587–1604,' in Cogswell, T, Crust, R and Lake, P (eds), *Politics, Religion and Popularity in Early Stuart Britain: Essays in Honour of Conrad Russell* (Cambridge, 2002), pp.21–44

Tytler, PF, *The History of Scotland From The Accession of Alexander III to the Union* (London, 2023)

Watkins, J, *Representing Elizabeth in Stuart England, Literature, History, Sovereignty* (Cambridge, 2002)

Weir, A, *Elizabeth the Queen* (London, 1999)

Weir, A, *Mary, Queen of Scots and the Murder of Lord Darnley* (London, 2003)

Weir, A, *The Lost Tudor Princess: A Life of Margaret Douglas, Countess of Lennox* (London, 2015)

Williams, N, *Elizabeth the First, Queen of England* (London, 1968)

Williamson, GC, *Lady Anne Clifford, Countess of Dorset, Pembroke & Montgomery, 1590–1676. Her life, letters and work* (Wakefield, 1967)

Wilson, D, *Sweet Robin: a biography of Robert Dudley, Earl of Leicester, 1533–1588* (London, 1981)

Wilson, DH, *James VI & I* (London, 1963)

Wilson, VA, *Queen Elizabeth's Maids of Honour and Ladies of the Privy Chamber* (London, 1922)

Wood, A, *Athenae Oxonienses: An Exact History of All the Writers and Bishops Who Have Had Their Education in the University of Oxford*, 4 vols. (London, 1813–1820)

Woolf, DR, 'Two Elizabeths? James I and the Late Queen's Famous Memory,' *Canadian Journal of History*, 2 Part 2 (1985), pp.167–91

Wright, C (ed), *Sir Robert Cotton as collector: essays on an early Stuart courtier and his legacy* (London, 1997)

PICTURE ACKNOWLEDGEMENTS

Alamy Stock Photo: 1 below left/Pictorial Press, 2 above left/incamerastock, 2 centre right/National Trust Photographic Library, 3 above left and centre right/Picture Art Collection, 3 below left/ Royal Armouries Museum, 4 above left/Logic Images, 5 above left/ incamerastock, 6 above right/National Trust Photographic Library, 6 centre left/Historic Images, 6 below right/GL Archive, 7 above right/Picture Art Collection, 7 below right/Penta Springs Limited, 8 above right and below right/Picture Art Collection, 9 above right and centre left/Picture Art Collection, 9 below left/Ian Dagnall, 10 below left/1 Collection, 10 below right/Niday Picture Library, 11 above left and below left/Picture Art Collection, 11 centre right/ Pictorial Press Ltd, 12 below/Classic Collection 3, 13 above left/ Balfore Archive Images, 13 above right/World History Archive, 14 below/CBW, 15 above/Art Collection 2, 16 above left and above right/Picture Art Collection.

© Ashmolean Museum, University of Oxford/Bridgeman Images: 14 above.

© Blair Castle, Perthshire: 2 below left.

The British Library Archive/Bridgeman Images: 4 centre right.

© The British Library Board: 16 below/British Library, Cotton MS Faustina F III, f. 111r.
A page of William Camden's *Annals of Queen Elizabeth* photographed using specialist imaging techniques, and funded by the British Library Collections Trust.

INDEX

PLACES OF INTEREST

London

Greenwich. The now lost Tudor palace was the birthplace of Elizabeth I and her father Henry VIII. In 1543, the latter concluded the Treaty of Greenwich with Scotland, pledging Elizabeth in marriage to James Hamilton, son and namesake of the Scottish regent, the first Earl of Arran.
Hampton Court Palace. Elizabeth almost died at the palace after contracting smallpox there in 1562, prompting a long-running succession crisis. James held a conference there in 1604 to try to resolve the vexed issue of religion. It resulted in the publication of the King James Bible.
Nonsuch, near Cheam. Another lost royal residence, Nonsuch was a fairytale palace built by Henry VIII and a favoured retreat of his younger daughter Elizabeth. It was here that she signed the Treaty of Nonsuch with the independent Dutch provinces in 1585.
Richmond Palace. Richmond was Elizabeth's favourite residence. She called it her 'warm box' because it boasted a sophisticated heating system. It was here that she died in March 1603. Only the gatehouse now remains.
St Paul's Cathedral. A pageant was staged here as part of Elizabeth's coronation procession in January 1559. Forty-four years later, the proclamation of her successor James I was read out before the citizens of London.
Somerset House. James held peace negotiations here with Spain in 1604 and concluded the Treaty of London. His consort, Anne of Denmark, later made the house one of her favoured residences.
Tower of London. Elizabeth was imprisoned in the Tower in 1554, during her sister Mary's reign. She returned in triumph when she inherited the throne four years later. Both she and James spent a night before their coronation in the fortress, as long-established royal tradition dictated.

Westminster Abbey. Elizabeth and James were both crowned here, along with almost every monarch of England and Britain since 1066.

Whitehall Palace. The largest Tudor palace in London, it was destroyed by fire in 1698. It was here that Lady Margaret Douglas, mother of Lord Darnley and grandmother of Arbella Stuart, was imprisoned on Elizabeth's orders in 1565. James I was proclaimed King of England outside the palace gates in 1603. His son Charles I was executed outside the palace's Banqueting House in 1649.

England and Scotland

Ashby-de-la-Zouch, Leicestershire: St Helen's Church. Henry Hastings, sixth Earl of Huntingdon, had one of the strongest claims to Elizabeth's throne. He never pursued it, and when he died in 1596 the grateful queen ordered a lavish burial in his native Leicestershire church.

Bedfordshire: Wrest Park. Arbella Stuart was imprisoned here in early 1603 on suspicion of conspiring against the dying queen.

Cumbria: Workington Hall. Mary, Queen of Scots spent her first night here after fleeing to England in 1568. She did not then know that far from being Elizabeth's honoured guest, she was her prisoner.

Edinburgh: Holyroodhouse Palace and Abbey. The principal residence of the monarchs of Scotland, Holyrood was the site of Mary, Queen of Scots' coronation, her marriage to Lord Darnley and the murder of her favourite, David Riccio. James was staying at the palace when he allegedly plotted to have Elizabeth assassinated in 1598. Five years later, he received the news that he was King of England.

Edinburgh: Kirk O'Field. Mary, Queen of Scots' estranged husband Lord Darnley was staying here in February 1587 when it was destroyed by a huge explosion. Darnley's body was discovered in the grounds, bearing the marks of strangulation.

Hertfordshire: Hatfield House. Elizabeth was staying at Hatfield, her favourite residence as a princess, when she found out that her sister Mary had died and she was Queen of England. James never liked the residence so gave it to Robert Cecil, who had smoothed his path to the English throne.

Hertfordshire: Theobalds. The house was owned by Elizabeth's most trusted adviser, Lord Burghley. He entertained the queen and her court there in 1587, including Arbella Stuart, a claimant to her throne. Burghley's son Robert Cecil inherited the house and met James there for the first time in May 1603. He later gave Theobalds to the King in exchange for Hatfield

House. James died there in 1625. The palace was demolished during the Commonwealth established after the execution of James's son Charles in 1649.

Knowsley, near Liverpool: Knowsley Hall. The ancestral home of Ferdinando Stanley, fifth Earl of Derby, a claimant to Elizabeth's throne.

Lancashire: Lathom House. Another of the Stanley homes, it was here that Ferdinando died after a sudden illness in 1594. The main part of the house was demolished in 1925.

Northamptonshire: Fotheringhay. Mary, Queen of Scots was tried in the Great Hall of Fotheringhay Castle in October 1586 and executed the following February. The castle was dismantled in the 1630s, leaving only the earthworks.

Perth: Gowrie House. Home of the treacherous Ruthven family, Gowrie House was the scene of a dramatic attempt to either kill or kidnap James VI in 1600. It was demolished in the early 1800s.

Perth: Lochleven Castle. Mary, Queen of Scots was imprisoned in this island fortress after her arrest in June 1567. It was here that she signed the deeds of abdication the following month. She escaped in May 1568 and made the fateful decision to flee to England.

Peterborough Cathedral. Mary, Queen of Scots was laid to rest here in 1587, a studied insult by Elizabeth, who refused to have her buried in Westminster Abbey. It was also the final resting place of Henry VIII's first wife, Catherine of Aragon.

Staffordshire: Chartley Manor. It was during her imprisonment at Chartley that Mary, Queen of Scots sealed her doom by leaving a paper trail of her involvement in the Babington Conspiracy of 1586. The manor house was destroyed by fire in 1781.

Stirling Castle. The birthplace of James VI and the site of his coronation in July 1567 when he was just thirteen months old. It was also here that James's firstborn child, Henry, was born in 1594.

Weybridge, Surrey: Oatlands. The now lost palace of Oatlands was the last stop on Elizabeth's final, spectacular summer progress in 1602.

Oxfordshire: Woodstock Palace. Elizabeth was imprisoned in this now lost palace during her sister Mary's reign. She was rumoured to have considered having Arbella imprisoned there in the early weeks of 1603, as she lay dying at Richmond Palace.

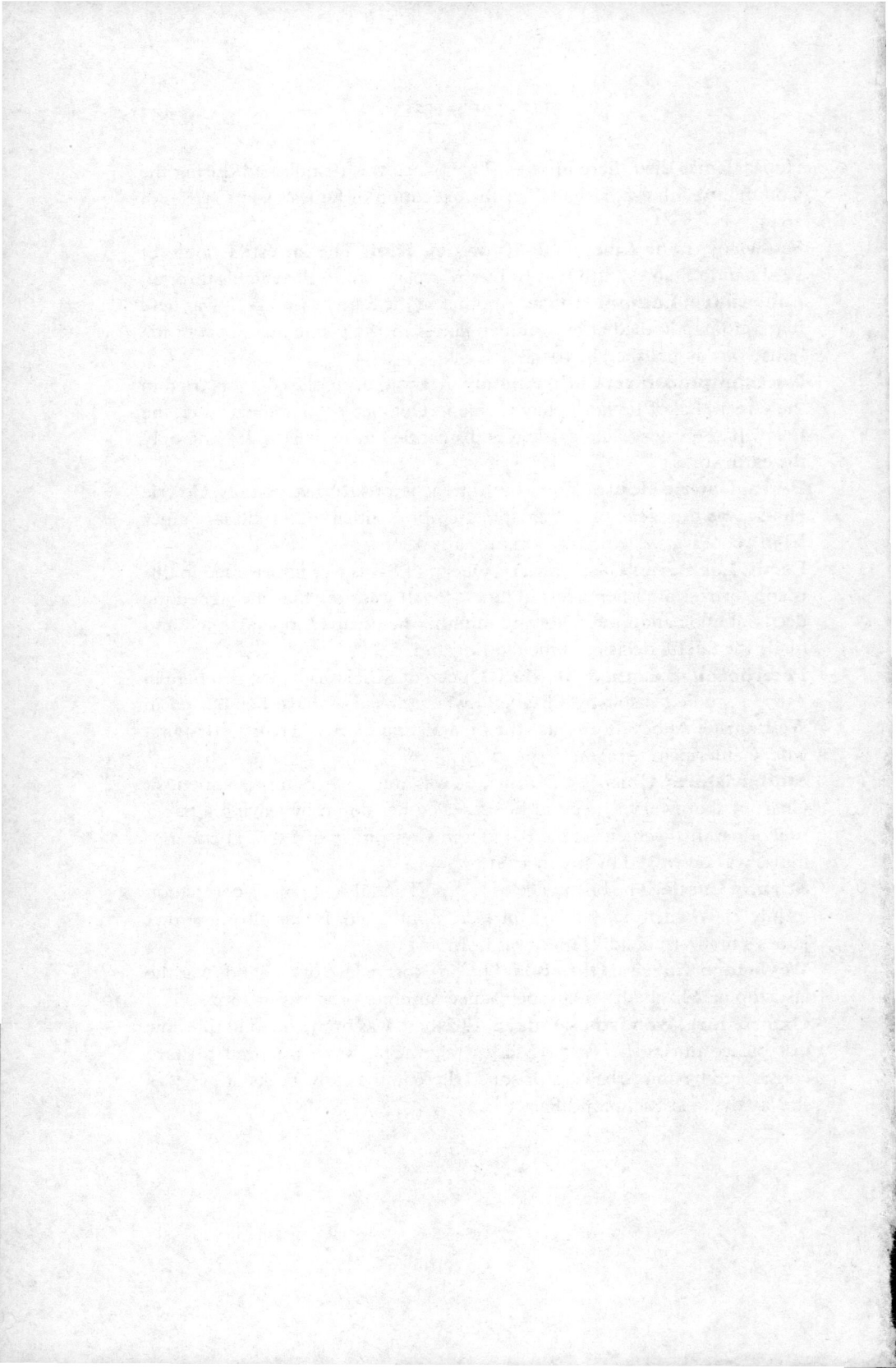